GOVERNANCE NETWORKS IN PUBLIC ADMINISTRATION AND PUBLIC POLICY

PUBLIC ADMINISTRATION AND PUBLIC POLICY

A Comprehensive Publication Program

EDITOR-IN-CHIEF

EVAN M. BERMAN

Distinguished University Professor
J. William Fulbright Distinguished Scholar
National Chengchi University
Taipei, Taiwan

Founding Editor

JACK RABIN

1. *Public Administration as a Developing Discipline,*
   Robert T. Golembiewski
2. *Comparative National Policies on Health Care,* Milton I. Roemer, M.D.
3. *Exclusionary Injustice: The Problem of Illegally Obtained Evidence,*
   Steven R. Schlesinger
5. *Organization Development in Public Administration,* edited by
   Robert T. Golembiewski and William B. Eddy
7. *Approaches to Planned Change,* Robert T. Golembiewski
8. *Program Evaluation at HEW,* edited by James G. Abert
9. *The States and the Metropolis,* Patricia S. Florestano
   and Vincent L. Marando
11. *Changing Bureaucracies: Understanding the Organization before
    Selecting the Approach,* William A. Medina
12. *Handbook on Public Budgeting and Financial Management,* edited by
    Jack Rabin and Thomas D. Lynch
15. *Handbook on Public Personnel Administration and Labor Relations,*
    edited by Jack Rabin, Thomas Vocino, W. Bartley Hildreth,
    and Gerald J. Miller
19. *Handbook of Organization Management,* edited by William B. Eddy
22. *Politics and Administration: Woodrow Wilson and American Public
    Administration,* edited by Jack Rabin and James S. Bowman
23. *Making and Managing Policy: Formulation, Analysis, Evaluation,*
    edited by G. Ronald Gilbert
25. *Decision Making in the Public Sector,* edited by Lloyd G. Nigro
26. *Managing Administration,* edited by Jack Rabin, Samuel Humes,
    and Brian S. Morgan
27. *Public Personnel Update,* edited by Michael Cohen
    and Robert T. Golembiewski
28. *State and Local Government Administration,* edited by Jack Rabin
    and Don Dodd
29. *Public Administration: A Bibliographic Guide to the Literature,*
    Howard E. McCurdy
31. *Handbook of Information Resource Management,* edited by Jack Rabin
    and Edward M. Jackowski

Available Electronically

PublicADMINISTRATION*netBASE*

GOVERNANCE NETWORKS IN PUBLIC ADMINISTRATION AND PUBLIC POLICY

CHRISTOPHER KOLIBA

JACK W. MEEK

ASIM ZIA

CRC Press
Taylor & Francis Group
Boca Raton   London   New York

CRC Press is an imprint of the
Taylor & Francis Group, an **informa** business

CRC Press
Taylor & Francis Group
6000 Broken Sound Parkway NW, Suite 300
Boca Raton, FL 33487-2742

© 2011 by Taylor and Francis Group, LLC
CRC Press is an imprint of Taylor & Francis Group, an Informa business

No claim to original U.S. Government works

Printed in the United States of America on acid-free paper
10 9 8 7 6 5 4 3 2 1

International Standard Book Number: 978-1-4200-7126-9 (Hardback)

Library of Congress Cataloging-in-Publication Data

Koliba, Christopher.
 Governance networks in public administration and public policy / Christopher Koliba, Jack W. Meek, and Asim Zia.
  p. cm. -- (Public administration and public policy ; 158)
 Includes bibliographical references and index.
 ISBN 978-1-4200-7126-9
 1. Intergovernmental cooperation. 2. Interagency coordination. 3. Public-private sector cooperation. 4. Intergovernmental cooperation--United States 5. Interagency coordination--United States 6. Public-private sector cooperation--United States. I. Meek, Jack W. II. Zia, Asim. III. Title. IV. Series.

JC355.K593 2011
352.1--dc22   2010006571

Visit the Taylor & Francis Web site at
http://www.taylorandfrancis.com

and the CRC Press Web site at
http://www.crcpress.com

This book is dedicated in sweet remembrance of my grandmother, Patricia King, who encouraged me to follow the beat of a different drum, and to my family, Erica, Naomi, Orielle, and Jasper, who make it all worthwhile.

This book to is also dedicated to Caitlin, Ursula, Anika, Rustum, and our future generations.

Contents

List of Figures

List of Tables

Preface

The purpose of this book is to offer a conceptual framework for describing governance networks, and in so doing we provide a holistic way to conceive of their construction.

Our hope in writing this book, this way, is that readers engage in these ideas, apply them to the governance networks in their midst, and deepen their understanding of the dynamics unfolding around them. We wish to address the practical applications of the conceptual framework for public administrators, policy analysts, policy makers, students, and researchers. To a certain extent, then, we hope that this book is both accessible and practical, a tall order for a topic as complex as governance networks.

Much of the context for this book is premised on the description of governance networks and political and administrative trends founded within the United States. We deeply acknowledge that the development of policy and governance network frameworks, theories, and models has been led by researchers drawing on examples from many different national and international contexts. We particularly need to acknowledge the leadership of scholars from the United Kingdom, Denmark, Belgium, the Netherlands, and others who have made and continue to contribute to the evolution of these concepts and constructs.

The courses in which these concepts have been discussed have included Foundations of Public Administration, Administrative Theory and Practice, Policy Systems, a Collaborative Management Institute, and Systems Analysis and Strategic Management, taught at the University of Vermont and several research seminars at the University of La Verne as part of the Regional Studies Project. A special thanks goes to the numerous graduate students at the University of Vermont including: Renea Bordeau, Marcia Bristow, David Curtis, Haley Dienst, Nicole DuBois, Jennifer Kenyan, Chong Kim, Emilie Kornheiser, Leslie Langevin, Santina Leporati, Patty McShane, Alissa Robertson, Catherine Symans, Marc Bilodeau, Meghan Butler, Katherine Gleeson, Kelly Houston, Mercy Hyde, Tracey McCowen, Micheal Loner, Kristen Wright, Erica Spiegel, Kevin Stapleton, Robin Kemkes, Forest Cohen, Emily Bibby, and Carol Beatty.

The authors owe their gratitude to a number of gifted scholars and practitioners who have greatly influenced them and the content and framing of this book. In particular, Chris Koliba thanks those who have served as collaborators on parts of this work. Substantial credit needs to be given to the following colleagues, with whom he has collaborated: Rebecca Gajda, Jean Lathrop, Daniel Bromberg, Russell Mills, Clare Ginger, Michael Gurdon, Joshusa Farley, and Erica Campbell. Additional thanks go to Rachel Weston, Tony Habinshuti, Qin Zhou, and Alison Siemianowski for their research and editorial assistance on aspects of this work. Special thanks also goes to Fred Bay, Kathleen Kesson, Jane Kolodinsky, Rachel Johnson, Ken Becker, Owen Bradley, Mary Whalen, Jean Berthiaume, Matthias Finger, Sam Marullo, Marjorie DeVault, Ralph Ketcham, and Mary Stanley, and to the memory of Manfred Stanley, whose wisdom and early guidance continue to shape his thinking.

Jack Meek wishes to especially acknowledge H. George Frederickson for sharing his ideas and papers on governance and offering feedback on drafts on numerous occasions over the past decade and more. There is no doubt the interpretation of governance networks presented here is deeply influenced by these conversations and shared readings.

Asim Zia thanks the John D. and Catherine T. MacArthur Foundation for sponsoring relevant research applications on biodiversity conservation and international development. He also thanks Michael Glantz and CU Boulder's Center for Capacity Building for supporting his research on global climate change applications. Finally, he thanks Malte Faber, Bryan Norton, Barry Bozeman, and Bruce Hannon for enabling the evolution of his learning on complex systems and environmental governance.

We also thank those scholars who offered feedback on papers presented at the September 2008 Minnowbrook Conference, several American Society of Public Administration conferences, and the June 2009 Trans Atlantic Dialogue 5, held in Washington. Their guidance has informed the direction and tone of the book. We also thank those who have reviewed pieces or all of this manuscript, including Craig Wheeland, Curt Ventriss, Fran Berry, Joop Koppenjan, Frederique Six, Marc Holzer, Taco Branson, Pam Mischen, Görtug Morçöl, Naim Kapucu, and Chris Skelcher. We thank Evan Berman for his gracious support of this project from its inception. We also thank the folks at Taylor and Francis, particularly Stephanie Morkert, Jay Margolis, and Rich O'Hanley for their editorial assistance.

The true worth of the book will be determined by those who view the framework as useful to understanding governance networks and defendable in the face of empirical scrutiny. As we note in Chapter 11, we believe these are critical next steps to advancing our understanding of governance networks. We look forward to learning more about the nature of governance networks and how we can improve our understanding of their dynamic nature.

Introduction: Why Governance Networks?

All men [*sic*] are caught in an inescapable network of mutuality, tied in a single garment of destiny.

—**Martin Luther King, Jr. (1986, p. 290)**

Some problems are so complex that you have to be ... well informed just to be undecided about them.

—**Laurence J. Peter (n.d.)**

This is a book for policy makers, public administrators, and policy analysts who find themselves working in, accountable to, influenced by, or otherwise interested in governance networks. Governance network administration and policy analysis has always been a complicated undertaking. We will argue that it is often a complex enterprise as well, and provide the reader with some ways to make sense of this complexity.

The Complex Nature of Today's Policy Problems and Solutions

Take the instance of the local town manager who is faced with the challenge of rectifying a several-decade's-old dispute over who is responsible for a town road that gets washed out after every significant rainfall. The owners of the hillside land adjacent to the road claim that the agricultural practices of the farm farther up the hill are the cause of poor runoff, and therefore the farmer should be responsible for ameliorating the problem. The farmer up the hill claims that the roadway culverts were not constructed right. The state's agency of natural resources is interested in the site because of the extensive pollution that this situation is causing to the nearby wetland down the hill. The town manager is caught between a host of public and private actors with interests defined by the narrowness and expansiveness of their concerns (Houston, 2009).

Take, as another instance, the city administrator faced with an even greater problem: the toxic water table that sits under the city's business district. Faced with challenges from the Environmental Protection Agency (EPA) to declare the district a Superfund site, this manager must work with the city's elected representatives, the private businesses in the area, and the main polluters to work out a compromise that will clear up the aquifer while preserving the economic vitality of the downtown business district (Rosegrant, 1996).

Moving up in magnitude, consider the challenges that a Federal Emergency Management Agency (FEMA) administrator faces when asked to coordinate the processing of "requests for assistance" during the response and recovery phases following the landfall of Hurricane Katrina in August 2005 (Government Accountability Office, 2006). As the coordinator with the bureaucratic authority to manage the system, she is asked to coordinate the fulfillment of requests for assistance with a regional unit of the Red Cross, an entity that she has no jurisdictional power over. Or consider the long-term Red Cross volunteer who has been assigned to work with FEMA to make sure that the affected area's needs are met. How should relationships between FEMA and the Red Cross be designed? What if there is no time to sort out the details?

Consider the contract manager for the U.S. Department of Defense who has documented the repeated failures of a contractor to effectively deliver the supplies and services specified within the contract, but who has no authority to ensure that the contractor comply. Or the leader of a small nonprofit organization who is considering what role his or her organization should play within an emergent coalition of advocacy groups and service providers. Or the regional planner who needs to work with a variety of state agencies, regional and local governments, developers, and area businesses to design regional land use, transportation, and economic development plans. Or the financial securities regulator who observes the mounting risks arising out of an unregulated mortgage products industry?

Also consider the policy analyst who is asked to recommend an implementation strategy for a new public health care insurance option. Or the policy analyst who is asked to determine which social service partnerships are providing adequate care to his or her clientele and why. Or the policy analyst looking for ways to frame a problem in such a way as to build support for a given policy tool.

What do all of these public administrators and policy analysts have in common? Their work is undertaken within networks formed when different organizations align to accomplish some kind of policy function. To be effective, they must find ways to navigate complexity in such a way as to generate effective results.

We describe a variety of trends and movements that have contributed to the complexity of these systems, as well as the challenges that public administrators, policy makers, and policy analysts face as a result. Globalization has inextricably linked nations, institutions, organizations, and individuals. The public interest gets molded and shaped by coalitions of interest groups using the next advances in information technology and marketing strategies to influence governance systems toward their desired ends. The increasing complexity and "wickedness" of public problems, the expansion of information technologies, the moves to contract out, privatize, and partner, coupled with globalization, have fueled interest in the application of network frameworks to the study of public administration, public policy, and governance structures. These trends have contributed to the emergence of governance structures that have become, essentially, innovations in governing. There is growing evidence to suggest that these trends have and will continue to shape interjurisdictional landscapes, and represent new kinds of reform with regard to how government interacts with for-profit and not-for-profit organizations to design and deliver public goods and services. We describe these arrangements as *governance networks*, defined here as interorganizational networks comprised of multiple actors, often spanning sectors and scale, working together to influence the creation, implementation, and monitoring of public policies.

The fact that policy makers, public administrators, and public policy analysts have to operate within environments that are complicated has been recognized in the collective appreciation of "bounded rationality" (Simon, 1957) and incremental decision making (Lindblom, 1959), which are now commonly held assumptions in the field. The limited capacities that policy makers, implementers, and evaluators possess to carry out their work using purely rational logic and action have been demonstrated in some of the classic studies shaping the field, including Allison's (1971) and later Roberto's (2004) studies of the decision-making processes of the Bay of Pigs and Cuban Missile Crisis, Pressman and Wildavsky's study of the Oakland Redevelopment Initiative (1984), Kingdon's critique of the rational policy cycle and introduction of the policy stream model of political agenda setting (1984), and studies of failures in the *Challenger* explosion (Romzek and Dubnick, 1987), the Teton dam disaster (Schmidt, 2002), the emergency response following the 9/11 attacks (Comfort, 2002), the response and recovery efforts following Hurricane Katrina (Kiefer and Montjoy, 2006; Derthick, 2007; Koliba, Mills, and Zia, accepted for publication), and the near meltdown of the mortgage, insurance, and finance industries in 2008. The events described in these studies were not only complicated by the bounded rationality of the individuals implicated within them, but they were complex because they involved many networks of actors, oftentimes spanning many social sectors and geographical boundaries, who were relating to one another through a variety of ties, oftentimes with competing aims and priorities. Complicated features involved in executing the public's interests become complex when it becomes impossible to predict outcomes and successfully "steer" collective action. Complex systems exert qualities that are emergent, evolving, and dynamic. They possess certain capacities to self-organize. Their actions may not be defined through a rational set of assumptions regarding causes and effects and linear reasoning.

In spite of this complexity, policy makers, public administrators, and policy analysts are required to do their best to make sense of what is happening around them. We write this book at a time when not a great deal is known about how the performance of these networks is measured, or about the long-term effects of public-private partnerships, contracting out, and other collaborative arrangements as they have grown more common. We assert that governance networks are *not*, unto themselves, a social good. Ineffective networks exist. We believe that a turn toward networks (not at the exclusion of hierarchies and markets, but in relation to) in public administration and policy studies is useful in ultimately determining questions of the normative worth (e.g., questions of ethics, norms, and values) of networks and the proper role of public administrators in upholding these values.

Traditional views of management and administration that rely on the study of hierarchical arrangements are not enough to explain the changing conditions that public managers find themselves working within (Goodsell, 2006). Shifting the delivery of public goods and services entirely to "the market" is not sufficient enough either, as we will argue that business management principles and practices are not sufficient enough to ensure democratic accountabilities.

The Network Turn in Public Administration and Public Policy

This book focuses on a third way of understanding how public goods and services get framed and delivered. Substantial literature describing the rise of the "network society" may be found within both the academic and popular presses. Managing *within* networks gives rise to new challenges that our previous theories of hierarchy and markets do not account for. Most theoretical frameworks used to study hierarchical and market structures make certain assumptions about how power is structured, decisions are made, and collective actions are undertaken. Compared to these two traditional frameworks, we know very little about how power, decisions, and collective actions unfold within partnerships, strategic alliances, and other collaborative arrangements. As we will see, social network and social capital theories may be used to understand how cooperation and collaboration exist as essential features of network management.

Because so little is known about what accounts for success and performance in governance networks, we will offer very few prescriptive judgments or definitive "how to's." We avoid rendering generalizations about how governance networks *should* be structured and managed, although we invite the readers to do so themselves by applying the tools and frameworks introduced here to the study of the governance networks within their midst.

We opt to provide the reader with guidance for developing a deeper situational awareness of how governance networks operate. Pilots, engineers, emergency management professionals, and military strategists have emphasized the importance that situational awareness brings to understanding complex systems. Situational awareness hinges on a combination of systems thinking, the acquisition and filtering of information, and the application of descriptive patterning that may only be developed through extensive experience built up over time. We introduce the reader to a range of characteristics endemic to interorganizational networks and interpersonal, collaborative relationships. As a result of applying the methods introduced in this book, we hope that the reader will be able to discern the systems dynamics that persist within governance networks.

Over the course of the book we describe a framework that governance network administrators as well as policy makers and analysts can use to develop enough situational awareness to carry out their work efficiently, effectively, and democratically. In Chapter 8 we discuss some of the network administration competencies that are employed by network administrators who draw on their awareness of the complex and complicated situations to shape network structures and functions. These skills and strategies include oversight, resource provision, negotiation and bargaining, facilitation, collaborative governance, and systems thinking. We suggest that network administrators need to utilize these skills and competencies with an awareness of the network properties that exist within their governance networks. In Chapter 11 we discuss some of the options available for analysts and researchers to study and model governance network dynamics. The results of the analysis of governance networks may, ultimately, be used to evaluate their performances, and be used to design and coordinate public policies.

We present a taxonomy of network characteristics that has been derived as a result of blending the network literature found within the policy studies and public administration fields with interdisciplinary theories and frameworks such as social network analysis, systems theory, and complexity theory. We believe that such a framework can be used to guide practice, learning, and research. To better explain the larger approach of this book, we reference the distinctions that Nobel Prize winner Elinor Ostrom (2007) makes between frameworks, theories, and models:

1. A *conceptual framework* identifies a set of variables and the relationships among them that presumably account for the asset of phenomena. The framework can provide anything from a modest set of variables to something as extensive as a paradigm.
2. A *theory* provides a denser and more logically coherent set of relationships. It applies values to some of the variables and usually specifies how relationships may vary depending upon the values of critical variables.
3. A *model* is a representative of a specific situation. It is usually much narrower in scope, and more precise in its assumptions, than the underlying theory. Ideally, it is mathematical (as paraphrased by Sabatier, 2007, p. 6).

In this book we provide readers with a *conceptual framework* of governance networks to help understand and manage governance networks. It is our hope that the framework is relevant to a broad range of situations as readers are likely to experience.

We present and use the "network" as a symbol of the capacities of organizations, groups, and individuals to coordinate their activities in some way to achieve aims associated with public purposes. In building a theoretical framework through which we may describe governance networks, we rely heavily on network metaphors and analytical tools, as well as some of the central tenants of systems and complexity theories. We also draw on theoretical frameworks found in policy studies, public administration, and governance studies to provide a foundation for what anthropologists refer to as a "thick description" (Geertz, 1973) of interorganizational networks that have been designed to create, implement, or monitor public policies. By doing so, we hope to contribute to the development of a systematic and transdisciplinary study of governance networks, and advance the field's capacity to conduct ethnographic research, undertake hypothesis testing, as well as eventually engage in complex, computational modeling of the phenomena we describe in this book.

We make a critical assumption about the state of public administration in this book. We assert that the application of traditional views of government roles, responsibilities, and structures is not enough to account for the complexities inherent to modern governance systems. We are not, however, declaring the "death of the public bureaucracy." Nor are we suggesting that governing can occur without the state and its institutions. Instead, we believe that the application of networks to questions that are of importance to public administration and policy studies may lead to answers found in reinvigorated, "smarter" roles and functions for the institutions of government. Thinking in terms of governance networks also calls for a deeper examination of the role of the nonprofit and business sectors in providing public goods and services. Informed by the shift of focus from *government* to *governance*, we see the turn to networks as a moment when our methodological, empirical, and theoretical tools finally catch up with a phenomenon that has, as we will explore in Chapter 1, been in our midst since the first human beings decided that it was in their best interest to live and work together.

Outline of the Book

In Chapter 1, our review of the literature on governance networks leads us to suggest that networks have always been an integral feature of democratic governments and intersector arrangements; however, contemporary trends have accentuated the importance that governance networks play in modern democracies. These trends include the emergence of "wicked problems," the move to privatize government services, the move of government to partner with sector stakeholders to provide public goods at reduced costs, and the more recent turn to regulate and nationalize. Recognizing that while governance networks have been with us since the beginning of the American democratic experience, it is clear that the range and depth of innovations in governance networks places them in a different stage of development, which raises serious questions that deserve our attention. While there are positive benefits to governance networks, there are also significant challenges, particularly with regard to how governance networks are to be administered, the nature of "democratic anchorage" of these networks, and constructing ways in which governance network performance can be understood.

In Chapter 2, we offer a conceptual framework to assess governance networks that conceives of networks as a kind of participant relationship that is evident in all forms of macro relations: markets, hierarchies, and collaboratives. With this analytic frame, we assert that "mixed-form governance networks" account for markets and hierarchies as network forms alongside of "collaboratives" or partnerships. In this perspective, it is evident that mixed forms of governance networks operate across multiple sectors and in multiple geographic scales where mixed administrative authorities comprise of vertical, horizontal, and diagonal relational ties. To get to this perspective, we develop an understanding as to the ways in which network metaphors and analytical frameworks have been employed within the public administration, policy studies, and governance fields, and highlight discrepancies across the literature and their concerns in regard to the relationship between network structures, and markets and hierarchies.

Central to our work presented here is the belief we hold that the presentation of a conceptual framework of mixed-form governance networks allows us to develop a means for creating a taxonomy of governance networks characteristics, and ultimately describing the many different ways that stable governance networks arise and carry out one or more functions related to the policy stream. The next task is to develop a set of network characteristics as a matter of developing multiple layers of analysis—from the characteristics of individual network actors, to the nature of the ties between actors, to the nature of network-wide characteristics, to ultimately, systems-wide characteristics that position governance networks within broader external environments.

In Chapter 3, the focus is placed on the network actor: the most basic component of governance networks. We refer to network actors as nodes that represent social actors with various unique goals and roles within the network shaped by the sector they represent (public, private, or nonprofit). These nodes are to be understood to have a definitive geographic scale (local, regional, province/state, national, or international) as well as a social scale (the nesting of individuals, groups, organizations, and networks of organizations) that shape their interests and role in the network. Nodes are also influenced by their place in the network (center and periphery) and capital resources. The characteristics of each node noted above uniquely shape nodal behavior and influence the nature of network patterns and the roles played in the emergent social exchange of resources.

Chapter 4 focuses on the ties among and between nodes in the network. The central feature of nodal ties is resource exchange. From social network analysis, we assert that the relation among nodes shapes the kinds of administrative authorities among the nodes, and that the nature of resource exchange is shaped by the formality, strength, and coordination of nodal ties. We refer to these as the vector of ties, or the ties among administrative authorities. Both the social ties (strength and coupling) shaped by nodal context characteristics (outlined in Chapter 3) and the vector of administrative ties shape the governance network and determine resource exchange. This "multiplex" of ties can assist in assessing network stability.

In Chapter 5, interorganizational governance network configurations and operations are described and placed within policy streams. Emphasis in this chapter is placed on the nested nature of three network-wide functions that are performed by governance networks: operating functions (coordination, mobilization, information sharing, capacity building, learning), policy stream functions (defining and framing problems, policy planning, policy coordination and implementation, policy evaluation, policy alignment), and policy domain functions that are issue or domain specific.

Chapter 6 reviews six kinds of network-wide structures: intergovernmental, intragovernmental, interest group coalitions, regulatory subsystems, grant and contract agreements, and public-private partnerships. These arrangements are linked to use of "policy tools" in the work of Lester Salamon (2002b). From a systems perspective, governance networks are viewed in terms of functions needed within the system and the structures designed to achieve these functions.

In Chapter 7, we shift again the level of discourse on governance networks and examine them within the perspective of system dynamics. Relying on certain elements of complex systems theory, we offer a way to conceive of governance networks as a series of inputs, processes, outputs, and outcomes with positive and negative feedback that contribute to understanding the nature of regulation and governance of governance networks. The imagery we attempt to offer allows for the reader to consider the dimensions of governance networks as working patterns of a holistic, dynamic system. We believe the systems perspective provides one avenue to examine the role and function of governance networks shaped by the interplay of the parts of the system and how these contribute or detract from system-wide goals. We believe that this perspective will contribute to discussions later in the book with regard to critical considerations regarding governance networks, namely, administrative, accountability, and performance considerations. This chapter sets the stage in providing perspective to address the central challenges concomitant with the emergent character of mixed-form governance networks.

In Chapter 8, we argue that mixed-form governance networks reflect selective administrative characteristics of four paradigms of public administration: classical, new public management, collaborative public management, and governance network management. From this integration, the chapter directs its attention to the roles that individual public administrators take within governance networks. Clearly, public managers play a critical role participating in and administering governance networks, particularly ensuring democratic anchorage and network performance. These are difficult challenges given the complexity of administering across boundaries. Our review of the literature in this chapter suggests a number of promising administrative skills and management strategies in active and performing governance networks. We highlight the avenue available for the public administrator to enhance participatory governance. Most important, we assert that the role of the public administrator in governance networks should be viewed as evolutionary and emergent, as one of continuous adjustment, calling upon skills that assert both adaptive and directive qualities. Such is the demand on the public administrator managing in interdependent contexts.

With Chapter 9, we turn to the challenge of governance network accountability. From a systems perspective, we view accountability as representative of the structures that participate within the governance network and guided by the nature of the interdependencies of network participants and their sector characteristics. This view of accountability is very different than ones traditionally conceived between two participants bound within a hierarchy and reflects a more interdependent and complex character of governance networks. Simply put: Network accountability is a system-level construct—one that is shaped by the accountability structures of the individual parts of the network. As such, the accountability structures examined in this chapter are constructed around accountability regimes that represent the participants and the operations of the network.

With Chapter 10, we explore network performance. Performance measurement is often viewed as the systematic application of information to assess success. To assess network governance performance, we again turn to a system frame of reference and discuss the kinds of challenges that are operable within interorganizational governance networks. The administrative challenge here is developing appropriate information that enhances participation and improves the functioning of feedback loops. Clearly, performance measurement is challenging within organizations, and when we move our attention to governance networks, these challenges are accentuated.

Chapter 11 highlights the central themes that are discussed in this book. What is apparent is that the use of governance networks is expanding, along with their complexity in terms of size and scope. We feel one way to begin to assess governance networks is to understand their basic components (nodes, ties, and functions), their arrangements, and the challenges related to their administration, accountability, and performance. We believe this taxonomic approach provides a basis to build our knowledge about governance networks and to improve our understanding of the challenges and opportunities they offer.

We conclude in Chapter 12 by returning to the need to understand and support the normative basis through which governance networks obtain their democratic legitimacy. We discuss the relationship between public values, public interests, and governance networks and make the claim that governance network analysis is rooted in theories of democracy, in addition to the range of systems and network theory discussed in this book.

Approaches to Reading This Book

We have written this book for several audiences: practicing public administrators (who we describe as "governance network administrators"), policy analysts, policy makers, students, and researchers. Below we suggest some of the ways that different kinds of readers can approach this book.

The Public Administrator

You are responsible for managing or coordinating some aspect of a governance network's operating or policy functions. As agents responsive and accountable to citizens, interest groups, or elected public officials working within a government or nonprofit organization, you are concerned with making good decisions, wisely using your professional discretion, and achieving your organization's policy goals or strategic mission.

Carrying out your work within the complicated and complex contexts found within governance networks will likely require that you take on a variety of roles. We define these roles in terms of being a regulator, a resource provider, a negotiator, a facilitator, and a broker. It requires that you are accountable to a variety of constituencies and stakeholders. It will also be likely that you will be expected to provide results, essentially performing your duties with due diligence and achievement.

You will want to approach this book as a guide for interpreting the governance networks in your midst. You will want to ask questions about who are the actors or players in your network, what motivates them, and how power and authority are welded. You will want to consider how horizontal, collaborative ties differ from vertical, command and control ties. You will want to know when you need to negotiate with other actors or facilitate interactions. You will want to think about where the boundaries of your governance network are drawn and why.

For the practicing public administrator, this book may be used as a guide for ascribing a language to a set of practices and structures that have always been in your midst. You may begin to incorporate some of this language into your strategic planning efforts or your performance management systems. You may use this language to decide which tools and strategies to pursue, when to enter into a new venture, or when to leave a dysfunctional one.

The Policy Analyst

You are responsible for analyzing public or social problems, identifying a set of possible solutions or policy tools and instruments, or evaluating the implementation and success of existing policies. You may be looking to develop models and forecasts to determine which combinations of policy actors and policy tools work best and under what circumstances. You may be looking to draw some conclusions about the impacts of a given policy to its ascribed policy goals.

You will likely be interested in using this book to define the kind of process and structural variables found within policy implementation structures and functions. You may use some of the theories referenced in the book to describe, analyze, and evaluate public policy problems and solutions. For the policy analyst, this book may be used to provide a conceptual basis for the analysis of public policies.

The Policy Maker

You are in a position to make decisions that will shape the design and coordination of public policies. You are responsible for selecting policy tools, providing incentives for certain kinds of policy actors to participate in a governance network. You may be in a position to determine what kind of resources will be available to the network. You will likely want to know if particular governance networks are performing well or not, and want to understand what is needed to sustain the desirable ones.

You will want to know that the governance networks that are accountable to you, and those to whom you are accountable, are capable of progressing, changing, or evolving into a desirable state. You will want to know what actions can be taken to effectively steer these networks. You will also want to know why some networks fail and which networks are detrimental to society.

For the policy maker, this book provides a mental framework for thinking about the relationship between policy actors, the nature of the ties between them, and the overarching structures and functions that determine how and to what extent the whole network adds public value, meets the public's interests, performs, and succeeds.

The Student of Public Administration and Public Policy

You are interested in learning how governance networks work and how best you may be able to study, survive, and thrive within them. You will likely be looking to compare one governance network to another. You will want to apply the framework or some of the language from this book to the study of written cases or living examples. You may cull the newspapers and news sites for examples of governance networks. You may write papers or reports using some of this framework to explain who is implicated in a particular network, the ties that bind them together, networks structures and functions, and the roles of feedback and performance indicators in the governance of the network as a whole. You may be interested in studying governance networks as the basis of a thesis, dissertation, or class assignment.

For the student, this book provides a foundation for understanding how some of the basic properties of network governance combine with trends like privatization, devolution, and partnership to shape your field of interest. This book is best used in relation to written case studies (some of which are recommended later in the book) and the active exploration of living examples.

The Researcher or Theorist

You are interested in building a body of empirical evidence pertaining to the governance of networks and developing theoretical constructs to describe and explain these social phenomena. You are interested in employing certain combinations of factors and variables to study the efficiency, effectiveness, and sometimes the failures of the governance networks in our midst.

You will be interested in how the conceptual framework described here holds together. If you are a quantitative researcher, you will likely be interested in determining which characteristics and variables are operationalizable and how the framework discussed here can be used to generate testable hypotheses. If you are a qualitative or case study researcher, you will be looking to see how aspects of this framework can be used to code narratives and explain observable social phenomena.

For the researcher or theorist, this book provides a synthesis of a wide-ranging array of literature. Perhaps something in this book inspires you to ask a new research question or frame a new thesis. Perhaps you will find something to critique here, tear apart, and perhaps reconstruct using other theoretical frameworks.

On the Web

Go to our website: www.uvm.edu/~cmplxgov <mailto:complexgovernance@uvm.edu> to find educational support materials such as power point presentations to use in courses and professional development opportunities, writable case study templates, and other news and useful items relating to building the field's capacity to describe, evaluate and design governance networks using the framework of this book. Post case studies of governance networks. Draw on other's case study materials. Learn about research and educational opportunities tied to this work. Be a part of building governance networks 2.0!

About the Authors

Christopher Koliba is an associate professor in the Community Development and Applied Economics Department <http://www.uvm.edu/cdae> at the University of Vermont (UVM) and the director of the Master of Public Administration (MPA) Program <http://www.uvm.edu/mpa> at UVM.

He possesses a Ph.D. and an MPA from Syracuse University's Maxwell School of Citizenship and Public Affairs. His research interests include organizational learning and development, governance networks and complex adaptive systems, action research methods, civic education, and educational policy. He has published articles in *Public Administration Review, International Journal of Public Administration, Administration & Society, Administrative Theory & Praxis, American Journal of Evaluation, Ecological Economics, Educational Policy, Journal of Public Affairs Education, Journal of Higher Education Outreach and Engagement, Michigan Journal of Community Service Learning, the American Behavioral Scientists,* and the *American Journal of Education.* Chris teaches courses pertaining to public policy and public affairs, public administration, governance networks, collaborative management, and the intersection of science and society. He is married, father of three children, and lives in central Vermont.

Jack W. Meek is professor of public administration at the College of Business and Public Management at the University of La Verne where he serves as Coordinator of Graduate Programs & Research and director of the Master of Public Administration Program. His research focuses on metropolitan governance including the emergence of administrative connections and relationships in local government, regional collaboration and partnerships, policy networks and citizen engagement.

Jack has published articles for encyclopedias, chapters for several books and articles in academic journals including the *International Journal of Public Administration, Public Administration Quarterly, The Journal of Public Administration Education, Administrative Theory and Practice,* and the *Public Productivity and Management Review, Public Administration Review/ and Emergence: Complexity and Organization.* Jack serves on the editorial boards of the International Journal of Organizational Theory and Behavior, State and Local Government Review and Social Agenda.

Asim Zia is an assistant professor in the Department of Community Development and Applied Economics at the University of Vermont. His professional career began as a civil servant in the Ministry of Finance and Economic Affairs of the Federal Government of Pakistan. He has a Ph.D. in public policy from the Georgia Institute of Technology. In 2005, the Association for Public Policy Analysis and Management (APPAM) honored him with its best doctoral dissertation award. His research is focused on the policy analysis of complex systems, governance networks and decision analysis in three substantive arenas. First, in the domain of environmental policy analysis and evaluation, he investigates descriptive, dynamic and normative dimensions of space-time scale choices, and subsequent valuation trade-offs, for designing and implementing public policies. Second, he is assessing the synergies and trade-offs among climate change mitigation and adaptation policies from the perspective of complex systems. Third, Asim is engaged in the modeling of metropolitan planning organizations as complex governance systems to improve the integration of transportation, air quality and land-use policies.

Chapter 1

The Emergence of Governance Networks: Historical Context, Contemporary Trends, and Considerations

> Inter-organizational, inter-governmental, and inter-sectoral coordination, of course, has always been important in American administration.
>
> **—Donald Kettl (2006, p. 13)**

In this opening chapter we make two arguments: (1) that governance networks have always been an integral feature of democratic governments and intersector arrangements, and (2) that several contemporary trends have accentuated the importance that governance networks play in modern democracies. Recognizing what is at stake here, we lay out several areas of consideration around which we organize the book. These critical considerations include descriptive, administrative, accountability, and performance challenges.

We anchor our first argument around a thought experiment first introduced by Thomas Paine in his classic pamphlet *Common Sense*. We use this thought experiment to argue that modern democratic governments are dependent on the evolution

1

of informal social networks into more formalized and complex network structures. We argue that the separation of power embodied in the U.S. Constitution (and borrowed from the trilateral form of government first developed in Great Britain) can be interpreted in terms of basic network structures. We also recognize how the early discussions about states' rights and the federalist system ultimately structured the networked features of intergovernmental relations that we find in the United States today. Drawing again on Paine's thought experiment, we briefly trace the history of intersector relations that emerged out of colonists' concerns about the roles of religious organizations and trading companies. We conclude this section by recognizing that a "politics of structure" (Wise, 1994) has always marked the relationships between governments, corporations, and nonprofit organizations.

We then turn to some of the contemporary trends that are influencing the development of new "innovations in governance." We chart how the moves to devolve, privatize, regulate (nationalize), and partner are contributing to the evolution of governance network structures. We lay the foundation for considering how these trends help shape who participates in governance networks, what roles and authorities they wield, and what functions they take on.

As we note in the opening pages of the chapter, the design and implementation of governance network structures need to be understood within the context of democratic systems. Drawing historical and contemporary developments we ask: Just what is at stake here? We discuss the extent to which the network turn that we describe here is leading to the undermining of state sovereignty or may be serving to form the basis of new forms of "democratic anchorage."

We conclude the chapter with an overview of the four major themes that will guide the remainder of the book. We lay out these themes as a series of considerations. We frame descriptive considerations as a matter of articulating many of the critical characteristics that may be used to describe, and ultimately analyze, governance networks. We frame administrative considerations in terms of the evolution of public administration theory and practice, suggesting that the field needs to deepen its understanding of how administrative roles and responsibilities are shaped by network configurations. Drawing on two of the major developments in public administration theory and practice of the last three decades, we highlight the importance that accountability and performance considerations need to play in the development of a comprehensive understanding of governance networks.

Networks as an Inherent Property of the U.S. Government

During the late 1700s, in what came to be the United States, some critical discussions were being had about the proper roles and configurations of government. We are reminded of the debates being had at the time concerning power, who had it, and how was it was to be exercised. These debates were not occurring simply as a rhetorical exercise, but to inform the construction of new institutions and social structures. As we have noted, the weighing of these ideas led to active experimentations that, some argue, are still going on today. Applying the network metaphor to the empirical study of networked configurations sheds new light on some of these enduring questions. We conclude that network configurations are engrained within our democratic structures and across our intersector relations.

In 1776 Thomas Paine authored the most widely read pamphlet of his era, *Common Sense.* In laying out an argument for the overthrow of the British monarchy, Paine provided his readers with a thought experiment designed to surface what he believed to be the place of government in the lives of free citizens. The thought experiment begins with a vision of a small band of settlers arriving in a pristine natural environment, with no signs of an existing human civilization. He asks the readers to think about what life would be like if there were no governments:

> A thousand motives will excite them thereto; the strength of one man is so unequal to his wants and his mind so unfitted for perpetual solitude that he is soon obliged to seek assistance and relief of another, who in his turn requires the same. Four or five united would be able to raise a tolerable dwelling in the midst of a wilderness, but no man might labor out the common period of life without accomplishing anything; when he had felled timber, he could not remove it, nor erect it after it was removed; hunger would urge him from his work and every different want call him a different way....
>
> Thus necessity, like a gravitating power, would soon form our newly arrived emigrants into society, the reciprocal blessings of which would supersede and render the obligations of law and government unnecessary while they remained perfectly just to each other; but as nothing but Heaven is impregnable to vice, it will unavoidably happen that ... they will begin to relax in their duty and attachment to each other, and this remissness will point out the necessity of establishing some form of government to supply the defect of moral virtue.
>
> Some convenient tree will afford them a statehouse, under the branches of which the whole colony may assemble to deliberate on public matters. It is more than probable that their first laws will have the title only of regulations, and be enforced by no other penalty than public disesteem. In this first parliament every man by natural right will have a seat.
>
> But as the colony increases, the public concerns will increase likewise, and the distance at which members may be separated will render it too inconvenient for all of them to meet on every occasion as at first.... This will point out the convenience of their consenting to leave the legislative part to be managed by a select number chosen from the whole body, who are supposed to have the same concerns at stake which those who

appointed them and who will act in the same manner as the whole body would act were they present.… And as [these representatives engage in] frequent interchange will establish a common interest with every part of the community, they will mutually and naturally support each other, and on this … depends the strength of government and the happiness of the governed. (Paine, as quoted in Adkins, 1953, pp. 5–6)

At first, Paine claims, this small band of settlers would have to fend for themselves, relying on each other to build each other's homes, hunt and forage for food, and eventually, cultivate the land. As the population grows, the informal ties that bind this small group are not enough to meet the needs of community. Certain members of the community may begin to specialize based on their particular skill sets and interests. This community soon has its share of carpenters, blacksmiths, farmers, etc. At its smaller scales, conflicts may be worked out between community members. However, at some critical point the complexity of living and working together gets to be too much to handle through informal means. Paine asks the reader, rhetorically, what would this community do? He describes what happens next. Community members would convene under "some convenient tree" to determine the rules of the community and, ultimately, how these rules are to be set and enforced. A fledgling government would be born out of what had been previously an informal network of settlers. Paine essentially argues that governments exist because communities of human beings reach a certain size at which point their informal networks need to be formalized, leading to the establishment of government institutions. Revisiting Paine's thought experiment reminds of us that our first governments emerged out of informal social networks.

Paine made the argument that monarchies were not a suitable form of government because they place control of society out of the hands of ordinary citizens. The founders recognized that displacing kings and queens as sovereign rulers did not do away with a more rudimentary consideration, namely, who had the power to decide and act on behalf of the public? The later feudal systems of Europe were arranged as hierarchies, with the monarch at the top. Power flowed from the top down. Rejecting monarchies, the founders understood that power needed to flow through some form of institutional structure. They placed a great deal of faith in the capacity of institutional structures to mitigate wanton exercise of power. Steeped in assumptions regarding the self-interested nature of human behavior, these founders sought to devise a structure of government designed to defuse the concentration of power from the hands of the few to the institutional structures of

"The founders sought to devise a structure of government designed to defuse the concentration of power from the hands of the few, to the institutional structures of the many."

the many. Although they did not explicitly use the term, the founders essentially turned to network structures for a solution.

The framers of the Constitution had a problem to solve. They were chiefly concerned about the concentration of power into the hands of a monarch, and wary of humans' capacity to act selfishly and concentrate power around them. "By 1787, not only had the theory of self-government been widely debated, but virtually every conceivable device for implementing it had been suggested, if not tried" (Ketcham, 1986, p. 3). The framers' ultimate solution was to devise a network of three separate institutions of authority (what network theory refers to as nodes) that we now describe in terms of legislative, judicial, and executive branches. Each branch would have its own combinations of checks and balances in relation to the other branches.

These checks and balances may be explained in terms of one branch having authority *over* the others, as well as all branches sharing authorities *with* each other. Thus, the *separation of powers* flows through relational ties that may be vertically, horizontally, or diagonally articulated (Figure 1.1).

In essence, the founders intuitively understood one of the major contributions that separate, distinct, yet interdependent institutions (networks) bring to the study and design of systems of governance, namely, that relational power may be conveyed through both vertical (hierarchical) and horizontal (collaborative) ties. Because each branch of government has its share of checks and balances vis-à-vis the others, they are encouraged to find ways to build strong horizontal ties between them and, when substantive disagreements persist, wield vertical authority to keep the other branches in check.

In Table 1.1 we adapt Thomas Birkland's matrix, in which he describes the separation of powers, identifying instances when the legislative, executive, or judicial branch of government exerts authority over the other branches. We have added descriptors for instances of when one branch has authority over the others (see the first row) and instances of when one branch defers authority to one of the others (see the first column). As an example, the executive branch may wield principal authorities over the legislative branch when laws are recommended or vetoed, and

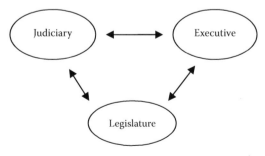

Figure 1.1   Separation of powers.

Table 1.1 Authority Distributed across the Separation of Powers

		Principal Authority Over ⇩		
		Legislature	Executive	Judiciary
Agent Authority To ⇧	Legislature	Make laws	Recommend laws; veto laws; make regulations that have the force of law	Review laws to determine legislative intent; new interpretations = law making
	Executive	Override vetoes; legislative vetoes of regulation; impeach president	Enforce and implement laws	Review executive acts; restrain executive actions
	Judiciary	Impeach judges; call witnesses in hearings	Pardon criminals; nominate judges	Interpret laws

Source: Adapted from Birkland, *An Introduction to the Policy Process: Theories, Concepts, and Models of Public Policy Making,* M.E. Sharpe, New York, 2001, p. 47.

make regulations that have the force of law, and in so doing, exert a certain measure of power and authority over the legislative branch.

Donald Kettl observes that "the Constitution—in its drafting, its structure, and its early function—was a remarkable balancing act of complex issues, political cross-pressures, and boundary-defined responses.... For generations since, flexible, bend-without-breaking boundaries have been the foundation of American government" (2006, p. 11). To this end, the network configuration of government conceived by the framers of the Constitution allows for frequent "border crossings" between branches and levels of government as well as between agencies and units within a particular branch. Because governments are network structures in their own right, we must be careful not to assume that government interests are represented by one, unified actor.

The public administrators responsible for operating within and across these network arrangements have always been confronted with challenges associated with the jurisdictional boundaries existing across levels of government. These challenges have most often been understood within the context of federalism, a topic that we turn to next.

Federalism

In addition to Paine's indirect ascertainment that governments emerge out of informal network ties, and the founders' reliance on network structures to devise a separation of powers, we find networks implicated in the decisions leading to the formulation of the relationship between federal and state governments, a debate codified in the federalist-antifederalist exchanges of 1787. The central concern in these debates centered on the relationship between a national government and its states. The antifederalists sought to codify the Articles of Confederation, which imbued the states with greater autonomy vis-à-vis the federal government. The federalists won this debate. The arguments of Alexander Hamilton regarding the need for a strong central government to ensure economic prosperity, coupled with James Madison's concerns about human nature and the need for a strong central government of checks and balances, compelled the framers of the Constitution to devise a strong federal government. However, this federal governance structure still made room for the existence of substantive state power. The federal government was not to rule over the states with an iron fist. That the Civil War, which has been described as the "war between the states," occurred brings this point home. Although the Civil War did not result in the dissolution of the United States, it provides us with an important reminder of what can happen when networks fracture to the point of breaking.

The Constitutional structure that was eventually enacted positioned the federal government as having vertical authority over state and local governments in some policy arenas, shared authority in other areas, and no authority over states and localities in still other areas. The Tenth Amendment reserve powers clause provides that "the powers not delegated to the United States by the Constitution, nor prohibited by it to the States, are reserved to the States respectively, or to the people." Phillip Cooper observes that "over time that provision has been read to mean that the power to regulate in matters of health, safety, and public welfare, commonly

THE 80,000 GOVERNMENTS OF THE UNITED STATES

1 national government
50 state governments
3,000+ county governments
35,000+ municipal governments
45,000+ special districts

Source: **Nownes,** *Pressure and Power: Organized Interests in American Politics,* **Houghton Mifflin, Boston, 2001, p. 31.**

**U.S. PUBLIC SECTOR
WORKFORCE COMPOSITION
(AS OF 1990)**

17% federal
25% state
58% local

Source: **Cigler, in Stivers, Ed.,**
Democracy, Bureaucracy, and
the Study of Administration,
Westview Press, Oxford, 2001, p. 356.

referred to as the police powers, are reserved to the states. Indeed, the Supreme Court has been increasingly willing in recent years to support that state authority and limit federal power. For this reason the federal government has had to rely on a system of intergovernmental grants and contracts to make important policies in these fields" (2003, p. 22).

The relationship between states and local governments is also implicated in this history, having been described as "the nation's oldest intergovernmental relationship (Walker, 1995, p. 267)" (Krane, Ebdon, and Bartle, 2004, p. 514). This history has been marked by the 1868 Supreme Court ruling in the *Clinton v. Cedar Rapids and Missouri River Railroad* case, eventually known as Dillon's rule. This ruling essentially made local governments agents of state legislatures (Miller, 2002, p. 30), requiring any changes to local government charters to be voted on by state legislative bodies. Although some states have moved away from relying on Dillon's rule, thirty-nine states currently rely on this structure to dictate state-local government relations (Richardson and Gough, 2003). The relative autonomy of local governments, vis-à-vis their state principals, has a bearing on the extent to which pushes for greater regionalization are possible (Richardson and Gough, 2003), a point we return to later in the book.

The distinctions between local, state, and national jurisdictions have been well captured in the voluminous literature pertaining to intergovernmental relations (IGR). Individual public administrators are often challenged by the need to seek clarification regarding the rules and roles governing intergovernmental relations. We argue that the crossing of intergovernmental boundaries gets mediated through legal interpretations of the U.S. Constitution and the legal and political precedence used to determine the distinction between national, state, regional, and local levels of government. Governance network administrators, particularly those immersed within intergovernmental networks, need to understand these legal, administrative, and political dynamics.

Networks as an Inherent Property of Intersector Relations in the United States

Governments at every geographic level are connected to a diverse array of private and nonprofit organizations, resulting in a complex array of intersector ties. In this section we provide a tertiary look at the history of these ties within the U.S. context, framing this history in terms of the "politics of structure" (Wise, 1994) that have marked it. We will explore how these ties may persist as one sector's attempt to influence the structures and behaviors of other sectors, or as collective attempts to engage in collective action and resource exchanges through governance networks. In this section we discuss intersector relations as a matter of macro-level considerations, focusing broadly on generalizations made about the relationship between governments and corporations, and government and nonprofit organizations. These generalizations will be built upon in later chapters.

As a sovereign authority, governments have the moral and legal authority to regulate businesses and industries, a fact first asserted when states established the rights to issue corporate charters. Governments wield authority over the private and nonprofit sectors through the establishment and enforcement of social, economic, and environmental regulations. Governments also contract with businesses to provide goods and services to meet public priorities and needs.

In the United States, governments have always regulated the operations of nonprofit organizations through charters that are registered at the state level. Legally recognized nonprofit organizations are required to have governing boards and comply with a set of economic and social standards to ensure nonprofit and, at times, tax-exempt status. Governments issue grants and contracts to nonprofit organizations for the delivery of public goods and services.

Intersector ties are bidirectional. Historically, corporations and nonprofit organizations have exerted influence over the structures and functions of governments. Corporations can influence public policies through campaign donations, lobbying, and their active involvement in public relations campaigns. As voluntary associations, nonprofit organizations serve as a conduit through which interests may be organized to undertake collective action. Nonprofit organizations also monitor the activities of governments.

The fledgling government of Paine's thought experiment would be founded to run the affairs of the local community and likely coexist alongside of local churches, budding artisan guilds, and the establishments of area merchants. Because governments require resources to run, these nongovernmental institutions might be hired to provide services or goods used by the government in the course of carrying out its duties (early forms of contract agreements). These social institutions would also likely exert some measure of influence over who serves in the government and how the government's affairs are carried out. This was certainly the case in early Puritan settlements of New England, as churches and church leaders played key roles in government. The influence of private sector organizations in governmental affairs is evident in the early settlements around Jamestown and elsewhere in the mid and lower Atlantic areas. Charles Wise has noted how the history of intersector relations may be marked by "the politics of structure" (Wise, 1994, p. 85), which extend across the intersector ties between governments and nonprofits, and governments and corporations.

Government-Nonprofit Relations

The early influences of religion in the New England settlements on the structures and functions of early colonial America led the framers of the Constitution to put in checks and balances to check the power that religion, religious institutions, and religious leaders could have upon government. The role of religion in the shaping of early American governments was considered by the framers of the U.S. Constitution and incorporated into the First Amendment, which called for the separation of church and state. In essence, they created a constitutional distinction between governments and religious institutions, leading to what we now understand as the differences between the public and voluntary sectors.

In the 1800s religious institutions increasingly served as charitable organizations that performed important social services that would later be taken on by governments. Early social service organizations operating outside of the scope of formal government laid the foundation for the modern welfare state. With the growth in the size and number of nonprofits, an argument can be made that trends toward privatization and partnership have renewed a nineteenth-century dynamic, whereby governments are using indirect polity tools to enable nonprofit service delivery (Block, 2001). Today in the United States there are approximately 1.2 million registered nonprofits.

The nonprofit sector (often referred to in the literature as the third, voluntary, or independent sector) contributed $621.4 billion to the U.S. economy in 1996, employed 10.2 million people, and engaged 5.7 million full-time equivalent volunteers (Boris, 1999, p. 6). Nonprofits make up approximately 6% of the total number of organizations in the United Sates. Between 1987 and 1997, the nonprofit sector grew 65%, compared to the business sector's 26%. In Chapter 3 we note the roles that the nonprofit sector plays in providing the social and physical spaces for citizens to associate with one another outside of the context of the state and private spheres.

Figure 1.2 visually lays out the distinction that Lester Salamon makes between member-serving and public-serving nonprofits.

The nonprofit sector has "traditionally served as a voice for articulating public needs and preferences" (DeVita, 1998, p. 229). The importance of voluntary associations to the cultivation of democratic culture was first recognized by Alexis de Tocqueville in 1831. More recently, the value of voluntary associations to the health and vibrancy of "civil society" and social capital has been the subject of extensive study and consideration (Putnam, 2000). Voluntary organizations have been described in terms of their capacities to represent interests (Crensen and Ginsberg,

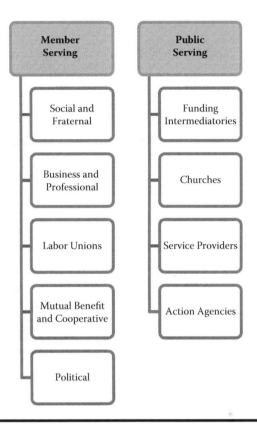

Figure 1.2 Anatomy of the nonprofit sector. (Compiled from: Salamon, in Ott, Ed., *The Nature of the Nonprofit Sector*, Westview Press, Boulder, CO, 2001, pp. 23–39.)

2003), an important factor when considering the "democratic anchorage" of the governance network.

The structures of nonprofit organizations have been mediated through governmental rules and regulations, such as charter requirements and a federal tax classification structure that places limits on the kinds of political influence that tax-exempt nonprofit organizations are able to wield. The U.S. Constitution contributes to the creation of interest group development by providing guarantees of free speech, association, and the right to petition the government for redress of grievances (Loomis and Cigler, 2002, p. 6).

Sector differences have been distinguished through Constitutional Law for reasons that have a significant bearing on how we come to understand governance networks. The separation of church and state and the evolving nature of corporate identity may be understood in terms of how power is structured within governance networks. The framers of the Constitution and, over time, the Supreme Court have had to consider how the public, private, and nonprofit sectors relate to each other.

The U.S. First Amendment right to free speech has been extended to corporations and interest groups. Arguably, interest groups have always had access to the levers of government, attempting to exert their influences through informal social ties between lobbyists and elected officials, as well as through the formation of interest group coalitions. "Historically, non-profits pioneered public programs that became government responsibilities when the demand grew beyond nonprofits' capacity to respond. These programs include primary education, kindergarten, disease control, and many more. People also created non-profits because the existing business or government services were not considered sufficient because they were inaccessible, costly, barebones, culturally or religiously inappropriate, ineffective, or not innovative" (Boris, 1999, p. 22).

Interest groups (sometimes referred to as factions, organized interests, pressure groups, and special interests) serve as "a natural phenomena in a democratic regime" (Loomis and Cigler, 2002, p. 3). Interest groups are formed to influence the structures, decisions, and actions of governments. Some types of interest groups, particularly lobbyists (and to an increasing extent, politically active think tanks), may become

> intensely focused and well informed on the issues of structuring government agencies that affect their interests.... [They] are in a position to pressure Congresspeople who have strong incentives to do what such groups want. Bureaucratic structure emerges from the battle of interests with features determined by the powers, priorities, and strategies of the various designers. (Wise, 1994, p. 85)

Given the nonprofit sector's capacity to be the space where interests are codified, defended, and advanced, they are "public-serving" organizations (Salamon, 2001) driven by their interests-centric missions.

Government-Corporation Relations

In early colonial Jamestown and some middle Atlantic colonies, British trading companies such as the Virginia Company and East India Company served as the primary colonizing agents. The early corporate-states were governed by these companies, which were eventually displaced as the settlements grew in size. The size and power of trading companies, most evident in their influence on British policies toward the colonies, led some colonists to distrust the role and influence that businesses and corporations might have in governmental affairs (Nace, 2005).

During the early decades of the United States, corporate power was reigned in through the use of corporate charters sanctioned by individual states, which often adopted substantial constraints around a company's mission and functions. This era of government-corporate relations was marked as a time of strong governmental influence over a corporation's activities. Some have

The boundaries created by early corporate charters included:

- Specification of performance function
- Life span ranging from 20 to 30 years
- Limited ownership rights
- Limited size
- Limited geographic scope
- Prohibition of intercompany ownership
- Performance criteria profit limitations

Source: Nace, *Gangs of America: The Rise of Corporate Power and the Disabling of Democracy*, Berrett-Koehler Publishers, San Francisco, 2005.

argued that government influence over corporations began to wane with the *Trustees of Dartmouth College v. Woodward* Supreme Court ruling of 1819. New Hampshire sought to turn Dartmouth College into a public institution and lost. This ruling initiated a steady shift in government-corporate relations, leading to the eventual treatment of corporations as legal citizens (*Santa Clara County v. Southern Pacific Railroad* (1886)), the overturning of charter limitations leading to development of a corporation's capacity to own other companies (Nace, 2005, p. 77), and having financial contributions equated with speech (*Buckley v. Valeo* (1976)). These extensions of rights and privileges have led some to assert that corporations wield too much power over the apparatus of governance (Nace, 2005).

Noting the coalescence of power in private firms, businesses, and corporations, Lowi observes that when "objective capitalistic practices are successfully employed privately for so many years ... institutions develop around them, classes of wealth emerge, power centers organize" (Lowi, 1969, p. 4). In the late 1960s and early 1970s Congress initiated some of the most extensive legislation related to the social regulation of business (Johnson, 2001), enacting over twenty major laws applying to social regulations, while passing statutes that initiated four more regulatory agencies (May, 2002) that would directly affect America's corporations. Under the Reagan administration, however, the strengths of these agencies were diminished. Social regulations were crippled due to new protocols that limited the creation of new regulations, and the degradation of compliance enforcement for older regulations (May, 2002). The Reagan administration's intent was to remove "the roadblocks that have slowed our economy and reduced productivity" (Reagan, 1981, para. 21), and extensively privatize as many government services as possible.

Private firms of all sizes and geographic locales have the capacity to organize their interests in attempts to influence how public problems are framed, policy solutions are selected and designed, and implementation decisions are made. These influences were accounted for in the early iron triangle model and more recently described as instances of "regulatory capture" (Peltzman, 1976).

Contemporary Trends Shaping Innovation in Governance Networks

Several social, political, and economic trends have shaped how contemporary governance networks are structured and function. These trends include the moves to devolve, privatize, partner, and more recently, re-regulate and even nationalize. Some have argued that these trends have arisen out of the collective recognition of the "wickedness" of prevailing social, political, and economic problems.

In this chapter we discuss how various types of mixed-form governance networks develop as a result of these trends. We define mixed-form governance as interorganizational networks comprised of relatively stable patterns of coordinated action and resource exchanges (Rhodes, 1997; Sorensen and Torfing, 2008) aligned around one or more policy functions. Within mixed-form governance networks, organizational and institutional actors are likely drawn from the public, private, and nonprofit sectors, and across geographic planes (local to international). They relate through a variety of vertical and horizontal administrative arrangements.

The Persistence of Wicked Problems

Social, public, and economic problems are increasingly viewed as "wicked problems" that lack clearly formulated definitions and ascriptions of cause and effect, are addressed through incremental decision making (Lindblom, 1959), and are moderated through "bounded rationality" (Simon, 1957). Referring to the persistence of implementation failure within the United States, Robert Behn has asserted that "most failures in performance are failures of collaboratives," recognizing that "in the United States, most public policies are no longer implemented by a single public agency with a single manager, but by a collaborative of public, nonprofit, and for-profit organizations" (2001, p. 72).

During the first decade of the twenty-first century, we find the failed performance of governance networks in the headlines. These performance failures include the poorly executed response and recovery efforts following landfall of Hurricane Katrina in 2005. This case highlights the challenges associated with applying the traditional structures of government bureaucracy to extremely complex and changing situations that call for the coordination of actors that span sectors and levels of government. In Iraq, we have seen controversies surrounding the role of private security forces and their seeming lack of accountability to democratic control. The reconstruction of Iraq has been marred by billions of dollars of cost

Wicked problems:

- Lack a definitive formulation
- Have no stopping rule
- Have solutions that are not true or false, but better or worse
- Lack immediate and ultimate tests of a solution
- Do not have an enumerable (or an exhaustively describable) set of potential solutions, or a well-described set of permissible operations that may be incorporated into the plan
- Are essentially unique
- Can be considered to be a symptom of another problem
- The existence of a discrepancy representing a wicked problem can be explained in numerous ways. The choice of explanation determines the nature of the problem's resolution (Rittel and Webber, 1984).

overruns, some of which having resulted from poorly structured and managed contracts. Most recently, the financial and economic crisis that hit in the fall of 2008 mainly centers on the underregulations of "innovative" mortgage products. These headline-grabbing cases underscore what we believe to be the proverbial tip of an iceberg. The challenges that we associate with managing in governance networks extend well beyond responses to catastrophic events or acts of war and occupation. These challenges may be found in any circumstance in which different actors, oftentimes with different operational characteristics, goals, and functions, work together to address any number of wicked problems that arise within the public domain.

The increasing complexity and "wickedness" of public problems (Rittel and Webber, 1984), the expansion of information technologies, and even globalization have fueled interest in the application of network frameworks to the study of public administration, public policy, and governance structures. We focus on three identifiable trends and perhaps one emerging trend that have influenced the development of governance networks, and will likely drive the proliferation of governance networks for many years to come. The first trend concerns the move to devolve government services and authority to lower levels of government. The second trend is the move to privatize or contract out. The third trend is the move to partnership. A fourth trend is re-emerging and may be characterized as the move to regulation, and perhaps even nationalize.

We argue that each of these trends contributes to the emergence of governance structures that have become, essentially, innovations in governing. Growing evidence suggests that these trends continue to shape interjurisdictional landscapes and represent new kinds of reform with regard to how government interacts with for-profit and not-for-profit enterprises in the design and delivery of public services

(Hula, 1999; Salamon, 2002b). In many cases, these reforms are geared toward seeking efficiencies in service production. In other cases, these reforms are advanced as "market solutions" or collaborative arrangements.

The Move to Devolve

Devolution is "based on the assumption that decisions are best made by people and governmental units closest to the problem" (DeVita, 1999, p. 213). The contemporary trends toward devolving government services and funding to more local levels of government began in earnest in the early 1980s in the United States. In the United States, devolution "fortified the role of state government by making them the administrators of national policies in such fields as low-income health care, cash welfare, education policy, and transportation" (Hovey, 1999, p. 4). According to Sawicky, "if we exclude Social Security, Medicare, net interest on the federal debt, and defense from the total expenditures of federal, state and local governments in the United States, 80% of what remains is administered by state and local governments" (Krane, Ebdon, and Bartle, 2004, p. 514).

The devolution of federal funding to the states was a key strategy in the Great Society programs. From 1960 to 1980 there was an "unprecedented outpouring of financial aid to states and localities," peaking in 1978 (Krane, Ebdon, and Bartle, 2004, p. 514). Beginning in 1980, funding from the federal government to the states began to decline, with federal grants-in-aid amounting to 26.5% of state and local spending in 1980 down to 19.1% in 1987 (Krane, Ebdon, and Bartle, 2004, p. 514). This second wave of devolution was predicated by the increasing decentralization of public services without substantial federal funding. Krane and his associates have noted the ideological thrust of the Reagan administration that marked this area of devolution in the United States. "In many respects, Reagan viewed the national government as if it were the *Leviathan*, a ruler or government that systematically seeks to maximize budgetary resources, even over the opposition of the

---

FACTORS CONTRIBUTING TO THE DEVOLUTION OF POWER TO SMALLER UNITS OF GOVERNMENT

■ Too much federal government
■ Loss of control and accountability
■ Cookie-cutter policies
■ Waste and inefficiency

Source: Hovey, *The Devolution Revolution: Can the States Afford Devolution?* Century Foundation, New York, 1999.

citizens. Devolution was the sword by which he could slay the beast (Krane, 1990)" (Krane, Ebdon, and Bartle, 2004, p. 519).

One consequence of devolution is the increasing reliance on regionalization, particularly in larger metropolitan areas. Writing about the trends impacting regionalization, David Miller observes that as "systems of local government are becoming more diffused or decentralized, they are becoming more coordinated … most lasting regional approaches emerge as negotiated agreements between players over time" (Miller, 2002, p. 4). The strong role that state governments play in mediating local government charters, particularly in states in which Dillon's rule is being adhered to, has been recognized as significant in either helping or hindering the application of regionalization as a response to the devolution of powers.

The Move to Privatize

Stressing reforms to make governments operate more like businesses has been an ongoing subtext within the public administration field since Woodrow Wilson first suggested that public administration is a "field of business" (Rosenbloom, 2004, p. 446). Subsequently, those who study the functions and structures of government have looked to the private sector as a model of efficiency and a talent pool from which to recruit qualified public servants. We examined the public-private connections of public service creation earlier in this chapter and discuss how the public sector has coevolved along with the private and nonprofit sectors since the birth of the United States. We noted how power and authority between these sectors have evolved from early corporate charters (Nace, 2005) and voluntary associations (Couto, 1999) to the contemporary privatization movement (Moe, 1987; Donahue, 1999; Savas, 2005) and the "post-regulatory state" (Crawford, 2006) of the modern era.

The desire to run governments more like businesses became a central tenant of U.S. federal government reforms with the proliferation of extensive privatization efforts beginning in the 1980s and the "reinventing government" efforts of the 1990s. Instead of relying on government as the sole producer of public goods and services, the Clinton administration advanced a "new public management" paradigm that placed an emphasis on the use of markets and market forces to deliver public goods and services. Those calling for deference to markets and market forces for the delivery of public goods and services "frequently begin with a reverential view of market competition and an assumption that such competition is superior to government monopoly. They assume that leaving things to the market will produce superior results" (Kettl, 2002, p. 491). As such, privatization became a commonly held, and sometimes dominant, perspective in the new public management paradigm.

Charles Wise has observed that "privatization is not a single policy but is an umbrella concept that has come to mean a variety of policies. These include transfer of ownership (sales of state-owned assets and enterprises); deemphasizing monopoly production of public services by introducing or increasing competition or reducing obstacles to it in the hope of increasing efficiency in the production of public services (contracting out portions of public activity); encouraging private production of services that are currently provided by government" (1994, p. 84). Privatization also "involves deregulation, policy decentralization, downsizing of government, outsourcing of public services and privatization of sectors previously assumed to be what economists called 'natural monopolies' including gas, electricity, telephones and so forth" (Linder and Rosenau, 2000, pp. 4–5).

There is strong reason to believe that recent reforms designed to turn more of the delivery of public goods and services over to market forces have led to profound shifts in how governments are structured and power is distributed. Indeed, by the winter of 2007, the U.S. federal government funded more contractors than civil servants, leading some to assert that private contractors have become the "fourth branch" of government (Shane and Nixon, 2007). In a study of the 1999 U.S. federal budget, Salamon found that only about 28% of the federal government expenditures supported the direct delivery of public goods and services, leaving the remaining 72% of expenditures used to support indirect policy tools (Table 1.2) (Salamon, 2002a).

These kinds of shifts in service design and funding support suggest that nonprofit and for-profit organizations are increasingly taking on functions once reserved to the state sphere. Kettl (2002) and Salamon (2002a) have described this shift as moving from direct government to indirect government, suggesting that indirect government is facilitated through *indirect policy tools*. Policy tools are "instruments of public action" that "can be defined as an identifiable method through which collective action is structured to address a public problem" (Salamon, 2002a, p. 19). We will explore how policy tools help to structure the "rules of the game" that dictate who participates and how they participate.

As the result of the proliferation of indirect policy tools, Salamon concludes: "Public problem solving has become a team sport that has spilled well beyond the borders of government agencies and now engages a far more extensive network of social actors—public as well as private, for-profit as well as non-profit" (Salamon, 2002b, p. 600). Salamon and his colleagues have asserted that policy tools play a major role in shaping network structures, a claim that we revisit in later chapters (2002b).

Several reasons are given to explain the recent proliferation of indirect policy tools. Indirect policy tools are said to "inject a degree of competition into the provision of public services, breaking the monopoly of governmental agencies and thereby potentially improving service quality and 'customer' orientation" (Salamon, 2002a, p. 31). Thus, the use of indirect policy tools is viewed as an extension of the new public management perspective in public administration by favoring the infusion of markets and market forces into the delivery of public goods and services.

Indirect policy tools are said to "provide access to talents and resources" that are needed to cope with complex public problems (Salamon, 2002a, p. 31). The increasing reliance on indirect policy tools gets presented as a matter of building and drawing on social and human capital to address what are increasingly being

Table 1.2   Scale of U.S. Federal Government Activity, by Tool of Public Action Fiscal Year, 1999

		Amount ($ bil.)	%
Direct Government	Goods and services	186.8	5.2
	Income support	550.4	15.4
	Interest	229.7	6.4
	Direct loans	38.4	1.1
Subtotal, Direct		1005.3	28.1
Indirect Government	Contracting	198.8	5.6
	Grants	286.4	8.0
	Vouchers	251.0	7.0
	Tax expenditures	602.0	16.8
	Loan guarantees	252.4	7.0
	Government-sponsored loans	409.2	11.4
	Deposit insurance	376.1	10.5
	Regulation	200.0	5.6
Subtotal, Indirect		2575.9	71.9
GRAND TOTAL		3581.2	100.0

Source: Salamon, 2002a. Permission granted by Oxford University Press.

perceived to be "wicked" and "swampy" public problems. Historically, the non-profit and for-profit sectors have always been tapped to provide necessarily public goods and services (Cooper, 2003). In recent decades, the move to privatize has accentuated this codependence.

Privatization has also impacted the development of regulations and the regulatory dynamics that arise through them. Recent trends, fueled by deference to markets, have led to a move away from traditionally defined regulatory relationships, in which governments served as the principal authorities over their regulated agents, toward more collaborative arrangements, characterized in terms of self-regulation and "regulatory capture" (Peltzman, 1976). We will be describing these governance networks as regulatory subsystems that involve governmental and nongovernmental actors in some kind of regulatory relationship.

INDIRECT TOOLS

■ Inject a useful degree of competition into the provision of public services, breaking the monopoly of governmental agencies and thereby potentially improving service quality and "customer orientation"
■ Provide access to talents and resources that are desperately needed to cope with complex public problems
■ Offer a greater degree of flexibility, making it easier for government to experiment, to change course when needed, and thus to remain responsive to new needs (Salamon, 2002a, p. 31)

Lastly, indirect policy tools have been described as offering "a greater degree of flexibility, making it easier for government to experiment, to change course when needed, and thus to remain responsive to new needs" (Salamon, 2002a, p. 31). Indirect policy tools such as grants and contracts are used to foster experimentation and innovation. When these experimentations are most successful, learning and knowledge transfer result, and arguably, society is said to benefit.

The work of E. S. Savas (2005) focuses on privatization of public services and public-private partnerships and reflects "public goods" logic with regard to the design and implementation of public services. Savas (2005) asserts that "we are experiencing a reorientation of government, a redirection away from a top-down approach" (p. 328) "Privatization ... is not merely a management tool but a basic strategy of societal governance" (p. 329). It is clear that governance in this perspective is one that seeks to deliver services in efficient and effective ways—through privatization and public-private partnerships.

The Move to Partner

The creative use of partnerships by public administrators allows for various stakeholders to jointly address seemingly borderless problems. Collaborative actions allow for both state and nonstate entities "to address certain kinds of highly complex problems that appear to be beyond the capacity of sovereign states alone to solve" (Karkkainen, 2004, p. 74). Partnering implies that there is a spreading of risk (Linder, 2000, p. 20) as well as common agreement around provisions to share or pool resources. Partnering is used to improve economies of scale and scope (Bovaird, 2004, p. 207).

Governmental actors may use indirect policy tools as a way to structure or contribute resources to public-private partnerships. Public-private partnerships (PPPs) are intersector partnerships that have been pursued to foster innovation, experimentation, and flexibility. As social, environmental, and economic problems become more complex and wicked, public-private partnerships are being pursued as a means of shifting risks, sharing power, and leveraging resources across sectors (Linder and Rosenau, 2000; Bovaird, 2005). "Partnering involves sharing of both responsibility and financial risk. Rather than shrinking government in favor of private-sector activity through devolution of public responsibility, or other forms of load-shedding, in the best of situations partnering institutionalizes collaborative arrangements where the difference between the sectors becomes blurred" (Linder and Rosenau, 2000, p. 6).

PPPs are a relatively recent development in governance network structures. Several reasons have been given for entering into PPPs. Table 1.3 illustrates Linder's review of why PPPs form.

The PPP was first widely used in the United States to advance local economic development. Writing on the history of PPPs, Linder observes that "despite momentum gathered since the late 1980s … the partnership is not new to governance. More than a decade earlier, without the fanfare or reformist cachet, partnerships were deployed by the federal government in the United States as a tool for stimulating private investment in inner-city infrastructures. Likewise, partnerships were key to coordinating federal initiatives in regional economic development. The record of these devices through the 1970s is at best mixed (Stephenson, 1991, pp. 109–127)" (Linder, 2000, p. 19). In Chapter 6 we explore the public-private partnership in greater detail.

Table 1.3 Rationale for Why Public–Private Partnerships Form

Partnership as:	Conceptions of Partnership
Management reform	Chance for government to learn business practices from the private entity it is partnering with
Problem conversion	"Commercialize problems" so private firms will be enticed to solve them
Moral regeneration	Market forces will instill government bodies with virtues
Risk shifting	Leveraging of government ability whereby a private sector entity buys into a public project
Restructuring public service	Cutting through government red tape by moving from a public to a private workforce
Power sharing	Replaces the adversarial relationship between government and private firms with a give-and-take one

Compiled from: Linder, in Rosenau, Ed., *Public Private Partnerships*, MIT Press, Cambridge, MA, 2000, pp. 19–36.

The Move to Regulate and Nationalize

Teske defines regulations as "policy choices made by governments that limit the private behavior of citizens or businesses. Sometimes these regulations are general decisions that are captured in laws or statutes and thus are the direct products of legislatures and [elected executives]" (Teske, 2004, p. 5). During the course of writing this book, the United States, and indeed the entire globe, experienced a profound shift in how privatization and the reliance on "market solutions" are viewed. The Obama administration is calling for a renewal of strong regulatory practices that may signal the reinvigoration of the state as a stronger authority. It would seem that the era of deregulation that had marked the last three decades is facing serious scrutiny. Deregulation has been cited as one of the causes behind the crisis in the real estate and credit markets, including the failure to intervene in the "housing bubble," financial deregulation and unchecked financial "innovation," private regulatory failure, and no controls over predatory lenders (Weissman, 2008). In Chapter 6 we explore some of the historical roles that governments have played in the regulation of industry. The era of deregulation and self-regulation that has marked the most recent era of government reform may in fact be waning, at least for the financial services and automotive industries.

The recent downturn in the economy and resulting threats of corporate bankruptcies have contributed to a rise in interest in nationalization. The move to nationalize reasserts the observation that "corporations are essentially political constructs. Informally, they are adjuncts of the state itself" (Berle and Means, 1968, p. xxvii). The extent to which the current economic crisis leads to greater regulation and even nationalization of some industries is still yet to be determined. We argue, however, that the move to regulate and nationalize bears significant implications for governance network theory and research.

Donald Kettl has suggested that the financial crisis of 2008 could be leading to the formulation of a new "social contract" between governments and industry (2009). The extent to which "the rules of the game" have been rewritten will be better known as time goes on. The questions pertaining to the regulation of industry and the extent to which some industries pose to become "moral hazards" that are essentially too big to fail is, we argue, an enduring trend that shapes the structures and functions of governance networks. We recognize this claim by accounting for networks that are built as a result of regulatory frameworks into the model.

Types of Networks Arising out of These Trends

We are left to conclude that these trends have stimulated the development of certain configurations of actors that are arranged into some distinct form of governance networks. We recognize that the development of mixed-form governance networks may be shaped through a variety of indirect policy tools and interorganizational arrangements that are either:

Developed as a result of inter- and intragovernmental relations. We assert that modern democratic governments organized around the separation of powers and levels of interlocking geographic scale can be understood in terms of network configurations. We refer to this kind of governance network as an intergovernmental network, relying heavily on Wright's models of intergovernmental relations (2000).

Structured through grant and contract agreements. We refer to this kind of governance network as a grant and contract agreement. Privatization and contracting out through grants and contract agreements is often touted as the harnessing of "private energies" by allocating public funds to private firms and nonprofits (Donahue, 1989) through the policy tools of procurement and purchase of service contracts, and grants.

Structured through regulations. We refer to this kind of governance network as a regulatory subsystem comprised of interorganizational networks of regulators and regulated entities. The traditional outlook on regulatory subsystems places government regulators as the principals over regulated agents. These traditional relational ties are grounded in the state's capacity to render coercive power to control the behaviors of regulated agents. The move away from coercive regulation to more voluntary forms of compliance has led some to raise concerns about the "regulatory capture" of government regulators (Levine and Forrence, 1990; Laffont and Tirole, 1991), leading to a shift of regulatory powers away from states and into the hands of the regulated agents. The financial crisis that came to the public's attention in September 2008 may lead to an increase in state regulatory powers.

Designed to influence the framing of public problems and derivation of policy solutions. We refer to this kind of governance network as an interest group coalition: interorganizational networks of organized interest groups, advocacy organizations, and collective interest groups. These coalitions engage in coordinated action to influence the framing of public problems, the design and selection of policies, or the evaluation of policy implementation. Interest group coalitions "are arguably the central method for aggregating the viewpoints of organized interests in American politics. They serve as institutional mediators reconciling potentially disparate policy positions, in effect 'predigesting' policy proposals before they are served to the legislature" (Hula, 1999, p. 7).

Formed when organizations from different sectors partner with each other to achieve public purposes. We refer to this kind of governance network as a public-private partnership (PPP), a strategic alliance between public, private, and nonprofit sector entities in which risk is shared and power between the partnering entities is relatively distributed in nature. PPPs are typically formed to "increase the scale and visibility of program efforts, to increase support for projects, and to leverage capital to enhance feasibility, speed, or effectiveness" (O'Toole, 1997, p. 46). The distribution of resource and power will likely vary across PPPs of differing functions and actor compositions.

We explore how these factors help to give shape to governance networks by drawing extensively on the relevant theoretical frameworks found across many fields of discourse. In this chapter we have argued that several trends have led to an increasing reliance on governance networks contributing to the proliferation of one or more of the factors cited above. We have argued that these trends are shaped largely through the proliferation of "indirect policy tools" (Salamon, 2002; Kettl, 2002) that position particular governmental actors as members of interorganizational governance networks. There is a great deal at stake when governments' roles get "hollowed out." Some of the administrative, accountability, and performance challenges that arise as a result of these changing dynamics are discussed in the final third of the book.

The Stakes: Withering State or Democratic Anchorage?

Not all view sector blurring in the design and delivery of public services as an apparent good. Concerns about "hollowed-out government" refer to the kinds of accountability and performance challenges that result from weakened state authority (O'Toole, 1997). In writing about the increasing role that interest groups play in the policy process, Theodore Lowi observed that these new forms of "pluralistic" relationships may lead to an "impotent" government. He goes on to add that "government that is unlimited in scope but formless in action is government that cannot plan. Government that is formless in action and amoral in intention (i.e. *ad hoc*) is government that can neither plan nor achieve justice" (1969, p. x). If governance networks form as unplanned, unintended, or *ad hoc* manifestations of incremental actions, the legitimate power and authority of the state is challenged.

Those most concerned about the withering of state authority have framed their critiques in terms of neoliberalism and the new public management as paradigms of public service that rely upon market incentives rather than public service motivations (Denhardt and Denhardt, 2003). Concerns regarding sector blurring can be viewed in terms of challenges associated with strong state roles. Nor do all view the kinds of collaborative arrangements found in certain kinds of networks as an inherent good either (Bardach, 1998). Although collaboration may be a viable means for leveraging human and social capital and, as we will argue, building democratic anchorage, it can be an ineffective means for delivering public goods and services. In the worst-case scenarios, collaboration can lead to decidedly undemocratic practices. We must account for the possibility that in the worst cases, collaboration can result

> "The shift in perception from government monopolies to governance as a 'team sport' involving actors from across social sectors calls for the reconsideration of two critical public administration concerns: the role of the state and the administrative functions undertaken by agents of the state."

in group think or collusion: a togetherness mentality lacking intelligent debate or a plotting together toward an unethical end.

The shift in perspective from government monopolies to governance as a "team sport" involving actors from across social sectors calls for the reconsideration of two critical public administration concerns: the role of the state and the administrative functions undertaken by agents of the state. As a result of the proliferation of indirect policy tools and partnership strategies, "the state has become a differentiated, fragmented, and multicentered institutional complex that is held together by more or less formalized networks," resulting in the blurring of boundaries between the public, private, and nonprofit sectors (Sorensen, 2006, p. 100). Some argue that "the model of a unitary, state-centered hierarchical political decision making structure has always been a fiction, quite remote from real-life decision making" (Adams and Kriesi, 2007, p. 132).

Traditional views of government roles, responsibilities, and structures are not enough to account for the complexities inherent to modern governance systems. The proliferation of these networks leads to the blurring of the lines between public, private, and nonprofit sectors (Sorenson, 2006, p. 100). Government agencies have been described as serving as brokers (Cooper, 2003, p. 47; also see Kettl, 2006) in addition to direct service providers and regulators. Governments have been described as playing roles as rowers *and* steerers (Denhardt and Denhardt, 2003); leaders *and* followers (Koontz et al., 2004); boundary spanners (Kettl, 2006); orchestrators, modulators, and activators (Salamon, 2002a); and mandaters, endorsers, facilitators, and partners (Fox et al., 2002) in governance networks. The extent to which these "new" roles are positive developments that are, in the long run, good for democracy is an unsettled matter. We need to ask some critical questions about these new roles, assessing how and to what extent the traditional responsibilities (or in some cases, the lack of responsibilities) assumed by the state are still relevant. This begs us to ask: Are governance networks contributing to the

REASONS TO BE OPTIMISTIC ABOUT NETWORKS

- Networks provide greater points of access for citizens and organized interests to be involved
- Market accountability may achieve greater efficiencies
- Collaboration builds capacity

REASONS TO BE CONCERNED ABOUT NETWORKS

- Insufficient democratic anchorage
- Regulatory capture (interest groups and political insiders manipulate the system for their own gains and to the disadvantage of those who do not have the resources to organize)
- Dark networks (inflict intentional social harm)
- Underperformance (don't achieve goals/results)
- Too complex to understand

withering of the state and the sovereign authorities that it carries, or does a positive assessment of governance networks hinge on the extent to which they remain democratically anchored?

Governance, as it is being used here and across the public administration and policy studies literature, is a concept deeply rooted in democratic theory that situates the state as a sovereign entity, vested with the legitimate power to use its authority for the betterment of the common good. At this point, it is unclear whether the expanded roles that governments take on in governance networks undermine their capacity to bring their sovereign authority to the network. Some views of network governance assume that the state plays a state-centric role in the activities of governance networks, with government institutions serving as lead organizations. Others view the state as being in a weaker role, subjected to some combination of broader societal factors or market forces (Pierre and Peters, 2005). The extent to which the state does bring its sovereign position to the governance networks is a critical consideration.

Those concerned that governmental authority is weakened in governance networks have employed terms like "governing without government" (Rosenau, 1992), the "postregulatory state" (Crawford, 2006), and the "disarticulation of the state" (Frederickson, 1999, p. 702). Cases of weakened state power may be found in studies of interest group coalitions' influence over policy design, coordination, and implementation (Hula, 1999) and in instances of regulatory capture (Peltzman, 1976). We also find evidence of weakened state powers in critical studies of privatization and contracting that examine contracting performance, oversight measures, and competitive bidding processes. The advancement of PPPs as a strategy has been described by their critics as a potential "Trojan horse," contributing to the steady erosion of state sovereignty (Miraftab, 2004).

Governments require adequate staffing and information and, arguably, the political will to enforce contracts and regulatory standards. They must be both responsive to and resistant against special interests, and negotiate the best deals on behalf of the public (Cooper, 2003). The political will to enforce contracts and regulatory standards is shaped, in part, by the formal and informal network relationships that occur between governments and the corporations and nonprofits that may attempt to exert political influence over contracting decisions. The same might be said for instances of regulatory capture as it exists between industries and their regulating governmental bodies.

For all intents and purposes, the complexity of governance networks can render them invisible, leading to a lack of transparency and the development of "centres of power and privilege that give structural advantage to particular private interests in the process of making or shaping public policy decisions (Lowndes, 2001)" (Klijn and Skelcher, 2007, p. 588).

Others assert that the "death of the public bureaucracy" is vastly overstated, often arguing that public institutions are not only still relevant, but still wield extensive power to carry out public affairs (Goodsell, 2006). Still others view governance networks as offering "one route to enhanced [democratic] accountability precisely because it has the potential to draw more actors into a process of deliberative policy-making and implementation" (Klijn and Skelcher, 2007, p. 594). In this view, network structures are both complex and adaptive and can "accommodate the changed nature of society and the complex policy problems it faces" (Klijn and Skelcher, 2007, p. 596). This complexity and adaptability can provide more "surface area" through which citizens and interest groups can enter and influence the actions of the network.

As we argued earlier in this chapter, the "politics of structure" (Wise, 1994) has always historically existed between sectors. As governance network structures are used with increasing frequency, greater "institutional and management capacity [is] necessary to meet the many new challenges before us. That will, in turn, require hybrid institutions that can both carry out a variety of what might be regarded as traditional responsibilities of governance and, simultaneously, emphasize various kinds of contractual agreements, both formal and informal, as a critically important mode of operation" (Cooper, 2003, pp. 47–48).

A governance network's capacity to support or hinder democratic accountability hinges on its capacity to be what Eva Sorensen and Jacob Torfing (2005) describe as "democratically anchored." Sorensen and Torfing assert that "governance networks are democratically anchored to the extent that they are properly linked to different political constituencies and to a relevant set of democratic norms that are part of the democratic ethos of society" (2005, p. 201). Similarly, the concept of "public value" has been advanced in terms of network governance. Stoker observes that "the judgment of what is public value is collectively built through deliberation involving elected and appointed government officials and key stakeholders. The achievement of public value, in turn, depends on actions chosen in a reflective manner from a range of intervention options that rely extensively on building and maintaining network provisions" (2005, p. 42). In Chapter 9 we discuss the extent to which democratic anchorage of a governance network can be construed as a matter of degree, rather than in absolute terms.

Governments play a critical role in governance networks by funneling symbolic power and cultural authority to the network; informing public perceptions of the network, lending it legitimacy; allocating distinctive (tactical) resources and providing sources of information through which interests are pursued; and serving as a backup of last resort with regard to other forms of control (Crawford, 2006, p. 459). States contribute to the democratic anchorage of a governance network most directly through the privileged position that elected officials play as representatives of a territorially defined citizenry. If government actors play informal or weak roles in a governance network, the democratic anchorage that they bring to the network will be limited. The resultant networks tend to "resist government steering, develop their own policies and mold their environment" (Kickert et al., 1997a, p. xii). Thus, we may conclude that governments are critical actors in governance networks if they maintain a sufficient level of democratic anchorage. Regardless, we must also recognize the roles that nonprofit organizations play as voluntary associations comprising civil society and facilitating democratic participation processes. We will also consider the ways in which corporations and businesses are accountable to a variety of stakeholders and social pressures. These considerations materialize in the adoption of "triple bottom line" standards and corporate social responsibility initiatives. All of these matters will be addressed in Chapter 9.

Government participation in governance networks is not, unto itself, the only critical consideration that we will address over the course of this book. Governance networks pose significant challenges to those concerned about their effective and efficient functioning. We discuss these challenges in terms of certain descriptive, administrative, accountability, and performance considerations.

Descriptive Considerations

What are governance networks? How are they structured? What functions do they carry out?

Having performed an extensive analysis of the literature relating to interorganizational networks, Provan, Fish, and Sydow conclude that "no single grand theory of networks exists" (2007). The interorganizational networks described in the public administration and policy studies literature are often of such complexity that it is difficult for one single theory to account for all possible variables and combinations of variables. George Frederickson observes that the current phase of theory development is "neither theoretically tidy nor parsimonious," and "at this point there isn't a single theory that puts its arms around third party governance" (Frederickson, 2007, p. 11). The sheer range of theoretical constructs that can conceivably be marshaled to describe governance networks calls for interdisciplinary approaches to the study of governance networks. Such an undertaking calls for some measure of comfort with ambiguity, and the potential for combining and recombining conceptual frameworks often associated with one theoretical tradition or another. The lack of theoretical tidiness around governance networks (and its related terms) may provide opportunities for conceptual innovations. A lack of theoretical tidiness should, ultimately, be mitigated as more empirical evidence is collected, a point that we will address in Chapter 11.

In this book we synthesize a diverse array of theoretically defined, and in some cases empirically tested, conceptual frameworks derived from a body of literature found across the sociology of organizations, organizational development and change, social network, systems theory, and complexity theory literature. We also draw heavily upon the multiple paradigms of public administration and management theory, policy network theory, and policy stream and governance models.

In a 1997 article titled "Treating Networks Seriously," Laurence O'Toole called for three kinds of theoretical and empirical developments needed to bring governance networks into sharper focus (O'Toole, 1997, p. 48): (1) Determine what networks, and what kinds of networks, can be found in today's administrative settings; (2) examine the historical dimension of network formation and development; and (3) explore the array of networks in a broadly comparative perspective. Throughout this book we directly tackle O'Toole's first objective, introducing a relatively comprehensive, but admittedly theoretically untidy, set of frameworks to describe mixed-form governance networks. In Chapter 2, we discuss some of the historical dimensions of network formation in relation to developments in intergovernmental and intersectoral ties. By contributing to the development of network descriptors, we hope to ultimately assist in the development of the field's capacity to carry out comparative analysis of governance networks of mixed forms.

A summary of the major conceptual developments that are relevant to governance network theory is provided in Table 2.1. As a result of our review of this literature, several conceptual questions are evident. Some of these questions emerge out of what appears to be conceptual contradictions apparent across the literature. We frame these conceptual challenges below as critical questions to guide governance network analysis.

> *Macro-level forms: Are hierarchies and markets forms of networks, or should networks be considered distinct from them?* The first question may be characterized in terms of the application of the term *networks* in relation to what some have described as alternatives to other macro-level organizational forms: hierarchies and markets. As we will discuss in Chapter 2, two schools of thought exist regarding the relationship between networks, hierarchies, and markets. One school of thought views networks solely in terms of the inherent nature of their horizontal ties, and another school of thought views hierarchies and

markets as variations of network form. We argue that the former position limits our capacity to describe, compare, and evaluate network configurations that possess certain combinations of vertical, horizontal, and competitive ties within them.

Administrative authority: How do we account for mixed (vertical and horizontal) administrative ties in networks? If networks are to be conceived as comprised of both vertical and horizontal relationships, as is recognized in Agranoff and McGuire's (2003) case studies of local community economic development networks, and in the literature on network management (Koppenjan and Klijn, 2004), then it becomes important to develop a conceptual framework that accounts for mixed forms of administrative authority. The question of mixed-form authorities is posed in terms of the need to develop a theoretical framework of public administration that establishes authority for networks that work across vertical and horizontal ties.

Sectoral composition: How do we account for multisector arrangements in networks? Grant and contract agreements, regulatory systems, and public-private partnerships have been described as involving actors from across the public, private, and nonprofit sectors. The importance of cross-sector relationships has been described in terms of boundary blurring (Kettl, 2006), as instances of regulatory capture (Peltzman, 1976), and most recently, in the context of re-regulation and nationalization. The implications of sector blurring have been framed as classical trade-offs between markets and democracy (Stone, 2002), governments and businesses (Moe, 1987), and public funding and charitable giving (Horne, Van Slyke, and Johnson, 2006). Sector blurring also raises important questions pertaining to public and democratic accountability, suggesting that the relationship between sectoral characteristics and the roles, resources, and influences they bring to governance networks needs to be understood.

Policy functions: How do we account for networks taking on functions related to multiple policy streams? Some network configurations have been associated with policy functions ascribed to a particular segment of the policy cycle (Patton and Sawicki, 1986) or policy stream (Kingdon, 1984). Early renditions of the iron triangle and issue networks, for instance, focused on the roles of interorganizational networks in the problem-framing and policy creation phases (Heclo, 1978). Drawing on studies of policy implementation (O'Toole, 1990), network configurations have also been associated with postenactment phases. However, the line between pre- and postenactment phases of the policy cycle is rarely discrete. Kingdon's policy stream model is used as a nonlinear approach to policy development and implementation. According to Kingdon, agendas are set and policy windows open when various components of the policy stream (problems, policies, and politics) couple. He alludes to the roles that network configurations play in facilitating this coupling. The relationship between network configurations and policy functions needs to be addressed. We suggest that Bovaird's (2005) classifications of policy functions offer guidance in this regard.

Geographic scale: What role do the geographic scale of network actors and the nature of public problems play in determining governance network structures and functions? Governance networks will likely defy clear demarcation of jurisdictional boundaries. Individual network actors may be accountable to a predefined constituency at local/municipal, county, state, federal, or international geographic scales. The scale of each actor combines, comingles, or competes with the scale of the problem that a governance network addresses. Governance networks may have a spatial focus at local scale (e.g., a brownfield development), but they may contain members from outside the local scale. Or conversely, a governance network's focus could be global (e.g., addressing global climate change), but it may contain very localized actors. Governance networks may also defy political or administrative boundaries, as in the case when watersheds or air sheds provide a scope that defies traditional jurisdictional and administrative boundaries. Many governance networks arise out of the need to address boundary conflicts. In this book, we argue that systems analysis and complexity science can provide clues to untangling the paradoxes of geographic scale within which governance networks operate in real-world situations.

Social scale: How do we account for actors of mixed social scale operating within a network? A question arises when the social scale of network actors is considered. These considerations have been recognized by modelers in terms of questions of scalability (Miller and Page, 2007). In their view, interorganizational networks are, essentially, complex systems that are comprised of social actors understood across multiple social scales: individuals organized into groups, groups organized into organizations and institutions, organizations and institutions organized into interorganizational networks. We consider the extent to which this "nested complexity" is evident in the extensive case studies of interorganizational networks that have been undertaken. These cases often describe the roles that organizations; groups—task forces, committees, and teams; and individuals play in the networks. The resulting nested complexity needs to be not only recognized, but also highlighted with regard to mixed actor operations.

Administrative Considerations

How are networks governed? What does it mean to manage a network? To manage within a network?

Theodore Lowi defines administration as "a process of self-conscious, formal adaptation of means to ends. Administered social relations are all those self-conscious and formal efforts to achieve a social end, whether expressed as a general condition like predictable conduct, legality, productivity, public order, or as a more concrete organizational goal" (1969, p. 30).

At this point, we know very little about how power, decisions, and collective actions that comprise administrative functions unfold within partnerships, strategic alliances, and other collaborative arrangements. Likewise, we know little about how power, decisions, and collective actions unfold across contractual and regulatory relationships. As we will see, social network and social capital theories may be used to understand how cooperation and collaboration exist as essential features of network management. Although much has been written about the increasing reliance on negotiation and bargaining in public administration, this literature primarily focuses on negotiation and bargaining in terms of formalized protocols designed to mediate conflicts and derive collective agreements.

Governance networks have been described as taking on certain configurations of administrative authority that shape the flow of power between them. Agranoff and McGuire's studies of community development networks highlight the role that vertical and horizontal relationships play within them (2003). Conceptual frameworks designed to analyze social power dynamics are abundant, and can be found across the literature of virtually every social science. Of particular interest to us are the kinds of conceptual frameworks that describe the flow of administrative power and authority within or across organizations.

Drawing on theories of social exchange (Rhodes, 1997) and the definitions of administrative power as discussed across classical public administration, management, and organizational development studies, power is viewed as being predicated on the coordination of the flow of resources that get exchanged across network partners (nodes). This is particularly true when one node controls the flow of resources (be it funding, information, etc.) to other actors within the network.

We can find examples of vertical resource control dating back to Weber's first introduction of bureaucratic theory, where we find considerations of power being explored as a matter of supervisor-subordinate relations. Classical organization development theory, found in the works of Gulick (1937), and later in the works of Simon (1957) and others, establishes the basis for describing the "command and control" structures of bureaucracies. More recently, principal-agent theory has emerged from economics and studies of contractual arrangements to provide a picture of vertical relations as they exist in social networks (Milward and Provan, 1998).

In regard to shared power or horizontal resource control and relations, there is a growing body of literature that explores the nature of power in terms of the voluntary bonds forged through shared values and norms. Social psychologists, sociologists, and more recently, behavioral economists have studied how cooperative behaviors come about. Social capital and game theories are particularly useful here. Beginning with Axelrod's now classic "iterated prisoner's dilemma" experiments conducted in the early 1980s, game theorists have studied the nature of cooperative and collaborative behaviors that manifest between two social actors construed as equals or peers (1980).

Table 1.4 provides a brief overview of the relationship between the classical public administration (PA), new public management (NPM), and collaborative public management with a network administration framework that combines all of them.

In addition to the vertical and horizontal vectors of relational power, we must recognize the possibility that the structure of power relations between two or more actors in a governance network may be comprised of a mixture of both vertical and horizontal relations. We find diagonal ties manifesting as principal-agent "problems" resulting from information asymmetries between agents "on the ground" and closest to the work, and their principal overseers. With greater access to information, agents possess a measure of power over their principals, positioning the agent as more of a negotiating and bargaining partner. Although principals may possess formal vertical authority, informally, they must rely on the development of horizontal ties, oftentimes through extensive negotiation and bargaining. Diagonal ties bring with them the burdens of certain kinds of transaction costs that come with extensive concession and compromise.

Table 1.4 The Convergence of Four Public Administration Paradigms into Governance Network Administration

Public Administration Paradigm	Dominant Administrative Structure	Central Administrative Dynamics
Classical public administration	Public bureaucracies	Command and control
New public management	Public bureaucracies or private firms	Competition Concession and compromise
Collaborative public management	Partnerships with private firms, nonprofits, and citizens	Collaboration and cooperation Concession and compromise
Governance network administration	Mixed-form governance networks	Command and control Competition Concession and compromise Collaboration and cooperation Coordination

Given the existence of vertical, horizontal, and diagonal ties, Donald Kettl observes: "The basic administrative problem [becomes] developing effective management mechanisms to replace command and control" (2002, p. 491). According to Kettl, networked public managers "have to learn the points of leverage, change their behavior to manage those points of leverage, develop processes needed to make that work, and change the organizational culture from a traditional control perspective to one that accommodates indirect methods" (2002, p. 493). Although classical paradigms in public administration have tried to distinguish administration from politics, in the networked environs of the "disarticulated state" (Frederickson, 1999), politics is understood as an integral feature of administrative action. "Politics can be seen as aggregating individual preferences into collective actions by some procedures of rational bargaining, negotiation, coalition formation, and exchange" (March and Olsen, 1995, p. 7). A conceptual framework is needed to account for the fragmented and dynamic confluence of multiple forms of administrative authority that emerge in networked environs.

The blurring of sector boundaries leading to more dynamic authority structures found in governance networks has led to serious reconsiderations of managerial roles and functions, which in turn has led to reconsiderations of accountability (Mashaw, 2006; Koliba, Mills, and Koliba, accepted for publication) and performance (Frederickson and Frederickson, 2006). The development of the governance network as an observable and, ultimately, analyzable phenomenon has been suggested as a means through which to establish management and administrative practices that can contribute to a richer understanding of cross-jurisdictional relations that are characterized by both vertical and horizontal relations. Because of the combination of mixed-form authority structures that persist in governance networks, the classical public administration considerations of public bureaucracies and command and control forms of management are still very relevant. In mixed-form governance networks, public bureaucracies still play a very pivotal role, even within the most highly decentralized governance networks. Their cultures and command and control hierarchical structures help shape the public bureaucracies' participation in governance networks. Because governance networks often engage actors from multiple social sectors, including those private firms guided by markets and market forces, new public management (NPM) considerations of public-private partnerships, contracting out, and reliance on market forces are useful in the study of governance networks. The central premise behind NPM is to bring market efficiencies to the delivery of public goods and services. Governance networks are also likely to involve some collaborative alignments, oftentimes directly with citizens. The emerging body of literature pertaining to "collaborative public management" (Agranoff and McGuire, 2003; Bingham and O'Leary, 2008) is very relevant as well, and needs to be woven into a differentiated theory of network management. The ongoing studies of collaborative management will deepen our understanding of the kind of skills, attitudes, and dispositions needed to foster effective horizontal administrative relationships.

A picture of network management is emerging that may be described as the combination of "governance and public management in situations of interdependencies. It is aimed at *coordinating strategies of actors with different goals and preferences with regard to a certain problem or policy measure within an existing network of inter-organizational relations*" (Kickert, Klijn, and Koppenjan, 1997a, p. 10). We argue that effective network management requires the use of all forms of administrative dynamics, including command and control, competition, concession and compromise, and collaboration and cooperation. We conclude that all three PA paradigms are useful to the study of governance network management and combine to form the basis of a network management framework. A dilemma only surfaces when we constrain our assumptions to one paradigm.

Although there are many different ways that social power has been framed, we view administrative power within governance networks as being wielded through the representation of authority. Power flows in social networks through authority wielded *against, over, shared,* and *negotiated between* two or more nodes in a social network. Taking into account the complexity of relational ties that are possible in governance networks, Sorensen and Torfing argue that the policy actors may not "be equal in terms of authority and resources (Mayntz, 1993, p. 10). There might be asymmetrical allocations of material and immaterial resources among the network actors" (2008, p. 9).

Power relations may be complicated by the shifting nature of more innovative working relationships found within contemporary workplace environments. This observation leads us to suggest that a diagonal dimension of power relations may be said to exist. Metaphorically speaking, the steepness and the direction of the ties may vary over time and be contingent on environmental factors. We also argue that the existence of certain macro-level structures found within markets, hierarchies, and collaboratives helps to dictate how and to what extent which administrative authorities are at work.

Accountability Considerations

To whom are actors operating within a network accountable? To whom are governance networks accountable? How much democratic anchorage do they have?

As we have noted, in polycentric governance systems the "state has become a differentiated, fragmented, and multicentered institutional complex that is held together by more or less formalized networks." The proliferation of these networks leads to the blurring of the lines between public, private, and nonprofit sectors

(Sorenson, 2006, p. 100). Sector blurring is complicated by the multiple ways in which administrative authority is structured. "The current public governance problem is how to ensure that third parties, who often have independent bases of political power, asymmetric information, potentially conflicting goals, and only partial views of the public interest (Posner, 2002; Salamon, 2002b), act in ways that meet public goals" (Stone and Ostrower, 2007, p. 427).

Considering the potential for sector blurring that may occur in some forms of mixed-form governance networks, we must consider how and to what extent distinctions between the accountability structures of the governments, for-profit firms, and nonprofit organizations contribute to the development of network-wide accountability regimes. We must recognize that accountability in democratic societies has traditionally been predicated on the legitimacy that accompanies the kinds of sovereign entities found in local, state, and national governments. This has resulted in a substantial shift from accountability predicated on governments to accountability predicated around complex network dynamics occurring within and across governance networks. These considerations beg for more discussion concerning the fate of state sovereignty and the qualities of democratic anchorage that have been traditionally ascribed to it.

Many have noted how the shift from a monocentric system of *government* to a polycentric system of *governance* raises some serious accountability challenges (Behn, 2001; Posner, 2002; Page, 2004; O'Toole and Meier, 2004b; Goldsmith and Eggers, 2004; Pierre and Peters, 2005; Scott, 2006; Mashaw, 2006; Mathur and Skelcher, 2007). Because it can no longer be assumed that the state possesses the same kind of authority as traditionally ascribed to public organizations, governing these interorganizational networks gives rise to new accountability challenges. These challenges arise when states are displaced as central actors, market forces are considered, and cooperation and collaboration are recognized as integral administrative activities. We introduce a tripartite accountability framework (Figure 1.3) for discerning how accountability is structured within governance networks that include democratic, market, and administrative accountability frames, through which eight accountability types may be identified based on which stakeholders "to whom" accounts are rendered.

Discerning the accountability structures amidst the complexity that persists in cross-sector, cross-jurisdictional settings requires us to consider the dynamics at work when the accountability structures of one network actor comingle, compete, or complement the accountability structures of other network actors. As a result of unpacking these dynamics, we may be able to ascertain the extent to which "hybrid accountability regimes" (Mashaw, 2006, p. 118) emerge within governance networks.

Figure 1.3 Tripartite model of governance network accountability.

Performance Considerations

Are governance networks successful? Effective? Who determines what high performance looks like?

We have already noted how Robert Behn has asserted that "most failures in performance [of policy implementations] are failures of collaboratives," recognizing that "in the United States, most public policies are no longer implemented by a single public agency with a single manager, but by a collaborative of public, nonprofit, and for-profit organizations" (2001, p. 72). In recent years, we find the failed performance of governance networks screaming across the headlines, ranging from troubles with the response and recovery efforts following the landfall of Hurricane Katrina, to gross malfeasants relating to defense contracting in Iraq. These cases highlight the challenges associated with applying performance standards associated with the traditional structures of government bureaucracy to extremely complex and changing situations that call for the coordination of actors that span sectors and levels of government. We assert that these headline-grabbing cases underscore what we believe to be the proverbial tip of the iceberg. The challenges that we associate with managing in governance networks extend well beyond responses to catastrophic events or acts of war and occupation. These challenges may be found in any circumstance in which different actors, often with different operational characteristics, goals, and functions, work together to address any number of wicked problems within the public domain.

There have been relatively few studies that look at the efficacy of network structures in achieving ascribed outputs or outcomes (see as representatives: Marsh and Rhodes, 1992; Heinrich and Lynn, 2000; Koontz et al., 2004; Imperial, 2005; Frederickson and Frederickson, 2006; Koliba, Mills, and Zia, accepted for publication; Rodriguez et al., 2007). We conclude from some of these studies that governance networks may be ineffective organizational strategies for achieving public outputs or outcomes. Despite these cases, identifying network-wide performance measures appears to be a very big challenge here.

Focusing on governance network performance management may be one way to guard against the proliferation of ineffective networks and lead to improvements in public policy outcomes, deepened citizen engagement, the provision of some measure of transparency, and the equitable distribution of power, and sustain effective networks (Bovaird and Loffler, 2003, p. 322). Definitions for what constitutes effective outcomes of governance networks will need to be addressed.

The performance measures of a governance network may be oriented toward fostering greater citizen access to the apparatuses of governance; it may build social ties and social capital that lay the foundation for future collaborative undertakings; or it may legitimize the activities of the governance network itself. Thus, we are left to consider that if we were ranking the kind of performance outcomes ascribed to governance network, the capacity of the governance network to foster greater democratic connectivity would be at the top of the list. Creating democratic anchorage may be framed as the process goal, becoming an ultimate outcome for the governance network. Such process outcomes are often embodied in efforts to promote "good governance," a governance framework that is defined by Bovaird and Loffler as "the negotiation by all stakeholders in an issue (or area) of improved public policy outcomes and agreed governance principles, which are both implemented and regularly evaluated by all stakeholders" (2003, p. 316.)

Building an argument for interpreting network performance as one based on process indicators may be difficult. Although the conceptualizations of social ties may be intuitively accessible to all, rarely do processes dynamics capture the interest or attention of those to whom accounts need to be rendered. Much more needs to be done by researchers and educators to inform critical stakeholders about the importance of the kind of good governance that comes via the democratic anchorage of governance networks. Very often, these efforts are framed in terms of developing performance measures designed to achieve "results" (Durant, 2001).

The development of performance measures, however, hinges on how the governance network defines the problem, i.e., what social, political, economic, physical, chemical, and biological factors are assessed as key causes of the policy problem that need to be addressed by a governance network. Ulrich (1998) calls this management choice the "system of concern" or "boundary judgment." We call this dynamic the phenomenon of micro- or macro-scoping: Micro-scoping occurs when a governance network shrinks its spatial and temporal boundaries to define a system of concern (or define a policy problem). Conversely, macro-scoping occurs when a governance network expands the boundaries of a system of concern. Micro- or macro-scoping leads to a differential development in the choice of performance measures by a governance network. We explore this issue in more detail in Chapter 10.

Viewed outside the context of governance network, performance measurement initiatives face a number of challenges that have been summarized by Robert Durant as "Confusion around outputs and outcomes; Inadequate training and technical know-how for developing performance measures; Lack of resources for measurement design, data collection and monitoring; Different expectations about what performance measures are designed to do and for what they will be used; Fear by agencies that they will be asked to develop outcomes measures for results that are not easily measured, that are shaped by factors outside their control … and, that are not amenable to assigning responsibility to particular actors" (Durant, 2001, pp. 702–3). Studies of performance measurement initiatives across governance networks accentuate all of these factors as major challenges to applying performance measurement frameworks to the networks (Posner, 2002; Page, 2004; Frederickson and Frederickson, 2006).

Determining how performance is defined between collaborators is complicated by the capacity of collaborators to possess their own unique perspectives around what matters, what counts, and why. As Page puts it, "Reasonable people may disagree about which results to measure, and appropriate data can be difficult to track" (2004, pp. 591–92). Despite these challenges, the application of performance measurements to governance networks is important because of the links between measurement and accountability. Those to whom accountability must be rendered may be inclined to rely on certain kinds of performance measurement data (construed here in terms of both quantitative and qualitative forms) in the execution of their obligations as accountants. We will argue that governance networks are guided by the existence or lack of certain hybridized accountable regimes.

CRITICAL QUESTIONS AND CONSIDERATIONS

In sum, we believe that this book provides a framework for eventually answering the following kinds of questions:

■ How are governance networks structured? What functions do they carry out? How are their boundaries distinguished?
■ How are governance networks governed? What does it mean to manage a network? To manage within a network?
■ To whom are actors operating within the network accountable? How much democratic anchorage do they have?

■ Are governance networks successful? Effective? Who determines what high performance looks like? What are the performance indicators?

We acknowledge that some will be looking to apply these generalized questions to specific kinds of governance networks. Some may want to ask more specific questions, like: How are health care networks structured? Who governs environmental management networks? Who is accountable within an emergency management network? How is performance evaluated in a regional planning network? We strongly encourage the reader to begin to ask such questions. We believe that asking these and other questions helps to facilitate the development of situational awareness and provides the reader with a basis for thinking about the framework and how it relates to actual practice.

At this juncture we invite the reader to identify a governance network of interest to him or her. It may be the governance network that you work in or are trying to influence the direction of. It may be a public-private partnership that is being pursued by your local town to foster economic development. It might be a regulatory subsystem in need of reform discussed in the news. It could be an interest group coalition that you are a part of that is trying to advocate for a particular social cause or policy action. You may be thinking of pursuing a grant from a federal agency and wondering about what you need to do to land the grant or work with others once the grant is awarded.

Ask yourself what do you know about this governance network? Think about where you can find out more information about it. The following chapter begins to lay out some of the characteristics that you might consider looking for.

Chapter 2

Defining the Governance Network

> Call it a clan, call it a network, call it a tribe, call it a family: Whatever you call it, whoever you are, you need one.
>
> **—Jane Howard (1999, p. 234)**

In this chapter we look at how the public administration and policy studies fields have employed network metaphors and network analysis to describe the range of interorganizational configurations that have arisen to create, implement, and evaluate public policies. In order to orient the reader to understanding the dynamics of governance networks, we feel it is useful to begin with an overview of social network analysis as it has evolved within the social sciences. We note that the concept of the social network as a configuration of social actors arranged in some form of relationship with other social actors has been a mainstay of classical sociology and management studies. We then synthesize the extensive literature that has applied network and systems metaphors and analytical tools to the study of public administration and public policy and draw inferences around which a theoretical framework may be developed. We then make a case for using the term *governance networks* to describe the range of network configurations alluded to in Chapter 1.

Fundamentals of Social Network Analysis

Network metaphors and analytical tools are being used widely across all fields of natural and social science. The prevalence of network configurations as a dominant natural and social structure should hardly be a revelation to most readers. What is "new" is our heightened capacity to apply network metaphors and tools of analysis to the study, design, implementation, and monitoring of the networks that persist across the natural and social domains.

Network analysis has been a staple of social science research for many decades. Alfred Radcliffe-Brown was the first to make the case that *any* observation of social phenomena needs to be anchored in "the patterns of behavior to which individuals and groups conform in their dealings with one another" (1940, p. 228). Network concepts have a long and rich history of being used to study organizational form and the diffusion of information across social structures. Berry et al. (2004) trace the origins of social network analysis to the early Hawthorn experiments of 1924 to 1932, marking the first use of "network configurations to analyze social behavior" (p. 540). These social experiments are often cited as an important milestone in the evolution of management and organizational development, leading us to conclude that network analysis has been a part of our field for quite some time and embedded within our studies of hierarchies.

Social network analysis has been used to study the diffusion of knowledge, beginning with Coleman, Katz, and Mentzel's ground-breaking study of information diffusion in physician networks (1977). Stanley Milgram's "small world" research is often cited as an important breakthrough in social network analysis, demonstrating the "six degrees of separation" that exist between any two people (1969). Over the last few decades, the progress of social network analysis has benefited from advances in statistical methods and high-speed computing.

Noted anthropologist A. R. Radcliff-Brown is credited with first using the network metaphor to draw links between natural and social phenomena. In a speech given in 1940, he asserted:

> Social structures are just as real as are individual organisms. A complex organism is a collection of living cells and interstitial fluids arranged in a certain structure; and a living cell is similarly a structural arrangement of complex molecules. The physiological and psychological phenomena that we observe in the lives of organisms are not simply the result of the nature of the constituent molecules or atoms of which the organism is built up, but are *the result of the structure in which they are united*. So also the social phenomena which we observe in any human society are not the immediate result of the nature of individual human beings, but are the result of the social structure by which they are united. (1940, p. 223)

Radcliffe-Brown's observations here underscore a central challenge facing researchers looking to apply network metaphors and analytical tools to the study of any social or natural phenomena—the relationship between the parts of the system and the system as a whole. As we consider the relationship between the parts of a governance network and the governance network as a whole, we must build in the capacity to view a governance network as being more than the sum of its parts. The extent to which the characteristics and actions of individual nodes (e.g., the network's parts) help to shape the actions of the network as a whole is an extremely important, albeit complicated, consideration. Networks need to be treated as active agents operating of their own volition. This assertion is often associated with the premise of network "holism." Degenne and Forse (1999, p. 5) lay out the three propositions of holism common to any network form:

a. Structure takes precedence over the individual [nodes]
b. Structure cannot be reduced to the sum of individual actions
c. Structure exerts absolute constraint on individual actions

The joint, coordinated actions that occur between nodes of networks need to eventually be understood in terms of acts of the network as a whole. The matter gets complicated by the challenges posed by differences in scale that can occur between nodes in social networks.

Thomas Catlaw describes "the network" as being a metaphor for human relationship. He notes that is serves as a "root metaphor" that "has come to be 'a fundamental image of the world from which models and illustrative metaphors may be derived' (Brown, 1976, p. 170)" (2008, p. 3).

The network metaphor is a powerful symbol for comprehending complex natural and social phenomena. It also runs the risk of being overused, employed to explain nearly every phenomenon. Some fear that "networks have become a ubiquitous metaphor to describe too many aspects of contemporary life. And in so doing, the category has lost much of its analytical precision" (Thompson, 2003, p. 2). We must, cautions Graham Thompson, be concerned about analytical precision if we are to ever translate the network metaphor into an analytical tool to guide managerial and design decisions.

Network structures are often described in terms of "nodes" tied together through coordinated actions and resource exchanges (Figure 2.1) (Wasserman and Faust, 1994; Rhodes, 1997). In social networks, nodes may be described as existing across several levels of social scale: from the micro level of interpersonal relationships to the more macro-level interorganizational relationships. We describe governance networks, first and foremost, in terms of their organizational nodes and ties between nodes. However, we also understand governance networks in terms of their multiscalable properties: as being comprised of individuals, groups of individuals, *and* organizations. Governance networks are distinguished from other forms of social networks based on the characteristics of network actors and the kinds of

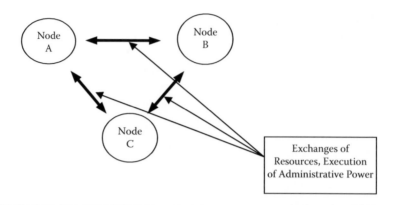

Figure 2.1   Nodes and ties.

functions and collective actions they take on. These functions are aligned with the pursuit of one or more policy streams, a point that we explore in Chapter 6.

The resources to be exchanged between nodes (regardless of their social scale) can take a material (as in the case of exchanges of electrical pulses between neurons or the transfer of financial support from one network actor to another) or social form (often construed in terms of knowledge, information, or social norms).

This basic framework for describing and analyzing social networks has been described by Samuel Leinhardt as a paradigm that

> operationalizes the notion of social structure by representing it in terms of a system of social relations tieing [*sic*] distinct social entities to one another. Within this framework the issue of structure in social relations becomes one of pattern or systematic organization. It also involves the corollary issues of the interdependence of the patterns formed by differ-ent relations, the implications that patterns have for the behavior of the individual entities, and the impact that the qualities of the entities have on the patterns. (1977, p. xiii)

The Place of Interorganizational Networks in Public Administration, Policy, and Governance Studies

There have been many explicit efforts to employ network concepts to the study of complex social structures that arise when public policies are made, implemented, and monitored within the policy studies and public administration fields. Hugh Heclo (1978) is credited with first applying the term *network* to the study of public policy and administration with his introduction of "issue networks" (Rhodes, 1997). Heclo presented the issue network concept in reaction to what he found to be the more restrictive (and less pervasive) "iron triangles"—the relatively closed networks of government agencies, legislative committees, and interest groups.

Interorganizational networks have been implicated in descriptions of policy or government "subsystems" (Baumgartner and Jones, 1993), the advocacy coalition framework (ACF) (Sabatier and Jenkins-Smith, 1993, 1999), policy coalition (March and Olsen, 1995), and policy network (Rhodes, 1997b; Kickert et al., 1997; Koppenjan and Klijn, 2004). This literature in particular has employed elements of systems dynamics and exchange theory to the study of interorganizational network configurations. We also find interorganizational networks described across much of the policy implementation (Gage and Mandell, 1990; O'Toole, 1997; Hill and Hupe, 2002), intergovernmental relations (O'Toole, 2000; Wright, 2000), and policy tools (Salamon, 2002b) literature. Interorganizational networks have also been described as third-party government (Salamon, 2002b; Frederickson and Frederickson, 2006), public sector networks (Agranoff, 2007), governance networks (Sorensen and Torfing, 2005, 2008; Bogason and Musso, 2006; Klijn and Skelcher, 2007), cross-sector collaborations (Bryson, Crosby, and Stone, 2006), public management networks (Milward and Provan, 2006; Frederickson and Frederickson, 2006; Agranoff, 2007), and certain kinds of strategic alliances (Wohlstetter, Smith, and Malloy, 2005).

Interorganizational networks have also been described in terms of the functions that they perform, whether service contracts, supply chains, *ad hoc* channel partnerships, information dissemination, civic switchboards (Goldsmith and Eggers, 2004), problem solving, information sharing, capacity building and service delivery (Milward and Provan, 2006), learning and knowledge transfer (McNabb, 2007), or civic engagement (Yang and Bergrud, 2008). Interorganizational networks have also been described as existing across many policy domains, including social service delivery (Provan and Milward, 1995; Milward and Provan, 1998), land use planning (Koontz et al., 2004), watershed management (Leach and Pelky, 2001; Imperial, 2005), health care (Frederickson and Frederickson, 2006; Rodriguez et al., 2007), transportation (Albert, Gainsborough, and Wallis, 2006), emergency management (Comfort, 2002; Kapucu, 2006a), community economic development (Agranoff and McGuire, 2003), and food systems (Sporleder and Moss, 2002; Smith, 2007; Jarosz, 2004). In addition to these uses of network metaphors and tools of analysis, particular types of network configurations have been described in the literature, including interest group coalitions (Hula, 1999), regulatory subsystems (Krause, 1997), grants and contract agreements (Kelman, 2002; Cooper, 2003; Goldsmith and Eggers, 2004), and public-private partnerships (O'Toole, 1997; Linder and Rosenau, 2000; Bovaird, 2005).

As a synthesis of the literature we offer seven characteristics concerning the structures and functions of interorganizational networks operating across public administration and policy studies:

1. Networks facilitate the *coordination of actions* and *exchange of resources* between actors within the network.
2. Network membership can be drawn from some combination of *public, private, and nonprofit sector actors.**
3. Networks may carry out one or more *policy functions*.
4. Networks exist across virtually all *policy domains*.
5. Although networks are mostly defined at the interorganizational level, they are also described in the context of the *individuals, groups, and organizations* that comprise them.
6. Networks form as the result of the selection of particular *policy tools*.
7. Network structures allow for *government agencies* to *serve in roles other than lead organizations*.†

These characteristics form the fundamental basis of developing an understanding of interorganizational governance networks. In Table 2.1 we highlight some of the important milestones in policy network and governance network development.

The Networked Properties of Governance Processes

Governance has been defined as "the empirical manifestation of state adaptation to its external environment" as well as denoting "a conceptual or theoretical representation of co-ordination of social systems and, for the most part, the role of the state in that process" (Pierre, 2000). A generic use of the term will likely be centered on defining governance as "the means by which an activity or ensemble of activities is controlled or directed, such that it delivers an acceptable range of outcomes according to some established social standard" (Hirst, 1997, p. 3). A more expanded view of governance construes the process of coordination and control as an integral dimension of public policy making and implementation. In this larger, democratic context, "governance refers to sustaining co-ordination and coherence among a wide variety of actors with different purposes and objectives such as political actors and institutions, corporate interests, civil society, and transnational organizations." To this end, "governance could be said to be shorthand for the predominant view of government in the *Zeitgeist* of the late twentieth century" (Pierre, 2000, pp. 3–4).

There has been a conceptual shift away from a singular focus on unitary *government's* delivery of discrete policies to that of processes of *governance* (Cleveland, 1972; Frederickson, 1999). This shift has paralleled the incorporation of network metaphors in public administration and policy studies. As a result, governance,

---

* With the obvious exception of intergovernmental networks, which may be described as networks of governments of different geographical scope.
† With the obvious exception of intergovernmental networks, which are relegated to networks of public sector organizations.

Table 2.1   Major Conceptual Developments in Governance Network Theory since 1990

Conceptual Ground Covered	Author(s)
Intermittency of network coordination; importance of the goal orientation of network members. Differentiates between intermittent and permanent network coordination (2003). Discusses the goal orientation of network members, how members are linked and aligned around common efforts, and network-wide purposes.	Gage and Mandell, 1990; Mandell and Stellman, 2003
Collective action theory; institutional analysis and development (IAD) framework. IAD presents an integrated framework for linking conditions, attributes, and rules to actions and patterns of interaction. Provides the basis from which to understand collective action and resource pooling.	Ostrom, 1990, 2007
Implementation networks. Looks at the whole network level, distinguishing between degrees of hierarchy and levels of integration found in governance networks.	O'Toole, 1990
Policy subsystems; role of feedback; punctuated equilibrium. Integrated systems analysis within a public policy framework by drawing on negative and positive feedback concepts to describe systems dynamics. Discusses system stability and change in terms of agenda-setting processes that are evidenced by instances of punctuated equilibrium through which rapid changes to the system are evidenced. Asserts that systems dynamics can be viewed in terms of any policy domain.	Baumgartner and Jones, 1993
Advocacy coalition framework (ACF); power concentrating in clustered elites. ACF relies on the roles that informal ties between "policy elites" play within and across policy subsystems. In this model, policy elites form clusters, which in turn form into organized interest groups. Emphasizing more the functional capacities of the policy subsystem itself, ACF does not analyze the policy subsystem as an interorganizational network. However, ACF does anticipate the role that coalitions and coalition formation plays as a matter of the development of formal network ties between organizational and institutional actors.	Sabatier and Jenkins-Smith, 1993, 1999

(continued)

Table 2.1 Major Conceptual Developments in Governance Network Theory since 1990 (Continued)

Conceptual Ground Covered	Author(s)
Policy networks; governance. Rhodes describes how policy networks can be characterized as degrees of network stability, the relative openness of network membership, and the role of vertical and horizontal articulation of network relationship (Rhodes, 1997). Differentiates between types of networks based on these characteristics, distinguishing between fluid and open "issue networks" and stable and closed "policy communities." Adapts a framework from Marsh and Rhodes (1992) that distinguishes the size of the network based on the number of members, the types of interests network members bring to the network, the frequency of their interactions, the continuity and consensus that exist between them, and the distribution of resources within the network and within the participating organizations (Rhodes, 1997, p. 44).	Rhodes, 1997
Policy network characteristics; network management functions. Kickert et al. (1997) define policy network characteristics in relation to rational, classical, and network perspectives. Juxtaposes differences between the new public management paradigm and emergent network management paradigm. Highlights the role of game theory in network management, later expanded by Koppenjan and Klijn (2004).	Kickert, Klijn, and Koppenjan, 1997b
Network closedness. Schaap and van Twist (1997) distinguish between social and cognitive closedness, underscoring the importance that the orientation of individual network members plays in determining the degree of closedness found within governance networks.	Schaap and van Twist, 1997
Macro- and micro-level tools that structure and manage governance networks. Tools are instruments that can be used both to influence goal-oriented processes and to create the conditions that facilitate the mutual formulation of targets.	De Bruijn and ten Heuvelhof, 1997
Network forms of organization. Advances the notion that networks are an inherent organizational structure within all organizational forms, including hierarchies and markets.	Podolny and Page, 1998

Table 2.1 Major Conceptual Developments in Governance Network Theory since 1990 (Continued)

Conceptual Ground Covered	Author(s)
Policy tools. Suggests ways in which the characteristics of macro-level policy tools help to shape network structures and functions.	Salamon, 2002b
Vertical and horizontal administrative roles; types of networks. Agranoff and McGuire (2003) introduce a set of micro-level "public action tools" that are used to support vertical and horizontal collaborative management activities. These public action tools are later elaborated on by Agranoff (2007).	Agranoff and McGuire, 2003
Distinguishing networking from network structures. Keast, Mandell, Brown, and Woolcock (2004) distinguish between formal and informal bonds that form through network ties.	Keast, Mandell, Brown, and Woolcock, 2004
Governing through networks. Goldsmith and Eggers lay out some considerations for how network configurations may be shaped through grant and contractual agreements (2004). Pays particular attention to the role that communication technologies play in facilitating coordinated action and resource exchange, differentiating between types of technologies based on levels of collaborative technologies and their consequences (p. 99).	Goldsmith and Eggers, 2004
Decision-making models and problem solving in networks. Koppenjan and Klijn (2004) situate the development of policy networks within the context of wicked problems, and the range of uncertainties that result from them. Relying heavily on game theory, breaks down the relationship between the realm of uncertainty that occurs across the domains of content, process, institutions, and governance, and the types of decision-making structures that occur within complex network arrangements. Actor characteristics and behaviors are described. A vision of network management emerges based around the cultivated capacity of network managers to leverage and manage the range of games that emerge within and across interorganizational arrangements.	Koppenjan and Klijn, 2004

(continued)

Table 2.1   Major Conceptual Developments in Governance Network Theory since 1990 (Continued)

Conceptual Ground Covered	Author(s)
Government roles in networks. Several researchers frame government roles in terms of following, encouraging, and leading. Suggests relationship between government strategy and network configuration.	Koontz et al., 2004; Pierre and Peters, 2005; Klijn and Skelcher, 2007
Functions of public management networks. Milward and Provan (2006) distinguish between service implementation, information diffusion, problem-solving, and community capacity-building networks, differentiating networks based on core operational functions undertaken within interorganizational networks.	Milward and Provan, 2006
Democratic anchorage of governance networks. Sorensen and Torfing (2005) discuss the role of democratic accountability in networks in terms of elected officials' roles, citizen participation, and democratic norms. Builds on the work of March and Olsen (1995).	Sorensen and Torfing, 2005
Network performance measurement; alignment with government agency goals; measurement characteristics. Frederickson and Frederickson identify key variables that they use to interpret how performance measurement systems are used across federal health care networks (2006). These variables include the degree of directness of government involvement, the alignment of health care networks with federal purposes, the degree of network articulation of authority and control, network goal characteristic, and levels of goal agreements, and the level of centralization of policy implementation.	Frederickson and Frederickson, 2006
Centrality and betweeness in interorganizational networks. Drawing on the factors used in network analysis, Provan, Fish, and Sydow (2007) discuss the roles that actor centrality and relational betweenness play in shaping network structures.	Provan, Fish, and Sydow, 2007

Table 2.1   Major Conceptual Developments in Governance Network Theory since 1990 (Continued)

Conceptual Ground Covered	Author(s)
Network governance model. Provan and Kenis (2007) introduce network governance model, based on three forms of interorganizational coordination: shared governance, lead organization, and network administrative organization.	Provan and Kenis, 2007
Network functions; internal arrangements; role of communities of practice. Agranoff (2005, 2007) distinguishes between types of actions and decisions made across public management networks. Recognizing the link between decision making and actions, differentiates between information exchanges, agenda setting, research report and study writing, the facilitation of forums, strategic planning, reviewing of plans, adjusting policy or program designs, and creating new public policies. In much the same vein as Milward and Provan's (2006) efforts to create a typology of public management networks, Agranoff describes differences between informational, developmental, outreach, and action networks. Identifies three types of internal arrangements and groupings that persist within the twelve different public management networks that he has studied (2007, p. 111).	Agranoff, 2005; 2007

rather than government, takes into account the "lattices of complex network arrangements" (Frederickson and Frederickson, 2006) that arise when networks are said to form. Governance dynamics align interorganizational network structures to the public policy process, "whether 'upstream' in policymaking, 'midstream' in policy implementation, or 'downstream' in policy enforcement'" (Bingham, Nabatchi, and O'Leary, 2005, p. 553).

Over the last several decades an interdisciplinary body of "governance" literature has emerged across the public administration, policy studies, nonprofit management, and corporate governance fields. Variations of governance in public administration, and policy studies in particular, have been described in terms of the "new governance" (Durant, 2001; Salamon, 2002), "third party governance" (Salamon, 2002b), "collaborative governance" (Ansell and Gash, 2008), "public governance" (Stone and Ostrower, 2007), or "meta governance" (Sorensen, 2006). A substantial focus on network governance (Rhodes, 1997; Lynn, Heinrich, and Hill, 2000; Goldsmith and Eggers, 2004; Provan and Kenis, 2007; Sorensen and Torfing, 2008) has emerged. Within most public administration, public management, and public policy literature, governance has been understood as a construct either loosely or tightly tied to the role of the state (and its governmental institutions) as central actors in the network (Pierre and Peters, 2005).

The shift from government to governance within the public administration literature has coincided with the new public management movement and the accompanying "reinvention" and "reengineering" initiatives tied to it (Durant, 2001). New governance frameworks have been advanced, designed to account for the prospects for "market solutions" to address pressing social problems (Durant, 2001). Others have focused on how third parties impact governance arrangements (Salamon, 2002b). New governance frameworks are also informed by conceptualizations of the quasi-legislative and quasi-judicial tools used to garner greater citizen participation within governing networks (Bingham, Nabatchi, and O'Leary, 2005).

Public governance is another term ascribed to interorganizational networks tied to some component of the policy process (Lynn, Heinrich, and Hill, 2000; Bovaird and Loffler, 2003; Stone and Ostrower, 2007). "Public governance entails (a) looking up to the broader authorizing environment that established policy and legal parameters in which implementation takes place and (b) looking down to the operating environment where daily policy implementation takes place" (Stone and Ostrower, 2007, p. 430). Authorizing environments are described as shaped by the "rights, rules, preferences and resources that structure political outcomes" (March and Olsen, 1995; Bogason and Musso, 2006, p. 5). Operating environments are said to be shaped by the managerial considerations that arise within vertically and horizontally aligned network actors (Agranoff and McGuire, 2003; Heinrich, Hill, and Lynn, 2004; Rodriguez et al., 2007). These views of the new governance and public governance frameworks assume that the state plays a state-centric role in the activities of governance networks (Pierre and Peters, 2005). However, other models of governance have been proposed that view the state in a weaker role, subjected to some combination of broader societal factors or market forces (Pierre and Peters, 2005).

The rationale for participatory governance and collaborative governance is rooted in a number of concerns, including the decline in social capital (Putnam, 2000), the decline in citizen participation (Macedo et al., 2005), the role and power of experts and expert knowledge (Yankelovich, 1991; Fischer, 2000), the intractability of "wicked problems," and the ingrained conflicts that persist between stakeholders. These and other concerns have been cited as factors feeding into this renewed interest in collaborative governance through deliberative democracy tools (Henton and Melville, 2008, pp. 6–7).

Advocates of participatory governance mechanisms seek to take advantage of the greater number of access points afforded ordinary citizens in some complex governance network structures. If governance networks can accommodate greater citizen involvement and, ultimately, allow for citizens to exert influence over them, the democratic anchorage of the networks can be assured, leading to, what some argue is, greater "public confidence in government and the public's willingness to expand its 'comfort zone' for new solutions and policy directions in which government plays a part" (Henton and Melville, 2008, p. 4).

Archon Fung (2006) offers a way to interpret various participatory strategies with respect to the democratic outcomes of legitimacy, justice, and effectiveness of public action. He addresses participatory designs based upon ranges of three governance dimensions: participant selection, communication and decision, and authority and power. In this effort, each design is examined in light of the ability to achieve democratic outcomes. Fung argues that "no single participatory design is suited to serving all three values simultaneously; particular designs are suited to specific objectives" and that "direct participation should figure prominently in contemporary democratic governance" (Fung, 2006, p. 74).

Citizen administration consensus-oriented deliberation (Yankelovich, 1991) continues to receive a great deal of attention that suggests a basis for optimism in neighborhood councils (Berry, Portney, and Thomson, 1993; Kathi and Cooper, 2005), urban neighborhoods (Fung, 2006), and a number of other sectors, such as participatory budgeting (Weeks, 2000) and environment and land use planning (Lukensmeyer and Torres, 2006).

While there is a great deal of optimism with regard to the promise and exercise of the various kinds of participatory governance, there remain a number of issues concerning how participatory governance is designed and implemented. One concern centers upon the political nature of governance, where participatory governance cannot overcome the trade-offs between democratic values and norms, and pragmatic realities fueled by the desire for greater efficiencies or tacit power struggles (Roberto, 2004). Another concern is related to the way in which participatory governance is designed and perhaps misapplied by government. Klijn and Skelcher (2007) note how some of this literature "starts from the theoretical premise that networks are predominantly characterized by horizontal relationships, self-steering and pluralism, and that too easily draws an association with deliberative forms of democracy, when, in essence, their dynamics are inherently more complex" (p. 605). Citizen governance strategies that are mandated by law, such as public hearings and citizen advisory boards, may influence governance practices very differently than strategies that are based on citizen-centered or bottom-up initiatives. Rodrigues et al. (2007) studied the dynamics within governance networks devised to coordinate the delivery of health care within Canada. Quasi-governmental boards worked with networks of large, regional hospitals and local health clinics, all of which were forced through legislative mandate to collaborate in an effort to coordinate health care delivery within their regions. They found that in this setting, at least, top-down oversight from the quasi-governmental board was needed in order to advance and deepen coordinated activities. In those instances in which actors were left to reach consensus around objectives of their own volition, tangible results were hard to come by (Rodriguez et al., 2007). Thus, any logic of governance constructed for governance networks needs to account for both vertical and horizontal relationships that exist within them (Heinrch et al., 2004; Stone and Ostrower, 2007, p. 425).

A related concern is the use of participatory governance strategies for bureaucratic rather than network-wide interests. A factor hampering the proliferation of deliberative forums concerns the coupling of deliberative processes to tangible decision making within the governance network itself. The results of citizen deliberations may be effectively communicated to actors within the governance network, only to have this feedback summarily ignored or reframed to meet the desired ends of the real power brokers within the network. In essence, deliberative forums may do more to co-opt citizens than provide them with real power within networks.

In this book, we view governance as a property of the interorganizational network. In order to adequately describe how these networks are governed, we view governance as a matter of systems dynamics. From a systems perspective, governance may be understood as the processes that regulate the flow of feedback to and within the social system (Katz and Kahn, 1978). Such feedback may be derived through the internal dynamics occurring across the network or unfolding within individual actors of the network. Feedback may also be directed to the system from its external environment or be grounded in the internal dynamics that unfold between network actors.

A. W. Rhodes (1997) was one of the first scholars to deeply consider the relationship between governance and interorganizational networks, arguing that governance occurs as "self-organizing phenomena" shaped by the following characteristics:

1. *Interdependence* between organizations. Governance is broader than government, covering nonstate actors.
2. *Continuing interactions* between network members, caused by the need to exchange resources and negotiate shared purposes.
3. *Game-like interactions*, rooted in trust and regulated by rules of the game negotiated and agreed by network participants.

Governance, therefore, is characterized by the interdependency of network actors, the resources they exchange, and the joint purposes, norms, and agreements that are negotiated between them. Phillip Cooper describes the evolving forms of governance this way:

> The point has increasingly been to move away from the use of mechanisms of authority and toward governance by agreement, whether that means negotiated arrangements with regulated enterprises, service contracts with profit-making or nonprofit nongovernmental organizations, interjurisdictional agreements with other agencies of government at any level, [or] service agreements with citizen clients. (Cooper, 2003, p. 47)

Considerations of network governance lead to an inevitable consideration of the bargaining and cooperative systems of more horizontally-arranged ties, in addition to the traditional, vertically-oriented command and control systems of monocentric government systems (Kettl, 2006, p. 491). We argue that mixed-form governance networks may incorporate all forms of administrative authority.

Summing up the current state of understanding of governance as a property of networks, Stone and Ostrower conclude: "Those who study governance must regard it as a nested or multilayered construct (Ostrom, 1990; Lynn et al., 2000; Milward and Provan, 2000; O'Toole, 1997, 2000). Governance occurs at several interrelated levels of analysis and necessarily involves multiple actors" (2007, p. 424). These assertions lead to the supposition that governance becomes "the property of networks rather than as the product of any single centre of action (Johnston and Shearing, 2003, p. 148)" (Crawford, 2006, p. 458). Over the past fifteen years a "logic of governance" (Lynn et al., 2000) for governance networks has emerged from the literature that places "performance or outcomes of public programs at the individual or organizational level as the ultimate dependent variable" (Stone and Ostrower, 2007, p. 423). This logic of governance has also emphasized the role of the public administrator as the guardian of sound, good governance practices and the importance of hybrid accountability regimes of the network (Mashaw, 2006).

Discerning the Properties of Governance Networks

With roots in the multigovernment context of the European Union, governance network theory originated out of the Dutch school of governance (Pierre and Peters, 2005), which combines policy network frameworks (Heclo, 1978; Rhodes, 1997), elements of systems and network analysis, and democratic theory. The role of the state, its institutions, and sovereign obligations in interorganizational networks has become one of the central considerations of governance network theory (Sorensen and Torfing, 2005; Bogason and Musso, 2006; Klijn and Skelcher, 2007; Sorensen and Torfing, 2008). Governance networks have been described as possessing a degree of "democratic anchorage" (Sorensen and Torfing, 2005) that hinges on the extent to which there are links to elected officials, ordinary citizens, and democratic norms.

Sorensen and Torfing assert that governance networks can take many different forms: "They can either be self-grown or initiated from above. They might be dominated by loose and informal contacts or take the form of tight and formalized networks. They can be intra- or interorganizational, short-lived or permanent, and have a sector-specific or society-wide scope" (Sorensen and Torfing, 2005, p. 197).

Governance networks may be described in terms of systems and subsystems. Baumgartner and Jones conclude that "the American political system is a mosaic of continually reshaping systems of limited participation.… Some are strong, others are weak … created and destroyed" (1993, p. 6). Although we recognize how some interorganizational networks exist as informal, dynamic "issue networks" (Heclo, 1978; Rhodes, 1997) or "policy subsystems" (Baumgartner and Jones, 1993) created and destroyed with some measure of frequency, we will be focusing on those interorganizational governance networks that are relatively stable, emerging as the result of combinations of certain policy functions, policy tools, and policy actors. Early forms of governance networks may first exist as loosely coupled, informal issue networks, only to merge as stable, more formally recognized arrangements.

At the cross-institutional level, interorganizational arrangements are often referred to as networks and have been discussed as a third kind of organizational form in comparison to two existing forms: hierarchies and markets. Two schools of thought exist regarding the comparisons among these organizational forms. The first, adhered to by Sorensen and Torfing (2005, 2008), as well as others who have introduced network analysis to public administration (O'Toole, 1997; Goldsmith and Eggers, 2004; Provan, Fish, and Sydow, 2007; Provan and Kenis, 2007), posits that hierarchies, markets, and networks are distinct organizational forms from one another. Because much of traditional social network analysis has emphasized the role of horizontal ties, the network gets introduced as its own form of macro-level social structure alongside of hierarchies and markets. In this view, networks are akin to collaborative arrangements or partnerships. Proponents of the hierarchy, market, *and* network model often view macro-level networks as relatively recent governance phenomena built around the establishment of cooperative ties.

A second view posits that markets and hierarchies are variations of network form. In this view, "markets and hierarchies are simply two pure types of organization that can be represented with the basic network analytic constructs of nodes and ties (Laumann, 1991)" (Podolny and Page, 1998, p. 58). "From a purely structural perspective," this view considers that "the trichotomy among market, hierarchy, and network forms of organization is a false one" (Podolny and Page, 1998, p. 58). In both natural and social networks "clustering" of nodes tends to take place. Ravasz and Barabasi have noted how these clusters may be described in terms of hierarchical structures, suggesting that hierarchy is an inherent phenomenon of network structures (2003). In addition, the notion of the "network organization" (Borgatti and Foster, 2003) has been advanced, suggesting that network dynamics exist within any form of social organization. Writing about the relationship between hierarchies and networks, Frederickson and Frederickson observe: "It is not so much that networks have replaced hierarchies but more that standard hierarchical arrays, or parts of them, have often been enmeshed in lattices of complex networks arrangements (O'Toole, 2000; Agranoff and McGuire, 2001)" (Frederickson and Frederickson, 2006, p. 12).

Markets have been widely recognized as networks of buyers and sellers, arranged in their own latticework of marketing, sales, manufacturing, and service functions. The basic buyer-seller dyad is based on laws governing economic activity and norms associated with buyer preference and taste. Classical economic theory is built on assumptions about the relationship between buyers and sellers, as well as between competitors. As maximizers of their personal utility, market sellers compete for their market share. Buyers and sellers need to cooperate with one another in order to engage in an exchange of goods and services. In an attempt to get the best value or maximize profit, each actor in the network may engage in negotiation and bargaining.

Viewed in terms of their network and systems features, markets exhibit the more emergent and essentially scale-free elements of any of the three macro-level forms. Writing about the dynamics of market exchange systems, F. H. Knight observes:

> [The exchange system's] most interesting feature is that it is automatic and unconscious; no one plans or ever planned it out, no one assigns the participants their roles or directs their functions. Each person in such a system seeks his own satisfaction without thought of the structure of society or its interests; and the mere mechanical interaction of such self-seeking units organizes them into an elaborate system and controls and coordinates their activities so that each is continuously supplied with the fruits of the labor of one vast and unknown multitude in return for performing some service for another multitude also large and unknown to him (Knight, 1965, p. 29). (Porter, 1990, pp. 15–17)

Knight's description of market dynamics may be critiqued for its idealization of market interactions. March and Olsen have noted how certain "voluntary" exchanges found in market interactions can be coerced (1995, p. 10). The predilection that markets are populated by a multitude of "economic men" acting on their own personal utility-maximizing interests is being heavily critiqued within the literature in behavioral economics, social and community psychology, and sociological studies of market-like behavior.

In order to represent markets and hierarchies as variations of network forms, and still account for the existence of cooperative ties, we may distinguish between markets, hierarchies, and collaboratives, with the latter being interorganizational network structures that rely on norms of trust and reciprocity. For a summary of the characteristics of the three forms of macro structures discussed, see Table 2.2. Collaborative structures emerging within the policy stream have been described as public-private partnerships (Linder and Rosenau, 2000; Bovaird, 2005), strategic alliances (Wohlstetter, Smith, and Malloy, 2005), cross-sector collaborations (Bryson, Crosby, and Stone, 2006), and interest group coalitions (Hula, 1999) in the literature. Although many governance networks get shaped, in part, by the organizational structures of the actors that comprise them, we suggest that all governance networks possess, to one degree or another, certain collaborative characteristics. The collaborative as a third form of network is introduced here as a value-neutral construct. As network accountabilities and performance get considered, the question "Collaboration to what end?" may be asked. Cautioning against viewing collaboration as a panacea for solving complex public problems, Bardach suggests that we should "not want to oversell the benefits of interagency collaboration. The

Table 2.2   Macro-Level Network Forms

	Market	*Hierarchy*	*Collaborative*
Relational tie	Competitive	Command and control	Collaborative and cooperative
Public administration paradigm	New public management	Classical public administration	Collaborative public management
Institutional frame	Businesses/ corporations	Public bureaucracy	Partnerships; coalitions

Source: Modified from Powell, *Research in Organizational Behaviour, 12,* 295–336, 1990; Grimshaw et al., in Marchington et al., Eds., *Fragmenting Work: Blurring Organizational Boundaries and Disordering Hierarchies,* Oxford University Press, Oxford, 2005.

political struggle to develop collaborative capacity can be time consuming and divisive. But even if no such struggle were to ensue, the benefits of collaboration are necessarily limited" (Bardach, 1998, p. 311). We must be able to take into account that collaborations and partnerships may be an ineffective means for delivering socially desirable outcomes. Collaboratives can be undertaken in closed networks, leading in their worst cases to "group think" or collusion. The social capital derived through horizontal ties may support "dark networks" (Raab and Milward, 2003) that exist to do social harm. We also need to be able to take into account collaborations that are carried out without sufficient democratic anchorage (Sorensen and Torfing, 2005), and develop the means to ascertain the degree of democratic anchorage that exists within any given governance network.

The collaborative as a third form of network is introduced here as a value-neutral construct. As network accountabilities and performance get considered, the question of "Collaboration to what end?" may be asked. Cautioning against viewing collaboration as a panacea for solving complex public problems, Bardach observes:

> We should not be impressed by the idea of collaboration per se. That collaboration is nicer sounding than indifference, conflict, or competition is beside the point. So, too, is the fact that collaboration often makes people feel better than conflict or competition. I do not want to oversell the benefits of interagency collaboration. The political struggle to develop collaborative capacity can be time consuming and divisive. But even if no such struggle were to ensue, the benefits of collaboration are necessarily limited. (Bardach, 1998, p. 311)

We must be able to take into account that collaborations and partnerships may be an ineffective means for delivering socially desirable outcomes.

We conclude that by allowing for the possibility that network forms take on characteristics of some combination of market, hierarchical, and collaborative arrangements, we can begin to recognize the trade-offs and opportunities that occur when one form of administrative authority is compared to, contrasted against, and combined with one another. If for-profit firms participate in an interorganizational network, they bring to the network facets of the market structures to which they belong. Their engagement in public-private partnerships, regulatory subsystems, or grants and contract agreements is carried out with one proverbial eye over their shoulder, judging their participation, in part, on the impacts that their involvements have on fostering their own competitive advantage. The potential impact that network-wide actions have on the participating firm's economic standing is often an important consideration guiding network-wide actions.

If public sector organizations such as government agencies formally participate in an interorganizational network, they bring with them elements of their bureaucratic, hierarchical structure. Official public agency participation is often predicated on the will and desires of the agencies' principals, be they the elected chief executive officers, their appointees, or supervisors imbued with the authority to dictate the agencies' scope and type of involvement. Those who distinguish governance networks from markets and hierarchies fail to take into account the influence that the market and hierarchical structures of the participating organizations and institutions have in the structures and functions of the network itself. At the meso and micro levels, these mixed ties surface as distinctions between vertical, horizontal, and competitive ties, a matter we turn to in great depth in Chapter 4.

The Conceptual Architecture of the Book

We classify the types of network structures and characteristics found across the literature in terms of a nested configuration of levels of analysis. Looking across this literature, we find some frameworks focusing exclusively on the whole network as the unit of analysis (O'Toole, 1990; Rhodes, 1997; Schaap and van Twist, 1997; Milward and Provan, 2006; Frederickson and Frederickson, 2006; Agranoff, 2007; Provan and Kenis, 2007; Provan, Fish, and Sydow, 2007), while others combine individual member characteristics *and* whole networks (Agranoff and McGuire, 2003; Mandell and Steelman, 2003) into their frameworks. At the core of this nested configuration are the characteristics of the particular network actors or nodes, and the orientations they bring to their networked activities. At this level we contemplate actors' goals, motivations, interests, and ultimately, the resources they bring to a network. At the next level of analysis are the ties that exist between network actors or nodes, described in terms of the strength, formality, and vector of relational ties that get established between any two social actors or nodes. With the characteristics of the individual actors and the ties forged between then defined, we may move to considerations of network-wide characteristics. At this level we characterize network structures in terms of the degree of openness and closeness that governance networks may have, the relative stability and formality of governance networks, and the network-wide policy and operation functions undertaken. We are capable of describing network-wide governance structures (Provan and Kenis, 2007). At the broadest level of consideration are systems-wide considerations that view governance networks as being embedded in systems dynamics that include the external environment, input/output flows, and feedback loops. Table 2.3 lists the major components of the taxonomy of the book. Appendix A provides all of the major architecture in one place.

The definition of governance networks that we use here is premised on the notion of markets, hierarchies, and collaboratives as types of interorganizational network structures that influence the kinds of administrative authorities, accountability regimes, and performance standards employed. *Governance networks are defined as relatively stable patterns of coordinated action and resource exchanges; involving policy actors crossing different social scales, drawn from the public, private, or nonprofit sectors and across geographic levels; who interact through a variety of competitive, command and control, cooperative, and negotiated arrangements; for purposes anchored in one or more facets of the policy stream.* We also add that governance networks are found within specific policy domains (such as health, environment, transportation, education, etc.) as well as exist across policy domains.

The mixed-form governance networks that we describe in this book are characterized as variations of some combination of actors, ties, and network-wide and systems characteristics. Over the course of the next few chapters we discuss each of these variations. We offer some suggestions for ways in which each variation may be labeled or categorized. The selection of these variations has been grounded in the literature review outlined earlier in this chapter. A scan of the major developments in governance network analysis provides some reference to additional typologies and frameworks that have populated the literature.

Summary

In this chapter we synthesize some of the expansive bodies of literature that have arisen over the last few decades that we believe contribute to the development of an interdisciplinary theoretical framework to describe and ultimately evaluate governance networks. We began the chapter reviewing the ways in which network metaphors and analytical frameworks have been employed within the public administration, policy studies, and governance fields. We noted that one of the major discrepancies across the literature concerns the relationship between network structures, and markets and hierarchies. We have argued for the development of a view of mixed-form governance networks that accounts for markets and hierarchies as network forms alongside of collaboratives and partnerships. We introduced the mixed forms of governance networks as pertaining to the multiple sectors,

Table 2.3   A Taxonomy of Governance Networks 1.0

Level/Type of Variable	Variable	Variable Descriptors
Actors (nodes)	Social scale	Individual Group Organizational/institutional Interorganizational
	Social sector (organizational level)	Public Private Nonprofit
	Geographic scale	Local Regional State National International
	Role centrality	Central-peripheral Trajectory
	Capital resources actor provides (as an input)	Financial Physical Natural Human Social Cultural Political Knowledge
	Providing accountabilities to	Elected representatives Citizens and interest groups Courts Owners/shareholders Consumers Bureaucrats/supervisors/principals Professional associations Collaborators/partners/peers
	Receiving accountabilities from	Elected representatives Citizens and interest groups Courts Owners/shareholders Consumers Bureaucrats/supervisors/principals

(continued)

Table 2.3   A Taxonomy of Governance Networks 1.0 (Continued)

Level/Type of Variable	Variable	Variable Descriptors
		Professional associations Collaborators/partners/peers
	Performance/output and outcomes criteria	Tied to policy function and domain
Ties	Resources exchanged/pooled	Financial Physical Natural Human Social Cultural Political Knowledge
	Strength of tie	Strong to weak
	Formality of tie	Formal to informal
	Administrative authority	Vertical (command and control) Diagonal (negotiation and bargaining) Horizontal (collaborative and cooperative) Competitive
	Accountability relationship	Elected representatives Citizens and interest groups Courts Owners/shareholders Consumers Bureaucrats/supervisors/principals Professional associations Collaborators/partners/peers
Network-wide characteristics	Policy tools	Regulations Grants Contracts Vouchers Taxes Loans/loan guarantees

Table 2.3 A Taxonomy of Governance Networks 1.0 (Continued)

Level/Type of Variable	Variable	Variable Descriptors
	Operational functions	Resource exchange/pooling Coordinated action Information sharing Capacity building
	Policy functions	Define/frame problem Design policy solution Coordinate policy solution Implement policy (regulation) Implement policy (service delivery) Evaluate and monitor policy Political alignment
	Policy domain functions	Health, environment, education, etc.
	Macro-level governance structures	Lead organization Shared governance Network administrative organization
	Network configuration	Intergovernmental relations Interest group coalitions Regulatory subsystems Grant and contract agreements Public-private partnerships
Systems-wide	Properties of network boundaries	Open-closed permeability
	Systems dynamics	Systems-level inputs, processes, outputs, and outcomes
	Feedback loops via	Policy tools Representation Administrative authority Accountability Performance management

(continued)

Table 2.3   A Taxonomy of Governance Networks 1.0 (Continued)

Level/Type of Variable	Variable	Variable Descriptors
	Hybridized accountability regimes	Elected representatives
		Citizens and interest groups
		Courts
		Owners/shareholders
		Consumers
		Bureaucrats/supervisors/principals
		Professional associations
		Collaborators/partners/peers
	Performance management system	Governing communities of practice
		Data collection regimes
		Decision heuristics

multiple geographic scales of network actors, and mixed administrative authorities comprised of vertical, horizontal, and diagonal relational ties. We also noted that mixed-form governance networks may be coupled with multiple policy functions found within and across the policy stream. We believe that the presentation of a model of mixed-form governance networks allows us to develop a means for describing the many different ways that stable governance networks arise and carry out one or more functions related to the policy stream. Lastly, we scanned the literature that has arisen to describe governance network structures, concluding that we may look upon the task of developing a set of network characteristics as a matter of developing multiple layers of analysis—from the characteristics of individual network actors, to the nature of the ties between actors, to the nature of network-wide characteristics, to ultimately, systems-wide characteristics that position governance networks within broader external environments.

CRITICAL QUESTIONS AND CONSIDERATIONS

This chapter focuses on the basic components of social networks that are simultaneously comprised of individuals, groups, and organizations. The basic architecture of the book hinges on the basic structures of any network: nodes linked together by ties. These nodes have unique characteristics. The ties between nodes have unique characteristics as well. As nodes develop multiple ties with multiple nodes, network-wide properties take shape.

Consider your level of awareness of the social networks that you are a part of. Map these relationships using basic node and tie structures. Consider how and to what extent these social networks intersect. Think about what binds you together and how strong or weak these ties are.

In your approach to understanding governance networks, how would you address the following kinds of questions?

- What kinds of governance networks can you identify? Who participates in these networks? Do participants have roles or responsibilities in other networks or organizations?
- Can you identify the policy domain of a selected governance network? What type of influence does the governance network exert within the policy domain? What policy tools does the governance network rely upon in exerting influence?
- Where is the governance network structure located in the public policy process: upstream in policy making, midstream in policy implementation, or downstream in policy enforcement?
- How are citizens represented in governance networks? What role do citizens play within the governance network? How are citizens selected for participation in governance networks? What kind of participation takes place in governance networks?
- What is the geographic reach of the governance network? What kinds of jurisdictions are involved with the governance network?

Chapter 3

Characteristics of Actors Participating within Governance Networks

All the world's a stage, and all the men and women merely players.
They have their exits and their entrances and one man in his time plays
many parts.

**—William Shakespeare (As You Like It, Act II, Scene VII,
Lines 139–166) (Thurber, 1922, p. 39)**

In this chapter we address some of the characteristics of the potential nodes that
populate a governance network. These nodes are described as social actors who
possess certain goals and take on certain roles within a governance network. We
argue that these goals and roles are shaped, in part, by the social sector to which
the actor belongs. We discuss how an actor's sector characteristics (public, private,
or nonprofit) impact the actor's goal and role orientations. We also set the stage for
a deeper discussion of sector governance and the range of accountability frameworks and performance expectations found within each sector. We then acknowledge that network actors will be attuned toward certain levels of geographic scale:
local, regional, statewide (in a U.S. context), national, and international. We then
broach a subject that has been given scant attention within the network literature
in public administration and policy studies, namely, the social scale of participating actors. In the previous chapter we touched on the roles that citizens and public
administrators play in certain kinds of collaborative or participatory governance

structures. These concerns raise the topic of the social scale of a network actor. We view social scale as a nested concept that includes individuals, groups, organizations, and networks of organizations. We argue that discerning the level of social scale is critical to describing and analyzing actor characteristics. We then explore the relationship of an actor with a network in terms of the metaphor of center and periphery. Lastly, in anticipation of describing network ties in terms of resource exchange theory, we lay out the range of possible resources that specific network actors may bring to their involvement. We describe these resources in terms of nine different distinctions of "capital resources."

As the component parts of the larger whole, the characteristics of the individual actors within a governance network matter. Although we believe there to be an almost limitless capacity to define the characteristics of individual network actors, we settle on a few critical features that appear to be most relevant in describing the structures of governance networks. We note that there has not been a great deal of attention paid to the characteristics of individual network actors in the literature cited in Chapter 2. Although there has been some recognition of the problems associated with the social scale of network actors (Koontz et al., 2004; Provan, Fish, and Sydow, 2007; Koppenjan, 2008), as well as questions raised concerning the compatibility of public, private, and nonprofit goals (Salamon, 2002a), we find little discussion to date laying out distinctions between the central characteristics that individual network actors bring to their collective undertakings.

Goal and Role Orientation of Network Actors

The importance of goal setting and attainment has long been recognized as a central feature of organizational behavior and leadership development (Hall, 1980). Etzioni first observed that "an organizational goal is a desired state of affairs which the organization attempts to realize" (1964, p. 6). However, such a "desired state of affairs is by definition many things to many people" (Hall, 1980, p. 88). Thus, we may conclude that goals, be they set at the individual, group, or organizational level, are essentially statements shaped by abstract values. Goals carry meaning because they project a desired state of being, and must, ultimately, be converted to specific guides for action on an operational, and essentially practical, level.

Focusing particularly on the nature of "complex" organizational goals, Charles Perrow first distinguished between "official" and "operative" organizational goals. Official goals are "the general purposes of the organization as put forth in the charter, annual reports, public statements by key executives and other authoritative pronouncements" (1961, p. 855). Official goals are often reified, appearing as written standards or explicit pronouncements. Reification means "to treat [an abstraction] as substantially existing, or as a concrete material object" (Wenger, 1998, p. 58). Official goals are "constraining or guiding principles" from which rules, policies, procedures, and habits emerge (Hall, 1980, p. 90). We may relate official goals with Argyris and Schon's concept of organizational "theories *of* action" (1995).

Operative goals, on the other hand, "designate the ends sought through the actual operating policies of the organization; they tell us what the organization actually is trying to do, regardless of what the official goals say are aims" (Hall, 1980, pp. 89–90). Operative goals are produced through participation, engagement, and practices of organizational actors. Operational goals serve as "theories *in* action" (Argyris and Schon, 1995). According to Hall, operative goals are produced through a combination of official goals and other internal and external factors (1980). He views operational goals at the level of the rules, policies, procedures, and habits that emerge out of actual experience.

As we consider the particular goals of different network actors and how these goals contribute to the wider network, we must recognize the differences between official goals and those that actually guide the operations of nodal actors. Case studies of governance networks often highlight the disparities that exist between an organization's official positions and those that exist "in use" (Koontz et al., 2004; Frederickson and Frederickson, 2006; Rodriguez et al., 2007). A pattern that may sometimes emerge in interorganizational governance networks is the difference between the official positions held by organizations and institutions, and the unofficial positions taken up by their respective individual representatives. One may also find that an individual actor in a network may state that he or she does not officially represent the interests of his or her organization. In some cases, official participation may even be prohibited by law or statute, as in the cases when legislatures or executives limit governments' roles in networked activities.

Thus, the goals that particular network actors bring to their participation in a governance network need to be understood in terms of their official positions and operational positions. The goal compatibility between network actors becomes a central consideration as network ties and network-wide functions are explored.

The roles that particular network actors take will, in large part, be predicated on the depth and breadth of capital resources each brings to the network. We will note in the section to follow that resource exchanges between network actors are rarely equal. Lead organizations supplying the bulk of a governance network's financial resources and network staffing are common. Arguably, those contributing the most, or at least the most valuable, capital resources to a network will be in a better position to wield some measure of authority over other network actors. Being resource rich often positions network actors as the principals in a principal-agent dynamic. Resource-poor network actors will more likely be positioned as network agents, often giving authority to those who bring more resources to the table. When two or more actors enter into a network relationship as partners we may assume one of two things: (1) Either there exists a sufficient balance in the distribution of resources, meaning network actors bring equal amounts of resources to the network, or (2) gaps between resource distributions do not matter to network members. The latter case may arise when resource-rich actors voluntarily forgo the latent and manifest authorities that may be tied to their resources. The characteristics of the kinds of ties said to exist between network actors, we will elaborate further on the relationship between resource distribution and the vector of social ties.

Particular network actors may take on any number of roles within a network that extend well beyond the kind of principal-agent partnership roles described above. Roles may be tied to the central resources that a network actor brings to the network, be it taking on the role of funder (financial), expert (knowledge and human), or boundary spanner (social). Across the literature, particular attention has been paid to the roles that governments take on in governance networks. In describing the kind of roles that governments take on in public-private partnerships, regulatory subsystems, and grant and contract agreements, Koontz et al. (2004) describe governments as leaders, followers, and encouragers. Donald Kettl (2006) has discussed the ways in which governments play the role of "boundary spanner." Lester Salamon (2002a) describes the orchestrating, modulating, and activating roles that government actors can and do play in governance networks. After examining the ways in which governments can influence corporate social responsibility through a variety of regulatory and partnership initiatives, Tom Fox and his colleagues (2002) discuss how governments play mandating, endorsing, facilitating, and partnering roles. We may recognize that these roles can be taken on by nonstate actors as well.

Social Sector

We believe that one of the central distinguishing features that exist between particular nodal actors is the social sector from which the actor originates. Although we will look at sectoral differences as they relate specifically to governance, accountability, and performance measures in later chapters, we focus here on the distinctions between the goals of the public, private, and nonprofit sectors at the organizational scale. The model of public, private, and nonprofit social sectors is a widely adapted framework that draws distinctions between the public, private, and voluntary natures of these sectors. Extensive consideration has been given to the differences between the public and private spheres (Bozeman, 1987, 2007; Janoski, 1998). Economists sometimes couch these differences in terms of public and private goods, while political scientists draw on these distinctions when discussing the relationship between democracies and markets. Over the course of the last several decades, the importance of "civil society" has become a focus of much interest, resulting in the addition of what has been labeled the "voluntary," "third," or "nonprofit" sector. Although these terms have been used interchangeably, we will settle on the nonprofit sector here. Although a strong case could be made for characterizing civil society as the voluntary sector, we opt to use the term *nonprofit organizations* to represent the range of "voluntary associations" first recognized by Alexis

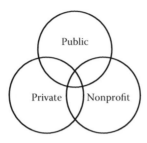

Figure 3.1   Three social sectors model.

de Tocqueville more than 178 years ago. The three social sectors are represented in Figure 3.1 as a Venn diagram.

Public sector organizations are the formal institutions of the state, spanning the legislative, executive, and judicial branches of government. As sovereign entities, these institutions have a contractual obligation to serve the interests of their citizenry. The governmental institutions of the state are guided by public interests and public policy goals. Private sector organizations are driven by market forces and the pursuit of profit as the dominant performance measure. Businesses, corporations, firms, and other labels ascribed to for-profit organizations make up the private sector. Property rights and ownership play a critical role in defining corporate governing structures. The nonprofit sector is comprised of voluntary associations that are prohibited from earning profits. Nonprofit organizations are driven by social missions designed to represent interests, advocate positions, inform the public, or deliver social services. Table 3.1 provides a summary of some basic social sector characteristics.

The primary official goal of private sector organizations appears to be profit. We may be inclined to view profit as a clearly articulated and defined goal. However, "the readily quantifiable profit goal is not such a simple matter.… It is confounded by such issues as the time perspective (long-run or short-run profits); the rate of profit (in terms of return to investors); the important issue of survival and growth in a turbulent and unpredictable environment that might in the short run preclude profit making" (Hall, 1980, p. 88). Despite these important caveats, suggestions that private firms exist to provide goods and services that customers and consumers need and want, and even allusions to an increasing interest in "triple bottom lines" and "corporate social responsibility," the profit motive remains the central goal of private sector actors in governance networks. As actors guided by market forces, the profit goal drives competitive efforts to wield authority against.

The official goals of public sector organizations are wrought with much more ambiguity (Stone, 2002), as it is now commonly observed that policy goals get framed through the lens of different policy actors. As Charles Lindblom (1959) first noted in his classic article "The Science of 'Muddling Through,'" the successful attainment of public policy goals may be determined when an agreement between policy actors exists on the proper actions to undertake. In Deborah Stone's (2002)

Table 3.1 Characteristics of Social Sectors

Characteristics Unique to the Sector	Private Sector	Public Sector	Nonprofit Sector
Organizational actors	For-profit firms, businesses, and corporations	National, state, regional, and local level governments (including legislative, judicial, and executive branches)	Nonprofit organizations; nongovernmental organizations (NGOs); informal community groups
Individual actors	Business managers; owners; consumers	Public managers; elected officials; citizens; judges	Nonprofit managers; citizens; clients
Official goal Predominant performance standard(s)	Profit	Making and enforcing laws and regulations; meeting public needs; delivering public policy	Fulfilling mission
Overarching goals determined by those to whom accountabilities are rendered	Board of directors; shareholders/owners; business managers	Elected officials; citizens; public managers	Board of directors; clientele/interests

Source: Modified from Block, in Ott, Ed., *The Nature of the Nonprofit Sector*, Westview Press, Boulder, CO, 2001, pp. 97–111.

book *Policy Paradox*, she describes how goal ambiguity serves as an essential feature of the public policy-making process. The role of ambiguity in framing public policy goals obviously brings a certain measure of uncertainty to the participation of a public sector organization (or public official) in a governance network. Official public goals may be clearly specified in laws and regulations. However, the fact that such laws and regulations may be subject to the interpretation of the individuals charged with enforcing, enacting, and implementing them renders even clearly articulated public policy goals ambiguous. Noting this phenomenon, Hall observes that "if it [a public sector organization] is staffed by personnel who have values above and beyond simply administering the existing laws ... their own values toward social action or inaction can clearly modify the stated goals of the organization" (Hall, 1980, p. 88). In instances where laws, regulations, and policy directives are clear and those responsible for enforcing, enacting, or implementing them understand and comply with the original intent behind them, we may find some measure of alignment between official public sector goals and their operative goals. However, in cases where certain internal and external factors bring ambiguity to public policy goals, we find these goals the subject of dynamics found in the "polis," and the continuous negotiation of authority between policy actors that is said to exist within the polis (Stone, 2002). As we have considered in Chapter 1, when we discussed the role of democratic anchorage, governance networks can and do serve as spaces through which common, and essentially public, goals may be derived.

The official goals of nonprofit sector actors are shaped in large part by the mission of the organizations and the interpretation of these missions by nonprofit managers and their boards of directors (Stone and Ostrower, 2007). Both the official and the operative goals of nonprofit actors may be influenced by external funders who articulate their own funding priorities and, indirectly, influence how nonprofit actors officially define their missions or operate on a day-to-day basis. Nonprofit organizations are generally founded to serve a social or public need. As conduits through which collective interests may coalesce, this sector's goals are also shaped through a process of "negotiated meaning" between those sharing common interests. We will argue that nonprofit actors are the most susceptible to being influenced by the goals of other members of the governance network, resulting, in the worst cases, in unwanted "mission creep." In the best cases, nonprofit actors are, overall, in the best position to adapt to changing conditions and respond to emergent needs, new priorities, and altered conditions. Nonprofit organizations do wield significant power as representatives of certain collective interests. Nonprofit organizations are often used to exert influence over the political system. In cases like these, nonprofit governance structures allow for special interests to collectivize power and operate from a significant position of strength.

A review of the differences in the performance standards across the public, private, and nonprofit sectors allows us to draw a continuum of clearly defined measures: nearly universal measures (such as profit), to the ambiguity-riddled challenges of measuring successful public policies (Stone, 2002), to the highly context-specific and mostly localized performance standards ascribed to individual nonprofit organizations (Stone and Ostrower, 2007). Although there is some literature that has discussed the differences between social sectors, and how these differences impact contractual agreements and public-private partnerships (Gazley and Brudney, 2007), a full accounting of intersector dynamics is largely missing from the literature reviewed here. The challenges associated with principal-agent problems get compounded when private contractors are viewed as interest groups capable of capturing contractual and regulatory authorities. These considerations lead us to conclude that we need to evolve our capacities to evaluate multisector arrangements.

At this juncture, very little is known about how the different governance and administrative structures of the public, private, and nonprofit sectors inform the governance of an entire governance network. The role that sector blurring plays in governance networks has been extensively discussed in Koppell's analysis of "hybrid organizations" (2003). Koppell defines the hybrid organization as entities, "created by the [U.S.] federal government (either by act of Congress or executive action) to address a specific public policy purpose. It is owned in whole or part by private individuals or corporations and/or generates revenue to cover its operating costs" (2003, p. 12). Hybrid organizations are embodied in many (but not all) government corporations, authorities, and some commission structures. Koppell reviews how certain hybrid organizations in the housing and mortgage, export promotion, and international development industries are held accountable through various forms of bureaucratic control. However, his study of hybrid organizations is largely relegated to describing how bureaucratic control is exerted over the hybrid organization. Although he richly describes how and to what extent there exist a set of apparent trade-offs between public missions and private funding, his conceptual model for analyzing these dynamics stays focused on the examination of principal-agent relations guided by certain assumptions regarding the centrality of state sovereignty.

In later chapters we discuss the role that social sector characteristics play in crafting network-wide accountability regimes. We suggest that the study of accountability across complex intersector arrangements needs to be understood as a series of trade-offs between the democratic anchorage of the state (and sometimes collective interest groups), market accountabilities (when private firms and corporations are implicated), and administrative accountabilities (introduced below in terms of the vertical or horizontal nature of administrative authorities).

Geographic Scale

Governance network actors pursue their goals at multiple geographic scales, which in turn are typically driven by the spatial scope of the organizational goals with which the network actors are primarily affiliated. We suggest the need to differentiate among actors based on the geographic scale of their primary organizational affiliations. While geographic scale can be represented as a continuous function, here, for simplicity, we break down the discussion of geographic scale in discrete terms that corroborate typical political-administrative boundaries. We enunciate this as the spatial boundedness of network actors and break it down into four concrete spatial scopes: localism, regionalism, nationalism, and internationalism.

> *Localism*: Public sector actors operating in local (e.g., county or municipal) governments typically focus their system of concern at the local level. Though the dynamics at larger spatial scales may constrain the actions of local public sector actors, the actors at the local scale are typically the ultimate implementers,

or what Lipsky (2004) calls "street level bureaucrats." Local actors thus operate in action arenas (Ostrom, 2007). Similarly, small nonprofits or community organizations and small businesses typically operate at local levels. The politics and social dynamics of local level actors are much more interpersonal than the politics at larger spatial scales. We can also argue that governance networks at local levels provide very interesting empirical test beds for modeling purposes, as system complexity increases at larger geographical scales.

Regionalism: Network actors operating at regional, statewide, or multistate geographical levels (in the U.S. context) can be grouped as regional/state level actors. These include representatives of metropolitan or state governments in public sector organizations. Nonprofits are typically larger at this scale than the local level nonprofits, and so are the private sector organizations, which are typically LLCs or small corporations (in the U.S. context). A lot of public policy implementation, including transportation, health, education, economic development, and so on, occurs at the regional scale. The system complexity at this scale is higher than that at the local scale, primarily because both the sheer number of network actors and their goal conflicts are higher at the regional scale than the local scale.

Nationalism/federalism: Various nation-states have different levels of centralized (federal) vs. decentralized (confederal) powers to raise taxes/revenues, legislate policies, and implement some of them (especially defense, foreign affairs, and national security). In modern democracies, policy-making legislatures are elected periodically through population-based or area-based representational systems. The public sector actors in the federal government are thus relatively unstable. Bureaucrats and judges, however, last longer than elected representatives. Large national level nonprofits and think tanks influence national level policy-making processes, as do large, even multinational level, corporations when they lobby national level policy makers. National level network actors in all sectors have typically larger geographical domains of concern than regional or local level network actors; however, democratic accountability and the need to be reelected forces many national level policy makers to pursue their respective regional or local level interests in the resource allocation done at the national level, such as budget making processes and so on.

Internationalism: Network actors operating at international scales include members of international public sector organizations, such as United Nations agencies; international nongovernmental organizations (NGOs), such as International Union for the Conservation of Nature (IUCN) and World Wildlife Fund (WWF); and multinational corporations, such as automobile and oil companies. Network actors operating at the international scale typically deal with cross-national resource extraction or resource allocation issues. Due to the lack of a stable international government, network actors at the international scale operate with very different rules of the game than typically observed at the national, regional, or local levels.

Within each of these three social sectors, organizations operate across varying levels of geographic scale. In Chapter 6, we examine how different levels of governments may nest inside of one another or coexist as a complex network of intergovernmental entities. Corporations, businesses, and firms get shaped by the geographic scale of their operations and ownership patterns, ranging from multinational corporations to small local businesses, while nonprofit organizations will likely tailor their missions around attending to a particular geographic scale: from the international aid agency to a local food bank. For our purposes, we draw distinctions between the local, state/regional, national, and international levels. Table 3.2 breaks down how social sectors and geographic scales converge within a particular organizational or institutional actor.

Table 3.2 Range of Governance Network Actors (U.S. Context) by Scale and Sector

	Social Sector		
Geographic Scale	*Private Sector*	*Public Sector*	*Nonprofit Sector*
International	Multinational corporations	United Nations; international regulatory entities	International nongovernmental organizations
National	Corporations	Federal government (legislative, executive, judicial)	National nonprofit organizations
State	Corporations/ businesses	State government (legislative, executive, judicial)	Statewide nonprofit organizations
Regional	Regional businesses	Regional government	Regional nonprofit organizations
Local	Local businesses	Local government (legislative, executive, judicial)	Local nonprofit organizations; community groups

Scale of Social Nodes

In social networks, nodes may represent very different kinds of *social scale*, ranging from individual people to small groups of people (individual teams, committees, departments, offices, etc.), to entire organizations. Although multiscale network modeling is beginning to be devised, at this current time, we argue that most network analysis within the public administration and policy studies literature has been rendered by observing the relationship between nodes of a comparable scale. We may classify the types of network structures and characteristics found across the literature in terms of a nested configuration of levels of analysis. Looking across the literature, we find some frameworks focusing exclusively on the whole network as the unit of analysis (O'Toole, 1990; Rhodes, 1997; Schapp and van Twist, 1997; Milward and Provan, 2006; Frederickson and Frederickson, 2006; Agranoff, 2007; Provan and Kenis, 2007; Provan, Fish, and Sydow, 2007), while others combine individual member characteristics and whole networks (Agranoff and McGuire, 2003; Mandell and Steelman, 2003; Koppenjan and Klijn, 2004; Koontz et al., 2004) into their frameworks.

In dealing with complex networks found within social systems, the matter of *social scale* is a preeminent consideration (Dodder and Sussman, 2002). This is particularly true if the social system is comprised of more than individuals, extending into the small group and organizational levels. In order to understand how social networks encompass multiple levels of scale, it is useful to consider how scale-free networks grow.

The basic premise behind scale-free networks is an assumption regarding the almost unlimited capacity to continue to add nodes to the network. Mathematically speaking, new nodes added to the network tend to demonstrate a preferential attachment to nodes with a greater number of existing links. Mathematician Albert-Laszlo Barabasi, who has done a great deal to popularize network analysis as well as serving as one of its preeminent scholars, describes preferential attachment as follows:

> We assume that each new node connects to the existing nodes with two links. The probability that it will choose a given node is proportional to the number of links the chosen node has. That is, given the choice between two nodes, one with twice as many links as the other, it is twice as likely that the new node will connect to the more connected nodes. (Barabasi, 2003, p. 86)

The picture of a scale-free network that gets painted here is a visual structure of individual nodes (be they individual Web sites, cells, human beings, or organizations), clumping together to form clusters. These clusters, in turn, cluster with other clusters, and so on. We have already noted how the clustering of clusters forms the basis of certain kinds of hierarchical arrangements (Ravasz and Barabasi, 2003).

We may view the scale-free dimensions of social networks as being represented in the nested nature of individual people, grouping into small groups, which in turn form organizations, which in turn form interorganizational networks.

Systems theorists have recognized the "nested complexity" of social networks (Dodder and Sussman, 2002). Sociologically, the matter of social scale has been framed as a distinction between macro, meso, and micro levels of analysis (Collins, 1988). Figure 3.2 provides a visual representation of the ways in which nodes of a smaller social scale (individual) may be understood as nesting within larger scales (organizational).

The nested complexity of many social networks can be recognized in some of the classical considerations of organizational leadership, and the extent to which individual leaders can influence the dynamics of an organization. Guiding much of this literature is the assumption that individual leadership can and does impact the operations of organizations. Likewise, it has been widely noted how organizations socialize individual members, suggesting ways in which a person's membership in an organization socializes him or her and, ultimately, shapes his or her professional identity (Wenger, 1998). The relationship between the individual person and the wider organizational context is an enduring theme within public administration, as evidenced in this quote by Paul Appleby:

> [Government] is a system, and the system cannot be understood except in terms of the public employees themselves, their conceptions of their positions, and the attitudes of the public about what is required in and from our civil servants. These elements together are what make government a system, for in combination they comprise what we call a bureaucracy. (Appleby, 2004, p. 132)

The conclusion that we may draw from this observation is that governance networks, as social networks, are multiscalable, with the nodes of a social network defined in terms of individual persons, groups of people, or organizations.

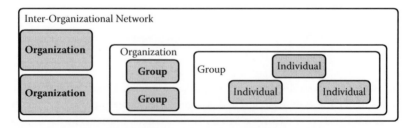

Figure 3.2 The nested complexity of social networks.

Nodes as Organizations and Institutions

The extensive bodies of literature that focus on the study, description, and evaluation of organizations and institutions across the public, private, and nonprofit sectors are relevant to the development of any metalevel theory of governance networks. Although the principles of holism (Degenne and Forse, 1999) are extremely relevant to the study of interorganizational social networks, the extensive body of literature drawn from institutionalism, neoinstitutionalism, and new institutionalism, as well as the organizational development literature found across many social science disciplines, are relevant resources in the development of an integrated theory of governance networks.

Institutional theory views institutions as forms of organization that are shaped by some combination of formal, explicit structures and implicit norms and routines (Peters, 2005). Empirical institutionalism "takes as a given the political and social institutions of a society and then attempts to determine whether those institutions have any impact on the behavior of their members" (Peters, 2005, p. 99). These approaches to institutional structures have been applied to institutional arrangements between two or more organizations. Although we believe that the theory of governance networks put forth in this book is highly compatible with institutionalism, we recognize the difference between institutions as organizations and institutional arrangements as the formal and informal standards, norms, and routines that guide any interaction between multiple social actors. Arrangements may be said to be institutionalized when they have achieved a certain level of stability, with routines leading to the "sedimentation" of certain structures and functions (Peters, 2005). Institutionalism also brings the notion of isomorphism into the picture. The isomorphic properties of one institution may be copied by other institutions. The development of parallel structures and functions between two or more organizations can, in certain instances, facilitate the flow of resources between two network actors, regardless of their social scale.

Nodes as Groups of Individuals/Communities of Practice

Case studies of governance networks often highlight the roles that groups of individuals play in the administration and governance of interorganizational networks. These small group configurations have been described as taking the forms of committees, task forces, advisory groups, and teams operating within governance networks. Small groups may take on formal roles and responsibilities within the network, operating as central coordinating mechanisms designed to steer the governance network. Rhode's social exchange theory discusses group configurations as "dominant coalitions" operating within the broader network (1997). Sabatier's ACF framework refers to these small groups as "advocacy coalitions" (Sabatier and Jenkins-Smith, 1993). Historically, the loci of power found in iron triangles were often described as formal and informal conferences, panels, and committee meetings. In some instances, as in cases in which committees, authorities, and task forces are given resources to create, maintain, or govern broader interorganizational networks, groups turn into formal network administrative organizations (NAOs) (Provan and Kenis, 2007), shaping how governance networks are led and, ultimately, governed.

The importance of group structures and functions to the operation of the wider network has been recognized across many of the case studies of network configurations in the literature (Wenger, 1998; Koontz et al., 2004; Agranoff, 2007, 2008). Some have isolated these groups for study, drawing implications for network-wide performance in fields such as health care (Rodriguez et al., 2007), education (Gajda and Koliba, 2007), and transportation (metropolitan planning organizations: Wolf and Farquhar, 2005). Oftentimes these groups, committees, task forces, commissions, and authorities serve as the nerve center for network-wide operations, providing the physical and virtual spaces for interpersonal coordinated actions and resource exchanges to occur. These groups have begun to be described as communities of practice (Wenger, 1998; Snyder, Wenger, and de Sousa Briggs, 2003; Goldsmith and Eggers, 2004; Agranoff, 2008; Koliba and Gajda, 2009), capable of spanning organizational boundaries, facilitating the alignment of practices, and coordinating action pertaining to network-wide objectives. Figure 3.3 displays how communities of practice may relate to one another. It should be noted that this figure does not account for the possibility (and inevitability) that individuals will be members of more than one community of practice.

Snyder, Wenger, and de Sousa Briggs (2003) define communities of practice as

> "groups of people who share a concern, a set of problems, or a passion about a topic, and who deepen their knowledge and expertise in this area by interacting on an ongoing basis." They operate as "social learning systems" where practitioners connect to solve problems, share ideas, set standards, build tools, and develop relationships with peers and stakeholders. (2003, p. 17)

It is believed "that communities of practice are valuable … because they contribute to the development of social capital, which in turn is a necessary condition for knowledge creation, sharing, and use" (Lesser and Prusak, 2000, p. 124). The value of looking at the community of practice as a node within a governance network lies in the capacities of communities of practice to transcend formal organizational boundaries. As spaces where knowledge is transferred and decisions are made, and learning is achieved, communities of practice serve as critical features of interorganizational networks.

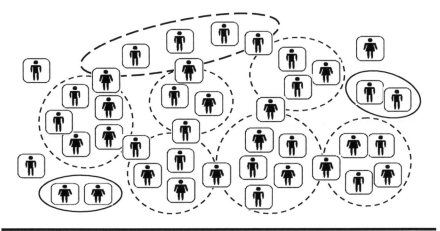

Figure 3.3 Communities of practice. (Source: Gajda and Koliba, *American Journal of Evaluation, 28,* 26–44, 2007.)

Nodes as Individual People

Distilled to their most rudimentary level, social networks must be composed of interlocking and clustering nodes of individual people. The importance of individuals to the governing, management, and ultimate success and failure of governance networks may be recognized in the countless case studies written describing and evaluating interorganizational network functions. The importance of individual leaders has been recognized in discussions of critical skills (Salamon, 2002a; Agranoff and McGuire, 2003; Agranoff, 2007) and differences between participants as individuals or as representatives of participating organizations and institutions (Koontz et al., 2004).

Those responsible for managing within and across governance networks, be they construed as collaborative public managers or network managers, are particularly relevant to those looking to understand how governance networks operate and ultimately, we will argue, are democratically governed. Individuals also play important roles in the accountability structures of governance networks.

Milward and Provan (2006) and Agranoff and McGuire (2003), among many others, have recognized that as administrators *of* and *within* governance networks, public managers play a critical role in ensuring that democratic and administrative accountability exists within all forms of governance network. It has been recognized that managing within networks brings a degree of complexity to administrative and managerial tasks. Mathur and Skelcher (2007) argue that network governance through the nodes of public-private partnerships and government-nonprofit collaboratives is reshaping the role of public administrators from "neutrally-competent servants of political executive" to "responsively competent players in a polycentric system of governance" (p. 231).

Spanning Social Scales

Among those who have studied governance networks, several have recognized the relationship between the individual and institutional levels of network actors. Koontz et al. (2004) distinguish between governmental actors as the "flesh-and-blood employees, elected officials, and other people in government who take action within the context of [the institutions they represent]" and governmental institutions themselves (p. 22). They conclude that individual "governmental actors and institutions, together or separately, constitute governmental roles in a particular collaborative effort" (Koontz et al., 2004, p. 22). Drawing on a series of case studies of environmental collaboratives in which governments play any number of roles (leading, following, facilitating, etc.), they observe the ways in which individual "governmental actors critically affect collaboration; in others, institutions may dominate; in yet others, both could be crucial; and in some cases, neither may make a substantial impact" (2004, p. 22). They also suggest that individuals and their institutions exist interdependently, with each providing constraints on the other. They conclude that "governmental roles in a particular case may be quite complex, particularly if the [individual] actors are seeking to change institutions in ways that promote or constrain collaboration" (2004, pp. 22–23). We may argue that the observations that they make regarding governmental actors and roles can be extended to private and nonprofit sector actors as well.

In examining the relationship between social scale and the roles of consensus and conflicts arising in policy networks, Joop Koppenjan explores the relationship between institutional level actors, group level actors, and individual actors, and, following Koontz et al.'s observations (2004), suggests ways in which actors at various levels of social scale bring certain measures of interdependence and autonomy to their network participation (2008, p. 151). Thus, we are left to conclude that network actors may or may not represent the interests of the actors from other levels of social scale, suggesting that an individual may actively participate in a governance network without officially representing the groups or organizations to which he or she belongs. We are left to conclude that the consideration of social scale as a critical characteristic in the operations of governance networks brings a measure of complexity into any study of their composition and behavior.

Center, Periphery, and Trajectories

"Structure conditions the expression of human agency" (Worsham, Eisner, and Ringquist, 1997, p. 4). The location of a given node within a social network matters, having a potential bearing on the strength and vector of the ties within it. The centrality of network nodes and the features of closeness and betweeness between nodes is a standard feature of most traditional network analysis (Provan, Sydow, and Fish, 2007). To determine the centrality of a given node requires access to an extensive

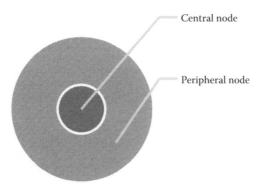

Central node

Peripheral node

Figure 3.4   Center-periphery metaphor.

amount of data concerning the relationships that nodes have to one another. We may consider centrality in terms of a given node's place within the network using a center-periphery metaphor first introduced by Edward Shils (1975) (Figure 3.4).

The visual that may be useful here is the classic bull's-eye. Central actors in a social network are positioned as network hubs, serving as mediators between other nodes (being positioned between two nodes). Other actors may be positioned on the periphery of the network.

According to social exchange theory, the centrality of an actor has a bearing on the power that it possesses. "Those who are centrally located have many alternatives and are not constrained by their actions by ties to a few organizations. The centrally located have access to resources such as information and are able to increase others' dependence on them" (Stevenson and Greenberg, 2000, p. 2).

The degree of centrality that a social node has in a network structure is not a proxy for determining the power of that node in the network. "Those who appear less powerful, such as the peripheral actors, may not be powerless. As agents, peripheral actors may be aware of the network and their position within it. They may exert influence by strategic uses of the network, use brokers who bring together parties to a transaction, or use more centrally located actors to mobilize support for their agenda" (Stevenson and Greenberg, 2000, p. 3). Case studies of governance networks, for example, demonstrate the ways in which more peripherally situated network actors can leverage their place to affect an impact on network outputs and outcomes. Peripheral actors need not be perceived as possessing less power. Peripheral actors may possess resources that are central to network stability and success.

The centrality of any given social node within a network will likely change over time. Involvement may deepen or lessen. The movement of social network actors has been described in terms of outbound and inbound trajectories (Wenger, 1998). As dynamic, adaptable systems, governance networks get shaped by these trajectories. These trajectories may be viewed in terms of their inbound or outbound nature. Network actors with inbound trajectories are joining the network with the prospect of becoming full participants in its practice. Their identities are invested in their future participation, even though their present participation may be peripheral. While other network actors will be on outbound trajectories leading out of a network. "What matters then is how a form of participation enables what comes next" (Wenger, 1998, pp. 154–155). By introducing the notion of trajectories into social network analysis, we account for the dynamics that the march of time brings to social networks. The trajectory metaphor adds an element of movement to the strength and vector of ties. Trajectory also accounts for the development of emergent network properties, a topic that we touch on in Chapter 7.

Variation in Actor Resources and Stock of Available Resources *to*/Provided *by* Actors

Network actors will possess their own stock of resources, which provides a foundation for their capacity to participate. We may characterize network actors in terms of the resources they bring to the network. Although governance networks often create resources that, in turn, support or aid in the collective undertaking of others (as, for instance, a piece of public infrastructure that is constructed through a public-private partnership), we are discussing resources here as a characteristic that specific network actors bring into (or perhaps withhold from) a governance network.

Each member of a governance network, whether construed as existing at the organizational, group, or individual level, brings some measure of capital to its involvement. The essence of network dynamics may be distilled down to the social ties that are formed between two nodes to exchange resources and engage in collective action. We have already noted how exchange theory underscores the capacity of two or more network actors to exchange resources. For instance, in a grant and contract agreement, a lead government agency will bring financial capital to the network. Contracted agents will bring some combination of human, knowledge, physical, social, and cultural capital to the relationship. In regulatory subsystems, lead government regulators may assert their political capital to ensure compliance, requiring regulated entities to supply them with information and the appropriate paperwork supplied by the regulated entity's human capital. In interest group coalitions, network actors may contribute virtually any form of capital to the collective endeavor. Likewise in public-private partnerships, in which some measure

A *resource* is a "source of supply, support or aid, especially one held in reserve."

—Webster's Dictionary (1989, p. 1221)

of risk sharing may be achieved as partners contribute a host of capitals, including financial, to a collective undertaking.

According to the basic tenants of social exchange theory, the range of resources that an actor "brings to the table" helps to determine its roles and functions within the network. In Chapter 4, we describe how resources are exchanged or combined with the resources of other network actors. In Chapter 7, we discuss how resource production or preservation may be characterized as the outputs and outcomes of governance networks.

Although there are many ways to categorize the kinds of resources that exist within social systems, we will rely on a multidimensional model of resource "capitals." We describe resources in terms of eight different types of capital. Capital is defined as "assets available for use in the production of further assets" (Wordnet, 2009). We use the term *capital* here to refer to the variety of assets that may be transferred between actors. The term *capital* is most often associated with wealth, and by inference, financial resources. However, over the last several decades social scientists have begun to widen the use of capital to encompass other supplies or stocks of resources. In addition to financial capital, we find allusions to physical, human, social, natural, political, cultural, and intellectual/knowledge capital across a broad swath of social science disciplines.

We recognize that the equation of capital to wealth and the building of wealth is a common way of referring to capital. We divorce these two meanings, equating capital, instead, with assets that may be traded or combined through network connections. Although some actors may engage in resource exchange and pooling to build wealth, other actors will likely be motivated by other ends, such as solving a public problem or delivering a public service.

Within a governance network framework, inputs into the system may be understood as stocks and flows of resources or capital. Financial, physical, human, social, natural, and intellectual capital may be used by individual network actors or by the network as a whole. Financial inputs into a governance network may be understood in terms of funding streams, as inputs entering the network from external sources, or as the flow of financial resources within the network. Physical capital includes any equipment, meeting space, or other material possessions owned by individual network actors used on behalf of the network, or owned by the network on the whole. The human capital of individual networks actors, construed at the organizational, group, or individual level, may contribute to the functioning of the governance network. Social capital, what may be deemed as the by-product of horizontal ties, may be brought into a governance network by an individual network actor serving as a "boundary spanner" (Wenger, 1998; Kettl, 2006), linking social networks together. Social capital may be generated as an outcome within the governance network as well and be cycled back into the system as an input. Informational or knowledge capital not explicitly embodied within the expertise of particular network actors may be used as a critical input into the governance network, as in the instance when the network is reacting to the release of new data.

Table 3.3 offers definitions of these resources and lists some common ways that stocks of each particular capital can be described.

Financial Capital

Principles essential to the development and maintenance of financial capital are "leverage, financing, capital structure, appropriate levels of growth and spending, proper evaluation and accountability on spending projects" (Wattanasupachoke, 2009). Financial capital is the purchasing power of the individual, group, or organization that owns it. Financial capital includes both cash holdings of firms, governments and nonprofits. Measurable indicators of financial capital include wealth and savings. This form of capital can be held collectively by shareholders or citizens or privately by individuals. Resource input in the market by individuals, shareholders, and organizations generates the capacity to buy and sell goods and services. Financial capital is also recorded in budgets and revenue streams, and accounts payable and receivables. In most instances, financial capital is viewed as a tangible, measurable capital. Grants and contracts are most likely structured to facilitate the exchange of financial capital for other forms of capital.

Physical Capital

Physical capital is manifested in the form of physical goods, either fixed capital or stocks and work in progress (Rosen, 2008). Physical capital is also referred to as built capital (Mulder, Costanza, and Erickson, 2006). Physical capital takes the form of assets created through human agency, including croplands, buildings, and machines. They are tangible, observable, and quantitative assets. Physical capital can be defined as "productive, tangible assets such as production sites, machines, infrastructure and buildings" (Svendsen and Sorensen, 2007, p. 455). Physical capital clearly exists as an observable and measurable asset. The purpose and benefits of physical capital are found in how it is used to generate income. Physical capital can be held in both individual and collective ownership. An example of individually owned physical capital would be a truck used for transporting goods. An example of collectively owned physical capital would be state-owned bridges and roads.

Natural Capital

A taxonomy of natural capital has been posited by Foldvary (2006), who divides it into three categories: (1) space, (2) nonliving matter, and (3) biological natural resources. We represent this taxonomy below, recognizing that each of these categories is worth a deeper description. We refer the reader to Foldvary's article.

Table 3.3   Capital Resources Possessed and Exchanged by Network Actors

Type of Capital Resource	Definition	Examples of Stock of Resources
Financial	Any liquid medium or mechanism that represents wealth or other styles of capital. It is, however, usually purchasing power in the form of money available for the production or purchasing of goods.	Cash; securities; loans
Natural	"Stocks or funds provided by nature (biotic or abiotic) that yield a valuable flow into the future of either natural resources or natural services" (Daly and Farley, 2004, p. 437).	Watersheds; farmland; air; wildlife; recreation areas
Physical	"Productive, tangible assets such as production sites, machines, infrastructure and buildings" (Svendsen and Sorensen, 2007, p. 455).	Buildings; office space; equipment; property
Human	"The present discounted value of the additional productivity, over and above the product of unskilled labor, of people with skills and qualifications" (Rosen, 2008).	Skills; individual expertise; labor
Social	Egocentric: Prestige or high status in a stratified social structure as a result of association, identification, alliance with, or appropriation by others (Ogbu, 1987; Swartz, 1990). Sociocentric: The accumulated trust, reciprocity, and durability built up between two or more actors that allows for the development of human knowledge (Coleman, 1986, 1988; Lesser and Prusak, 2000) and political capital (Putnam, 2000).	Social ties forged through bonded, bridging, and linking ties; common norms forged as a result of social ties: trust and durability

(continued)

Table 3.3 Capital Resources Possessed and Exchanged by Network Actor (Continued)

Type of Capital Resource	Definition	Examples of Stock of Resources
Political	Representational: Political power built on the premise of representation, representing the other's interests. Reputational: Political power based on one's reputation (Lopez, 2002).	Favors; persuasive powers
Cultural	Social norms and traditions, evidenced in verbal facility, information about social institutions, and requirements for advancement in social class (Bourdieu, 1986); rituals, mythic lore, symbolic experiences (Swidler, 1986); skills, habits, styles adopted by a social group (Farkas, 1996, 2003).	Cultural values; habits; customs; rituals; artistic tradition
Intellectual/ Knowledge	"Intellectual material—knowledge, information, intellectual property" (Stewart, 1997, p. 7).	Information; knowledge

Spatial land
1. Territorial space, that is, the surface-spatial soft-shell envelope at the earth's surface in which life is located, including the space holding the waters
2. Spectral space, or the frequencies of the electromagnetic spectrum
3. Routes for satellites and other spacecraft

Material natural resources
1. Solid substances, such as minerals and coal, oil in solid substances such as shale and tar sands, and ice
2. Liquid substances, such as water and oil
3. Gaseous substances, such as air and natural gas, as well as properties of gas, such as the capacity to carry sound waves
4. Other states of matter, such as plasma

Biological natural resources
1. Living beings
2. The genetic base of life
3. The ecological relationships among living beings, including the habitat

ECOSYSTEM SERVICES

Supporting: Soil formation and nutrient cycling.
Regulating: Water/air purification and pest regulation.
Provisioning: Fuel wood, oil, sunlight, minerals, food, airspace for air travel, waterways.
Cultural: Aesthetic enrichment, quality of life, recreation, and enjoyment.

Source: Costanza et al., *Nature, 387,* 253–260, 1997.

These natural resources have been described as providing some measure of "eco-system services" that contribute to the sustainability of life and the quality of life engendered within human civilization. Ecosystem services have been divided into supporting, regulating, provisioning, and cultural. Ecosystem services are "ecosystem functions of value to humans" (Daly and Farley, 2004, p. 432).

Human Capital

Human capital can be seen "as abilities that are either innate or acquired (Schultz, 1993)" and "wisdom gained through experience" (Davenport, 1999, p. xi). Human capital includes both technical know-how, and the skills of the workforce. Human capital is used to describe the assets that individual people possess: "innate abilities, behaviors, personal energy, and time. These elements make up human capital, the currency people bring to invest in their jobs. Workers not organizations own this capital" (Davenport, 1999, p. 7). Human capital is situated in the individual who possesses it. Economically, human capital is defined as "the present discounted value of the additional productivity, over and above the product of unskilled labor, of people with skills and qualifications" (Rosen, 2008). Human capital is defined by Thomas Davenport (1999) as the maximizing of knowledge, skills, talent, and behaviors of workers. He sees that maximization process happening through a variety of means, such as the workplace environment, an investment framework, education and training, increasing worker and employer value, and strengthening ties.

Social Capital

Social capital is formed in the bonds between actors. Bourdieu (1986, p. 248) first defined social capital as "the aggregate of the actual or potential resources which are linked to possession of a durable network of more or less institutionalized relationships of mutual acquaintance and recognition ... which provides each of its members with the backing of collectively-owned capital."

TYPES OF SOCIAL CAPITAL

Bonding social capital: Characterized by strong bonds (or "social glue"), for example, among family members or among members of an ethnic group.

Bridging social capital: Characterized by weaker, less dense, but more crosscutting ties ("social oil"), for example, between business associates, acquaintances, friends from different ethnic groups, friends of friends, etc.

Linking social capital: Characterized by connections between those with different levels of power or social status, for example, links between the political elite and the general public, or between individuals from different classes.

Social capital has its roots in social exchange theory and the notion that social networks are formed through the aggregated behaviors of individuals and actor/environment relations. Eric Lesser (2000) writes of the differences in types of social capital, one being egocentric and based on the connections between individual actors; and the other being sociocentric and based primarily on measures in the capacity to access large amounts of information and relationships, such as a liaison between two departments, agencies, or organizations. Egocentric social capital is based on prestige and high status in a stratified social structure as a result of association, identification, alliance with, or appropriation by others. Sociocentric social capital is based in the communities of practice that emerge as groups share information and build networks that lend themselves to mobilizing assets. Social capital has been linked to social and organizational learning (Lesser and Prusak, 2000) and knowledge transfer, suggesting that sociocentric social capital is strongly tied to the development of knowledge capital.

Political Capital

Political capital is accumulation and selective use of influence and power. Political capital has been defined as "the sum of combining other types of capital for purposive political action or the return of an investment of political capital which is returned into the system of production (reinvestment)" (Casey, 2008, p. 7). Casey observes that "political capital is ill-defined, little understood, yet an important concept for understanding political exchange and relationships in the political arena" (Casey, 2008). It can be seen, it can be felt, yet no aspect can be touched.

This form of capital is collectively generated through representation and reputation, which can be held by one individual in power, by an effective leadership team, or an entire organization. Generally, it is the situation that determines how political capital is exchanged. Political capital can be structural, illustrating the linkage between political party, ideology, administrative authority, accountability, and leadership. It can be instrumental, for instance, pertaining to rights, access, and political connections. There are also distinctions made between representational and reputational political capitals. Representational political capital is built on the premise of representation, representing the other's interests. Reputational capital refers to political capital that is developed based on one's reputation. Each is important when trying to both sustain and develop political capital (Lopez, 2002).

Political capital is observed qualitatively by studying behaviors as indicated in public opinion or public policy support. Quantitative measurements can be examined through the use of political polls, campaign contributions, and election results. It is arguably one of the more abstract capital forms because of relationships and social perception. "Political capital refers to the individual powers to act politically that are generated through participation in interactive political processes linking civil society to the political system. As such, the term political capital refers to three factors related to local political actors' ability to engage in political decision making: the level of access that they have to decision-making processes (endowment); their capability to make a difference in these processes (empowerment); and their perception of themselves as political actors (political identity)" (Sorensen and Torfing, 2003, p. 613).

Cultural Capital

Cultural capital is defined as knowledge of social norms and traditions, evidenced in verbal facility, information about social institutions, and requirements for advancement in social class (Bourdieu, 1986); rituals, mythic lore, and symbolic experiences (Swidler, 1986); and the skills, habits, and styles adopted by a social group (Farkas, 1996, 2003). Pierre Bourdieu coined the term *cultural capital,* introducing the concept to explain the role that cultural predilections play in determining the success of children in school. According to Weininger and Lareau, "Bourdieu broke sharply with traditional sociological conceptions of culture, which tended to view it primarily as a source of shared norms and values, or as a vehicle of collective expression. Instead, Bourdieu maintained that culture shares many of the properties that are characteristic of economic capital. In particular, he asserted that cultural 'habits and dispositions' comprise a *resource* capable of generating 'profits'; they are potentially subject to *monopolization* by individuals and groups; and, under appropriate conditions, they can be *transmitted* from one to another" (2007, p. 1).

We may define cultural capital more broadly than Bourdieu. When considered at the organizational level, cultural capital takes the form of the norms, habits, customs, and other cultural characteristics ascribed to an organizational setting. The extensive attention paid to organizational culture is relevant here. The extent to which the cultural capital of one network actor negatively or positively impacts its roles and functions within the network is worth considering. We suggest that the cultural capital of a given network actor can be viewed qualitatively, as the embodiment of organizational values, norms, and customs. Although cultural capital is harder to exchange than most of the other forms of capital discussed here, we hold out the possibility that cultural capital can be exchanged between organizations—the cultural norms of one organization can be transferred or transmitted to other organizations.

Knowledge/Intellectual Capital

Knowledge capital is "the intellectual material—knowledge, information, intellectual property, experience—which may be resorted to in order to create wealth" (Stewart, 1997, p. 7). Knowledge or intellectual (these terms are often used interchangeably) capital is studied as a body of knowledge in the field of knowledge management, which focuses on the management and information technology systems in place to facilitate the transfer of knowledge. In summing up the value of knowledge capital to organizations and networks of organizations, Jay Chatzkel observes:

> Knowledge is not detached from the people, processes, or infrastructure of an organization and its network. It is part of all of these things and progressively a more pivotal part. The ability to mobilize knowledge resources has become even more critical than the ability to control and amass physical and financial resources. (Chatzkel, 2003, p. 3)

According to March and Olsen, "knowledge is a scarce good, a strategic resource, and a normatively charged possession" (1995, p. 112). In writing about the value of knowledge to democratic institutions, March and Olsen describe it as "a foundation for political capabilities in most democratic politics (Crozier, 1964; Weber, 1978), but the value of specific knowledge depends on such things as changing political agenda, changing beliefs in political means, and changing competition from groups with alternative knowledge and experiences" (March and Olsen, 1995, p. 94).

The capital resources introduced in this chapter may be construed as characteristics of network nodes—something that actors bring to the network. The capital that each network actor brings to the network essentially serves as an input into the system. Resource capitals can also be used to characterize the nature of the ties that bind two or more actors together, particularly ties built around some kind of exchanges of resources. In the next chapter we view these capital resources in terms of the outputs and outcomes that a governance network generates.

Actor Characteristics: A Review

We recognize that we have only scratched the surface of the many different ways that the characteristics of network actors can be described. We discussed actor characteristics in terms of actor goals and roles, actor sectors, geographic and social scale, role centrality, and the types of resources that they bring to the network, listed Figure 3.5.

ACTOR A
Social scale
Geographic scale
Social sector
Role centrality
Ownership of capital resources
Contribution of capital resources to network/relationship
Providing accountability to
Receiving accountabilities to
Performance, output & outcome criteria (decision heuristics)

Figure 3.5   Actor characteristics.

The range of possible actor characteristics offered in this chapter is by no means exhaustive. We suggest, however, that the range of characteristics introduced in this chapter provides a basic skeleton on which more muscle can be added. We remind the reader again that we are providing a basic architecture around which further details and characteristics can be added.

CRITICAL QUESTIONS AND CONSIDERATIONS

The reader is invited to return to the governance network that was identified at the end of Chapter 1. Now that we know more about some of the potential characteristics of actors, we can begin to focus on listing the central and peripheral actors involved in the network:

- Is the network dominated by one kind of sector?
- Are there actors operating at different geographic scales?
- What motivates the actors to participate in this network?
- What resources do they bring to the network?

As we think about the nested complexity of these social structures, we may consider the role that particular individuals play within the governance network. We may also think about the groups, committees, or boards that are important to the operations and governance of the network.

Chapter 4

Characteristics of Ties between Actors

The ties that bind
Now you can't break the ties that bind ...

—Bruce Springsteen (1980)

This chapter focuses on the nature of the ties that may exist between network actors. We begin this section with a discussion of social exchange theory and the assumptions regarding the distinctions between actor autonomy and interdependence that exist within ties that facilitate the flow of resources. Drawing on some of the core conceptual tenants of social network analysis, we discuss how ties may be characterized along a continuum of formality and strength. We then define social ties in terms of administrative authorities that flow between network actors, based upon a framework or taxonomy for describing the differences between vertical, diagonal, horizontal, and competitive ties, characterizing administrative ties in terms of the vector of ties. We argue that these are, perhaps, the most critical ties to consider when describing and analyzing governance networks.

The characteristics that particular network actors bring to the network (goals, resources, and roles) help determine the nature of the social ties forged within and across the network. Reminded of the principles of holism that exist in social networks, a viable argument could be made going in the opposite direction as well, implying that we must recognize that the characteristics particular network actors bring to a governance network get shaped, in large part, by the nature of the ties that are forged between them.

The characteristics of social ties have traditionally focused on the degree of strength and coupling, the extent to which the tie serves as a bridge to other clusters of nodes, and the vector of ties. Social ties serve as the material or social conduit through which resources flow from one node to the other. At the end of the previous chapter we discussed how the characteristics of the particular nodes in the network help to determine what resources get exchanged and how. We noted how these resource capitals may flow unidirectionally, from node to node, or exchanged across nodes.

After scanning the literature, Provan, Fish, and Sydow (2007) observe that there often exists a wide array of "multiplex" ties between network actors. The multiplexity of ties lends some measure of stability to the relationships, "because they enable the connection between an organization and its linkage partner to be sustained even if one type of link dissolves" (p. 11).

Drawing on the policy network, social network, and collaborative management literature, we discuss two features of network ties that play a central role in determining the relative stability and formality of the network, as well as network-wide governance structures. In this chapter, we explore Rhode's social exchange theory in greater depth, then discuss how social ties may be characterized in terms of their degree of strength and vector. We conclude this section by arguing that the characteristics of the ties between network actors help to determine the positionality of particular network actors in the wider governance network.

Social Exchange Theory

Underlying Rhode's social exchange theory is the notion that actors enter into a social network for a reason, often understood as a goal of resource acquisition or some kind of goal attainment. "The distribution, and type, of resources within a network explains the relative power of actors (individuals and organizations). Different types of governance networks will be distinguished by particular patterns of resource-dependency" (Rhodes, 1997, p. 11). When viewed through the lens of resource exchange, actors bring a certain measure of dependence on other actors for resources. A graphic representation of this exchange is depicted in Figure 4.1.

According to Rhodes (2007, p. 1245), the key ideas in exchange theory are as follows:

1. Any organization is dependent upon other organizations for resources.
2. In order to achieve their goals, the organizations have to exchange resources.
3. Although decision-making within the organization is constrained by other organizations, the dominant coalition retains some discretion. The appreciative system of the dominant coalition

influences which relationships are seen as a problem and which resources will be sought.

4. The dominant coalition employs strategies within known rules of the game to regulate the process of exchange.
5. Variations in the degree of discretion are a product of the goals and the relative power potential of interacting organizations. This relative power potential is a product of the resources of each organization, of the rules of the game, and of the process of exchange between organizations (Rhodes, 1981, pp. 98–99; 1999, pp. 78–79).

The social network exchange theory outlined above provides the basis for a relatively comprehensive description of the dynamics unfolding between two or more network nodes. At its core, exchange theory recognizes the interdependent nature of life itself. We find this assertion embedded in the thought experiment posed by Thomas Paine in his pamphlet of 1776, *Common Sense*, in which he viewed the emergence of governments out of social necessity. In essence, no individual person or social organization exists in a vacuum. Social entities are required to exchange resources with their external environment. This observation is why networks are such a powerful metaphor and analytical tool. Any social actor is required to exchange resources (money, information, material goods and services, social intimacy, etc.) with other social actors on a daily basis.

Considered in the context of a social exchange framework, power is said to be the inverse of dependence (Stevenson and Greenberg, 2000), meaning the less dependent a social actor is on others, the more control it has over its own fate, and thereby the more power it has. This view of power places value on the relative autonomy a network actor possesses. However, when collaborative network arrangements exist, dependence can lead to increasing the capacity of individual social actors to develop and wield power. In this context, the articulation of power shifts from that of authority *against* or *over*, to authority *with*. Schaap describes resource exchange

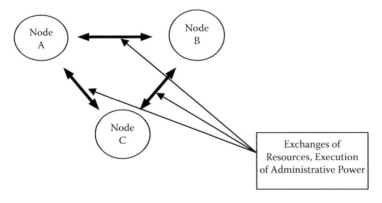

Figure 4.1   Nodes and ties.

Figure 4.2   The balance of dependency and autonomy.

as existing "in a field of tensions between dependence and autonomy" (Schaap, 2008, p. 121). Figure 4.2 depicts the tension between dependence and autonomy that exists within interorganizational governance networks.

Hertting (2008, p. 49) discusses the tension between dependency and autonomy this way:

> When the outcomes of the strategies of a set of actors interfere with each other, every single actor in the set is motivated to transfer a part of its right to autonomously choose and design strategies to the rest of the set of actors, in exchange for a similar right to control their choice of actions. By explicating this aspect of dependencies … perceived conflicts may be motives for a set of actors to develop governance networks (Stoker, 1991, p. 49).

Interdependencies between network actors may be more or less asymmetrical. Herrting understands dependency as a matter of the perception of the network actors involved. "It is possible to find situations where all actors are aware of strong mutual dependencies, while the intensity of their motives for handling the situation through some kind of coordination still differs slightly … even small asymmetries may cause big problem when it comes to institutionalizing governance networks among limited rational actors" (Hertting, 2008, p. 50).

Social exchange theory also accounts for the tendency of social nodes to cluster. Rhodes defines these clusters in terms of "dominant coalitions" (1997). In this book, we describe dominant coalitions in terms of the "communities of practice" chiefly responsible for governing governance networks. Exchange theory assumes that power is exercised through social clusters. Within interorganizational contexts, power may be exercised across organizational boundaries, coalescing in formal and informal constellations of individuals, groups, and organizations. This clustering effect possesses certain emergent, self-organizing qualities, a point that we will return to in Chapter 7.

Social exchange theory is also rooted in considerations of rationality and game theory. Rational behavior is said to follow certain patterns of reason and logic. Rational action is said to possess a certain element of predictability. Rational actors possess the capacity to bring certain measures of reason and logic to their decision making. Rational behavior has been studied quantitatively through rational choice and game theory. Although these theories are often constrained by the limits of rational behavior and the infusion of highly contextual factors, the emergence of certain patterns of behavior within social networks is an essential feature in ensuring a network's creation and sustainability.

The "rules of the game" in operation in most social networks can take one of two forms, both of which inform the other. Some rules are reified, existing as written rules, standards, and procedures. Laws and legally binding contracts help to structure the rules that structure and guide relationships in governance networks. The rules of the game also manifest in the "theories in use" (Argyris and Schon, 1995), the tacit knowledge and underlying norms and values that are formed within and across all social ties. These assertions about how the rules of the game are formed, utilized, and changed are essential features in any considerations regarding the administration and governance of governance networks.

The extent to which the rules of the game governing resource exchanges are explicitly recognized is a matter that concerns the formality of the ties, as well as the type of coordination of ties taking place between two or more nodes.

Resources Exchanged

Using the eight capital resources discussed in Chapter 3, we may anticipate a range of possible exchanges that may take place between any two actors within a governance network. These exchanges may be carried out as exchanges of the same kind of resources. One actor may exchange the same kind of capital resource, such as trading information (knowledge capital for knowledge capital), or trading one staff member's time and expertise with another's (human capital for human capital). More often, however, one kind of resource is exchanged for another kind of resource. Funders contribute money (financial capital) to support the purchase of natural, physical, and human resources. It takes human capital to build physical capital. Social capital is commonly associated with knowledge capital. The link between money and elections (financial and political capital) points to the possibility that some kinds of resource exchanges are carried out through more informal, loosely coupled means, leading some to suggest that these types of exchanges lack transparency.

Table 4.1 provides one way to understand the range of possible combinations of resource exchange. We have chosen to limit our discussion of possible exchanges of types of capitals to a few pertinent examples. We will likely need to leave it to others to "fill in the boxes."

The exchange of resources occurring between two social actors has been described by Elinor Ostrom as a system of common pool resources (1990). She differentiates between the types of rules that aid in the governance of resource exchanges and pooling (as described in Stone and Ostrower, 2007, p. 424):

Table 4.1   Range of Combinations of Resource Exchanges

		Resources Provided by Actor B							
		Financial	*Natural*	*Physical*	*Human*	*Social*	*Political*	*Cultural*	*Knowledge*
Resources Provided by Actor A	Financial								
	Natural								
	Physical								
	Human								
	Social								
	Political								
	Cultural								
	Knowledge								

1. *Operational rules* govern day-to-day activities of appropriators.
2. *Collective choice rules* concern overall policies for governing common pool resources and how those policies are made.
3. *Constitutional choice rules* establish who is eligible to determine collective choice rules.

In Chapter 5 we discuss the range of operational functions that are taken on within governance networks. These operational functions are governed by a complex array of operational rules, norms, habits, and customs. Collective choice theory has long been viewed as a central feature of resource exchange frameworks. Collective choice is shaped by individual and collective interests, all needing to be balanced in order to create an optimal level of autonomy and dependence. We have already touched on the importance of constitutional law on shaping intersector relations. Following Ostrom, we may argue that a complex variety of rules govern how and to what extent resources are exchanged and pooled together. However, we must admit that the extensive exploration of how different combinations of resources are exchanged is too vast an undertaking in a book of this nature.

Formality and the Coordination of Ties

The rules governing resource exchange are also shaped by the formality and depth of coordination between two or more network actors. These ties have been characterized in terms of the frequency of coordination (Mandell and Steelman, 2003) and the resulting degree of formality exhibited through the creation of explicit rules and procedures (Argyris and Schon, 1995). The frequency of coordination that occurs between members of an interorganizational network has been discussed by Mandell and Steelman, who, building on a framework first introduced by Gage and Mandell (1990), discuss how the formality of coordination of interorganizational networks may be articulated (2003). They describe how interorganizational networks are characterized in terms of intermittent coordination, through which network actors get physically (or presumably, electronically) convened and reconvened when occasions warrant. Other interorganizational networks may be supported through temporary coordination, thereby existing for limited amounts of time, dissolving when common goals or network-wide tasks are completed. Some governance networks may be governed through regular coordination, through which operational routines and goals get set and carried out.

A *formal* social structure is defined as "one in which the social positions and the relationships among [social actors] have been explicitly specified and are defined independently of the personal characteristics of the participants occupying these positions" (Scott, 1987, p. 17). Formal structures result through the joint recognition of the common ties that bind. The formality of governance networks may be ascertained by determining the extent to which set, prescribed, or customary methods have been established to govern network activity. Such methods may exist as the reified rules of the game, or in the establishment of explicit norms used to guide network interactions. Formal governance networks possess official goals around which network-wide coordination is to take place. Formal governance network ties will also develop extensive operational goals that the network uses to carry out its day-to-day activities.

Most studies of tacit knowledge in organizational settings underscore the proliferation of hidden or unspoken knowledge and norms within any social interactions (Senge et al., 1994; Argyris and Schon, 1995). When explicit norms become formalized, they often become reified, essentially becoming objective "things," such as written rules, standards, and contractual agreements (Wenger, 1998).

The frequency of coordination within a governance network and the degree of formality of the rules, norms, and procedures it possesses need not be coupled. We can envision scenarios in which a governance network that forms as a result of a grant and contract agreement is actively coordinated very infrequently, but relies on reified rules and standards found in the written contract between network actors to govern this coordination when they do meet and interact. We find this scenario also possibly taking place in regulatory subsystems, when a regulator's coordination with its regulated agents is infrequent, but the standards and operating procedures around which regulations are enforced are formally written, serving as the explicit guidelines around which compliance is sought.

Strength of Ties

Basic network structures require there to be links between two or more nodes. In social networks, these links have been described in terms of social ties. Some common conceptual tools to analyze social ties have emerged over the last forty years, including Granovetter's (1973) analysis of the "strength of weak ties," Charles Perrow's (1967) and Karl Weick's (1976) introduction of the "coupling" of ties, and Ronald Burt's (1997) "structural holes" argument. Systems theory has added the notion of open and closed social networks to the analysis of social ties. Social capital theory has emerged as a central construct in network analysis, having brought to the fore the importance of social ties and the requisite shared values and norms that are built as a result of them. Two types of social capital are said to exist: bonding and bridging (Putnam, 1993, 2000). In this section we present an overview of the various characteristics that have been used to describe social ties.

The relative strength of a social tie has been, historically, characterized in terms of the levels of duration of the contact, the emotional intensity and intimacy felt between two social actors, and the level of exchange of resources (Granovetter, 1973; Degenne and Forse, 1999, p. 109). Much of the seminal research on social ties has ascertained that the strength of ties between two actors is based on the frequency of contact (e.g., duration), the measurement of resources exchanged between the actors, and the subjective perceptions of an actor's ascertainment of the depth of emotional intensity of the relationship.

In Chapter 3 we discussed how the centrality of a network actor is a key characteristic of the individual network node. We noted that although more central actors possess access to certain kinds of power and authority, centrality does not necessarily mean that an actor is imbued with more power and authority than more peripheral actors. Granovetter's advancement of the "strength of weak ties" argument (1973) helps to explain this phenomenon. Weak ties that are characterized by infrequent contact, little emotional intensity, and little in the way of resources to be exchanged are often more effective at achieving certain kinds of common objectives, most notably, assisting one actor in a dyad to find gainful employment (harkening back to the old adage "it's not what you know, it's who you know"). The rise of social networking sites that have blossomed during the early years of the twenty-first century are facilitating the proliferation of weak ties. Social networking sites like "Linked-in" are viewed as essential tools for those seeking new employment opportunities.

The notion of coupling is a widely recognized analytical construct in organizational development theory (Perrow, 1967; Weick, 1976). Although the relative tightness or looseness of the coupling is not exactly synonymous with the strength of the tie, we bundle the terms here. The notion of tight coupling has often been associated with the analysis of bureaucratic control (Scott, 1987). More tightly coupled ties imply that the administrative authorities that govern the tie are more strongly reinforced. Traditionally, tight coupling has been equated with strong command and control or principal-agent relations. However, the challenges associated with principal-agent dynamics, often characterized in terms of the classical principal-agent problem (Donahue, 1989; Milward and Provan, 1998), suggest that, oftentimes, the coupling of vertical administrative ties is premised on weaker, more loosely coupled ties.

Later in this chapter we discuss the nature of more horizontally arranged ties, suggesting that these ties may also be characterized as being relatively stronger/ tighter bonds. The strength and tightness of ties have a significant bearing on how a governance network is governed. In later chapters we focus particular attention on how the strength and tightness of ties impact a network's accountability regimes and performance management systems.

We would be remiss to not mention the contribution that social capital theory can play to the understanding of ties' strength and tightness. Burt's study of the "structural holes" that persist in most any organizational (and by inference interorganizational) setting is particularly relevant here (1997). Essentially, Burt's research found that innovative practices require some measure of structural holes to persist within an organizational setting. Perceived gaps between social actors may be bridged by innovators. With these bridging ties, opportunities for new exchanges of resources (knowledge, for instance) facilitate new practices. Burt's work (1997), along with Putnam's research on

---

SOCIAL NETWORK ANALYSIS AND SOCIAL CAPITAL

1. Social capital shifts the focus of analysis from the behaviour of individual agents to the pattern of relations between agents, social units and institutions....
2. [It acts] as a link between micro-, meso-, and macro-levels of analysis....
3. [It is] multi-disciplinary and inter-disciplinary....
4. It reinserts issues of value into the heart of social scientific discourse....
5. It possesses a heuristic quality that allows for analysis, prescription and exploration.

Source: **Baron et al.,** *Social Capital: Critical Perspectives,* **Oxford University Press, New York, 2000, pp. 35–37.**

---

civil society in Italy and the United States (1993, 2000), has led to the common understanding that social capital may be described in terms of its bridging or bonding functions. Bridging social capital tends to be based on weaker, more loosely coupled ties. Bonding social capital tends to be based on stronger, more tightly coupled ties. Distinguishing between bonding and bridging social capital also has implications for the relative openness and closeness of the network, a point we will address in Chapter 7 when we discuss the boundaries of systems level constructs.

Flow of Authority across Ties

We argue that most forms of social network theory, as classically understood within the sociology and social psychology literature, have been unable to account for the ways in which social ties are structured through different ties of administrative authority.

We believe this has to do with the early association between social networks and horizontal ties. This association still persists in some characterizations of social network structures as being built exclusively through the development of trusting and reciprocal horizontal ties. To reiterate a point that was discussed in Chapter 2, hierarchies are a form of network. The move away from describing social networks merely in terms of their voluntary nature is critical to understanding how power is distributed within interorganizational networks.

The move to include both vertical and horizontal arrangements introduces vectors to the study of social ties. Conceptual frameworks designed to analyze social power dynamics are abundant, and can be found across the literature of virtually every social science. Of particular interest to us are the kinds of conceptual frameworks that provide the means for rendering a relatively simple structure for describing relational power. Theories of centralization-decentralization are helpful in this regard. We would argue that the reference to central and peripheral roles implied in discussions of decentralization is particularly useful in social network analysis. Top-down and bottom-up distinctions are also useful, particularly when hierarchical network structures are implicated. Dating back to Weber's first introduction of bureaucratic theory, we find considerations of power being explored as administrative authorities characterized as supervisor-subordinate relations. Table 4.2 lays out the multiple dimensions of administrative power and authority.

There is a smaller, yet still extensive, body of literature that explores the nature of power in terms of the voluntary bonds forged through shared values and norms (Mintzberg, 1983; Burt, 1997). Social psychologists, sociologists, and more recently, behavioral economists have studied how cooperative behaviors come about. Social capital and game theories are particularly useful in understanding horizontal ties (Hanaki et al., 2007). We have already discussed the relationship of social capital theory to the study of social ties. Essentially, social capital exists as a consequence of and a contributor to the development of horizontal ties. Beginning with Axelrod's now classic iterated prisoner's dilemma (1980), game theorists have studied the nature of cooperative and collaborative behaviors that manifest between two social

Table 4.2   Administrative Power and Authority in Governance Networks

Social Power	Direction of Power	Vector of Tie	Dynamic of Authority	Meta-Organizational Structure
Command and control		Vertical ties	Authority *over*	Hierarchy
Concession and compromise		Diagonal ties	Authority *negotiated between*	Mixed
Collaboration and cooperation		Horizontal ties	Authority *with*	Collaborative
Competition		No ties	Authority *against*	Market

actors construed as equals or peers. These developments have deepened our capacity to appreciate how power flows across horizontal relations.

In addition to the vertical and horizontal vectors of relational power, we must recognize the possibility that the structure of power relations between any two nodes in a social network may be comprised of a mixture of both vertical and horizontal relations. Virtually any comparison between an organization's formal (oftentimes hierarchical) structure and the nature of relations in actual practice underscores the fact that workers in organizations are often very capable of working across hierarchical boundaries, forging horizontal ties in the process. Thus, an individual may find himself or herself working with supervisors in capacities that look more like peer-to-peer relationships. More recent developments in leadership theory, such as servant leadership (Greenleaf, 2002), facilitative leadership (Stivers, 1993), participatory leadership (Kezar, 2001) and transformational leadership (Burns, 2003), have all underscored the value of working collaboratively with those who have been traditionally positioned as the followers and subordinates. We have discussed how weaker, more loosely coupled ties have been formed to facilitate the development of new working arrangements (Granovetter, 1973) and innovation (Burt, 1997). Power relations may be complicated by the shifting nature of more innovative working relationships found within contemporary workplace environments. This observation leads us to suggest that a diagonal dimension of power relations may be said to exist.

Metaphorically speaking, the steepness and the direction of the ties may vary over time and be contingent on a variety of environmental factors. Not only may roles and relationships shift over time, but also it is possible for two nodes to hold different kinds of relational power depending on the nature of the resources that are flowing between them. For example, we will be considering how government-sponsored grants and contracts place governments in the position of having some measure of vertical authority over the contracted agents. The principal-agent theory is premised on the existence of transaction costs associated with exerting this kind of authority. Transaction costs may be found in the resources needed to ensure adequate oversight. Transaction costs may also come in the form of information and the value that information garnered "on the ground" has to both the principals and agents (Milward and Provan, 1998). In this case, power relations may be structured by the flow of funding from government to contractor, as well as around the dynamics shaped by and through the transfer of knowledge from the agent to the principal. In this case, the challenges associated with principal-agent dynamics push this relationship away from a simple vertically arranged relationship to one that is decidedly more diagonal in nature. We characterize diagonal ties as falling into the category of negotiation and bargaining.

Lastly, we must account for the possibility that some degree of competitive ties exists, even in the most collaborative of governance networks. Given the nature of some intersector arrangements, private sector firms and business may be actors in a governance network. We have noted how more recent trends toward privatization and partnership have been mounted under the assumption that private sector actors bring a measure of market-based competition to the network. It is assumed that elements of competitive ties bring a measure of efficiency to the undertaking. We will discuss competition as an administrative authority that may exist as a feature of markets, as well as a feature of basic human interaction.

Command and Control

Dating back to Max Weber's initial introduction of bureaucratic theory, we find considerations of power being explored as a matter of supervisor-subordinate relations. Classical organization development theory, found in the works of Gulick and Ulrick, and later the works of Simon and others, establishes the basis for describing the "command and control" structures of bureaucracies. The social norms that undergird command and control relations include deference and submission to those in positions of authority. At the macro level, command and control has been used to describe the kind of authority that strong states employ when providing centralized direction over society. More recently, principal-agent theory has emerged from economics and studies of contractual arrangements to provide a picture of vertical relations as they exist in social networks (Milward and Provan, 1998). Theoretically, principals are to have authority over their agents. The typical question guiding the study of principal-agent dynamics in public bureaucracies has been: "Can principal A secure preference P from agent X?" (Koppell, 2003, p. 22).

In both the classical and more contemporary views of governance and control within vertical arrangements, real-world contexts arise that complicate matters. Bounded rationality (Simon, 1957) and information asymmetries may provide subordinates (or agents) with more power in the relationship. In essence, these complexities can lead to the "leveling of the playing field," potentially displacing positional authority with more lateral forms of authority even within the most tightly coupled bureaucracies (Durant, 2001).

> The relationship between power and dependence becomes more complex when one considers the multitude or variety of outcomes that may be considered relevant or in demand in organizations. Thus, *A* may control a particular outcome that is relevant to *B*, but *B* may control another, different resource that is desired by *A*. Thus, in order to acquire power in an organization, two conditions are necessary: actors must both decrease their dependence on others and increase others' dependence on them. (Brass and Burkhardt, 1993, pp. 193–94)

As a way to explain the kind of fragmented administrative authorities found in the principal-agent theory in hybrid organizations, Jonathan Koppell challenges the notion that vertical administrative authority may be simply understood in terms of

	Principal A		Preference P		Agent X?
	or		or		or
Can	Principal B	Secure	Preference Q	From	Agent Y?
	or		or		or
	Principal C		Preference R		Agent Z?

Figure 4.3 The complication of principal-agent theory. (*Source:* Koppell, *The Politics of Quasi-Government*, Cambridge University Press, Cambridge, 2003, p. 70.) Printed with permission of Cambridge University Press.

a principal-agent relationship (2003). He suggests that previous studies have tended to focus on understanding how principals can secure desired actions from agents. The roots for framing principal-agent studies as a top-down consideration may be found in the scientific management movement of the early twentieth century, and still very much pervades the management literature today.

Koppell critiques this view by questioning some of the central assumptions embedded in the root question (2003). He observes that rarely is there a clear sense of which principals are seeking which preferences from which agents, as outlined in Figure 4.3.

Koppell rightly recognizes that very often there exists a multiplicity of possible combinations of principals, preferences, and agents. He provides for the possibility that preferences may exist independently of the influence of any given principal. He also takes into consideration the view of the principal-agent relationship "from the bottom up," recognizing that agents bring resources to the relationship that may be mustered to renegotiate or bargain for certain power. Such negotiation and bargaining may be a part of explicit contracts and other legally binding agreements, or may be embedded in more tacitly undertaken negotiations and bargaining that operate at a more informal, yet politically charged level. The chronic and enduring nature of the principal-agent problem calls for the extension of principal-agent studies to studies of the formation of cooperative ties between peers, partners, and collaborators.

Concession and Comprise

In the kinds of interorganizational governance networks that are the focus of this book, the dynamics that shape one actor's authority over another is best described in terms of the principal-agent theory and, more importantly, the principal-agent problem that serves as a central thesis of the theory. Donahue describes the principal-agent problem:

> A *principal* commissions an *agent* to act on the principal's behalf. In general, the agent's interests do not entirely coincide with those of the principal; the principal does not have complete control over the agent; the principal only has partial information about the agent's behavior. The agency *relationship* consists in the reliance of a principal upon the agent with an agenda of his own. The agency problem is the difficulty, in all but the simplest such relationships, of ensuring that the principal is faithfully served and that the agent is fairly compensated. (Donahue, 1989, p. 38)

We argue that authority *over* becomes more a matter of *negotiated between* in most governance networks. In essence, in governance networks, "every group or organization which attempts to exercise control must also attempt to win consent from the governed" (Selznick, 2003, p. 155). Principal-agent theory focuses on the relevance of transaction costs associated with exerting this kind of authority. Reputation becomes an important element in the bargaining, negotiating, and mutual adjustment activities undertaken in networked relationships (Morris, Morris, and Jones, 2007, p. 95). In this case, the challenges associated with principal-agent dynamics push this relationship away from a simple vertically arranged relationship to one that is decidedly more diagonal in nature.

Organizational forms that rely on concessions and compromises that emerge through negotiation and bargaining are decidedly mixed in nature. Negotiated authority must rely on some combination of vertical and horizontal ties. Compliance in negotiated agreements is based on remuneration—the trading of one resource for another. These resource exchanges are shaped through incentives, concessions, and compromise.

Taking into account the complexity of relational ties that are possible in governance networks, Sorensen and Torfing argue that policy actors may not "be equal in terms of authority and resources" (Mayntz, 1993, p. 10). "There might be asymmetrical allocations of material and immaterial resources among the network actors" (2008, p. 9). To this end, the proliferation of negotiated authorities is all but ensured in most governance networks.

Cooperation and Collaboration

The word *collaborate* stems from the Late Latin term *collaborat(us)*, meaning to work or labor together. Collaboration and cooperation are often used interchangeably to describe the relationship forged between two or more peers. Power within these relationships is structured through the social norms of trust and reciprocity.

Social networks have traditionally been described in terms of horizontal ties and, for the purposes of this book, are described at the macro level in terms of collaborative partnerships, coalitions, and strategic alliances. Compliance in collaborative relationships is created through the social norms derived in trust. Drawing on

Koppell's model for describing the complexity of principal-agent ties as a template, some may distill cooperative ties into two simple questions: (1) Can A trust B? (2) Can B trust A?

Thompson describes how trust is a fundamental norm of social networks, observing that it is "established to precisely economize on transactions costs" (2003, p. 32). He goes on to add that "trust implies an expected action ... which we cannot monitor in advance, or the circumstances associated with which we cannot directly control. It is a kind of device for coping with freedoms of others. It minimizes the temptation to indulge in purely opportunistic behavior (Gambetta 1988)" (Thompson, 2003, p. 46). However, the feeling of trust is a subjective, socially constructed norm or belief that is predicated on the perceptions of the truster.

Ironically, it was Hobbes who first said, "To have friends, is power" (see Degenne and Forse, 1999, p. 115). The application of game theory to the study of cooperative behavior reveals that "the foundation of cooperation is not really trust, but the durability of the relationship." Durability is built up over time through "trial-and-error learning about possibilities for mutual rewards" and imitation of past successful relationships (Axelrod, 1980, p. 182). Sociologists and anthropologists who study trust tend to disagree with this, as they argue that the durability of relationship hinges upon trust and not vice versa Durability also requires network actors to not tolerate deviant behaviors. Axelrod's study of the iterated prisoner's dilemma underscores the need for networked actors to challenge such behaviors in an effort to bring about greater cooperation (1980, p. 184). As a result, the "reputational capital" of network actors becomes a key element within the establishment of durable, horizontally aligned relationships (Kreps and Wilson, 1982). Reputation becomes an important element in the bargaining, negotiating, and mutual adjustment activities undertaken in networked relationships (Morris, Morris, and Jones, 2007, p. 95).

The tools of social network analysis are often employed to study how cooperative behavior unfolds between two peers. The study of cooperative ties has been a long-standing interest of social psychologists and sociologists (Collins, 1988). In recent decades, biologists, economists, mathematicians, and computer scientists have examined social cooperation through the lens of evolution, behavioral economics, and game theory. Evolutionary biologists Stuart Kaufmann and David Sloan Wilson have popularized the importance that cooperative ties have played in the evolution of human civilization (Wilson, 2007; Kaufmann, 2004), essentially arguing that virtuous behavior (directed toward advancing the good of others) has always been a central feature of human development. Behavioral economists are turning to the study of cooperative behavior to better understand the behavior of consumers, the propensity of capitalists to cooperate with one another, and the underlying nature of common assets and public goods. Game theorists have described the underlying rules governing cooperative behavior as a series of "tit for tat" exchanges leading to the development of durable and relatively trustworthy relationships.

The role of reputation shifts our locus of attention from the question "Can A punish B for deviating from common expectations?" to the question "Does A even

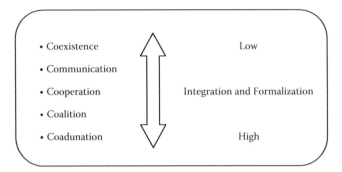

Figure 4.4 Degrees of collaboration. (Compiled from: Frey et al., *American Evaluation Association, 27*, 383–392, 2006.)

need to punish B? Might B punish himself or herself if he or she deviates from the common norm?"

We are left to conclude that in its purest form, collaborators are in such lock-step agreement on means and ends, goals and outcomes, that they approach what some have categorized as a merger, unification, or coadunation. We conclude, then, that collaborative ties may be understood as matters of degree. Several typologies for distinguishing differences between types of collaborative relationships have been posited (Gajda, 2004; Frey et al., 2006). Frey et al.'s (2006) synthesis of these degrees of collaboration is provided in Figure 4.4.

A range of terms have been posited to distinguish between types of collaboration that vary in depth and breadth of integration and formalization of ties. Frey et al. (2006) synthesize several of the typologies to have emerged within the program evaluation field, drawing distinctions between levels of collaboration ranging from mere coexistence to coadunation. In their weakest form, collaborative ties don't actually exist; however, the conditions that require mutual coexistence must first exist before collaborative ties are to form, a long-standing lesson drawn from international conflict mediation and negotiation (Watkins, 1999). At their most strongly and tightly coupled, collaborators merge to form a new unit, operating as one. Coadunation means to be closely joined or united. The potential for groups and organizations to merge with others is a very real and, some may argue, common practice.

Competition

We must also hold for the possibility that some administrative ties may be focused on defeating, winning, or otherwise getting a leg up on the competition. The importance of competition has been a mainstay of the theory of Darwinian evolution, under the theorem of the survival of the fittest. The combination of self-selection and variation serves as a compelling guideline for interpreting the importance of self-preserving behavior to the basic foundations of life. When resources are scarce, these dynamics become even more compelling.

The competitive drive is assumed by economists and social theorists to be a central driver of human nature. In politics, competition plays an integral role in elections and the policy-making process. Competition has been observed ecologically as "the struggle among organisms, both of the same and of different species for food, space, and other requirements for existence" (Webster, 1989, p. 300). Competition has been used to describe the relationship between cells, as, for instance, in descriptions of the competitive drive of cancer cells to take over space and functions once held by benign cells. Competition between social actors is defined as the "rivalry between two or more persons or groups for an object desired in common, usually resulting in a victor and a loser or losers, not necessary involving the destruction of the other" (Mintzberg, 1983).

Competition is understood as the central driver of market forces. As we view trends affecting the development of governance networks, such as contracting out and privatization, competitive forces are used, at least in theory, to engender greater efficiencies. Advocates of the new public management framework who place value on the role that market forces can play in delivering better public goods and services essentially make the argument that the infusion of competition facilitates the promulgation of "fitter" actors and agents.

A challenge of this notion to the study of the evolution of human civilization (and social insects like ants and bees) is that there are other forces at work as well to ensure the survival of the hive, the colony, the village, the town, or the nation-state. We recall again the conclusions we drew from Paine's thought experiment: that effective governance structures emerged to ensure the survival of the community. Those who view competition with skepticism, or at least as a value-neutral construct, call for better understanding of how competitive ties influence other forms of administrative authority.

It should be noted that in most instances of social competition there exists a set of underlying rules that govern competitive behavior. These rules imply the consent of all competitors in order for fair competition to take place, whether these are the rules of engagement that dictate warfare, the rules of a competitive sport, or the rules and regulations that govern market transactions. Just as our exploration of the other forms of administrative authorities has suggested that there exist less than cut and dry distinctions between them, we also need to account for the propensity that competitive ties exist as a matter of degree.

Characteristics of Ties: A Review

As a result of our discussion, a picture of multiplex ties (Provan, Fish, and Sydow, 2007) forged between two or more actors in a social network may be formed. In the previous chapter we discussed how different nodal actors, construed across any level of social scale, will bring a composite of official and operative goals and a range of capital resources into the network. These goals and resources, in turn, shape the official and operative functions and roles that each actor takes on. Two or more social nodes enter into networked relations in part because they are resource dependent on other actors in the network. According to the tenant of social exchange theory, this dependency may be shaped as a matter of resource scarcity—meaning a social actor needs the resources from another social actor in order to survive, or as a matter of resource codependency—meaning that a social actor believes it needs to coordinate its actions with other social actors in order to achieve a goal or objective.

The characteristics of the ties through which resource exchange get facilitated have been described in terms of the frequency of coordination of the tie, the degree of formality and explicitness of the tie, the strength of the tie, and the vector or flow of authority between actors. As a result of the complex combinations of ties built up between network actors, a picture of internodal structures and functions begins to take shape. These internodal structures take on internodal functions that, following the tenants of network holism, form network-wide structures and functions. We now turn to the range of characteristics that may be found at the network-wide level.

CRITICAL QUESTIONS AND CONSIDERATIONS

We now have some language to describe the kind of ties that exist between actors. Returning again to your governance network, select one or more dyadic relationships (e.g., a specific relationship between two actors).

- How do these two actors relate to one another?
- What type of administrative tie binds them together?
- What resources do they exchange? Pool?
- Is the tie formal or informal? Strong or weak?

Ask these same questions to other combinations of actors within the network. Begin to build models of dyads and triads.

Chapter 5

Network-Wide Functions

> Conjunction junction, what's your function?
> Hooking up two boxcars and making 'em run right.
> Milk and honey, bread and butter, peas and rice.
>
> **—Bob Dorough,** *School House Rock* **(1973)**

Whole network or network-wide characteristics form the third layer of analysis of this book. We present these network-wide characteristics in terms of their structures and functions. We begin the chapter with an overview of the range of meta-governance structures that have been ascribed to interorganizational governance network configurations. We then discuss the range of operational functions that have been attributed to governance networks. Next, we address how governance networks may be described in terms of the policy streams in which they function. We also acknowledge how governance networks have existed across a wide array of policy arenas, concluding that the contexts relating to specific policy arenas ultimately need to be relied upon to describe the entire range of functions undertaken by a governance network.

Governance networks are more than the sum of their parts. We have noted the goals and resources that particular nodes bring to a governance network. We have noted the ways in which the characteristics of the ties between nodes help to guide the positionality of the network's actors. Individual nodes form ties, which form clusters, which in turn form into large clusters as we move up the social scale.

The principle of holism suggests that the structure of the network should take precedence over any individual node, and that this network structure "exerts absolute constraint on individual actions" (Degenne and Forse, 1999, p. 5). We envision cases where this may very well be so, as in instances of resource scarcity or

115

strict adherence to formalized regulations or laws. Although we are not comfortable going as far as to suggest network-wide characteristics exert an absolute authority over the structures and functions of individual nodes, we must consider the kind of network-wide characteristics that have been used to describe them.

Network-Wide Functions

Throughout this book we have described governance networks as undertaking coordinated action and resource exchanges to achieve certain policy ends—be it problem framing, policy creation, or policy implementation. We argue that this definition accounts for operational functions that get carried out within virtually any interorganizational network: coordinated actions and resource exchanges, as well as other operational functions, such as information sharing, capacity building, and learning and knowledge transfer. Governance networks are distinguished from other forms of interorganizational networks (as, for instance, found in many market-oriented networks that exist between private firms in a supply chain) because they carry out policy functions. In this section we distinguish between operational, policy stream, and policy domain functions found in governance networks.

We begin with an overview of the range of operational functions taken on with a governance network. We argue that all governance networks, and indeed any interorganizational network, will likely carry out one or more operating functions. We view these functions as the most pervasive and common functions. We then discuss how the functions of governance networks may be described in terms of the policy stream functions the network takes on. Lastly, the most specific kinds of possible functions carried out concern the type of policy domain a given governance network falls under.

We have already considered how the goals of individual network actors are shaped through the comingling of official and operative goals. Following Hall (1980), we define goals as abstract expressions of prescribed values and beliefs. Goals are expressed in anticipation of actions that are to be undertaken in the pursuit of achieving the desired ends that are prescribed in them. Simply put, goals anticipate functions.

We find efforts to label governance networks in terms of their operational functions resulting out of the extensive research undertaken by Milward and Provan (2006) and Agranoff (2007). Other network types have been more loosely affiliated with one aspect of the policy stream, be it policy implementation networks (O'Toole, 1990) or the types of policy networks associated with the policy development or formation process (as found in discussions of iron triangle, issue networks, and the lobbying efforts of interest group coalitions (Hula, 1999)). Drawing on Baumgartner and Jones's distinctions between policy domains (1993, 2002), we identify the range of policy domains (for example, health, education, and the environment) that may distinguish certain governance network functions from others, leading us to be able to label some types of governance networks based on their policy domain (e.g., health care governance networks, environmental management governance networks, etc.).

We argue that the operational, policy stream, and policy domain functions of a governance network coexist with each other within governance networks. We assume that functions may exist in tandem with other functions, in much the same way that social ties may be described in terms of their multiplexity. Instead of ascribing a single function to an entire network, for instance, deeming a governance network as being "informational" (Agranoff, 2007) or "information sharing" (Milward and Provan, 2006), we suggest that information sharing may be one of many operational functions carried out within the governance network. We also suggest that governance networks may undertake more than one policy stream function, and in some cases more than one policy domain function, by serving as the space through which policy streams couple (Kingdon, 1984).

Operating Functions

We may equate operating functions with the kind of network-wide operational goals undertaken by the network as a whole. These operational functions exist for any interorganizational network, regardless of whether it ties its core mission back to matters of public policy. Although the classical debates in sociology regarding the relationships between the structures, functions, and roles of social organizations are too rich to explore in depth here (Collins, 1988), we will adopt a sociological perspective on social functions that assumes a link between social structures and social functions. Thus, the characteristics that particular network actors bring to their participation, the nature of the social ties built between, and the network-wide governance structures that combine, comingle, and sometimes compete within governance networks shape the kind of functions the network takes on. These factors help to shape which network actors take on particular functions, and which functions get more widely distributed across the network.

Discussions of the operating functions of organizations and groups have been taking place within the organizational development and management fields since Luther Gulick first introduced the POSDCORB framework in 1937. We present a few of the contemporary views of network-wide operational functions found within the public administration literature, making no allusion that the list of operative functions we discuss here is comprehensive. We focus on two very broad, but critically important operating functions: coordinated action and resource change. Comparing and combining the functions observed by a few pioneers of network analysis in public administration, we focus on three additional operating functions that appear to play critical roles in the operation of governance networks: information sharing, capacity building, and learning and knowledge transfer.

Coordinating Action

Our discussion of the characteristics of social ties and the types of coordination occurring between network actors has laid the foundation for us to consider the ways in which coordinated action unfolds in governance networks. At its basic form, coordinated action in any social network may be described as a series of coordinated "mutual adjustments" (Mintzberg, 1979). Writing on the role of coordination within a macro-level network context, Thompson viewed coordination as "the elements in the system are somehow brought into an alignment, considered and made to act together." He in turn aligns coordination with governance, which he views as "the regulation of these elements; the effectiveness of their reproduction, of their alignment and coordination" (Thompson, 2003, p. 37).

Examining the range of activities undertaken by different kinds of governance networks, Robert Agranoff coded for at least nine different types of coordinated actions (2007, pp. 45–47). This work builds on an earlier study of local economic development networks in which Agranoff and his partner Michael McGuire coded for different of types of public action that local governments and their partners used to coordinate activities (2003). Later in the book, we consider coordinated action in terms of the roles of public managers and the formation of internal governing coalitions or communities of practice. All of the functions described in this section, whether we consider them basic operating functions or policy functions, contribute to network-wide coordinated action.

Mobilizing and Exchanging Resources

Our discussion of the stocks of capital resources that particular network actors bring into a network and the process of resource exchange that occurs between them has underscored the importance that resource mobilization and resource exchange play in governance networks. Some of the most critical operational functions that a governance network takes on pertain to the kinds of resources that are exchanged, by whom, and at what time. Because we have discussed resource exchange extensively in previous chapters, we merely recognize the critical role that resource exchange plays in the operation of governance networks.

Diffusing and Sharing Information

Information is one of the critical capital resources that flows across virtually any social network. We may define *information* as "the organized data that has been arranged for better comprehension or understanding" (McNabb, 2007, p. 283). The flow of information within a governance network has been described as facilitating several other kinds of policy functions. Milward and Provan describe how information sharing contributes to the "shaping" of problems (Milward and Provan, 2006, p. 14). Information will likely serve as the chief function of networks taking on policy evaluation functions. How information flows across a social network plays a large role in how collective meaning and goals are established. In noting the role that information plays in social systems, Galbraith observes that "the greater the task uncertainty, the greater the amount of information that must be processed" among network members (1977, p. 105). Information sharing in a social network forms the basis for how coordination takes place, what roles network actors assume, and importantly, how network performance is measured. As Henry Mintzberg first observed in 1979, "mutual adjustment achieves the coordination of work by the simple process of information communication" (p. 3). Information exchange takes place within governance networks, and serves as the possible basis around which a governance network interfaces with its external environment. Information sharing may serve not only as a critical function in a governance network's internal processes, but also as an official goal of the network and one of its critical outputs. It is important to recognize that there are also instances of information withholding or strategic manipulation and framing of information that can occur within and across governance networks. In Chapter 10 we discuss how one type of information, performance measures/indicators, serves as the currency around which network performance can be monitored and directed.

Building Capacity

Social capital is another critical resource that flows across all social networks. Milward and Provan suggest that governance networks that carry out capacity-building functions build "social capital in community-based settings," arguing that capacity building is often viewed as "both current and future oriented" (2006, p. 11). Agranoff refers to capacity-building activities as instances of "outreach," through which client contacts may be pooled, expansion of network membership to new actors pursued, and the capacity of other networks to carry out their operational and policy functions built (2006, p. 10). Capacity-building functions entail the conscious building and strengthening of ties within and across governance networks.

Learning and Transferring Knowledge

Information sharing can lead to learning and knowledge transfer. Learning results "when experience and knowledge are consistently and extensively shared, valued, and promoted" (McNabb, 2007, p. 28). March and Olsen recognize that learning processes unfold within social systems in three integrated phases: "1.) Experimentation based on variation and risk taking; 2.) Selection and inference from experiments based on socially constructed evaluations; and 3.) Retention of learning in institutional rules and procedures that ensure a tacit, collective memory (March and Olsen, 1995, p. 199)" (Sorensen and Torfing, 2008, p. 105). In circumstances in which governance networks need to address complex, wicked problems that require extensive innovation and experimentation, the active promotion of learning and knowledge transfer serves as a critical operational function. Agranoff suggests ways in which capacity building is facilitated through "technical exchange" and mutual education (2007, p. 10).

We believe that a strong argument can be made that the range of operational functions introduced here may appear within and across virtually any interorganizational network delegated exclusively to exchanges undertaken by private actors for purposes of art, entertainment, or profit. In Chapter 2 we discussed how governance networks are distinguished from other interorganizational networks because of the inherent policy functions that they take on. Although we feel safe in asserting that all interorganizational networks carry on the operating functions discussed earlier, governance networks are distinguished by the range of policy functions they take on.

Policy Stream Functions

Within the policy studies and policy analysis field, several conceptual models have been used to describe the creation, implementation, and monitoring of public policies. Process models include the classic policy cycle (Patton and Sawicki, 1986), institutional analysis and development (Ostrom, 2005), social construction and policy design (Ingram and Schneider, 1993), the punctuated equilibrium theory (Jones and Baumgartner, 1993), and the advocacy coalition framework (Sabatier and Jenkins-Smith, 1993). We focus here on the policy stream model first proposed by Kingdon (1984). Kingdon proposed that three streams (problem, policies/solutions, and politics) operating distinctly and in conjunction with one another provide another conceptual model of the policy process.

Unlike the classic policy cycle, Kingdon's policy stream model does not assume linearity or rational behavior on the part of policy actors. The problems, policies, and politics streams may couple, and in fact need to couple, for agendas to be set and policy windows to open. Kingdon (1984) recognizes that policy streams are created and directed through social networks and indirectly asserted that social networks form as a result of one stream, or some coupling of multiple streams. Kingdon recognizes that a number of policy actors, including interest groups, academia, media, and political parties, coordinate actions within and across the policy stream. Kingdon focuses on the coupling of policy streams leading to agenda setting and policy windows. He grounds the policy stream model in the coordinated actions that arise during the preenactment phases of policy selection and design.

To account for the postenactment of policy tools, Tony Bovaird builds on the policy stream model by combining some of the stages of the policy cycle with the characteristics of policy streams and differentiates between stages in the policy development and policy coordination process (2005). He also distinguishes between regulatory policy implementation and services policy implementation, and allows for policy evaluation and monitoring as a "stream" in the policy stream.

Referring to networks created to enact policies, Gage described "implementation networks" as "systems of actors from different organizations that have become involved in accomplishing a policy goal, a collective good, quite possibly for widely different reasons. Implementation networks typically have substructures for policy making" (Gage, 1990, p. 131). These networks tend to have a "less extensive, but more cohesive degree of functional integration." Gage also observed that "it is likely to have a membership that has a higher degree of functional integration. For example, there will be close symbiotic relationships and members who have worked out guarded truces" (Gage, 1990, p. 131). We note here how networks predicated around the enactment of policies need to begin with the basic ties of coexistence.

We conclude that governance networks can be aligned with various layers of the policy stream. These streams may be understood in terms of the preenactment of public policies and the postenactment of public policies. Network configurations have been described in terms of the preenactment phases of the policy stream in the literature pertaining to iron triangles, issue networks (Heclo, 1978), policy subsystems (Baumgartner and Jones, 1993), advocacy coalitions (Sabatier and Jenkins-Smith, 1993), interest group coalitions (Hula, 1999), and policy networks (Rhodes, 1997). Postenactment network configurations have been described as third-party government (Salamon, 2002b), implementation networks (O'Toole, 1997), and public management networks (Milward and Provan, 2006; Frederickson and Frederickson, 2006; Agranoff, 2007). The selection and implementation of particular policy tools or suites of policy tools (Salamon, 2002b) play a central role in the organization of governance networks and their alignment within and across policy streams.

It may as well go without saying that networks carrying on particular policy functions or combinations of particular policy functions are more likely to rely on certain combinations of policy actors than others. The extent to which it is important to compare network configurations that appear over multiple policy streams ranging across the preenactment, enactment, and postenactment phases of policy development and implementation has yet to be fully explored within the literature.

Drawing particularly on Kingdon (1984) and Bovaird (2005), we discuss how each stream, phase, or facet of the policy process is distinguished. Figure 5.1 depicts the relationship between the phases of the policy process and the development of networks oriented to fulfilling these functions.

Defining and Framing Problems

Governance networks that exist to define or frame a public problem exist, at least in part, to bring a public problem into sharper focus or, in some cases, remove a

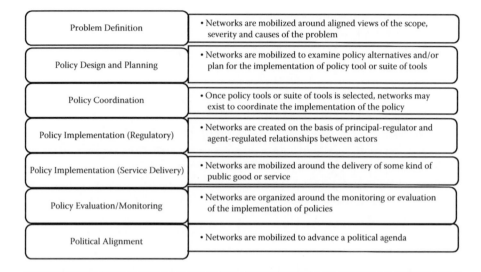

Problem Definition	• Networks are mobilized around aligned views of the scope, severity and causes of the problem
Policy Design and Planning	• Networks are mobilized to examine policy alternatives and/or plan for the implementation of policy tool or suite of tools
Policy Coordination	• Once policy tools or suite of tools is selected, networks may exist to coordinate the implementation of the policy
Policy Implementation (Regulatory)	• Networks are created on the basis of principal-regulator and agent-regulated relationships between actors
Policy Implementation (Service Delivery)	• Networks are mobilized around the delivery of some kind of public good or service
Policy Evaluation/Monitoring	• Networks are organized around the monitoring or evaluation of the implementation of policies
Political Alignment	• Networks are mobilized to advance a political agenda

Figure 5.1 Governance network relations to the policy stream. (Adapted from Bovaird, *International Review of Administrative Sciences, 71,* **217–228, 2005.)**

particular policy problem from the public agenda. Examples of governance networks attempting to frame a public problem can be found in recent efforts of the scientific community to highlight the perils of global climate change. A variety of interest group coalitions coalesced around the problem with the official goal of bringing global climate change onto the public agenda. We find interest group coalitions forming around most any policy arena. Within the literature, iron triangles, issue networks, and even intergovernmental networks have been described in terms of problem framing. Arguably, one of the only ways a public problem garners the attention of policy makers is through the collective actions of governance networks that have put pressure on or convinced or informed the perceptions of key decision makers. Other governance networks may exist to provide data, information, or new knowledge pertaining to public problems, as found in the many public-private partnerships and grant and contract agreements created to advance research and development.

Designing and Planning Policy

A simple definition of a public policy is that it is a solution to a problem (Stone, 2002). The design and enactment of a particular policy may be the official or unofficial goal of a governance network. Kingdon (1984) first described how policy actors may align around the promotion of a particular policy solution. Interest group coalitions, iron triangles, and issue networks may advocate for the design and enactment of particular policy tools, waiting for policy windows to open through which they may couple the policy with a pressing public problem. We found this happening when certain neoconservative interest group coalitions pressed for the incorporation of school vouchers and the relaxation of certain labor laws during the reconstruction efforts following Hurricane Katrina (Farley et al., 2007). We find interests coalescing around the adoption or repeal of particular policy tools, ranging from environmental regulation to tax credit and loan guarantee programs. With the promotion (or repeal) of particular policy tools as their official goal, certain interest group coalitions and public-private partnerships may view the policy solution as one of their central outcome goals.

Governance networks may also be created to collectively design policy solutions. Without predetermined outcomes, public-private partnerships are created to undertake collaborative planning processes. Across the literature we find deliberative democratic forums, neighborhood planning processes, and other participatory planning processes undertaken by and through public-private partnerships.

Coordinating Policy

Public policies need to be coordinated. In some instances, as in the coordination of complex policy rollouts in which entire suites of policy tools are called for, governance networks may be created to coordinate implementation. Frederickson and Frederickson's studies of health care networks, such as the regulatory subsystems and grant and contract agreements found in Medicare/Medicaid and the grants programs of the Health Resources and Services Administration (2006), provide rich examples of governance networks aligned around the coordination of an array of policy tools.

Implementing Policy through Regulation

The policy implementation literature is rich with descriptions of governance networks (Hill and Hupe, 2002, p. 83) designed to either regulate or deliver public goods or services. We have already discussed the roles and functions that regulatory subsystems take in attempting to regulate the economic, environmental, or social behaviors of nongovernmental organizations. A substantial body of literature has focused on the relationship between governments and their regulated entities (Krause, 1997; Teske, 2004; Frederickson and Frederickson, 2006). The principal-agent dynamics common in regulatory subsystems, in which government regulators serve as principals wielding authority over regulated agents, have been marked by waves of reforms, swinging from eras of expansion of government's regulatory powers to eras of deregulation. Some of the critical considerations that arise in regulatory subsystems accounted for in our governance network model concern the extent to which information asymmetries and regulatory capture shape the structures of regulatory subsystem networks.

Implementing Policy through Service Delivery

A second form of policy implementation network is those that provide or deliver public or social goods and services. In service delivery networks, "government funds the service under contract but doesn't directly provide it; a fiscal agent, [usually the government] acts as the sole buyer of services" (Milward and Provan, 2006, p. 11).

There exists a substantial body of literature pertaining to contracting out and privatization movements discussing the roles that grants, contracts, and other enabling policy tools play in structuring the nature of these service delivery networks. The policy implementation literature dates back to Pressman and Wildavsky's (1973) initial study of the Oakland Redevelopment Program, and extends to Sabatier and Mazmanian's (1981) discussion of the roles that governments play in executing top-down control through the utilization of grants and contracts. Subsequently, the substantial literature pertaining to the role of contracts (Kelman, 2002; Cooper, 2003) and grants provides some very useful insights into the ways in which certain configurations of grant and contract agreements take on service delivery policy functions. Public-private partnerships are created to provide public goods and services, leveraging the resources of contributing public, private, and nonprofit organizations.

Evaluating Policy

Many configurations of governance networks form to evaluate policies. Interest group coalitions may undertake extensive evaluation of policies in efforts to provide greater transparency of government activities, mounting persuasive arguments to reframe public policies into problems. Public-private partnerships involving private or nonprofit research firms and universities may be created to study the impacts of public policies (Koontz et al., 2004). Federal entities such as the National Institutes of Health (NIH) and the National Science Foundation (NSF) (Frederickson and Frederickson, 2006) use grants and contract agreements to carry out evaluation of public policy impacts. These evaluative functions provide data to elected policy makers and those looking to influence them.

Bringing Political Alignment

The importance of politics and political alignments between policy actors in the framing of public policies, creating public policies, and implementing public policies has been the focus of much of the policy studies and implementation literature in recent decades. Political processes are often equated with negotiation and bargaining, trade-offs leading to compromises and concessions, and the shear execution of power in efforts to control the outcome of public deliberations. We hope that it comes as an understatement at this point to conclude that governance networks of all forms exist, in part, due to the political alignments of policy actors.

Policy Domain Functions

In addition to the operational and policy functions, the functions of a governance network may be characterized by the policy domains that it functions within. These domains are shaped by at least two factors: the coalescence of policy actors around a particular set of interests or concerns, and the very nature of the wicked problems that are said to encompass a given policy arena or domain. In other words, the domains that a governance network functions within get predicated simultaneously by the type of actors engaged in the collective action, and the characteristics of the policy domain itself. Joop Koppenjan notes how it was Theodore Lowi who recognized the relationship between policy arena and multiactor configurations. "Lowi (1969), for instance, using the term arenas in this context, argued that depending on the nature and intensity of the conflict or the clash of interests between a set of actors, a specific configuration of actors or 'arenas' develops. Some arenas have a more pluralist (open) character; others tend towards a more elitist (exclusive) structure" (Koppenjan, 2008, p. 145).

Baumgartner and Jones (2002), building on a policy domain categorization scheme devised by OMB, have laid out one of the most comprehensive typologies for distinguishing between different policy domains that apply to the study of policy systems and governance networks. A list of these major policy domains is provided in Figure 5.2.

Baumgartner and Jones have studied governance networks, which they refer to as policy systems and subsystems (1993, 2002), within and across these domains. Space precludes a deeper exploration of the range of discrete functions taken on within a particular policy domain. We need to also hold out for the possibility that some governance networks carry out functions from more than a single policy domain. For example, some governance networks, like those engaged in regional planning efforts, will likely take on functions found within the community development, environmental management, transportation management, and even emergency management policy domains. One potential value that a governance network brings to wicked problems lies in its capacity to be a conduit for combining policy domains, policy streams, and operating functions.

There have been many seminal studies that have applied network metaphors and frames of analysis to the study of particular policy domains or the coupling of policy domains. Milward and Provan have studied how certain kinds of network configurations led to effective or ineffective delivery of mental health and social services (1998). Agranoff and McGuire's extensive research on local community development efforts has shed light on a range of characteristics common to governance networks within this policy domain (2003). Health care networks have been the focus of several studies (Frederickson and Frederickson, 2006; Rodriguez et al., 2007). Environmental management networks have been the focus of study as well (Koontz et al., 2004; Imperial, 2005). We likely may generate an extensive

1.	Macroeconomics
2.	Civil rights, minority issues and civil liberties
3.	Health
4.	Agriculture
5.	Labor, employment and immigration
6.	Education
7.	Environment
8.	Energy
9.	Transportation
10.	Law, crime and family issues
11.	Social welfare
12.	Community development; housing issues
13.	Banking, finance and domestic commerce
14.	Defense
15.	Space, science, technology and communications
16.	Foreign trade
17.	International affairs and foreign aid
18.	Government operations
19.	Public lands and water management'

Figure 5.2 Policy domains of Baumgartner and Jones's (2002) policy agendas project.

list of studies that have applied network frames of analysis to the study of policy implementation efforts across all of the policy domains listed above.

We suggest that within each of these policy domains an additional set of domain functions may be identified. We refer you to Baumgartner and Jones's classification scheme for a set of such functions that they derived for each policy domain (2002). We provide two examples in Table 5.1, one relating to health and the other to the environment, to illustrate the relationship between policy domain and domain functions.

By allowing for governance network functions to be dictated by the specific goals ascribed to within each policy arena, a wide array of functions and subfunctions emerge. We may consider ways to label governance networks by the policy domain they function within, suggesting that we may want to speak of "environmental governance networks" or "health care governance networks." In Chapter 6 we offer a set of possible network configurations that may be used to specify which kinds of governance network configurations are in operation, leading us to consider identifying governance networks as "environmental public-private partnerships" or "health care grant and contract agreements." Given the generalist approach to governance networks taken up in this book, we will simply note the wide array of potential policy domain functions that are possible.

We also must add that a governance network may extend across more than one policy domain. Just as governance networks are spaces within which policy streams are coupled (Kingdon, 1984), they may also serve as spaces where multiple policy domain functions overlap. Some of our own research using the governance network frameworks described in this book has focused on governance networks that serve as spaces where policy domains are integrated. Emergency management networks are often charged with coordinating functions that span the policy domains of health, transportation, environment, government operations, community development and housing, energy, law, crime and family issues, social welfare, and even defense-related issues. We have described regional planning networks through which transportation, community development, environment, and social welfare policy domains converge around the development and implementation of regional planning processes (Koliba, Campbell, and Zia, 2009). A third area of integrated policy domains that we can identify concerns the coordination of policies addressing climate change. Climate change issues are implicated in the environmental, transportation, energy, community development, social welfare, international affairs, science, technology, and communications domains, among others.

We conclude that the policy domain functions of a given governance network may reside within a specific policy domain, such as those found in Table 5.1, or span more than one policy domain. We anticipate that the policy domain categories put forth by Baumgartner and Jones will likely be expanded to account for the rise of these integrated policy domains.

Network Functions: A Review

In this chapter we have distinguished basic operational functions from policy functions and argued that the policy functions and policy domains of a given governance network are what distinguish governance networks from other types of interorganizational networks. The basic operation functions of coordinating action, resource mobilization, exchange and pooling, information sharing, learning and knowledge transfer, and capacity building may be found within interorganizational networks of many different forms—including those organized to pursue decidedly private/nonpublic functions. Borrowing from Kingdon's notion of policy streams

Table 5.1   Two Examples of Policy Domains and Domain Functions: Cases of Health and the Environment

Policy Domain	Domain Functions
Health	• General • Health care reform; health care costs; insurance costs and availability • Medicare and Medicaid • Regulation of prescription drugs, medical devices, and medical procedures • Health facilities' construction and regulation; public health service • Mental illness and mental retardation • Elderly health issues • Infants, children, and immunization • Health manpower needs and training programs • Military health care • Drug and alcohol treatment and education • Specific diseases • Research and development • Other
Environment	• General • Drinking water safety • Waste disposal • Hazardous waste and toxic chemical regulation, treatment, and disposal • Air pollution, global warming, and noise pollution • Recycling • Indoor environmental hazards • Species and forest protection • Coastal water pollution and conservation • Land and water conservation • Research and development • Other

Compiled from: Baumgartner and Jones, *Policy Dynamics*, University of Chicago Press, Chicago, 2002.

and Bovaird's adaption of it to networks, we presented a set of policy functions ranging from policy framing to policy evaluation, suggesting that governance networks may serve as the spaces through which different facets of the policy stream couple. We concluded the chapter by introducing the notion that governance networks will take on specific policy domain functions that will vary drastically from domain to domain. As the most specific type of function, the range of possible policy domains that can be used to describe governance network activities can be quite extensive.

The relationship between organizational functions and structures has been widely discussed within the field of sociology. Following the dictates of complexity theory, which tends toward nonlinearity and ascriptions of cause and effect, we suggest here that governance network functions and structures coexist and influence one another. At times, preexisting structures help to facilitate the development of new or emergent functions, as in the case of high "automaticity," when existing infrastructures and relationships lead to the implementation of certain policy solutions (as, for instance, in the case of using existing banking networks to implement student loans or low-income mortgages). Likewise, the need for social actors to mobilize to address a public need, for instance, in cases of natural disasters, facilitates the development of network structures designed to provide response and recovery efforts.

CRITICAL QUESTIONS AND CONSIDERATIONS

With this chapter we begin to address governance network questions in regard to the role the network plays in terms of functions the network performs.

- Returning again to your governance network, identify the governance network's operating functions, policy functions, and policy domain functions.
- What combinations of operational, policy, and policy domain functions does the network take on?
- How and to what extent do these functions complement one another? Compete with one another?
- Who determines which functions to carry out? Which actor or combinations of actors carry out specific functions?

Chapter 6

Network-Wide Structures

Form follows function—that has been misunderstood. Form and function should be one, joined in a spiritual union.

—Frank Lloyd Wright (Clayton, 2002, p. 303)

In this chapter we consider the kinds of network structures that can be found within governance networks of various configurations. We begin with a discussion of the roles that "policy tools" play in structuring network arrangements. We build on the policy tools framework first introduced by Lester Salamon and his associates and the links they draw between the selection and use of policy tools and the inherent network structures that arise as a result. We then explore Michael Provan and Patrick Kenis's network governance model, suggesting that their model is a useful starting point around which to describe macro-level, network-wide structures. We conclude the chapter with a look at five different kinds of governance network configurations: intergovernmental relations, interest group coalitions, regulatory subsystems, grant and contract agreements, and public-private partnerships.

There is a long-standing debate within sociology regarding the relationship between form and function. Adopting a systems view, we see the relationship between the range of functions outlined in Chapter 5 and the kind of structural characteristics raised in this chapter as being indelibly linked. Determining whether functions lead to structures or structures lead to functions is a matter that is highly contextual and likely contingent on the life cycle of the network. Governance networks may be catalyzed around the goals of fulfilling certain functions. These functions, in turn, help determine network structure. Governance networks may also emerge out of existing network structures, with functions arising from the collective decisions made by network actors operating out of these structures. For our

131

purposes, we skirt the "chicken or egg" question and simply offer this discussion of network-wide structure as yet another set of characteristics around which governance networks may be described.

Policy Tools

In laying out a framework for interpreting the place of policy tools in relation to contemporary public administration and policy frameworks, Michael Howlett observes that policy tools or instruments "are techniques of governance that, one way or another, involve the utilization of state authority or its conscious limitation" (Howlett, 2005, p. 31). The origins of the policy tool frameworks have been traced back to the work of Lowi (1969) (Landry and Varone, 2005, p. 107). Policy tool typologies have been introduced by Hood (1984), McDonnell and Elmore (1987), and Doern and Phidd (1992). Lester Salamon has been one of the chief proponents of a new governance framework that provides a focused study of the policy tool as a unit of analysis (2002a,b). He and his colleagues assert that the increasing uses of indirect policy tools have contributed greatly to the proliferation of governance networks. Salamon describes how policy tools structure the interactions of actors within a governance network. Policy tools may also be understood as "boundary objects" (Wenger, 1998) that serve to help structure the flow of resources and services, and with which actors are mobilized and participate. According to Salamon, "a [policy] tool or instrument of public action can be defined as an identifiable method through which collective action is structured to address a public problem" (Salamon, 2002a, p. 19). Policy tools structure action. Table 6.1 illustrates the relation of the policy tool to the policy stream. Although many different typologies of policy tool types have been introduced,* the policy tool typology presented in Salamon et al.'s (2002b) *The Tools of Government: A Guide to the New Governance* provides the most extensive overview of policy tool definitions and characteristics to date.

The selection of particular policy tools can become the intended outcome of a governance network. Networks that exist in the preenactment phases of the policy stream (described within the literature as iron triangles, issue networks, and interest group coalitions) function to influence the selection and design of particular policy tools, contributing to the "politics of structure" (Wise, 1994) that has historically marked intersectoral relations (see Chapter 2 for a discussion of this phenomenon). Noting the relationship between policy tool selection and design and political alignment, Salamon observes that "tools often take on an ideological coloration that makes them attractive on *a priori* grounds regardless of their fit with the problem to be solved" (Salamon, 2002b, p. 602). Thus, the selection and design of

---

* See Birkland (2001) for a breakdown of policy tools introduced prior to the publication of *The Tools of Government* (Salamon, 2002b).

Table 6.1   Relation of Policy Tool to Policy Stream

Stage of Enactment	Place in the Policy Stream	Policy Tool as Input or Outcome
Preenactment	Problem definition	Policy tools are viewed as problems/contribute to problems (input)
	Policy design	Policy tool is the design (output)
Postenactment	Policy coordination	Policy tool structures network (input)
	Regulation	Regulation structures network (input)
	Service delivery	Service grants and contracts structure network (input)
	Policy evaluation	Policy tool is the subject of an evaluation (output)
Pre- and postenactment	Political alignment	Policy tool enactment (or nonenactment) is output

particular policy tools may serve as the desired outcome of a particular governance network. The selection of the policy tool becomes "a central part of the political battle that shapes public programs. What is at stake in these battles is not simply the most efficient way to solve a particular problem, but also the relative influence that various affected interests will have in shaping the program's post-enactment evolution" (Salamon, 2002a, p. 11). Table 6.2 provides a basic listing of policy tools as laid out by Lester Salamon and his colleagues.

Policy tools can serve as a critical input into a governance network, structuring how authority and resources flow through it. "Tools importantly structure the post-enactment process of policy definition by specifying the network of actors that will play important roles and the nature of the roles they will perform" (Salamon, 2002a, p. 18). Speaking of the policy tool's function as an input factor, Salamon observes that the "choice of tool helps determine how discretion will be used" and authority carried out (2002a, p. 18). Postenactment (e.g., after a policy tool is selected and allocated sufficient resources), policy tools will structure how authority gets distributed across a governance network and, in some cases, how resources get distributed.

Policy tools possess certain characteristics that play a part in how they impact the mobilization, composition, and function of a governance network. Some tools are

Table 6.2 Policy Tool Definitions

Government Tool	Definition
Economic regulation	Specialized bureaucratic process that combines aspects of both courts and legislature to control prices, output, or entry and exit of firms in an industry (Salamon, 2002c, p. 117).
Social regulation	Social regulation is aimed at restricting behaviors that directly threaten public health, safety, welfare, or well-being (May, 2002, p. 157).
Environmental regulation	Variations of economic and social regulation design to ensure the sustainability of natural resources and the quality of ecosystem services.
Government insurance	Governments agree to compensate individuals or firms for losses from certain specified events. Eligible recipients are usually charged a fee, or premium, for participation in the program (Feldman, 2002, p. 187).
Public information	Policy makers seek to inform an audience of target actors about an issue or pattern of behavior to influence what people think, know, or believe when they engage in the target behavior (Weiss, 2002, p. 218).
Corrective taxes, charge, tradable permits	Use of price and other market mechanisms to create financial incentives to change behavior in ways that reduce social harms or secure benefits for society at large (Cordes, 2002, p. 256).
Procurement contracts	A business arrangement between the government and a private for-profit or not-for-profit entity in which the private entity promises, in exchange for money, to deliver certain products or services to the government agency or to others on the government's behalf (Kelman, 2002, p. 282).
Purchase of service contracts	Agreements under which a government agency enlists a private organization to deliver a service to an eligible group of clients (third party) in exchange for money (DeHoog and Salamon, 2002, p. 320).
Grants	Payments from a donor government to a recipient organization (typically public or nonprofit) or an individual (Beam and Conlan, 2002, p. 341).

Table 6.2   Policy Tool Definitions (Continued)

Government Tool	Definition
Loans and loan guarantees	Credit is provided as a way to encourage funding for borrowers or activities that are considered important, either politically or economically. Government makes a direct loan when it borrows from the Treasury to lend money; when the government guarantees a loan, a private lender makes the loan to the borrower (Stanton, 2002, p. 381).
Tax expenditures	A provision in the tax code used to encourage certain behavior by individuals or corporations by deferring, reducing, or eliminating their tax obligation (Howard, 2002, p. 411).
Vouchers	A subsidy that grants limited purchasing power to an individual to choose among a restricted set of goods and services (Steuerle and Twombly, 2002, p. 446).

Compiled from: Salamon, Ed., *The Tools of Government: A Guide to the New Governance*, Oxford, New York, 2002.

more coercive than others. "Coercion measures the extent to which a tool restricts individual or group behavior as opposed to merely encouraging or discouraging it" (Salamon, 2002a, p. 25). Most forms of regulation, for instance, are viewed as coercive by the regulated agent. To avoid having to force compliance, governments have moved toward more voluntary forms of compliance and self-regulation. Other tools, such as grants and contracts, call for contracted agents to voluntarily enter into a principal-agent relationship with the government. Within these relationships there is a clear remunerative quality to the relationship. Still other policy tools facilitate noncoercive relationships, such as vouchers, in which individual citizens are given latitude in where to spend the voucher, and public information, in which governments may partner with educational or media outlets to provide public service announcements. Howlett discusses the relationship between tool selection and the degree of compulsion inherent to the tools, suggesting another way of thinking about tools and coercion (2005).

Another characteristic of a policy tool concerns the degree of automaticity that is required to implement the tools. Some policy tools draw on an existing infrastructure to be implemented. "Automaticity measures the extent to which a tool utilizes an existing administrative structure to produce its effect rather than having to create its own special administrative apparatus" (Salamon, 2002a, p. 32). In some cases, such as loan guarantees, governments work with the banking industry to execute guaranteed loan programs. Some forms of social regulation, such as new criminal laws, may be difficult to enforce because the infrastructure to arrest or prosecute offenders is not robust enough. It should be noted as well that the existence of an infrastructure to implement a given policy tool may be the impetus for mobilizing a governance network.

The visibility of a policy tool is a third characteristic that structures collective action. Salamon and his colleagues view visibility chiefly in terms of the manifestation of the costs associated with the policy tools within a public budget (2002a). "Visibility measures the extent to which the resources devoted to a tool show up in the normal government budgeting and policy review process" (Salamon, 2002a, p. 35). Visibility may also be construed in terms of public awareness of the existence of the policy tool. Visibility within a budget may be helpful for providing network actors with insights into the extent of the financial resources that are being devoted to implementation, while the visibility of the policy tool in terms of public awareness may have a bearing on which actors get mobilized, as in the case of the release of a request for proposals, or the visibility of a competitive bidding process.

Howlett describes the "second generation" of policy tools study as being interested in the policy context out of which tool selection and implementation emerge and "the nature of instrument mixes" (2005, p. 33). Salamon refers to the mixing of multiple policy tools within a particular context as the "suit" of policy tools (2002a). Howlett observes that the result of mixing policy tools is "less well understood than are choices to select specific types of instruments" (2005, p. 33). Bressers and O'Toole observe that "almost always, the influence of policy instruments is effectively, a blend, or combination, of different instruments, sometimes enacted at different times and often for somewhat different purposes" (2005, p. 135). They note that policy tools may be enacted at different levels of the social and geographic scale (2005, pp. 137, 146).

Drawing on some of the classical distinctions used within policy tool description, Howlett divides policy tools into substantive and procedural instruments (2003). Procedural instruments such as public information tools, collaborative agreements, and mediated conflict resolution fall into this category, as does the funding of public services, policy evaluations, and strategic planning processes. Howlett stresses the importance of searching for "new network appropriate procedural policy instruments to meet the challenges of governance" (Howlett, 2005, p. 46).

Hans Bressers and Laurence O'Toole necessarily dampen our expectations around placing a premium on the selection of policy tools. They aptly warn, "The tools of government are not at the unencumbered disposal of formal policy makers. While instruments of governance may sometimes seem like so many arrows in a quiver, like options merely waiting selection and application at appropriate strategic moments by public officials, this appearance is deceptive" (2005, p. 132). They go on to add that "[policy] instruments are best regarded not as initial shapers of behavior in policy setting but as potential shifters of ongoing processes of policy action over time" (Bressers and O'Toole, 2005, p. 133). The choice of policy tools is "shaped by the networked pattern characteristics of the initial state from which policy-oriented change is sought." They add that "even more fundamental, any instrument must work its way through and be expected to perturb an existing set of processes involving actors in the policy system" (2005, p. 151). We conclude that policy tools play a role in shaping network-wide structures and that network structures, in turn, shape which policy tools are selected and implemented. As a characteristic of network-wide structures, policy tools contribute to the network in ways endemic to the complex arrangements between network actors.

Macro-Level Network Governance Structure

Having reviewed the growing body of literature on interorganizational networks, Provan and Kenis introduce three models of interorganizational form: the self-governed network, the lead organization network, and the network administrative organization (2007).

The most collaboratively structured network governance arrangement is the self-governed network, characterized by balanced flows of ties and authorities. Figure 6.1 shows a visual representation of these kind of arrangements.

In participant-governed or shared governance networks (presented in Figure 6.1 in the "perfect" form), authority and power are distributed across the network, as each organizational network node bears social ties between one another. The dominant relational ties operating in participant-governed networks are horizontal, as a participant-governed network depends, to a large extent, on the qualities of social norms that exist between network nodes. "Shared participant-governed networks depend exclusively on the involvement and commitment of all, or a significant

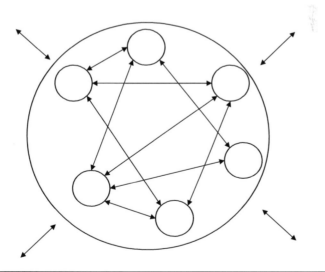

Figure 6.1   Self-governed network. (*Source:* Milward and Provan, IBM Center for the Business of Government, p. 23, 2006.)

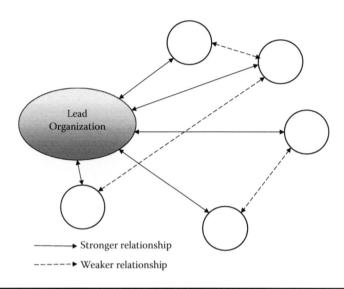

Figure 6.2 Lead organization network. (*Source:* Milward and Provan, IBM Center for the Business of Government, p. 23, 2006.)

subset of the organizations that comprise the network" (Provan and Kenis, 2007, p. 234).

A second form of network governance is the lead organization configuration, which is represented in Figure 6.2.

In lead organization networks (presented in Figure 6.2), authority and power are more likely to be concentrated within (or through) the lead organization. Following our discussion of strong and tight ties in Chapter 4, we suggest that the stronger the social ties between the lead organization and the other organizations in the network, the stronger the lead organization's authority. In lead organization networks, "all major network-level activities and key decisions are coordinated through and by a single participating member, acting as a lead organization" (Provan and Kenis, 2007, p. 235). In the context of governance networks, governments may take on the role of lead organizations within regulatory systems, exerting certain measures of command and control, and as in the cases of regulatory capture, concessions and compromises provided to their regulated entities. Governments may also serve as the lead organization in grants and contracting arrangements, in which they serve as principals to their contracted agents. Lead organizations may also rely on more cooperative and collaborative ties. Writing about the role that cooperation plays in bringing legitimacy to lead organizations, Mandell observes that "the lead agency's strong base of power must ... be tempered by its need to maintain the cooperation of members of the network.... These types of networks therefore have a great deal of potential conflict built into them, relating to the need for the lead

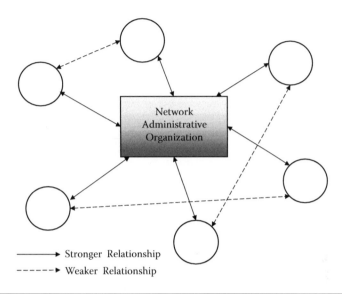

Figure 6.3   Network administrative organization. (*Source:* **Milward and Provan, IBM Center for the Business of Government, p. 23, 2006.**)

agency to control the members of the network and the members' need to remain autonomous" (1990, p. 43).

The third form of network governance is the network administrative organization (NAO). This configuration is represented in Figure 6.3.

The network administrative organization is a coordinating body that exists to administer the activities of the interorganizational network. An NAO may exist formally as a distinct organizational node of its own, or informally as a coordinating body (e.g., steering committees, governing boards, etc.) that exists to administer many of the critical functions of the network. "Unlike the lead organization model, however, the NAO is not another member organization.... Instead ... the NAO is established ... for the exclusive purpose of network governance" (Provan and Kenis, 2007, p. 236). Although no extensive studies of NAO structures have been undertaken to date, we may surmise that NAOs will likely forge certain combinations of vertical, horizontal, and diagonal ties when governing their networks' actions.

Much like Bressers and O'Toole suggest that the selection of policy tools is contingent on policy actors' preferences and characteristics, Provan and Kenis observe that the selection of macro-level network governance structures will be based, "at least in part, on the discretion of key network decision makers" (2007, p. 236). They suggest that the adoption of particular governance structures is contingent upon several factors: the levels of trust, number of participants, and goal consensus. Table 6.3 lays out their key predictions of effectiveness.

Drawing on the core relationship between social network structures and horizontal ties, Provan and Kenis (2007) correlate levels of trust with network governance

Table 6.3 Key Predictors of Effectiveness of Network Governance Form

Governance Form	Trust Levels	Number of Actors	Consensus around Goals
Shared governance	High	Few	High
Network administrative organization	Moderate	Moderate to many	Moderately high
Lead organization	Low, highly centralized	Moderate	Moderately low

Source: Adapted from Provan and Kenis, *Journal of Public Administration Research and Theory, 18,* 237, 2007.

structures. Observing the limited capacity that shared governance structures have within large groups (recall Paine's thought experiment), they suggest that high levels of trust and shared decision making can only occur across networks of limited size. They also anticipate that the degree of consensus around network-wide goals will vary from moderately low in lead organization structures dominated by vertical authorities to the goal alignments necessary to achieve a shared governance structure. They suggest that certain trade-offs between efficiency and inclusiveness are apparent across these forms, with lead organization structures more often viewed as the more efficient structures. Provan and Kenis conclude their article by suggesting a number of hypotheses that may be generated from this model. We discuss some variations of the hypotheses in Chapter 11.

Configurations of Governance Network Structure

Given the range of functions, tools, and governance structures that exist at the network-wide level, we may identify certain types of persistent configurations of governance networks. We recognize that a great deal has been written about each type of governance network configuration that we represent here. We make no allusions to providing a comprehensive overview of these structures, nor will we offer an extensive review of the historical and empirical factors that shape them. As is the case in a lot of social science literature, labels are by no means uniformly agreed upon. In many cases, multiple terms are used to describe what essentially boils down to very similar phenomena.

Having conducted a review pertaining to the framing of interorganizational network configurations, we can now turn to examining some of the various patterns these configurations generally operate. We identify five major types of governance network configurations: intergovernmental relations, interest group coalitions, regulatory subsystems, grants and contract agreements, and public-private partnerships. These five patterns distinguish themselves by their role in the policy streams of governance. We explore some of the characteristics of these mixed-form governance network configurations for the remainder of the chapter. Table 6.4 lays out the five patterns in terms of some of the major causes, functions, and trends impacting each configuration. At the end of the chapter we add a sixth pattern that does not easily fit into this framework: regional and geogovernance structures.

Intergovernmental Relations (IGRs)

Intergovernmental networks have been described as possessing a combination of "vertical interdependence" and "extensive horizontal articulation" (Rhodes, 1997, p. 38). Because intergovernmental relations are marked by combinations of hierarchical and collaborative arrangements, there has been little consensus around a singular model of intergovernmental relations for the United States. Deil Wright's (2000) three models of intergovernmental relations represent the relationship between local, state, and national governments as taking one of three forms: coordinate, inclusive, or overlapping authority. Each model represents the possible types of relationships that exist between governmental institutions.

The first of these configurations is the coordinate authority model, represented in Figure 6.4. The coordinate authority model implies that national, state, and local governments are independent and autonomous (Wright, 2000, p. 75).

The second configuration of intergovernmental relations is the inclusive authority model, represented in Figure 6.5 as a series of nested, essentially hierarchical relations between levels of government.

The inclusive authority model implies that national governments exist as the principals over state and local governments, implying a hierarchical network arrangement (Wright, 2000, p. 79). Under this view, states exist as "administrative districts" for federally established policies (Wright, 2000, p. 82).

The third model of intergovernmental relations suggests that the different levels of government exist as arenas of overlapping authority, a configuration that is represented in Figure 6.6.

Wright (2000, p. 84) outlines the three critical characteristics of this particular model:

1. Substantial areas of governmental operations involve national, state, and local governments simultaneously.
2. The areas of autonomy between levels of government are comparatively small.
3. The power and influence available to any one jurisdiction is significantly limited.

Table 6.4 Network Type, Causes, Functions, and Trends

Type of Network	Cause for Network Formation	Policy Stream Function(s)	Trends Impacting Their Formation	Type of Intersector Ties	Macro-Level Governance Structure
Inter-governmental networks	Networks that persist across inter- and intragovernmental relations	All	Devolution; partnership	Public-Public	Lead organization; shared governance (for overlapping authority model)
Interest group coalitions	Designed to influence the framing of public problems and derivation of policy solutions	Problem framing; policy planning and design; policy coordination; political alignment	Devolution; partnership	Nonprofit-nonprofit; private-private; private-nonprofit → Public	Shared governance; network administrative organization
Regulatory subsystems	Structured through regulations	Policy implementation—regulation; political alignment	Regulate; partnership; privatize (nationalize)	Public-private	Lead organization
Grant and contract agreements	Structured through grant and contract agreements	Policy implementation—service delivery; political alignment	Privatize; partnership; devolution	Public-nonprofit; public-private	Lead organization
Public-private partnerships	Formed when organizations from different sectors partner with each other to achieve public purposes	All	Privatize; partnership; devolution (nationalize)	Public-private-nonprofit	Shared governance; network administrative organization

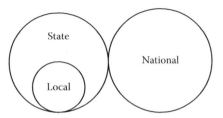

Figure 6.4 Coordinate authority model of intergovernmental relations. (Adapted from Wright, 2000.)

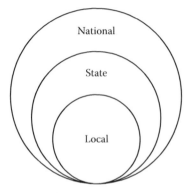

Figure 6.5 Inclusive authority model of intergovernmental relations. (Adapted from Wright, 2000.)

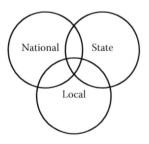

Figure 6.6 Overlapping authority model of intergovernmental relations. (Adapted from Wright, 2000.)

Wright notes that overlapping authority is established through substantial nego-tiation and bargaining. Federalism requires that governments of different scales cooperate with one another. Writing of the existence of such "cooperative federal-ism," Jane Perry Clark (1938) first recognized that

> much of the cooperation between federal and state governments has been found in the sea of governmental activity without any chart, com-pass, or guiding star, for cooperation has been unplanned and uncor-related with other activities of government even in the same field. Nevertheless, a *certain number of patterns* may be traced in the confu-sion. Cooperation has frequently been a means of coordinating the use of federal and state resources, of eliminating duplications in activity, of cutting down expenses, of accomplishing work which could not other-wise be carried out, and in general of attempting to make the wheels of government in the federal system of the United States move more smoothly than would otherwise be possible. (Agranoff and McGuire, 2003, pp. 37–38)

The articulation of power between levels of government is highly dependent on the context. Matters of constitutional law, for instance, take precedence over laws established at the local level, suggests the nested hierarchy found in Figure 6.5. In other areas, states are independent of federal authority, as in the case of determin-ing marriage rights, the setting of land use and zoning policies, etc. In still other cases, the federal government attempts to influence state and local polices with the powers of the purse.

Consider the matter of public education vis-à-vis intergovernmental relations. In the United States, states and localities are chiefly responsible for educating youth. In most communities in the United States, property taxes paid to towns and cities are coupled with federal (and some state) funds to pay for schools. Local school boards are often elected and charged with the fiduciary responsibility to ensure that a quality education is provided to all children. In the case of education, the federal government has somewhat limited authority. It may use the policy tools at its disposal, particularly block grants, as an incentive for state and local compli-ance. The federal government cannot mandate what schools teach and how they teach it. In essence, the federal government must rely on the networks that are structured through the flow of block grants to state governments and local school districts to exercise its power. This example illustrates the overlapping authority model. These contextually driven variations are outcomes very similar to what network theorists refer to as complex and adaptive systems, a subject that we will explore in Chapter 7.

The distribution of power across intergovernmental relations has been the subject of political reforms over the years. Devolution is the transfer of gover-nance responsibility for specified functions to subnational levels, either publicly or privately owned, that are largely outside the direct control of the central government. Devolution is used to describe the shift toward administrative decentralization, which transfers specific decision-making powers from one level of government to another (which could be from a lower level to a higher level of government), or government to nonprofit and private sector interests and constituencies.

Intragovernmental Relations

Network relationships are also established between institutions within a single branch of government, creating the basis for intragovernmental relations. This is most easily demonstrated in the bicameral structure of the U.S. Congress and state legislatures. The move to a bicameral Congress was another case in which the framers looked to network structures to balance power, in this case, between large and small states. The relationships between legislative houses are marked by combinations of horizontal and diagonal ties—by collaboration and cooperation as well as compromise and concession. Interagency networks may exist in the executive branch as well, as departments may collaborate or negotiate with one another around particular policy programs.

The role that intragovernmental relations plays in the design and execution of public policy and public service delivery has been described within the literature as joined-up government. The joined-up government literature is chiefly concerned with "coordination principally within a single tier of government" (Perri 6, 2004, p. 105). The nature of intra-agency coordination and collaboration is a topic that still demands further study. As governance agencies are asked to align practices around topics that transcend jurisdictional boundaries, the challenges and opportunities associated with joined-up government gain in importance. We suggest that these intra-agency configurations be considered as variations of the governance network form.

Interest Group Coalitions (IGCs)

Early variations of intersectoral studies focused on the "iron triangles" of congressional committees, executive branch agencies, and interest groups (Adams, 1981). Iron triangles have been historically presented as closed networks and have sometimes been referred to in the literature as "subgovernments" (Nownes, 2001, p. 198). It is an analytical construct that has fallen out of favor somewhat, following Heclo's critique that the iron triangle is too narrowly construed. The three points of the triangle are represented in Figure 6.7.

With the increasing number of organized interest groups, and the capacity of these groups to access elected officials, Heclo introduced the "issue network" as a counter to the iron triangle, viewing the issue network as temporary structures that are organized around particular interests and common agendas. When objectives

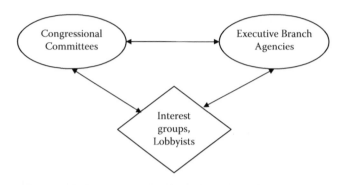

Figure 6.7   The iron triangle.

are met or conditions change, issue networks have the capacity to dissolve. Heclo's issue networks are relatively informal networks with permeable boundaries, and to an extent they possess easy entrance and exit. He originally presented the issue network as a "theory of non-structure" (Hula, 1999, p. 4), anticipating more recent interests in the self-organization and emergent qualities of complex adaptive systems. Heclo understood the issue network as social networks comprised of, essentially, policy elite. Issue networks are structured around informal, interpersonal ties that may be temporarily coordinated, if ever at all. Among the range of network types introduced within the public administration, policy studies, and governance literature, issue networks generally possess the largest number of participants and the least amount of formal coordination.* A simplified rendering of an issue network is provided in Figure 6.8.

The types of informal social networks that impact the creation of public policy have been described as networks of "interlocking directorates" that

> weld together men and women of high finance and industrial muscle who "decide" matters between themselves informally. Those decisions then have a profound impact on the economy and beyond. But how can any collective influence be effective if the power so controlled is neither

Figure 6.8   The informal configurations of issue networks.

---

* The issue network appears to be, conceptually, a scale-free form of governance network, a concept that we discussed in Chapter 5.

visible nor accountable? Indeed, how can elected representatives properly conduct their own legitimate business if they face similar obstacles?
The "establishment"—operating as a network of influential opinion
formers, agenda setters, and decision takers with a shared social, educational, and cultural background may act to usurp and undermine
genuine democratic government. (Thompson, 2003, p. 175)

Rhodes has suggested that issue networks may turn into more formalized networks. We choose to describe these networks as interest group coalitions that are
interorganizational networks of organized interest groups, advocacy organizations,
and collective interest groups engaged in coordinated action to influence the framing of public problems, the design and selection of policies, or the evaluation of
policy implementation. Discussing the proliferation of interest group coalitions
in legislative processes, Hula has noted that "a cursory glance through almost
any account of how a bill became law is likely to reveal a detailed description of
the coalitions that supported or opposed the legislation" (Hula, 1999, p. 22). He
goes on to add that "[they] are arguably the central method for aggregating the
viewpoints of organized interests in American politics. They serve as institutional
mediators reconciling potentially disparate policy positions, in effect 'predigesting'
policy proposals before they are served to the legislature" (Hula, 1999, p. 7).

Interest group coalitions operate to influence the development of public policy
by advocating for the existence or severity of certain public problems, calling for the
use of particular policy tools, or offering suggestions regarding how policies should
get coordinated. The interest group coalition also exists to align political actors into
a coherent and more powerful interest group.

There is reason to suggest that over the last few decades, the number and influence of interest group coalitions has risen. As evidence of this, Hula (1999) points
to the growth in the number of national associations in the United States, from
5,000 in 1955 to over 23,000 in 1999. A basic interest group coalition configuration is represented in Figure 6.9.

The basic interorganizational network structure of an interest group coalition is
one of formal or semiformal ties between various constituencies who join together
around common goals and interests they share. The ties between these constituencies
may be formalized through the development of a network administrative organization (NAO) designed to pursue the aims of the coalition (Provan and Kenis, 2007).

Figure 6.9 provides a possible governance structure for an interest group coalition organized by an NAO. Most trade associations fit such a structure, with the
trade association itself representing a formalized and permanent NAO. Other interest group coalitions may form an NAO to temporarily coordinate coalition activities. In these cases, we find the governance network coalescing around what Knoke
describes as the "collective action organization" (1990). It was sociologist Talcott
Parsons (1951) who first identified the role of collective action organizations as a
form of democratic association that straddle "the public and private sectors" and

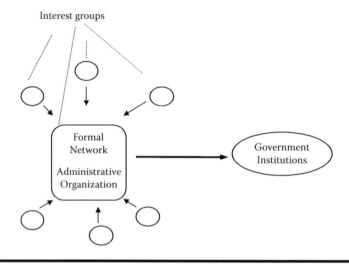

Figure 6.9 Configuration of interest group coalitions with formal network administrative structure.

"knit together the diverse institutions of modern civil society" (Knoke, 1990, p. 8). Collective action organizations are "founded on the premise of democratic member control. Ideally, officials [of a collective action organization] must attend to and be responsible to members' concerns" (Knoke, 1990, p. 15). Thus, in collective action organizations, the members of the interest group coalition share authority over the NAO with other members. Membership may be construed at the individual person level (as, for instance, when an individual person joins the Sierra Club) or organizational level (as in the case when individual corporations join a trade association to represent their interests). *The NAO is not, unto itself, the governance network*—an assertion that carries for any NAO in any governance network. Rather, the governance network gets recognized as the composite of the members of the collective action organization and the horizontal ties that the collective action organization forges with governments.

Although the formation of interest groups has long been hailed as a virtue of democratic societies, the growth of interest group coalitions and advances in their capacities to coordinate collective action and influence problem framing and policy creation have raised some serious concerns about the extent to which collective action organizations actually represent a coherent set of collective interests. In Crenson and Ginsberg's (2002) book, *Downsizing Democracy: How America Sidelined its Citizens and Privatized Its Public*, they track the evolution of collective action organizations from their early reliance on the active involvement of grassroots constituencies to "member-less" collective action organizations that rely on mass mailing lists, interpersonal social ties with people in position of power in the government, and the courts to exert influence. In these cases, the NAOs responsible for coordinating network actions become the principal actors, harnessing the legitimacy that comes with representing collective interests without having to be held accountable to those collective interests. The extent to which a collective action organization represents the actual interests of its individual members is a matter that we will be discussing in the context of the democratic anchorage of the governance network.

Regulatory Subsystems (RSSs)

The relationships forged between regulators and regulated entities take on network configurations that we describe as regulatory subsystems. The traditional outlook on regulatory subsystems places government regulators as the principals over regulated agents. These traditional ties are grounded in the state's capacity to render coercive power to control the behaviors of regulated agents. Today, governments most often play the role of lead organization, responsible for regulating the social, economic, and environmental behaviors of those defined as the regulated agents. A traditional structure of a regulatory subsystem as a hierarchical configuration is represented in Figure 6.10.

Jonathan Koppell describes the regulatory authority of governments along the lines of unified or divided concentration of regulatory authority, single-headed or multiheaded structures of agency leadership, and single- or multipurpose scope of regulatory authority (2003, p. 150). The points he makes regarding the nature of regulatory oversight suggest that regulatory subsystems cannot be defined in terms of a simplified principal-agent relationship, a point that we made in our discussion of vertical administrative authority in Chapter 4.

The earliest recorded efforts to protect the public's health date back to the thirteenth century, in which there is evidence of public health regulations concerning food quality in Great Britain. In the United States, the first food regulations were introduced through the Meat Inspection Act of 1907 (May, 2002). There was a growth in governmental or quasi-governmental agencies to regulate the private market during the first two-thirds of the twentieth century (Koppell, 2003; Nace, 2005).

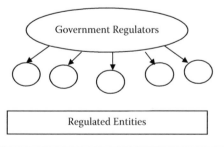

Figure 6.10   Traditional regulatory subsystem configuration.

The U.S. federal government took a more active role in the economic regulations of firms in 1887, with the introduction of the Interstate Commerce Act, initially designed to regulate the powerful railroad industry. The Interstate Commerce Act shifted the balance of power to regulate economic activities from the states to the federal government (Salamon, 2002c). States and local governments still hold onto the power to regulate industries like the telecom and utility industries. The economic regulation of markets took a firm hold as a result of the Great Depression when it became apparent that economic markets were far too sensitive to speculation and fickle investor psychology. The relative health of the market became a matter of public concern, leading to the development of regulations designed to influence the behaviors of the agricultural, airline, truck and freight, water transport, insurance, banking, and natural gas industries (Salamon, 2002c). Salamon notes that beginning in the 1970s, the use of government to regulate economic activities began to be pulled back in the United States. The deregulation of economic activities has continued on through to 2008.

Social regulations, designed to ensure food, drug, transportation, and workplace safety, have been standard features of governments' regulatory authority. Peter May defines social regulation as the rules that govern expected behaviors or outcomes; standards that serve as benchmarks for compliance; sanctions for noncompliance; and the administrative apparatuses designed to enforce sanctions (May, 2002, p. 158). Criminal and civil law are forms of social regulation. In recent years, social regulations have become more pervasive, as consumer movements have applied pressure on governments to regulate the quality of goods and services provided by corporations, firms, and businesses.

The publishing of Rachel Carson's *Silent Spring* (1962) is said to have given birth to the contemporary environmental movement. As concerns about water and air quality came to the fore, a new arena of regulation opened up. In response to the need to address the proliferation of pollutants into the environment, the Environmental Protection Agency (EPA) was created in 1970. Backed by a series of legislative acts designed to protect watersheds, oceans, and air quality, the EPA has instituted a series of environmental regulations designed to ensure that corporations stay within limits imposed by law. However, over the course of the relatively short history of the EPA, its use of coercive authority through regulation has often been a matter of last resort. Newer, self-regulation approaches to environmental regulation may be found, often relying on industries to police themselves, enter into voluntary compliance agreements, and use nonregulatory tools such as tradable permits to bring about desired behaviors.

The recent history of environmental regulation, in particular, illustrates how the interest group coalitions formed by industry have attempted to restructure the regulatory relationship between governments and industries. Crenson and Ginsberg discuss the evolving nature of regulatory systems in the quote below:

Public agencies and private interest groups discovered that they could help to resolve one another's problems. For the agencies, there was the complex task of regulating modern industries, which would have become incomparably more complex had the industries been disorganized and uncooperative. In effect, interest groups helped to prepare their industries for regulation by organizing the members into coherent and articulate alliances. The inclusion of these alliances in the regulatory process assured a high degree of voluntary compliance. [Government], for its part, used its coercive power to enforce the regulations that emerged from its deliberations with the regulated interests. If most firms cooperated with regulations, the occasional free riders who attempted to sidestep the costs of compliance in order to gain unfair competitive advantage could be targeted for regulatory sanctions. Compliant firms might therefore have some confidence that their political agreeability would not place them at an economic disadvantage with respect to lawless competitors. Voluntarism and coercion were two ends of the same bargain. (Crenson and Ginsberg, 2002, p. 122)

Recent trends across all forms of regulation have seen a move away from traditionally defined regulatory relationships, in which government serves as the principal authority over its regulated bodies, toward what may be described as more collaborative arrangements. Efforts to promote self-regulation have been common, particularly concerning environmental matters. In some aspects of food and drug regulations, the Food and Drug Administration has entered into cost-sharing agreements with the industries that they regulate (Frederickson and Frederickson, 2006). In some instances, such as the pharmaceutical industry, the regulated agent essentially pays for research on the safety and effectiveness of its own drugs (Frederickson and Frederickson, 2006).

One type of responsive regulation is "enforced self-regulation" (Ayres and Braithwaite, 1992, p. 101) or "management-based regulation" (Coglianese and Lazer, 2003). In this regulatory framework government provides broad compliance standards that organizations are expected to meet, though organizations are provided a great deal of flexibility in how they meet those standards (Hutter, 2001). The idea behind enforced self-regulation is that organizations will internalize the standards as their own, and therefore strive to comply normatively and, ultimately, voluntarily (Coglianese and Lazer, 2003).

The kind of relational ties that exist in governance networks through which self-regulating behavior is facilitated is one built around combinations of vertical and horizontal ties. These ties are presented in Figure 6.11 as a configuration of reciprocal ties between a regulator and the regulated.

The move away from coercive regulation to more voluntary forms of compliance has led some to raise concerns for the "regulatory capture" of government regulators (Pelzmen, 1976), shifting regulatory powers away from states and into the hands

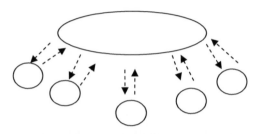

Figure 6.11   Regulatory adjustment seeking and capture.

of the regulated agents. Studies of regulatory capture have found that capture was more prevalent when one regulatory agency was responsible for overseeing a single industry (Lewis-Beck and Alford, 1980; Macey, 1992). In studying the dynamics that shape the development of regulatory subsystems, Terry Moe has gone as far as to suggest that some regulatory agencies are designed to fail (1989). Construing regulatory subsystems through the governance network framework is particularly useful in making sense of this kind of dynamics, particularly as the democratic anchorage of the governance network is considered.

We noted in Chapter 1 how the financial crisis of 2008 may be signaling a new era of regulatory practices. The extent to which the new regulatory era draws on, or reverts back to, the self-regulatory era marking the last fifty years is yet to be determined. The nationalization of the banking, parts of the auto, mortgage, and health care systems in the United States suggests the possibility of new forms of public-private partnership and hybridized arrangements.

Grant and Contract Agreements (GCAs)

During the American Revolutionary War the colonial government initiated its first contracts with seamstresses to make soldiers' uniforms (Cooper, 2003), beginning a long history of the U.S. government's reliance on private firms for the delivery of certain goods and services. Most early contracts were for the procurement of supplies and other material needs required by government. Over time, contracting out has become a widely accepted practice, used to provide a diverse array of public goods and services, ranging from sanitation services to certain features of military operations. In 1831, the Supreme Court ruled that "the government had inherent authority to contract," legitimizing a practice that had been in operation for several decades. However, it also ruled that "government could not contract away certain basic governmental power. Although we generally would include such matters as lawmaking within that restriction, the range of activities contracted out today makes the judgment about what is inherently or 'inalienable' government activity a continuing subject of debate" (Cooper, 2003, p. 28).

The privatization movement is often equated with contracting government services out to the private and nonprofit sectors. Privatization has come to mean many things, and is often aligned with the virtues of bringing market competition to the delivery of public goods and services. Privatization, simply defined, is the "enlisting [of] private energies to improve the performance of tasks that would remain in some sense public" (Donahue, 1989, p. 7). Most often, "private energies" are harnessed through the allocation of public funds to private firms and nonprofits through the policy tools of procurement and purchase of service contracts, and grants. Most procurement contracts are extended to private firms that have the capacity to deliver certain products or services to a government agency or to others on the government's behalf (Kelman, 2002, p. 282). Purchase of service contracts may be made with either for-profit or nonprofit organizations, which in turn deliver a service to an eligible group of "clients" (DeHoog and Salamon, 2002, p. 320). Grants, generally awarded to nonprofit organizations or to governments of a smaller geographical unit, are "payments from a donor government to a recipient organization or an individual," with the "aim of either 'stimulating' or 'supporting' some sort of service or activity by the recipient, whether it be a new activity or an ongoing one" (Beam and Conlan, 2002, p. 340).

Cooper recognizes that "many contracts are not simple purchases, but alliances, many involving critically important interdependent relationships between government and its contractors" (2003, p. 125). Contracts and grants are tools that structure the relationships occurring between governments and the contracted agent. As a legally binding agreement, a grant or contract binds the two parties together in a principal-agent relationship. In essence, the government, as the presumed lead organization, is said to exercise some measure of control over the contracted agent. However, for such a vertically arranged relationship to be maintained requires the contractor-contractee relationship to be robust. For a government to exert control over the contracted agent, it has to have enough administrative capacity and knowledge to do so. When governments lack the capacity to effectively manage grants and contracts, the authoritative role of government gets compromised. Power shifts to the contracted agent, who possesses more knowledge about what is happening on the ground.

Contracts and grants are also made with nonprofit and for-profit organizations because these entities are capable of filling a role or providing a service that government cannot. Thus, contracts and grants may be used as tools to develop an intersector network with the capacities to meet public needs. For the purposes of this book, we describe these kinds of network configurations as grants and contract agreements (GCAs).

Even as far back as the late 1700s, "it was becoming clear that contractors were quite willing to gouge the taxpayer and did not always live up to their promises about the level and quality of service. What we now call the problem of quality assurance, the need to guarantee, quite apart from price, that contractors deliver quality services and goods, was becoming important" (Cooper, 2003, p. 24). The principal-agent

OTHER MODELS USED TO CHARACTERIZE CONTRACT RELATIONSHIPS

Top-down model: "Based on two normative premises: that the federal system must be considered as a single system and that the de facto interdependence of the federal system mandates the application of executive-centered logic to the system."

Donor-recipient model: Involves "grantors and grantees based on actors within a collaborative system who depend on one another instead of operating by control at the top of the system. It recognizes that program collaborators must rely on each other within the parameters of a program that involves varying degrees of mutual, two-party control."

Source: **Agranoff and McGuire,** *Collaborative Public Management: New Strategies for Local Governments*, **Georgetown University Press, Washington, DC, 2003, pp. 56, 59.**

problem that we touched on in Chapter 4 can lead to information asymmetries and a shift in power. When government principals are not adequately staffed to monitor grants and contracts, the efficiencies once ascribed to the move to privatize government services get lost. As more complex and politically sensitive services get contracted out, such as in cases of intelligence and military security, the potential loss of democratic anchorage and public accountability becomes a serious concern.

Public-Private Partnerships (PPPs)

Public-private partnerships (PPPs) are a relatively recent development in governance network structures and have been described as cooperative ventures between states and private businesses. We define PPPs as strategic alliances between public, private, and nonprofit sector entities in which risk is shared and power between the partnering entities is relatively distributed in nature. PPPs are typically formed to "increase the scale and visibility of program efforts, to increase support for projects, and to leverage capital to enhance feasibility, speed, or effectiveness" (O'Toole, 1997, p. 46).

PPP arrangements differ from public goods and services grants and contract agreements (GCAs). In GCAs, resource exchanges occur between governmental principals and their contracted agents, with governments providing funding and oversight, and the contracted agent providing either goods or services. In PPPs, resource exchanges are more complexly arranged. Nongovernmental actors bring additional resources to a PPP: financial capital or the skills and expertise of their human capital. In PPPs, risks may be more equitably distributed across all individual network members.

PPPs may take on structures that are shaped, in large part, by the scope, scale, and policy arenas in which the PPP is operating. PPPs are created to provide services that meet public needs, such as public information campaigns, monitoring and research activities, and collaborative planning processes. Such projects may be carried out at local, small scales or large, international scales. These kinds of PPPs do not require the involvement of governments. However, government agencies may provide funding to support the coordination of the PPP. In still other cases, government may be an equal partner in a collective undertaking. Linder and Rosenau define partnering in this context as

> sharing of both responsibility and financial risk. Rather than shrinking government in favor of private-sector activity through devolution of public responsibility, or other forms of load-shedding, in the best of situations partnering institutionalizes collaborative arrangements where the difference between the sectors becomes blurred. (Linder and Rosenau, 2000, p. 6)

PPPs are also created to undertake large, capital improvement projects in which "at least one government unit, and a consortium of private firms" are "created to build large, capital-intensive, long-lived public infrastructure, such as highway, airport, public building, or water system, or to undertake a major civic redevelopment project." In such instances, "private capital and management of the design, construction, and long term operation of the infrastructure are characteristic of such projects, along with eventual public ownership" (Savas, 2005, pp. 15–16).

PPPs may be considered variations of "cross-sector collaborations." John Bryson, Barbara Crosby, and Melissa Middleton Stone synthesized the literature concerning the factors that contribute to the development of collaborative partnerships between two or more organizations from different social sectors. They define the cross-sector collaboration as "the linking or sharing of information, resources, activities, and capabilities by organizations in two or more sectors to achieve jointly an outcome that could not be achieved by organizations in one sector separately" (Bryson, Crosby, and Stone, 2006, p. 44). They lay out a series of propositions relating to the development of cross-sector collaborations that provide an initial look into the factors that give rise to the use of partnership development as a strategy. These propositions are laid out in Table 6.5.

The network configurations that arise in PPPs may take several forms. Because of the extensive need for coordination within most PPPs, either an NAO or lead organization structure is likely to be adopted. Quasi-public-private organizations, committees, or authorities may be charged with coordinating the PPP. Government

Table 6.5 Bryson, Crosby, and Stone's Design and Implementation Propositions for Cross-Sector Collaborations

Proposition 1	Like all organizational relationships, cross-sector collaborations are more likely to form in turbulent environments. In particular, the formation and sustainability of cross-sector collaborations are affected by driving and constraining forces in competitive and institutional environments.
Proposition 2	Public policy makers are most likely to try cross-sector collaborations when they believe the separate efforts of different sectors to address a public problem have failed or are likely to fail, and the actual or potential failures cannot be fixed by the sectors acting alone.
Proposition 3	Cross-sector collaborations are more likely to succeed when one or more linking mechanisms, such as powerful sponsors, general agreement on the problem, or existing networks, are in place at the time of their initial formation.
Proposition 4	The form and content of a collaboration's initial agreements, as well as the processes used to formulate them, affect the outcomes of the collaboration's work.
Proposition 5	Cross-sector collaborations are more likely to succeed when they have committed sponsors and effective champions at many levels who provide formal and informal leadership.
Proposition 6	Cross-sector collaborations are more likely to succeed when they establish—with both internal and external stakeholders—the legitimacy of collaboration as a form of organizing, as a separate entity, and as a source of trusted interaction among members.
Proposition 7	Cross-sector collaborations are more likely to succeed when trust-building activities (such as nurturing cross-sectoral and cross-cultural understanding) are continuous.
Proposition 8	Because conflict is common in partnerships, cross-sector collaborations are more likely to succeed when partners used resources and tactics to equalize power and manage conflict effectively.
Proposition 9	Cross-sector collaborations are more likely to succeed when they combine deliberate and emergent planning; deliberate planning is emphasized more in mandated collaborations, and emergent planning is emphasized in nonmandated collaborations.

Table 6.5 Bryson, Crosby, and Stone's Design and Implementation Propositions for Cross-Sector Collaborations (Continued)

Proposition 10	Cross-sector collaborations are more likely to succeed when their planning makes use of stakeholder analysis, emphasizes responsiveness to key stakeholders, uses the process to build trust and the capacity to manage conflict, and builds on distinctive competencies of the collaborators.
Proposition 11	Collaborative structure is influenced by environmental factors such as system stability and the collaboration's strategic purpose.
Proposition 12	Collaborative structure is likely to change over time because of ambiguity of membership and complexity in local environments.
Proposition 13	Collaboration structure and the nature of tasks performed at the client level are likely to influence a collaboration's overall effectiveness.
Proposition 14	Formal and informal governing mechanisms are likely to influence collaborative effectiveness.
Proposition 15	Collaborations involving system level planning activities are likely to involve the most negotiation, followed by collaborations focused on administrative level partnerships and service delivery partnerships.
Proposition 16	Cross-sector collaborations are more likely to succeed when they build in resources and tactics for dealing with power imbalances and shocks.
Proposition 17	Competing institutional logics are likely within cross-sector collaborations and may significantly influence the extent to which collaborations can agree on essential elements of process, structure, governance, and desired outcomes.
Proposition 18	Cross-sector collaborations are most likely to create public value when they build on individuals' and organizations' self-interests and each sector's characteristic strengths while finding ways to minimize, overcome, or compensate for each sector's characteristic weaknesses.

Source: Bryson et al., *Public Administration Review,* 66, 44–55, 2006. Printed with permission from Blackwell Publishing.

units, for-profit firms, or nonprofit organizations may serve as lead organizations in some PPP configurations. Depending on the flow of resources and collective norms developed in the PPP, all types of relational ties (vertical, horizontal, and diagonal) may be found. In cases of extensive investments of capital, PPP arrangements may be formalized through the eventual use of contracts to specify roles, responsibilities, and resource exchanges. Thus, grants and contracts are policy tools that can be applied to PPPs.

Challenges associated with PPPs often center on questions of risk, and which sectors or levels of scale are to shoulder the financial burdens of the more capital intensive PPP projects. Questions of who takes credit (or blame) for PPP successes and failures may arise. If principal funders exist, the amount of influence they wield may be questioned. A significant amount of bargaining and negotiation is often called for. The capacity for particular interest groups to enter into PPPs with an eye toward achieving individual gains is very real. These dynamics may be understood as a matter of who benefits from PPPs projects and how accountability gets rendered within and across them.

Regional and Geogovernance (GG)

It is useful here to briefly discuss a fifth kind of governance network configuration that represents an emergent form of governance networks that operate without borders. Of particular interest among some scholars is the emerging pattern of both regional governance (Miller, 2002) and global governance organizations (GGOs). As challengers to the territorial jurisdiction, both global governance organizations and regional governing institutions are examples, albeit different forms, of what Gilles Paquet (2005) refers to as geogovernance.

What geogovernance institutions hold in common are their cross-boundary characteristics and operations. Jonathan Koppell (2003) refers to global governance organizations as "hybrid" or "quasi-governments" that are quite prevalent and perform critical system-connecting functions. While critically important, these hybrid governments and administrative operations have a very different form of democratic anchorage than institutions that are territorially bounded. These institutions are subject to the accountability tensions addressed later in this book and can be viewed as lacking authority because they lack traditional forms of accountability.

The movement toward metropolitan regionalism as depicted in the work of David Miller (2002)—metropolitan councils of government, region-wide special districts, city-county mergers, metropolitan consolidations—is becoming prevalent and represents attempts to deal with jurisdictional fragmentation that is apparent in metropolitan regions and the general disconnect between jurisdictions and region-wide social, economic, and infrastructure problems. These regional associations often lack similar support as the hybrid institutions discussed above due to nontraditional accountability foundations and authority.

An important version of governance network configuration that emphasizes contemporary urban regions is the concept of "urban regimes" (Stone, 1989). The attractiveness of this concept for the study of governance networks is the urban regime focus on the inclusion of urban network actors beyond the government in the shaping of policy. These network actors may be narrowly defined, as in descriptions of alliance with powerful local and national economic interests, or broadly defined, as a coalition of private, public, nonprofit, and broader civic interests. For Stone, a regime "is specifically about the informal arrangements that surround and complement the formal workings of government authority" (p. 3) … "[they are] informal arrangements by which public bodies and private interests function together in order to be able to make and carry out governing decisions" (Stone, 1989, p. 6). Regimes involving "informal modes of coordinating efforts across institutional boundaries are what [he calls] 'civic cooperation.'" (Stone, 1989, p. 5). Of importance here in terms of network configuration are both the cross-jurisdictional and potentially broad representative nature of the urban regime. Regime theory (Stoker, 1995) offers the promise of understanding how urban stakeholders are interdependent in addressing common, cross-jurisdictional social and economic issues.

Thus, a central feature of geogovernance is the disconnection between locally established forms of accountability and the cross-boundary and lateral forms of operation and cooperation that operate in these institutions. In essence, politics is very much jurisdictional, while administration is interdependent. The challenge of bureaucracies operating without borders is the lack of institutional accountability because "geo-governance authority is essentially borrowed from member organizations … but represents a different kind of legitimacy based on a complex array of administrative accountability standards" (Frederickson and Meek, 2008). However, as these forms become more frequently employed, Paquet (2005) argues that the emerging forms of geogovernance will represent opportunities for new forms of collaboration and competition across jurisdictional and national interests.

Network Structures: A Review

In this chapter we have introduced a set of structural characteristics that maybe used to describe structural configurations at the network-wide level. We began by noting that governance networks are, by definition, implicated in either the preenactment, enactment, or postenactment of certain policy tools. Following Lester Salamon and his colleagues, we explored the relationship between policy tool characteristics and the structural configurations of governance networks. We then introduced Michael Provan and Patrick Kenis's framework of network governance, suggesting that this typology is useful in describing macro-level network structures. We then discussed five major forms of governance network configurations found within the literature. We noted how these configurations distinguish themselves by their place within the policy stream, the type of macro-level governance structures they take on, and their sectoral composition.

Although we have broken policy tools, macro-level network governance structures, and different types of network configurations down into discrete types, e.g., we distinguished between types of policy tools, governance structures, and network configurations, we need to consider the extent to which a particular governance network possesses more than one policy tool, more than one simple governance structure, and more than one type of configuration. The policy tools and instrument literature is clear in positing that policy tools are rarely offered independently of one another. Salamon refers to them as a suite of policy tools (2002a).

Some governance networks are quite extensive, possessing more than one center of power or activity, possessing pockets of self-governance, and other instances of lead organization behavior. Likewise, we may find instances of when a governance network can be described as a PPP or as a grant and contract agreement, or a regulatory subsystem that exhibits qualities of an interest group coalition. As we consider governance networks as existing in time and space, we must consider how the various combinations of structural forms discussed in the chapter evolve over time. Governance networks exhibit these qualities because they are complex, dynamic systems.

Over the course of the last several chapters we have steadily broadened our scope, beginning with the characteristics of individual network actors, to the kind of ties they have between them, and then in the last two chapters, the types of functions and structures governance networks take on. Although we have generally extended our view from the micro to the macro, we need to apply an additional descriptive layer to our architecture. So far, we have been describing network structures as being brought to life through a complex array of resource exchanges and collective actions orchestrated between certain configurations of policy actors. We now must turn our attention to describing governance networks in terms of their systems dynamics. In Chapter 7 we describe systems dynamics in terms of boundaries and borders, open and closedness, and feedback loops and logic models. In subsequent chapters on public management, accountability, and performance, we must rely on a combination of network analogies discussed in Chapters 3 to 6, and systems concepts that we will discuss in the next chapter.

CRITICAL QUESTIONS AND CONSIDERATIONS

With this chapter we can now begin to address governance network questions in regard to the role the network plays in terms of system-wide functions the network performs.

Revisit the governance network that you have been tracking.

- How is the network governed? Does it have a lead organization? A network administrative organization? A shared governance structure? Does the governance network have more than one of these structures operating?
- What policy tools or instruments are evident within the governance network? Are these tools and instruments used as an input into the network or as the objective of (an outcome of) the network? How do the properties of the tools or instruments impact which actors participate in the network? To what extent do policy tools help to structure the network? In other words, what is the relationship between the policy tools and the network structures?
- Describe the governance network in terms of one of the five network configurations introduced toward the end of the chapter. To what extent does your network exhibit more than one of these configurations.

Chapter 7

Governance Networks as Complex Systems Dynamics

How do you hold a hundred tons of water in the air with no visible means of support? You build a cloud.

—K. C. Cole (1999, p. 6)

In this chapter we describe governance networks in terms of complex systems dynamics. The application of systems frameworks to the description of governance networks allows for the consideration of external variables that help shape the structure and functions of governance networks. Systems dynamics have been characterized as a series of inputs, processes, outputs, and outcomes. A systems perspective also allows for the characterization of both positive and negative feedback that contribute to the regulation and governance of governance networks (Baumgartner and Jones, 1993).

Systems theory has become a widely utilized framework for understanding organizations and social networks. Systems metaphors and concepts have been used across the natural and social sciences. Although there is some controversy around who originated systems theory, Ludwig von Bertalanffy is often credited with introducing general systems theory to English-speaking audiences (Midgley, 2000; Hammond, 2003).

Systems theory has been used substantially across organizational psychology (Katz and Kahn, 1978; Mintzberg, 1979, 1983), organizational evaluation and intervention (Midgley, 2000), and management and organizational development (Scott, 1987; Senge, 1990). In public administration and policy studies, systems concepts have been applied to policy processes and subsystems (Baumgartner and Jones, 1993), the articulation of governance systems (Pierre and Peters, 2005), and the study of emergency management networks (Comfort, 2002). Systems concepts are embedded in the performance measurement literature, particularly when the "standard vernacular" of process, output, and outcome measures is used (Frederickson and Frederickson, 2006). Systems concepts also enter into the literature pertaining to organizational learning (Senge et al., 1994; Argyris and Schon, 1995) and descriptions of how knowledge is managed across systems and subsystems (McNabb, 2007). Systems have been ascribed to the group (Senge et al., 1994), organizational (Katz and Kahn, 1978; Mintzberg, 1979; Scott, 1987), and interorganizational (Mintzberg, 1983; Comfort, 2002) levels.

There is a great deal of overlap between network and systems theory and concepts. Our discussion of multiple social scales, multiplex social ties, and operational and policy functions has been presented in light of assumptions regarding the relationships between parts of a network and the network as a whole. The principles of network holism discussed earlier in this chapter are, essentially, assumptions derived from the basic tenants of systems analysis. Governance networks have boundaries and relationships with their external environments. They are shaped by input-output flows and feedback mechanisms. Governance networks are systems whose internal operations are shaped by forces and factors that occur as systems dynamics.

Systems dynamics may be distinguished from network dynamics by shifting frames of reference. The kinds of network concepts we discussed in previous chapters presented network dynamics as the accumulation of relationships between a complex array of social actors and ties. Our discussion of the kinds of functions taken on across a governance network shifts our focus toward the kind of processes that contribute to the joint productions of common goals, aligned practices, and collective products—outputs as well as outcomes. A systems view moves us from thinking of networks as a "tinker toy" configuration of nodes and links, to cycles of events and processes that materialize as the result of networked interactions.

In their classic text *The Social Psychology of Organizations*, Daniel Katz and Robert Kahn provide an extensive introduction of general systems theory to the social sciences. In describing how organizations are systems, they introduce a set of common characteristics found in "open" systems. They assert that "systems theory is basically concerned with problems of relationship, of structure, and of interdependence rather than with the constant attributes of objects" (Katz and Kahn, 1978, p. 24). They describe social systems as "cycles of events" that unfold between parts or subsystems of the system. When considered in terms of cycles of events, "structure is to be found in an interrelated set of events which return upon themselves to complete and renew a cycle of activities.... It is events rather than things which are structured, so that structure is a dynamic rather than static concept"

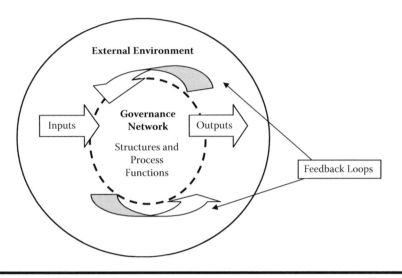

Figure 7.1   Systems dynamics impacting governance networks.

(p. 24). "Events are the observable nodal points in such cycles, and can be conceptualized as structures" (1978, p. 6).

Figure 7.1 encompasses some of the basic systems dynamics that we discuss in this section. We begin with a review of the literature pertaining to the permeability of network structures. We discuss how open social systems maintain an exchange of energy with their wider external environments and the ways in which a network's degree of openness relates to the kinds of boundaries that are established between governance networks and their external environment. The roles and influences of the external environment on a governance network are considered in light of the accountability structures that govern network actions. Figure 7.1 visually represents the relationship between a governance network and its external environment.

Systems are discussed here as relatively simplified models of reality (Miller and Page, 2007) that are arranged through a series of nested subsystems that are dynamic, adaptive, evolving, emergent, and resilient. More complex systems, which most governance networks are, defy simple linear explanation (Meadows, 2008).

Open social systems receive inputs from the external environment, which in turn shape the range of internal processes and functions taken on by different configurations of network actors. These inputs may be classified as capital resource inflows. We tie the processes and practices carried out within the "black box" of the network back to its operational and policy functions. A governance network will generate some kinds of outputs that it shares or distributes to the external environment. These outputs may or may not lead to a set of intended or unintended consequences or outcomes. A picture of systems dynamics emerges that views them as cycles of events involving the input to throughput to output to outcome cycle that is now common in organizational evaluation and performance management literature.

We then address the role that feedback loops play in regulating the behaviors of governance networks. We discuss the role that negative and positive feedback play in "steering" networks. We then briefly touch on some of the major concepts that the complexity sciences bring to the study of complex systems. Some of these concepts include adaptation, self-organization, and emergence. We conclude with a look at the relationship between governance mechanisms and systems dynamics. We believe that this discussion of systems dynamics paves the way for our discussions of administrative, accountability, and performance considerations, all of which will be explored through the context of systems and network analysis.

Permeability and Openness of Boundaries and Borders

In applying systems concepts to the study of social organization, Katz and Kahn conclude that "living systems, whether biological organisms or social organizations, are acutely dependent of external environments," asserting that they "must be conceived as open systems" (1978, p. 208). "Unless 'energy' of some sort is imported (see Katz and Kahn, 1978) into the social system that system will tend to break down" (Peters, 2008, p. 65). According to systems theorists, "that a system is open means, not simply that it engages in interchanges with its environment, but that this exchange is an essential factor underlying the system's viability, its reproductive ability or continuity, and its ability to change" (Buckley, 1998, p. 44). The importance of the external environment to the regulation of a social system has been long recognized as an important systems feature. As Mintzberg observes, "… external controls forces the organization to be especially careful about its actions. Because it must justify its behaviors to outsiders, it tends to formalize [these external controls]" (1979, p. 290).

We have discussed the multiplexity of social ties formed between two or more nodes. We may also view social ties in terms of their permeability or openness. Strong, formal ties give rise to tight bonds between actors, making it hard to bring new actors into the network. Granovetter's classic discussion of the "strength of weak ties" is built on the premise that social systems, as living systems, will require some kind of exchange of energy or resources with their environment. Weak ties are more permeable, and in their capacity to break we find their value. Weaker ties are more amenable to the development of new ties than are stronger ties. Open systems with permeable boundaries possess a greater capacity to build bridges or links to nodes or entirely other networks. The more that a system limits its exchanges with its wider environment, the more closed and essentially bonded a network is.

Linze Schaap discusses this permeability as a matter of network closure. "Closure," he observes, "occurs when certain actors are excluded from the interaction, for example because other actors fail to appreciate their contribution or dislike their presence and attendance" (Schaap, 2008, p. 118). He distinguishes between two kinds of closure: social and cognitive (Schaap, 2008, p. 119). "Social closure or exclusion means that actors are excluded from the interaction, excluded from membership of the governance network." Social closure is related to the capacity of the governance network to include or exclude members. Schaap suggests that cognitive closure can occur "when knowledge, information, ideas, or proposals are ignored and denied access to the agenda" (Schaap, 2008, p. 120). Cognitive closure may exist even when social openness between parts of the system exists.

Schaap suggests that when closure is used to create social exclusion it can be applied as a conscious and unconscious strategy (Schaap, 2008, p. 119). The capacity of a governance network to regulate its borders matters a great deal. "Closedness implies that steering signals [generated from the outside] do not penetrate into the system" (Kickert and Koppenjan, 1997, p. 55). The role of "steering signals" from their external environments is particularly relevant when accountability and governance structures are considered. Systems theory views these signals as feedback, a topic we will turn to later in this section.

The open or closed nature of governance networks may be found in discussions of differences between iron triangles, issue networks, and policy communities. Criticizing the iron triangle as being too closed and narrowly construed, Hugh Heclo posited the issue network to account for the relatively scale-free and open nature of policy networks. He defined issues networks as being comprised of "a large number of participants with quite variable degrees of mutual commitment or of dependence on others in their environment.... Participants move in and out of networks constantly" (Heclo, 1978, pp. 102–3). "Issue networks tend to be the broadest, most extensive, and evanescent of the various kinds of networks" found in the public administration and policy literature (Gage, 1990, pp. 130–31). The clash or complementarily of interests between potential policy actors serves as the primary coupling force in scale-free issue networks. According to Koppenjan and Klijn (2004), scale-free issue networks form:

1. When the need for interaction arises for the first time between actors who were not previously aware of their mutual dependencies
2. When new problems or actors manage to penetrate existing networks, thus creating chaos so that new forms of consensus must be developed in order to tackle previously unknown, politicized problems, or to enable interaction between old and new participants
3. When problems cut across networks so that actors from different networks must learn to interact with one another (Koppenjan, 2008, p. 145)

Issues networks arise when two or more policy actors recognize the mutual dependencies that develop when conditions change, ill-structured, wicked problems materialize, or as the result of the fragmentation of an existing network. Issue networks may evolve into more formalized and closed policy communities (Rhodes,

1997). Policy communities tend to include "limited numbers of participants and a conscious exclusion of some groups" (Schaap, 2008, p. 112). Because of their closed nature, policy communities may tend to favor the status quo. In essence, policy communities tend to exhibit the closed qualities of iron triangles, but involve a potentially wider array of policy actors.

We suggest that governance networks exhibit qualities of openness and closedness that will likely be structured through a variety of boundary-forming and boundary-brokering activities, which in turn will likely have differential effects on the level of policy change from the status quo (Adams and Kriesi, 2007). This view of the permeability of governance network boundaries also allows for the possibility that some parts of the network may exhibit greater degrees of openness or closedness than others.

System Boundaries

Boundaries, "no matter how negotiable or unspoken—refer to discontinuities, to lines of distinction between inside and outside, membership and non-membership, inclusion and exclusion" (Wenger, 1998, pp. 119–20). Boundaries appear in their most reified, official forms when the roles and capacities of particular network actors are distinguished or differentiated from one another. Boundaries form when some measure of autonomy of the individual network actors is preserved. The old adage that good fences make good neighbors is salient here (Kettl, 2006). The walls that are erected between actors allow for each actor to maintain its identity (Wenger, 1998), and likely manage its functions and stocks of resources independently from the network as a whole, or at least to a certain extent.

We again note Donald Kettl's observations regarding the importance that boundaries and boundary formation play in the administration of democratic governments when he asserts:

> The Constitution—in its drafting, its structure, and its early function—was a remarkable balancing act of complex issues, political cross-pressures, and boundary-defined responses. The boundaries were flexible because firm ones would have shredded the fragile coalition at the core of the new republic. For generations since, flexible, bend-without-breaking boundaries have been the foundation of American government. (2006, p. 11)

Kettl renders this observation during a time when the traditional, hierarchical boundaries of public bureaucracies are being broached by a cacophony of interorganizational governance networks that are bringing a host of new private and nonprofit actors into the spheres of governance. The range of border-blurring activities taking place leads Kettl to be less concerned about their existence per say. Rather, we need to determine which boundaries matter, how walls are erected, and to what extent the inevitable trade-offs matter when boundaries are drawn and redrawn.

From a systems perspective, we may articulate the difference between the boundaries internal to the governance network and those that are external to it. Internal boundaries will likely be influenced by the nature of the multiplex ties formed between actors in the network. Boundaries may also form around particular role and functional differentiations that give a governance network its internal dynamic structure. In interorganizational networks like governance networks, boundaries will likely form around organizational and institutional distinctions as well as discrete operational, policy, and domain functions. We have briefly touched on a few of the differences when discussing the differences that sector goals play in determining which boundaries, and by inference, which accountability and performance measures, matter and why.

The external boundaries of a governance network may be very difficult to discern. Determining who is a member of the governance network or not may be difficult to tell, particularly in those governance networks with informal structures. If a governance network takes on some of the scale-free qualities of issue networks, it may be virtually impossible to determine where the network ends and its external environment begins. Interest group coalitions and public-private partnerships may exhibit some of these qualities, particularly if there are few restrictions placed around who may participate in them.

"Border disputes" are perhaps most common when changes in intergovernmental jurisdiction exist. We have already noted how the structures and functions of intergovernmental and intragovernmental relations are subject to legislative or executive mandates, or the rise of wicked problems. We may point to the shifting nature of federalism and devolution as instances of the former, and the challenges of intergovernmental coordination following the landfall of Hurricane Katrina in 2005 (Cigler, 2007b) as an example of the latter. We also find the challenges associated with blurring borders across social sectors in the housing and banking crisis of 2008, during which debates concerning the nationalization of previously held private assets took place.

At the other end of the spectrum, as in cases of regulatory subsystems or grants and contract agreements, the boundaries of the governance network may be prescribed in the language of enabling legislation, written regulations, or contracts. In these cases, the boundaries of the network will likely exhibit more barriers to entry, as there are, after all, usually a limited number of grants or contracts to be let, or a ridged set of criteria determining which entities need to be the subject of regulatory oversight.

Katz and Kahn observe that

> system boundaries refer to the types of barrier conditions between the system and its environment that make for degrees of system openness. Boundaries are the demarcation lines or regions for the definition of appropriate system activity, for admission of members into the system,

and for other imports into the system. The boundary constitutes a barrier for many types of interaction between people on the inside and people on the outside, but it includes facilitating devices for the types of transactions necessary for organizational functioning. (Katz and Kahn, 1978, pp. 65–66)

There are several systems concepts that are important to determining how and to what extent boundaries are erected and, ultimately, broached. "Boundary objects" have been described as the "artifacts, documents, terms, concepts, and other forms of reification" that exist in social systems (Wenger, 1998, p. 105). Etienne Wenger has described boundary artifacts as the "nexus of perspectives" (1998, p. 107). Boundary artifacts may be the policy tools—the grants, contract, regulations, etc.—that dictate network membership (who is in/out), the flow of resources between actors, and how authority is structured. Boundary objectives may serve as inputs into the system or as discernable outputs of the system, particularly in cases where functions are carried out to build the capacity of others to expand and deepen ties.

A second systems concept that is important to boundaries and boundary setting is the instances in which boundaries break down, if only temporarily. Wenger refers to these as "boundary encounters" that occur when meetings and conversations are convened, and "brokering activities are allowed to take place" (1998, p. 112). It is important to note that boundary spanning occurs within the cycle of events that occurs in the social system. Boundary spanning occurs to build the internal cohesion within the governance network, as well as in instances when the governance network interfaces with its external environments.

Defining boundaries within governance networks can be a difficult task. When considered in terms of systems dynamics, Donnella Meadows observes that "there is no single, legitimate boundary to draw around a system" (2008, p. 97). Graham Thompson echoes this assertion, stating that "a network is a way of reducing the effects of certain boundaries by creating other ones. So in this approach boundaries in networks should never be conceived as given—neither in terms of the existence of actors or the boundaries they create" (Thompson, 2003, p. 232). Boundaries and borders in governance networks are defined by discontinuities between actors and subsystems. Wenger observes:

> Boundaries—no matter how negotiable or unspoken—refer to discontinuities, to lines of distinction between inside and outside, membership and nonmembership, inclusion and exclusion. Peripheries—no matter how narrow—refer to continuities, to areas of overlap and connections, to windows and meeting places, and to organized and casual possibilities for participation offered to outsiders or newcomers. (1998, p. 120)

According to systems theorist Donnella Meadows, the ties that bind subsystems together tend to be stronger than network-wide, systems-wide ties. Stronger subsystem ties are important to system-wide stability. She notes, "If subsystems can largely take care of themselves, regulate themselves, maintain themselves, and yet serve the needs of the larger system, while the larger system coordinates and enhances the functioning of the subsystems, a stable, resilient, and efficient structure results" (Meadows, 2008, p. 82). She adds that "complex systems can evolve from simple systems only if there are stable intermediate forms" (Meadows, 2008, p. 83).

Meadows cautions that "when a subsystem's goals dominate at the expense of the total system's goals, the resulting behavior is called suboptimization" (2008, p. 85). "To be a highly functional system, [there must exist a] balance [of] the welfare, freedoms, and responsibilities of the subsystems and total system—there must be enough central control to achieve coordination toward the large system goal, and enough autonomy to keep all subsystems flourishing, functioning, and self-organizing" (2008, p. 85).

Input-Output Flows

Systems theories describe the basic dynamics as the flow of inputs and outputs, which in turn give shape and function to the network (Bertalanffy, 1950). Katz and Kahn discuss the role of input and output flows as critical characteristics of open systems, noting how social systems require the importation of energy to support systems activities and how, in turn, systems export energy that becomes the requisite pool of stock resources available to other systems (1978). As cycles of events, we may dissect systems dynamics into input, process, output, and outcome functions. Breaking systems dynamics down this way is a widely accepted practice in program evaluation, manifesting in various versions of "logic models" (Poister, 2003). A version of the logic model is provided in Figure 7.2.

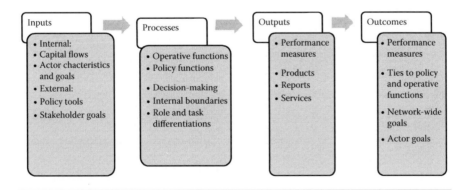

Figure 7.2   Systems logic model for governance networks.

Inputs

Although Katz and Kahn view inputs in terms of stocks and flows of energy, we have been building the case for interpreting inputs as stocks and flows of financial, knowledge, physical, human, social, natural, political, and cultural capital resources. Figure 7.2 displays the ways in which the "currencies" found in the types of capital resources flow across nodes in a social network. Capital resources were described as stocks of capital that particular network actors have available to contribute to a network. A systems view of inputs also underscores the role that resources flowing from an external environment into the governance networks can play in shaping network activities. Thus, we may view inputs that exist as internal features of a governance network. Network membership may be predicated on the depth and breadth of resources it will contribute to the operations of the whole. Inputs may also come from the external environment, passed on through to the governance network via the implementation of policy tools. For instance, a regulation formulated by an external legislative body may lead to the creation of regulatory subsystems designed around implementing their directives. External funders may contribute financial resources to the operations of governance networks without becoming a member of the network.

Inputs may also appear as goals or expressions of will, derived from either external principals or internal network members. We defined goals as abstract expressions of prescribed values and beliefs. In later chapters we interpret the goals and will of stakeholders as inputs that shape a governance network's accountability structures. We recognize that a governance network may render accounts to those internal members of the network, as well as those external to the network, such as broad swaths of atomized citizens and consumers.

Processes

Some models of input-output flows of systems describe the processes undertaken as a result of input factors comingling with actor characteristics and expressions of actors' desires and intentions as a "black box." The link between inputs and processes, described by Katz and Kahn as throughputs, is formed when an open system transforms the energy available to it. These processes "entail some reorganization of inputs" (1978, pp. 23–24). "The throughput of an organization is its responses to the objective task posed by the needs of the environment" (1978, p. 245). The processes that unfold in a governance network are often very complex. We argue that they are shaped through a combination of operative and policy functions taken on within the network; the boundaries and network configurations guiding the interactions between network actors; the roles, tasks, and actions undertaken by network actors operating individually or collectively; and the decisions made to guide these processes and direct future actions.

In the previous section we discussed the range of operative, policy stream, and policy domain functions undertaken in governance networks. We characterized these functions as types of activities undertaken by the network as a whole, or possibly by a subset of network actors. We differentiated between operative and policy functions, suggesting that the expression of operative and policy goals anticipates the kinds of processes undertaken within the system. These functions need to be treated as throughput processes of practice and participation. We will note that these functions may also, sometimes simultaneously, serve as intended system outcomes.

The processes undertaken with the governance network will be shaped by the internal governance structures (Provan and Kenis, 2007), as well as the informal and formal links between the "dominant coalitions" (Rhodes, 1997), advocacy coalitions (Sabatier and Jenkins-Smith, 1993) and "communities of practice" (Wenger, 1998) that shape the network's theories in use. We find processes shaped by the roles and tasks taken on by individual network actors as well as the manner in which decisions are made and implemented. In later chapters we will discuss these processes in terms of the administrative roles and responsibilities taken on by network managers and the collaborative dynamics that unfold between communities of practice.

Outputs

Katz and Kahn suggest that "open systems export some product into the environment" (1978, p. 24). Outputs are generally capable of being measured or counted (the number of clients served, the number of workshops put on, etc.) or represented as tangibly reified objects that represent the products of collective action (reports, plans, etc.). A variety of network outputs are described in the literature: land use plans (Koontz et al., 2004), scientific reports (Koontz et al., 2004; Agranoff, 2007), forums (Agranoff, 2007), Web sites (Agranoff, 2007), and program plans (Agranoff, 2007).

Although there has been some attention paid to process and outcome measures, the performance measurement movement has focused predominantly on the development of output measures to monitor workplace productivity. Frederickson and Frederickson (2006) have explored the role that performance measures play within governance networks operating within the health care arena, situating performance measurement within the context of descriptive (qualitative) to precise (quantitative) measures.

Outcomes

Within the logic of systems dynamics, outputs are said to contribute to short- or long-term outcomes. In the kind of governance networks that we have been exploring here, outcomes may be equated to goals and purposes. We have suggested that the goals of particular actors are brought into a network. In

Chapter 9 we discuss how actor goals relate to accountability structures. The systems outcomes implicated in governance networks may be framed in terms of meeting network-wide goals. These goals will likely be closely tied to the functions and structures operating at a network-wide level. In Chapter 10 we discuss outcome measurement as one way to describe and ultimately evaluate network performance. Significant challenges to measuring outcomes have been noted (Radin, 2006). Policy goals are often tied to vaguely worded or articulated objectives (Stone, 2002) that may only be described qualitatively, defying measurement (Radin, 2006). In formal social networks like governance networks, network outcomes are a matter best understood as a complex intersubjective terrain that is shaped through empirical evidence, social norms, and political processes. Within a systems context, this terrain may be described in terms of feedback loops.

Feedback

The concept of feedback is a critical dimension of complex system's dynamics. Most broadly, feedback is one way of characterizing the interactions between people, units, and data variables (Carver and Scheier, 1998, p. 11). Katz and Kahn view feedback as enabling a social organization to regulate its activities "on the basis of information about its functioning" (Katz and Kahn, 1978, pp. 55–56).

Figure 7.3, notes how the single loop has spaces within it for new inputs. These inputs help to control the system through feedback. In essence, feedback regulates the actions of the system. Regulation through feedback controls, in the very least, influences the behavior of the system. "Operational feedback is systemic information getting that is closely tied to the ongoing functions of the organization and is sometimes an integral part of those functions" (Katz and Kahn, 1978, p. 455).

Feedback loops are essential for maintaining the resilience of a system. Donnella Meadows has observed that "resilience is something that may be very hard to see, unless you exceed the limits, overwhelm and damage the balancing loops, and the system structure breaks down" (2008, p. 77). She goes on to add that "large organizations of all kinds, from corporations to governments, lose their resilience simply because the feedback mechanisms by which they sense and respond to their environment have to travel through too many layers of delay and distortion" (2008, p. 78). The same may be said for interorganizational dynamics as well.

A basic metaphor used to describe feedback within a system is that of the typical household heating system that regulates indoor air temperature. The thermostat takes continual readings of the air temperature. If the temperature falls below a certain threshold, a message is directed to the furnace to turn on. The regulator is the thermostat. The agent being regulated is the furnace. The outputs of the furnace not only impact the furnace's functioning, e.g., whether it will need to increase the flow of oil or natural gas, but this feedback loop has a bearing on a wider

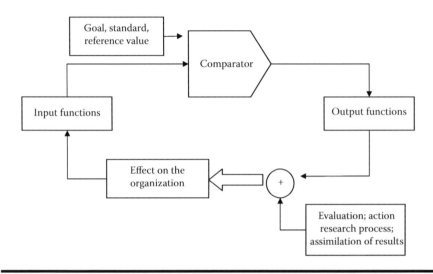

Figure 7.3 Principals of feedback control. (*Source:* Carver and Scheier, *On the Self-Regulation of Behavior*, Cambridge University Press, Cambridge, 1998, p. 11.) Printed with permission from Cambridge University Press.

environment, namely, the temperature of the house, which itself may be construed as a larger system. Figure 7.4 represents a schematic of a single-loop system.

Obviously, most systems are much more complex than systems designed to keep your home warm. Carver and Scheier point out that there may exist double- and triple-loop systems, some of which may be reinforced through a nested hierarchy of relationships. As systems add more inputs and outputs, many feedback mechanisms are at work, cycling into one another to guide the behaviors of the wider system.

Feedback operating within a system is construed as being either negative or positive in character. We should note that these labels do not carry with them value judgments—e.g., negative feedback is not, by definition, a form of feedback that is detrimental to a system's functioning. The same may be said for positive feedback. Baumgartner and Jones observe that "a complete view of the political system must include both positive and negative feedback processes because the events that make one of them possible also make the other one inevitable" (2002, p. 7).

Negative Feedback

Negative feedback is best described in terms of controls placed over the system that come into effect when the system deviates from a goal. "When a system's negative feedback discontinues, its steady state vanishes, and at the same time its boundary disappears and the system terminates" (Miller, 1955, p. 211). The example of the regulation of household ambient air temperature illustrates the case of negative feedback. The norm or threshold ambient temperature is the

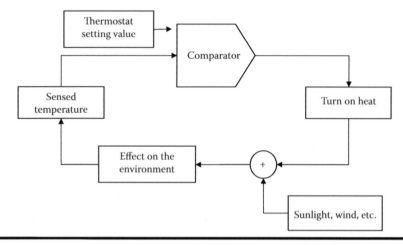

Figure 7.4 Principals of feedback control applied to home heating system. (*Source:* Carver and Scheier, *On the Self-Regulation of Behavior,* Cambridge University Press, Cambridge, 1998, p. 13.) Printed with permission from Cambridge University Press.

goal. When the room temperature as measured by the thermostat falls below the goal or temperature target, the heating system reacts by turning the furnace on. The elements of the system are altered to bring the system back into equilibrium or homeostasis. Similarly, in complex governance networks systems dealing with such policy domains as emergency management, when feedback information about the fragility or resilience of decaying infrastructure fails to reach emergency managers, exogenous shocks such as Katrina can result in system-wide collapse (Koliba, Mills, and Zia, accepted for publication).

In the realm of governance networks, negative feedback may be viewed in terms of sanctions or punishments within social systems. The use of regulations to correct deviant behaviors and the role of incentives to reward desirable behaviors are often described as some of the basic building blocks of public policy. Within the context of social systems, negative feedback may come in the form of information that is received by the system that then enables the system to correct its deviations from course. In Chapter 10 we discuss how negative feedback may be used to describe how performance measures and performance management systems may be used to regulate governance network behavior.

Positive Feedback

The central premise behind positive feedback is the notion that "success breeds success" or the "rich get richer." In essence, positive feedback operates on rewards to the system. The more profit a firm earns, the more profit it will seek to earn. "A positive feedback mechanism includes a self-referencing process that accentuates rather than counterbalances a trend" (Baumgartner and Jones, 2002, p. 13).

In describing how positive feedback unfolds within a governance network, Baumgartner and Jones observe that "positive feedback processes come about when issues are reframed, when institutional designs are altered, and when policy makers come to realize that other policy makers may be looking at old issues in new ways" (Baumgartner and Jones, 2002, p. 27).

In governance systems, positive feedback generally occurs as the result of one of two forces: mimicking and attention shifting. According to Baumgartner and Jones, mimicking "operates when people observe the behavior of others and act accordingly" (2002, p. 15). Mimicking leads to fads, cascading or bandwagon effects. Attention shifting occurs as a result of the boundary rationality of individuals, or what Herbert Simon refers to as "serial information processing" (1966). "They attend to only limited parts of the world at any given time. Since one cannot possibly simultaneously be attuned to all elements of the surrounding world, people use various informational short-cuts in order to make reasonable decisions" (Baumgartner and Jones, 2002, p. 15).

Baumgartner and Jones observe that positive feedback contributes to the coupling of policy streams. They note that conditions do not automatically translate into problems; that translation occurs when previously ignored aspects of a complex situation become salient, which occurs through the efforts of policy makers attempting to redefine public debates. They go on to add that the two mechanisms of positive feedback, mimicking and attention shifting, are "intimately related." They describe a phenomenon of how "previously ignored attributes of complex public policies become salient in a policy debate, setting off a cascade of interest through the calculations of expected action" (Baumgartner and Jones, 2002, p. 23).

The Medium of Feedback in Governance Networks

In discussing the interplay between negative and positive feedback within complex systems, Baumgartner and Jones note how Bendor and Moe (1985) have recognized "that in a negative feedback process, 'success is self-limiting' because the gains of one side lead to the mobilization of the opposing side. On the other hand, a different logic applies where positive feedback systems are operating: 'In such a world, the positive feedback of the Matthew effect—"To him who hath shall be given"—creates an unstable system of cumulative advantages' (1985, p. 771)" (Baumgartner and Jones, 2002, p. 13). Within governance networks negative and positive feedback loops combine, commingle, and sometimes counteract each other. Within governance networks, feedback gets mediated through a variety of processes, a topic that we turn to in the next section.

In social systems such as groups, organizations, and interorganizational networks communication flows through a series of nonlinear, face-to-face, and electronically mediated interactions between members of the organization, as well as with individuals and systems from outside of it. These interactions may also come in the form of written correspondence through which decisions are communicated, and through formal standards, rules, laws, and procedures in place to govern group behavior.

In social systems, feedback may be explicit or tacit. In addition to known and articulated logics used to guide group action, explicit feedback may be understood as the reified elements of an organization. Feedback manifests itself through artifacts and boundary objects, such as written rules, laws, strategic or action plans, standards, contractual agreements, and performance measures. Such artifacts may define the parameters through which feedback will be provided.

Gregory Bateson first examined the role of tacit feedback within social systems through observing the behaviors of dolphins that developed new tricks in response to changes in rewards, specifically fish. Bateson observed that they engaged what would eventually be understood as "double-loop learning" (Argyris and Schon, 1995). Many organizational development theories and frameworks have been evolved that take into account the role that tacit knowledge and communication play within organizational settings, including organizational learning and knowledge management theories. Thus, feedback may be understood as both conscious and subconscious communication within a complex system, or components of a complex system, and its environment.

Within the context of public administration, political science, and policy studies, systems of governance are regulated, and essentially governed, through a series of negative and positive feedback mechanisms that take on both explicit and implicit dimensions, as well as empirical and normative ones.

The medium through which feedback loops are communicated within governance networks takes many forms. The classical feedback mechanism within democracies is the policy tool selected by elected officials or public servants to solve a problem or, within the context of complex systems theory, achieve homeostasis within the system. The legitimacy of representative democracy and interest group dynamics hinges on the role of feedback. Anticipating the critical considerations to be covered in later chapters, we discuss how administrative dynamics, accountability, and performance management systems can be construed in terms of systems feedback.

Policy Tools and Feedback

One of the basic premises behind the policy tools framework is the sense that policy tools play a vital role in structuring governance networks, dictating collective actions, and determining resource flows. Policy tools also shape how and to what extent feedback is used within a governance network.

Within public administration, political science, and policy studies, the role of regulation is most often construed in terms of economic, environmental, and social regulation. Economic regulation is used in reference to the regulation of commercial or monetary activities. Social regulation usually takes the form of criminal and civil laws that seek to control or place parameters around social behavior and actions. Environmental regulation may exhibit qualities of both economic and social regulation that seek to promote behaviors and actions that are thought to be in the best interest of the natural environment. Within the discourses associated with public affairs, regulations are construed as policy tools (Salamon, 2002b; Howlett, 2005) that are implemented to achieve desired ends.

Other policy tools may be enacted as solutions to problems, acting as, essentially, attempts to regulate behavior and actions through incentives and sanctions. Grants and contracts are made by principals to agents who agree to terms that lead to the agent performing some service (conducting research, processing claims, collecting trash) or providing some good (photocopy paper, a fleet of vehicles, a piece of equipment). The written contract explicitly defines the parameters through which feedback will be used to regulate the grant and contract agreement.

Taxes, loans and loan guarantees, and vouchers are policies that, in essence, regulate the flow of financial resources within a governance system. Tax revenues provide the fuel through which the government functions. The intake of tax revenues gets regulated by elected officials who set tax rates and prioritize funding areas. Tax revenues provide a positive feedback mechanism for governance systems. Loans and loan guarantees and vouchers may be viewed as forms of feedback coming from government being directed at citizens. Vouchers, such as food stamps, may be awarded to citizens at a certain income threshold (gauged in terms of a determined poverty rate).

Representation and Interest Group Competition as Feedback

Representative democracy is premised on elected officials serving as surrogates for their constituencies within a legislative or executive governance network. Representatives receive feedback from their constituents, which in turn may influence their actions. If they respond adequately to this feedback, they get reelected, reaping the rewards of a classic positive feedback loop. Representatives also receive feedback from lobbyists and special interests, taking the form of campaign donations.

Baumgartner and Jones discuss how Peltzman's (1976) theory of regulatory capture represents positive feedback working within the context of interest group competition within a governance network:

> Members of these competing constituencies ... support or oppose the political decision maker depending on the action he has taken. Where the decisions veer too far in one direction, the disfavored group mobilizes to show its own power, supporting a challenging candidate, for example. With political support distributed between the two competing constituency groups, the decision maker is constrained to operate only within a certain band of action. The result is an equilibrium outcome that illustrates the negative feedback processes common to many theories of politics and policy. (Baumgartner and Jones, 2002, p. 9)

ETYMOLOGY OF GOVERNANCE

The English word *governor* stems from the Latin *gubernator* and the Greek *kybernetes* ("helmsman" or "steersman"), which in origin stem from the Latin *gubernare* and the Greek *kybernan* ("to steer" or "to govern"). The recent English word *cybernetics* shares the same etymology! Strictly or etymologically speaking, the word *governor* is therefore supposed to be a metaphor derived from *steersman* (spiritus-temporis.com/governor/etymology.html, 2009).

Acts of Administration as Feedback

In Chapter 8 we discuss the role of public administrators as critical actors managing over and within governance networks. We describe feedback in the context of the administrative authority they wield, as well as the range of administrative tools, skills, and attitudes that collaborative and networked public administrators employ within governance networks. Whether it be through the execution of oversight and mandates, resource provision, negotiation and bargaining, facilitation, brokering, or systems thinking, the skills and strategies that public administrators, operating as network managers, exercise provide opportunities for the execution of feedback, most often at the interpersonal level.

Accountability as Feedback

In Chapter 9 we define *accountability* in terms of feedback loops occurring between those to whom accounts are rendered and those rendering the accounts. We will note how and to what extent the characteristics of the accountability frame (democracy, market, and administrative) help to shape how feedback is structured and what medium through which the feedback flows—in this case, as explicit standards or implicit norms.

Performance Measurement as Feedback

In Chapter 10 we define performance measurement and management in terms of feedback loops as well. Performance management systems that are integrated into governance networks facilitate feedback loops that rely on the flow of performance data to correct for deviations and reward desired actions and behaviors. Noted system theorist Ackoff recognized that

> system performance depends critically on how the parts fit and work together, not merely on how well each performs independently; it depends on interactions rather than on actions. Furthermore, a system's performance depends on how it relates to its environment—the larger

system of which it is a part—and to other systems in that environment. (1980, p. 27)

Thus, the monitoring of system performance, both internally and externally, needs to be construed in terms of the conscious construction of data-driven and well as policy-framing feedback loops. As Beryl Radin and others have noted, just what accounts for high and low levels of performance is ultimately dictated by the construction of policy frames through an inherently political process. It is the combination of the technical capacities of data-driven decision making and the political capacities of policy actors that helps structure the feedback loops of governance networks. These feedback loops, coupled with network actor characteristics, the nature of the ties between them, network-wide characteristics, and other systems dynamics, give shape to governance as a systems construct.

The robustness of feedback loops operating within governance networks helps to dictate its stability. Baumgartner and Jones observe that "systems with more regular feedback processes built in are less likely to suffer extreme disruptions. To the extent that a system receives minor shocks on a frequent basis, it may be able to avoid major shocks" (Jones, 1994). They cite Berkamn and Reenock's research (2000), which has shown "where small-scale reforms are continually adopted, large-scale omnibus agency consolidations are less likely to occur. Where reforms are rare, they are more global when they finally do occur" (Baumgartner and Jones, 2002, p. 300). Baumgartner and Jones go on to assert that "systems designed to activate dormant interests when a system is under threat are more likely to survive more or less intact" (2002, p. 301).

Network Governance as a Systems Construct

According to the *Webster's Unabridged Dictionary*, to "govern" means "to rule by right of authority; to exercise a directing or restraining influence over; to hold in check; control" (Webster's, 1989, p. 612). An etymology of the term reveals that it stems from the Latin *guernátor* and Greek *kybernan*, meaning "to steer." The term *cybernetics* shares the same root as *govern*. The development of systems theory in the early twentieth century was undertaken with an aim toward discovering complementarity between human, mechanical, and electrical systems (Hammond, 2003). For engineers and mechanics, a "governor " is a "device used to maintain uniform speed, regardless of load." In machines, governors play the role of comparators, regulating the flow of fuel or energy into the system.

As we consider the relationship between systems dynamics and governance, we find these parallels, as well as the overlapping meanings found in the roots of the words *govern* and *governors* to possess a certain eloquence. The definition of *governance* that we are prepared to use throughout the rest of this book is therefore very much rooted in a systems framework. In this sense, governance needs to be understood in terms of the range of systems dynamics discussed in this chapter. To understand how the governance of any social structure operates, we need to clarify borders and boundaries, as well as the characteristics of these borders and boundaries, e.g., are they open or closed, permeable or impermeable? We may also ask: What are the inputs, processes, outputs, and outcomes over which, and through which, governance occurs? Lastly, we are reminded of the fact that the study of governance at the systems level can be, essentially, understood in terms of the ranges of feedback loops, cycles, and mechanisms found within the system.

A. W. Rhodes (1997) was one of the first scholars to deeply consider the relationship between governance and interorganizational networks, arguing that governance occurs as a "self-organizing phenomenon" shaped by the following characteristics:

1. *Interdependence* between organizations. Governance is broader than government, covering nonstate actors.
2. *Continuing interactions* between network members, caused by the need to exchange resources and negotiate shared purposes.
3. *Game-like interactions*, rooted in trust and regulated by the rules of the game negotiated and agreed upon by network participants.

We find elements of both classical network analysis and systems dynamics in this definition of governance. Governance is framed by the game-like interactions that give shape to the ongoing interactions of interdependent actors. These interactions are also shaped by the boundaries and borders constructed through them, inputs of resources, network-wide processes, outputs and outcomes ascribed to them, and various feedback mechanisms and loops that provide the network to self-correct and be corrected. We may construe that these three features of governance systems serve as a few of the simple rules that support the governance of complex governance networks.

Over the course of the remaining chapters, we explore governance through three frames of reference that have been advanced within the public administration and policy studies literature. We view governance in terms of the range of managerial and administrative roles and responsibilities found within the public administration field (Chapter 8). We explore how governance processes are shaped by certain sector characteristics and conclude that these characteristics need to be understood within the context of a robust accountability framework that is capable of accounting for the range of actors found within a governance network (Chapter 9). Lastly, we view governance in terms of expectations built up around performance by honing in on the potential role that performance data and performance management systems play in ensuring the governability of a governance network (Chapter 10).

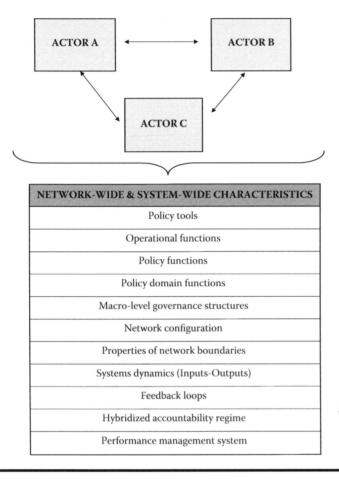

Figure 7.5   Systems, structures, and functions of whole networks.

Governance Networks as Complex Adaptive Systems

Governance networks are not simply systems, but rather *complex* systems capable of emergent qualities, adaptive to changing conditions, with the capacity to self-organize. Complex systems are "one whose component parts interact with sufficient intricacy that they cannot be predicted by standard linear equations; so many variables are at work in the system that its overall behavior can only be understood as an emergent consequence of the holistic sum of all the myriad behaviors embedded within" (Levy, 1993). Systems theory and complexity theory find a common denominator in the roles that "feedback and interactions" play as central factor in understanding society (Haynes, 2003, p. 90). Complex systems are understood as dynamic spaces governed by nonlinear processes. Donella Meadows notes, "Nonlinearities are important not only because they confound our expectations about the relationship between action and response. They are even more important because they *change the relative strength of feedback loops*. They can flip a system from one mode of behavior to another" (2008, p. 92). Thompson observes that "the non-linearity of complex systems means that small amounts of changes in inputs can have dramatic and unexpected effects on outputs" (2003, p. 136).

A central feature of complexity theory hinges on the notion that a few relatively simple rules can have tremendous effects on the behaviors of a system. These simple rules serve as the foundations of the development of "wildly diverse self-organizing structures" (Meadows, 2008, p. 80).

The consideration of governance networks as complex systems must allow for the development of the network-wide capacity to exhibit self-organizing qualities. According to Meadows, "the capacity of a system to make its own structure more complex is called self-organization" (2008, p. 79). Drawing on studies of complex adaptive systems in natural and social networks, Miller and Page suggest instances in which we "find robust patterns of organization and activity in systems that have no central control or authority. We have corporations—or, for that matter, human bodies and beehives—that maintain a recognizable form and activity over long periods of time, even though their constituent parts exist on time scales that are orders of magnitude less long lived" (Miller and Page, 2007, p. 7). In essence, we may understand self-organization as a property of both whole governance networks and particular subsystems of network actors.

Thompson applies a biological and evolutionary lens to the description of complex systems:

> Multistranded clumped networks that form a kind of non-linear (rhizome-like) organizational structure, containing different relational principles of connectivity and heterogeneity, are always "pregnant" with the possibility of breakdown and breakup, leading to new trajectories and transformations in a self-organizing framework that overcomes the twin obstacles presented by "necessary evolutionary advance" and "path-dependency." (Thompson, 2003, p. 11)

A picture of governance networks as organic, ever-evolving ecosystems of organizations, groups (which we have been referring to as communities of practice), and individuals emerges. Considering governance networks as not simply *complicated* social structures, but as *complex* social structures, brings certain distinct features into focus. Complexity, in this context, "is equated with the number of different items or elements that must be dealt with simultaneously by the organization (Anderson, 1999). But its distinctive feature is to stress the world as a system in construction, a dynamic formulation encouraging the notion of continual process of spontaneous emergence (Thrift, 1999)" (Thompson, 2003, p. 136).

Although some traditional applications of social network analysis view networks as static systems, or at least treats them as a one point in time or snap shot of reality, we have been describing governance networks as being "relatively stable and complex pattern[s] of relationships among multiple interdependent and self-organizing element which also constitutes a self-organizing system as a whole" (Morcol and Wachhaus, 2009, p. 45). Goktug Morcol and Aaron Wachhaus have compared networks and complex systems and noted their conceptual similarities "(a) ... networks and complex systems are composed of multiple interdependent components (actors or agents); (b) both are relatively stable patterns of relationships, although complex systems are defined in more dynamic terms; (c) they are [both] self-organizing." (2009, p. 46). The value of applying the network structures of nodes and ties to the relationships between active agents operating within complex adaptive systems helps to make "the abstractions used by complexity theory concrete (Carroll and Burton, 2000; Costa et al., 2007)" (Mischen and Jackson, 2008, p. 316), meaning that the application of network metaphors are particularly useful in developing a deeper understanding of complex governance networks parts and whole. This is an important consideration as we contemplate building our capacities to model complex governance networks (see Chapter 11).

The body of literature that has applied complex adaptive systems to the study of social phenomena is long and growing (see for instance Axelrod and Cohen, 1999; Marion, 1999; Haynes,2003; Miller and Page, 2007) and there are a number of key complexity concepts that are relevant to our discussion of governance networks. These concepts include the role of feedback discussed earlier in this chapter, as well as the principle of holism introduced in chapter two (Degenne and Forse, 1999). Feedback loops operating within complex adaptive systems give shape to the interactions between agents (which is different from the interactions between variables as found in traditional stock and flow systems analysis (Newell and Meek, 2005)). Those wishing to study complex adaptive systems will be careful to avoid reductionism. Marion observes that, "Reductionism does not work with complex systems, and it is now clear that a purely reductionist approach cannot be applied when studying life; in living systems the whole is more than the sum of its parts... (Marion, 1999, p. 27-28). For the study of governance networks, the implication of the complex systems approach is that both reductionist and holistic approaches can yield improved understanding of governance operations and outcomes. Both approaches can be embraced but not at the expense of the other. In addition to feedback and holism, we may describe governance networks as complex adaptive systems by noting the latent capacity for self-organization and emergence, and the potential for designing robust and resilient governance systems.

Donnella Meadow defines self-organization as the " capacity of a system to make its own structure more complex" (2008, p. 79). Complex adaptive systems scientists understand that "... just a few simple organizing principles can lead to wildly diverse self-organizing structures" (Meadows, 2008, p. 80). These self-organizing capacities are a characteristic of the non-linearity of their dynamics. Unlike the linear cause and effect models of standard systems analysis (as well as many of our statistical modeling methods), "… nonlinearity means a disproportionate relationship between variables [and agents]: a small change in one may trigger a large, disproportionate change in the other…" (Morcol and Wachhaus, 2009, p. 49). Self-organization is understood as the emergence of new structures and functions. Miller and Page suggest that "… emergence is a phenomenon whereby well-formulated aggregate behavior arises from localized, individual behavior. More over, such aggregate patterns should be immune to reasonable variations in the individual behavior" (2007, p. 46). Thus, the emergence of new patterns of organization and behavior begin "from the bottom up" at the micro level, or in the case of governance networks, interpersonal level. This is why we are quick to privilege the roles of individual network administrators (Chapter 8), "accounters and accountees" (Chapter 9), and communities of practice designed to learn from performance data (Chapter 10). Our discussion of governance network administration is very much grounded in the view that a central role of individuals is to serve as the midwives of emergent properties through the use of certain skills and strategies, accountability relationships, and performance standards.

Self-organization is also characterized as the emergence of higher level order in otherwise chaotic systems (e.g. Holland 1995, Kaufman 2004). In conventional notions of systems, more chaos is equated with more disorder at all scales. In complexity theory, unanticipated orderliness and patterns of self-organization among the interacting elements in the system could emerge out of the chaotic behavior of individual elements (nodes) in the governance systems.

It is important to note that within social systems like governance networks, emergence "occurs when learning processes exist (Holland, 1995)" (Mischen and Jackson, 2008, p. 316). The relationship between emergent forms of self-organization and learning become critically important when we consider the role that performance management systems play within governance networks. In Chapter 10 following Moynihan (2008), we argue that effective performance management systems are intentionally designed to operate within the context of network learning processes. In essence, effective performance management systems will be designed with a view to "harness complexity." Axelrod and Cohen, in their classic book *Harnessing Complexity: Organizational Implications of the Science Frontier*, describe this process as "… deliberately changing the structure of a system in order to increase some measure of performance, and to do so by exploiting an understanding that the system itself is complex. Putting it more simply, the idea is to use our knowledge of complexity to do better. To harness complexity typically means living with it, and even taking advantage of it, rather than trying to ignore or eliminate it" (Axelrod and Cohen, 1999, p. 9).

The picture of governance networks as complex adaptive systems is a model of constant dynamism, with some components of the network (what we may construe as its subsystem) are embarked on a processes of emergence and adaptation, with other components of the network remaining relatively stable and perhaps even actively resisting emergent functions and structures. Meadows reminds us that "Complex systems can evolve from simple systems only if there are stable intermediate forms" (2008, p. 83). These stable intermediate forms most likely exist at the meso levels of established organizations and institutions, and long standing, institutionalized communities of practice.

The stability of some network actors can influence the stability of the network as a whole, or some portion of the governance network's subsystem. Viewed through the lens of complex adaptive systems, these stable actors have more "fitness" than other network actors. Marion observes that "… fitness accrues to those who are best able to garner resources and that ability goes to organizations that can create mutually supportive networks with other systems; it does not accrue to those whose sole goal is to serve self at the expense of others. The motivation to elaborate, then, could be as simple as survival, and cooperation is the best tool for achieving it" (1999, p. 55). We may understand fitness of actors in terms of the need for interdependence. It is this structure of stability that allows for governance networks to maintain a certain measure of resilience.

Meadows observes that the resilience of complex adaptive systems " is something that may be very hard to see, unless you exceed the limits, overwhelm and damage the balancing loops, and the system structure breaks down" (2008, p. 77). Ascertaining the resilience of what appears to be a stable governance network becomes a critical feature in managing uncertainty and anticipating risk (Koppenjan and Klijn, 2004). This is why feedback becomes such an important dimension of network governance. "Large organizations of all kinds, from corporations to governments, lose their resilience simply because the feedback mechanisms by which they sense and respond to their environment have to travel through too many layers of delay and distortion" (Meadows, 2008, p. 78), and the same may be said for governance networks on the whole.

The resilience of complex governance networks becomes important for two reasons: when governance networks fail to be resilient (as in the recent cases of failed emergency management networks); and when governance networks fail to adapt to changing conditions (as in the recent cases of financial regulation networks). Sorensen and Torfing observe that "… the learning-based adaptiveness of governance networks might be impeded by the lack of capacities for experimentation, the conservative identities of actors who want to preserve the status quo, and the failure to resolve the internal conflicts between the actors that struggle over the assessment of experiments and the formulation of strategies for institutional reform" (2008, p. 105).

To view governance networks through the lens of complexity theory offers very important theoretical and practical potential. Addressing governance networks as pattern of relationships that evolve in ways that are unknown and uncertain gives rise to the notion of adaptive qualities of human relationships in governance. This governance network adaptation, as we noted early in this work, can work in positive and negative ways and gives rise to serious questions about governance network performance and democratic anchorage. As governance networks evolve, so will the need for an evolutionary pattern of democratic anchorage. On the pragmatic side, emergent and learning governance networks are exciting enterprises but they will also call upon new kinds of leadership and managerial practices to be viewed as both productive and accountable.

CRITICAL QUESTIONS AND CONSIDERATIONS

Based on the material presented in this chapter, we can assess governance networks from a systems perspective. Return once again to your governance network and consider the extent to which is it shaped by systems dynamics.

- What are the boundaries of the network? Are they open or closed? What distinguishes one component of the network from the other? To what extent is the network bifurcated into subsystems?
- Has your governance network been studied using a systems model (e.g., in terms of a system of inputs, processes, outputs, and outcomes)? If not, what would such an analysis look like? Who is contributing resources to the network? What processes does the network undertake? What are the outputs and outcomes of the network?
- Examine the extent to which the governance network is governed by feedback loops. What policy tools, elected representatives, citizens, and interest groups influence the network's behavior? The behaviors of specific actors in the network?

Chapter 8

How Are Governance Networks Managed?

> Good management is the art of making problems so interesting and
> their solutions so constructive that everyone wants to get to work and
> deal with them.
>
> **—Paul Hawken (1988, p. 39)**

Over the course of this book we have described the interorganizational governance network in terms of network nodes and ties. In Chapter 3, we discussed the differing levels of social scale found in interorganizational networks. We noted the nested complexity of social actors operating across the interorganizational, intraorganizational, group, and individual levels. In this chapter we focus on the role of one particular kind of network actor, the individual public administrator who takes on the role of network manager by either managing within the network or managing the network itself.

In the opening chapter of the book we noted Donald Kettl's observations that as a result of the network turn in public administration, "the basic administrative problem [becomes] developing effective management mechanisms to replace command and control" (2002, p. 491). According to Kettl, networked public managers "have to learn the points of leverage, change their behavior to manage those points of leverage, develop processes needed to make that work, and change the organizational culture from a traditional control perspective to one that accommodates indirect methods" (2002, p. 493).

In this chapter we focus on the roles that individual public administrators take within governance networks. We argue that as administrators *of* and *within*

189

governance networks, public managers play a critical role in ensuring that democratic and administrative accountability exists within all configurations of governance networks. We argue that managing within networks brings a degree of complexity to administrative and managerial tasks and requires a variety of administrative tools and skill sets, some of which are embodied in classical views of administrative roles and responsibility, and others of which have surfaced as the result of an emerging understanding of collaborative and network dynamics. The picture of public administration within a governance network context is one first described by Mathur and Skelcher, who argue for the need to reconsider the role of the public administrator away from being "neutrally-competent servants of political executive" to "responsively competent players in a polycentric system of governance" (2007, p. 231). The development of the governance network as an observable and, ultimately, analyzable phenomenon establishes management and administrative practices that contribute to a richer understanding of cross-jurisdictional relations that are characterized by both vertical and horizontal relations.

In this chapter we discuss the management of governance networks through the context of the major paradigms of public administration theory and practice. We suggest that a picture of governance network management emerges when the three previous paradigms—classical public administration, new public management, and collaborative public management—combine into an emergent framework of governance network management.

The Convergence of Public Administration Paradigms

In this section we argue that three public administration paradigms that have existed within the field converge or "sediment" into an emerging fourth paradigm that has been described as "network management" (Kickert and Koppenjan, 1997). Although there have been several other paradigms that might be included here, including the new public administration and the new public service movements, we focus on classical public administration, new public management, and collaborative public management paradigms because these frameworks contribute different outlooks on what accounts for administrative authority. We make the argument that these three paradigms converge to provide the basis for what we characterize as an emergent governance network management paradigm. Table 8.1 lays out the differences between the four public administration paradigms.

The Contribution of Classical PA to a Network Administration Paradigm

Throughout this book we have noted how the classical view of public administrative practice as unfolding in public bureaucracies through the implementation of

Table 8.1   The Convergence of PA Paradigms into Governance Network Administration

Public Administration Paradigm	Dominant Administrative Structure	Central Administrative Dynamics
Classical public administration	Public bureaucracies	Command and control
New public management	Public bureaucracies or private firms	Competition; concession and compromise
Collaborative public management	Partnerships with private firms, nonprofits, and citizens	Collaboration and cooperation; concession and compromise
Governance network administration	Mixed-form governance networks	Command and control; competition; concession and compromise; collaboration and cooperation; coordination

vertical administrative authorities needs to be understood as one potentially useful and necessary strategy to be employed within governance networks. To reiterate, classical public administration (PA) considerations of public bureaucracies and command and control forms of management are still very relevant. Public bureaucracies still play a very pivotal role, even within the most highly decentralized governance networks, largely because their cultures and command and control hierarchical structures help shape the public bureaucracies' participation in governance networks. The kinds of administrative authorities and roles found within hierarchical arrangements that have been the mainstay of classical public administration theory are critically important for several reasons:

1. *Vertical authority may persist within the organizational culture of individual network actors.* In Chapter 3 we argued that when bureaucracies participate within governance networks, the individuals representing their bureaucracy's interests must "serve two masters." They must be bureaucratically and politically accountable to their bosses and supervisors as well as be collaboratively accountable to their network partners. To this end, the picture of network management that we paint here must account for the fact that the individual public administrator will likely need to not only survive within the command and control authorities of his or her home organizations, but also negotiate these vertical arrangements and cultures in an effort to ensure that the interests of the home organizations are accounted for within network-wide functions and structures.

2. *Vertical authority may persist at the network-wide level.* Our discussions of regulatory subsystems and grant and contract agreements underscored the need to acknowledge that not all network ties are horizontal in nature. In some instances, a lead organization must exert control over other organizations in the network, either because of the need to seek regulatory compliance or as a function of effective contract oversight. Public administrators operating within regulatory subsystems or grant and contract agreements may be in a position to provide oversight over other network actors. In writing about the persistent need for the execution of vertical authority in grant and contract agreements, Phillip Cooper observes that it is important to recognize, and thereby manage, "the way that decisions get from the democratically elected political process through appointed executives and down through agencies to the contracting officer who is ultimately authorized to negotiate needs of the community and then to commit its resources in a legally binding relationship" (Cooper, 2003, p. 28). By the same token, public administrators may need to be subordinate to the authorities of other organizations within the network.

In both of these cases, the administrative dynamics described within the classical public administration literature are not only relevant, but of critical importance. Because there has been much written and researched about the arrangement of vertical command and control managerial roles and skill sets, we merely acknowledge their importance here and move on to discussions of the other administrative paradigms. We refer the reader to our discussions of principal-agent theory in Chapter 4 for deeper elaborations on these points.

The Contribution of New Public Management to a Network Administration Paradigm

Because governance networks often include actors from multiple social sectors, including those private firms guided by markets and market forces, the new public management (NPM) foci on public-private partnerships, contracting out, and reliance on market forces need to inform the study of governance networks. NPM became popular beginning in the late 1980s, with the era of privatization undertaken during the Reagan administration, and extending into the early 1990s, during the height of the Clinton administration's "reengineering government" reforms. The central premise behind NPM is to bring market efficiencies to the delivery of public goods and services. Klijn and Snellen (2009, p. 33) summarize the assumptions inherent to the NPM paradigm this way:

■ A strong focus on improving the effectiveness and efficiency of government performance

- A strong focus on ideas and techniques that have proven their value in the private sector
- A strong focus on the use of privatization and contracting out of governmental services, or (parts of) governmental bodies, to improve effectiveness and efficiency
- A strong focus on the creation or use of markets or semimarket mechanisms, or at least on increasing competition in service provision and realizing public policy.
- A strong interest in the use of performance indicators or other mechanisms to specify the desired output of the privatized or automized part of the government or service that has been contracted out

In Chapter 1 we discussed how privatization and contracting out have contributed to the evolution of governance networks. In Chapter 6 we recognized how the move toward indirect governance has led to the proliferation of grant and contract agreements and public-private partnerships. The emphasis that the NPM paradigm has placed on utilizing market mechanisms to engender greater efficiencies and better performance results cannot be divorced from the conceptualization of network management that we describe here. On one level, "the genie is out of the bottle." Contracting out is very much a reality that is not going away. Although we note, as many others have done, that network management is *not* synonymous with NPM, we need to keep in mind that NPM principles and practices are relevant for at least two reasons:

1. *The role of market forces and competition within governance networks needs to be accounted for.* The NPM concentration on the incorporation of market mechanisms in the delivery of public goods and services needs to be integrated into a conceptualization of network administration. The lessons learned from the implementation of sound contracting practices and the instances in which privatization has led to better services at cheaper costs speak to the continued relevance of NPM.
2. *Interest in monitoring network performance is a critical feature of sound network management.* In Chapter 10 we discuss the performance management and measurement movement and its relevance to governance network theory and practice. As Moynihan (2008) has noted, this movement has its roots in NPM. Although we cite how performance measurement has been critiqued as sometimes ignoring the bounded nature of rationality (e.g., performance measurement existing as an overly rationalized ideal type that ignores the social construction of knowledge and the politicized nature of problem and solution framing) (Radin, 2006), the attention that NPM brings to performance management is a major contribution to network management.

In laying the foundation for distinguishing NPM from network management, Klijn and Snellen observe how "NPM attempts to dismiss or reduce [the] complexity [found within networked arrangements] by abstaining from detailed [study] of governance, and focuses instead on governing by output criteria and organizing the playing field" (2009, p. 34). They go on to add that as a result, "the manager tries to keep as far away as possible from the complex realities of in interaction system itself. It treats the system as a black box and reacts to the emerging characteristics of the system by changing the output criteria" (2009, p. 34). We argue that network managers must consider much more than tinkering with output criteria. They need to "get inside" the black box, understand it, and when possible, interject themselves as active agents of influence.

The Contribution of Collaborative Public Management to a Network Administration Paradigm

The third paradigm of importance to network management is collaborative public management (CPM), which has focused on the skills of the public manager in collaborative settings. Robert Agranoff and Michael McGuire introduce collaborative management as "a concept that describes the process of facilitating and operating in multiorganizational arrangements to solve problems that cannot be solved, or solved easily, by single organizations. Collaboration is a purposive relationship designed to solve a problem by creating or discovering a solution within a given set of constraints" (Agranoff and McGuire, 2003, p. 4). The importance of collaborative skills, collaborative processes, and collaborative governance strategies for public administrators has been the subject of a great deal of literature, beginning with Axelrod's application of game theory of cooperative behavior (1980), Barbara Gray's articulation of collaborative processes (1989), and extending into the more recent literature concerning collaborative public management (Bingham and O'Leary, 2008).

Rosemary O'Leary and Lisa Bingham have noted the paradoxical nature of collaborative management (2007), observing that collaborative managers must work with both autonomy and interdependence; collaborative managers and their networks have diverse and common goals; they must work with both a fewer number and a greater variety of groups that are increasingly more diverse; and they need to be both participative and authoritative. Within some of the collaborative management literature the possibility that collaboration is mixed with more vertical forms of authority is raised. Agranoff and McGuire differentiate between vertical and horizontal collaborative activities, suggesting that collaborative management is not relegated to the management of horizontal ties built solely through voluntary engagement. Their comprehension of collaborative management appears to be very similar to the description of network management found in the literature.

What distinguishes collaborative management as a unique paradigm is the emphasis placed on the role of the collaborative manager as enabling greater citizen

COLLABORATIVE PUBLIC ACTION TOOLS

VERTICAL COLLABORATION ACTIVITIES

Information seeking

General funding of programs and projects
New funding of programs and projects

Interpretation of standards and rules
General program guidance
Technical assistance

Adjustment seeking

Regulatory relief, flexibility, or waiver
Statutory relief or flexibility
Change in policy
Funding innovation for program
Model program involvement
Performance-based discretion

Horizontal Collaborative Activities

Policy making and strategy making

Gain policy-making assistance
Engage in formal partnerships
Engage in joint policy making
Consolidate policy effort

Resource exchange

Seek financial resources
Employ joint financial incentives
Contracted planning and implementation

Project-based work

Partnership for a particular project
Seek technical resources

Source: **Agranoff and McGuire,** *Collaborative Public Management: New Strategies for Local Governments,* **Georgetown University Press, Washington, DC, 2003, pp. 70–71.**

GRAY'S ADMINISTRATIVE BENEFITS TO COLLABORATION

- Broad comprehensive analysis of problem domain improves the quality of solutions.
- It ensures that interests are considered in any agreement and that acceptance of the solution is greater.
- Parties retain ownership over a solution.
- Mechanisms for future coordination can be established.

Source: **Paraphrased from Gray,** *Collaborating: Finding Common Ground for Multiparty Problems,* **Jossey-Bass, San Francisco, 1989, p. 21.**

participation. According to Lisa Bingham, Tina Nabatchi, and Rosemary O'Leary (2005, p. 548) the central questions being drawn in collaborative public management are: How does one best coordinate multiple players and stakeholders in indirect government and networks? How and when does a public manager attempt to engage the public and how broadly? Which forms of citizen or stakeholder engagement are most effective? Thus, collaborative public management as a paradigm places emphasis on participatory processes that enable citizens to better influence the actions of the governance networks in their midst. To this extent, CPM has much in common with the new public service framework advanced by Denhardt and Denhardt (2003). The collaborative public management paradigm privileges collaboration grounded in a strong normative foundation of democratic participation and deliberation. To this extent, CPM serves as the counterweight to NPM, which relegates citizen involvement to the realm of customer service and customer satisfaction.

A Governance Network Administration Paradigm

Borrowing characteristics of each of the three previous paradigms, a picture of network administration is emerging that can be described as the combination of network governance and public management under conditions of interdependence. From the interdependence perspective, network administration is aimed at "coordinating strategies of actors with different goals and preferences with regard to a certain problem or policy measure within an existing network of inter-organizational relations" (Kickert, Klijn, and Koppenjan, 1997a, p. 10). We argue that effective network management requires an understanding of all forms of administrative dynamics, including command and control, competition, negotiation and bargaining, and collaboration and cooperation. All three public administration paradigms described above are useful to the study of governance network administration and represent a confluence of per-spectives that offer opportunities for integration by network participants, including public managers. It is the role of the public manager in governance networks, charac-terized by intersecting administrative dynamics, that we will examine next.

Determining the role of the public administrator in governance networks has received a great deal of attention in recent years among a number of scholars. It now seems clear that managing governmental hierarchies is not synonymous with managing in governance networks. In fact, *managing* governance networks may not even be feasible; *facilitating* governance networks seems to be a more appropri-ate application. Given the nature of mixed-actor relations in governance networks, we believe it is important to identify and evaluate the roles that public managers play as leaders of, and members in, governance networks.

Network administration takes place when the operations of the whole network, or at least those subsystems of the network that are visible or known, are consid-ered. "Network management ... involves steering efforts aimed at promoting these cooperative strategies within policy games in networks. Thus, network administra-tion may [be] seen as *promoting the mutual adjustment of the behaviour of actors with diverse objectives and ambitions with regard to tackling problems within a given frame-work of interorganizational relationships*" (Kickert and Koppenjan, 1997, p. 44). A network administration paradigm will blend a range of administrative roles and functions, leveraging the mechanisms of authority found in command and con-trol environments with administration through formal and informal agreements. Network administration must also account for the administration of horizontal ties built on the establishment of trust, reciprocity. and durability. Bressers and O'Toole suggest that network administration "involves such important but potentially mul-tilateral tasks as facilitating exchange, identifying potential options for multiactor agreement, and helping to craft patterns of communication as well as multilevel and multiactor governance arrangements" (2005, p. 141).

We explore some of the strategies that network managers have been described as undertaking within governance networks. Although the list of potential strategies at the disposal of network managers is long, we have settled on a few critical strate-gies and skill sets that appear to be pertinent. Realizing that entire volumes have been written on each of these strategies, we introduce a few of the more central strategies found within the literature. As interest in network governance has pro-liferated, a series of best practices or axioms have been put forth by some of the leading researchers and theorists in the field. We highlight a few of these suggested best practices here to give the reader a sense of the range of practice guides that are suggested.

The research of Stephen Goldsmith and William D. Eggers (2004) has provided a strong basis for understanding the skills of public managers for initiating and developing mixed-actor governance networks. These authors assert that working within a collaborative network model requires attitudes and behaviors beyond what is typically called for with a public manager accustomed to exercising hierarchical control. The central feature of network management is working in shared power relationships, an environment that requires flexibility and adaptability. Sharing power to achieve collective outcomes calls upon competencies to move networks toward performance outcomes, while still managing for high levels of performance against an agreed upon matrix (Goldsmith and Eggers, 2004).

The qualities of network managers are also reflected in the work of Robert Agranoff (2004), who examined managerial lessons evident in networks that have been established by network managers. These lessons are distinguishable from those represented in hierarchical structures. Among the ten lessons identified among network managers (see Table 8.2)—take a share of the administrative burden, operate by agenda orchestration, accommodate and adjust while maintaining purpose—public managers will need to rely upon interpersonal skills (lesson 8) that reflect working in a shared power arrangement.

As the result of studying fourteen collaborative networks represented in further research, Robert Agranoff provides additional observations regarding managing in networks. These observations include the recognition that managers still tend to do the bulk of their work within hierarchies. He recognizes that "most collaborative decisions or agreements are the products of a particular type of mutual learning and adjustment." These mutual learning adjustments lead to the proliferation of public sector knowledge management activities. He also observes that "despite the cooperative spirit and aura of accommodation in collaborative efforts, networks are not without conflicts and power issues" (Agranoff, 2006, p. 57).

With these findings, it is evident that network management calls upon the public manager to operate in very different ways and in many different settings. Some

Table 8.2   Ten Lessons on How to Manage in Networks

1.	Be representative of your agency and the network.
2.	Take a share of the administrative burden.
3.	Operate by agenda orchestration.
4.	Recognize shared expertise-based authority.
5.	Stay within the decision bounds of your network.
6.	Accommodate and adjust while maintaining purpose.
7.	Be as creative as possible.
8.	Be patient and use interpersonal skills.
9.	Recruit constantly.
10.	Emphasize incentives.

Compiled from: Agranoff, 2004.

of the skills will be less evident, or what Kettl refers to as indirect (Kettl, 2002). A review of these lessons from collaborative networks reveals that the role of the public manager is even more complicated with the additional burden of having to manage and participate in two kinds of settings, each with different kinds of responsibilities: hierarchical and network.

Not surprisingly, governance networks have been found to experience points of conflict. Conflicts are a critical, and some deem necessary, element of the kind of interorganizational networks that we discuss in this book. Conflicts may come about as the result of real, substantive differences of opinion and perspective. Rosemary O'Leary and Lisa Bingham studied the nature of conflict and conflict resolution in network settings. They concluded their study with the following observation about the complex nature of network conflict (O'Leary and Bingham, 2007, pp. 10–11):

- Members bring both different and common missions.
- Network organizations have different cultures.
- Network organizations have different methods of operation.
- Members have different stakeholder groups and different funders.
- Members have different degrees of power.
- There are often multiple issues.
- There are multiple forums for decision making.
- Networks are both interorganizational and interpersonal.
- There are a variety of governance structures available to networks.
- Networks may encounter conflict with the public.

The nature of these kinds of conflict will resonate, quite loudly, as we consider governance network accountability and performance management systems in Chapters 9 and 10. The notion that "adding actors does more than complexity, it tilts the balance of power" (O'Toole and Meier, 2004b) suggests that conflict in network contexts is all but inevitable. This makes advancing our capacities to describe and analyze the efficacy of accountability and performance standards all the more crucial.

The range of observations regarding what accounts for effective network management may be distilled into a smaller number of network management strategies. We believe that these strategies appear across the literature referenced here. These strategies also, coincidentally, align with the public administration paradigms discussed earlier in this chapter.

Governance Network Administration (GNA) Strategies

As a network administrator contemplates the range of strategies at his or her disposal, he or she must consider that a strategy "can be used both to influence goal-oriented processes (governance) and to create the conditions which facilitate the mutual formulation of targets (network management)" (Kickert and Koppenjan, 1997, pp. 120–21). These strategies are employed through the enactment of certain policy tools and the execution of certain network management skills. A variety of governance strategies have been recognized as being crucial to interorganizational networks, including leading and following (Koontz et al., 2004); boundary spanning (Kettl, 2006); and orchestrating, modulating, and activating (Salamon, 2002a). In addition to these roles, public managers can employ various governance strategies, including mandating, endorsing, facilitating, and partnering (Fox et al., 2002). Combined with the practices outlined above, a picture of some of the central network administration strategies emerges. Table 8.3 summarizes each of these strategies. In the section that follows, the characteristics of each strategy are described along with the corresponding role of the public administrator.

Oversight and Mandating

Oversight is a standard managerial function found in any hierarchical or principal-agent relationship. We have already discussed at length why command and control authorities persist even within governance networks. The establishment of administrative oversight may be premised on the designation of a lead organization or an individual leader of a governance network. When the authority is based on the position of the leader or overseer, the capacities of the leader to lead, and followers to follow become critically important. Administrative oversight may be derived through the issuance of executive orders, spelled out in contract agreement language, or agreed upon through memorandum of understandings.

Mandating provides "minimum standards for ... performance within the legal framework" (Fox et al., 2002, p. 3). The role of government in a mandating relationship is that of a traditional command and control orientation that is defined through legislation and implemented through agency regulation (Fox et al., 2002, p. 3). Tools associated with mandating roles include social and economic regulation, and fines and sanctions. For the public administrator, implementing mandates may be seen either in terms of the traditional command and control perspective or from an emergent perspective on mandates that explicitly provides regulated agents with more negotiating and bargaining power. The latter perspective suggests that government sets a framework within which regulated agents like corporations and industry must operate, but then corporations are given latitude in defining the ways that they may come into compliance. This process has been widely noted in the literature concerning regulatory capture and self-regulation. Thus, mandates do not necessarily imply coercion. Mandating sets parameters, but regulated interests may have room for "adjustment seeking" (Agranoff and McGuire, 2003, p. 75). The ability of public managers to grant "regulatory relief" is a critical component of managing across sectors (Agranoff and McGuire, 2003,

Table 8.3   Network Administration Coordinating Strategies

Governance Network Administration Coordinating Strategy	Strategy Characteristics	Classical PA	NPM	CPM	GNA
		PA Paradigm			
Oversight; mandating	Use of command and control authorities to gain compliance; employed in most classical hierarchical arrangements and regulatory subsystems	X			X
Providing resources	Provision of one or more forms of capital resources as inputs into the network	X	X	X	X
Negotiation and bargaining	Engaging in processes of mutual adjustment and agreements ultimately leading to common acceptance of parameters for resource exchange and pooling and other forms of coordinated action		X	X	X
Facilitation	Use of coordinating strategies to bring actors together and ensure the flow of information and joint actions between actors; usually relies on incentives and inherent agreements on common norms and standards		X	X	X
Participatory governance/ civic engagement	Use of administrative authority to ensure the participation of selected interests or citizens at large; relies on models of deliberative and consensus-seeking processes			X	X
Brokering; boundary spanning	The development and use of social capital to bridge boundaries, establish new ties				X
Systems thinking	The development of situational awareness of the complex systems dynamics that are unfolding within governance networks				X

p. 75). Regulatory relief can be viewed as what Ayres and Braithwaite (1992) call "responsive regulation."

Providing Resources

In Chapters 3 and 4 we discussed how the range of capital resources that a given actor brings to the network shapes public managers' functions and roles within the network-wide structure. In order to account for an actor's role as a provider of resources to a network, we distinguish the provision of resources as a distinct network management strategy. From a systems perspective, the provision of such resources serves as critical input and process factors. Such provisions may either require or lead to the establishment of a lead organization, as in the case when a funder enters into an agreement with those that it funds. The selection of which capital resources to provide, when to provide them, and on what conditions they are provided falls into the realm of network management strategies adopted by network managers.

We suggest that the selection of certain forms of capital resources predicates the kind of specific strategies employed. Those public managers responsible for managing the flow of financial resources into or out of a governance network will employ budgeting and accounting practices. Network managers may be stewards of physical or natural resources that are used by the governance network—bearing responsibility for the management of buildings, office equipment, and other built infrastructure or certain forms of ecosystem services at the disposal of the network. Network managers will likely provide human capital to the network, bringing with them certain skills sets and knowledge that are used by the network at large. Network managers may bring their social capital to the network, providing boundary spanning and bridging functions. As Agranoff has noted (2006), public managers may take a role in managing the flow of knowledge and facilitate learning. They may also bring political capital into the network, exerting influence or lending their legitimacy to network operations.

Lester Salamon refers to the provision strategy of network management in terms of the "modulation" of rewards (2002a, p. 17). Providing resources such as subsidies or other kinds of policy incentives may be used to get private parties to make investments in network-wide activities. The provision of resources in terms of modulating network activity is a critical facet of network management practices.

Negotiating and Bargaining

In studying the role that bargaining plays in the practice of public administration, Agranoff and McGuire ask the question: "Is bargaining a useful tool for advancing *mutual* interests?" (Agranoff and McGuire, 2004, p. 502). Clearly, "people negotiate to advance their interests and those of the institutions they represent" (Watkins, 1999, p. 245). It would appear that the use of negotiation and bargaining strategies, in the very least, allows for individual actors to represent their own interests in processes premised on mutual adjustments between two or more parties. Negotiation and bargaining skills appear to be a critical strategy employed by network managers if only for the reason that these kind of processes of mutual adjustment provide a space for alignment around common goals and expectations, as well as agreements around the parameters for resource exchanges and pooling.

Although negotiation and bargaining have been recognized as a critical skill set in contract management (Cooper, 2003), the integration of negotiation and bargaining strategies and processes into the public administration mainstream has been slow in developing. This is not to suggest that negotiation and bargaining skills and strategies have lacked attention in the wider literature. Texts on negotiation have proliferated within the business and international diplomacy fields, with Fisher, Ury, and Patton's *Getting to Yes* (1991) being the most popular text of this genre. Much of the literature on negotiation has presented negotiation processes in a linear or staged fashion, with negotiators "sitting at the table" to hammer out an agreement.

Michael Watkins (1999, p. 255) has suggested that negotiations take on nonlinear dynamics marked by:

- Sensitivity to early interactions: The beginning of negotiations set the tone for future interactions.
- Irreversibility: Sometimes negotiators "walk through doors that lock behind them."
- Threshold effects: Small incremental moves resulting in large changes in the situation.
- Feedback loops: Established patterns of interactions among actors readily become self-reinforcing.

Watkins' view of negotiation suggests that negotiation skills and strategies should be viewed more as a generative process. He outlines ten propositions that skilled negotiators should consider. We provide a summary of these propositions in Table 8.4.

Watkins studies negotiation as a generative, phenomenological process. Yet, his view of negotiation processes still advances negotiation as a formalized process involving two parties. Network managers may negotiate in less formal settings. We must also account for the possibility that negotiation processes unfold without conscious recognition that a negotiation is taking place. We suggest here that network managers recognize when negotiation is needed and being undertaken, and attempt to exert their influence over the processes as needed. Thus, whether negotiation follows a formal or informal line, the ten propositions laid out by Watkins are important.

Table 8.4   Ten Propositions for Negotiation

	Proposition	*Negotiation Skill*
1.	Negotiations rarely have to be win-lose, but neither are they likely to be win-win.	Skilled negotiators tailor their tactics to the type of negotiation, seeking both to create value and to claim value by crafting creative deals that bridge differences.
2.	Uncertainty and ambiguity are facts of life in negotiation.	Skilled negotiators seek to learn and shape perceptions through orchestrated activities taken at and away from the negotiation table.
3.	Most negotiations involve existing or potential sources of conflict that could poison efforts to reach mutually beneficial agreements.	Skilled negotiators often are called upon to mediate even as they negotiate, and intervention by outside parties is commonplace.
4.	Interactions among negotiators are fundamentally chaotic, but there is order in the chaos.	Skilled negotiators find opportunity in the fog of negotiation.
5.	While negotiations occurring in diverse contexts may appear to be very different, they often have similar underlying structures.	Structure shapes strategy, but skilled negotiators work to shape the structure.
6.	Most negotiations are linked to other negotiations, past, present, and future.	Skilled negotiators advance their interests by forging and neutralizing linkages.
7.	Negotiations are fragmented in time, and movement occurs in surges.	Skilled negotiators channel the flow of the process and work to build momentum in promising directions.
8.	Most important negotiations take place between representatives of groups.	Just as leaders often are called upon to negotiate, so too are negotiators called upon to lead.
9.	Organizations often are represented by many negotiators, each of whom conducts many negotiations over time.	Success in setting up organizational learning processes contributes to increased effectiveness, both individual and collective.
10.	Negotiation skills can be learned and taught.	Expert negotiators possess skills in pattern recognition, mental simulation, process management, and reflection in action, and these skills can be developed through carefully structured experience.

Compiled from: Watkins, *Negotiation Journal, 15,* 248, 1999.

Facilitation

As a facilitator, a network manager can "bring parties together" and create an "enabling environment" (Lepoutre, Dentchev, and Heene, 2007, p. 10) in which common goals or standards, or common agreements around resource exchanges and pooling, can be reached. In this role the public administrator can activate network partners in an effort to reach a policy goal or outcome. Lester Salamon recognizes network activation as a critical strategy undertaken by network managers (2002a). The activator is responsible for bringing together all available resources, such as money, expertise, and information, into one integrated network (Agranoff and McGuire, 2003). Salamon also identifies orchestration as an important network management skill set, equating the concept with the conscious facilitation of network activities as a matter of sustaining its collective action.

Camilla Stivers, among others, has promoted the notion of facilitative leadership within public administration. According to her, facilitative managers

> emphasize the possibility of leadership as facilitation rather than the giving of orders, and authority as accountable expertise rather than as chain of command. Ultimately, working within such a perspective, we should be able to ground administrative legitimacy in accountability that not only is exercised in the privacy of the individual conscience or in the internal process of a particular agency, but also tangibly enacted in substantive collaboration with affected others, including members of the general public. (2004, p. 486)

We may consider that facilitation is not synonymous with traditional forms of leadership. "Although many leaders can (and should) be effective facilitators, the facilitator differs from a leader in that the former is cognizant about the use of power, authority, or control and places limitations on uses of it" (Reed and Koliba, 1995, p. 4). The execution of effective facilitation skills is central for the development of mutual accountability structures within collaborative settings. We offer a few keys to facilitating group dynamics in Table 8.5.

To be successful, public managers will need to rely upon what Kickert and Koppenjan (1997) refer to as *reticulist skills*, or assessment skills to correctly determine involvement, interaction processes, and the distribution of information. Schaap describes facilitation strategies as providing the "means for creating procedures for ongoing interaction, discussions, negotiations, and decision-making." The effective facilitator helps "actors ... bind themselves to those procedures" (2008, pp. 126–27). Facilitation is central to the ongoing success of a governance network strategy.

Table 8.5 Keys to Facilitation Strategies in Network Management

Create a safe space	In order for group members to express their thoughts and opinions, they must feel that they can do so without fear of attack or condemnation. It is the facilitator's job to create such an environment, to monitor participant's comfort levels, and to take the necessary steps to maintain safety. This includes understanding and planning for individual differences in needs, abilities, fears, and apprehensions. Participants who feel safe are more likely to make honest and genuine contributions and to feel camaraderie and respect toward other group members.
Set ground rules	Ground rules establish a foundation upon which the group's communication will occur. They help to create a safe environment in which participants can communicate openly, without fear of being criticized by others. Ground rules that have been arrived at by all members are the most useful and can be repeated if tension rises.
Promote active listening	Staying quiet and considering others' remarks can be challenging when controversial topics are discussed, but is crucial to respectful communication. Facilitators should discourage participants from professing their opinions without considering and responding to others' comments. Instead, facilitators should model communication in the form of a dialogue, in which participants listen and respond to each other. The type of communication used (whether polite conversation is favored over informal or slang conversation) can vary, and should be determined according to such factors as the group's cultural background, familiarity with each other, goals for reflection, etc.
Manage disagree-ments	It has been said that whatever resists will persist. Facilitators must be adept at recognizing tension building in the group, and respond to it immediately. Among the most useful strategies is to repeat the ground rules established by the group, including a reminder that criticism should pertain to ideas, not people. In addition, facilitators should not permit any disrespect or insults and should clarify misinformation. It is important that negative behavior be handled immediately so that participants do not get the impression that the behavior is condoned by the facilitator.
Promote equality	Equality of participants should be communicated and modeled by the facilitator. Again, the facilitator must be an alert observer, identifying signs of a developing hierarchy, or of divisive factions within the group. He or she should not permit arguing against any group member(s), and should not take sides in any developing debate. Such situations can be counteracted by recognizing all members, and encouraging their participation equally.

Table 8.5   Keys to Facilitation Strategies in Network Management (Continued)

Be mindful of power and who has it	All groups have opinion leaders or people who most others look up to. Often, these opinion leaders will set the tone for a discussion, thereby limiting active involvement of the more reserved members. Identify who these opinion leaders are, and if it appears as though their power and authority are dominating the discussion, ask them, politely, to entertain other opinions.
Build in diversity	Facilitators must begin by recognizing their own attitudes, stereotypes, and expectations and must open their minds to understanding the limits these prejudices place on their perspective. The facilitator will be the role model that the group looks to, and should therefore model the values of multiculturalism. It is important that diversity be integrated throughout the reflection programming, rather than compartmentalized into special multicultural segments.

Source: Reed and Koliba, "Facilitating Reflection: A Guide for Leaders and Educators," 1995, retrieved November 30, 2009, from http://www.uvm.edu/~dewey/reflection_manual/index.html.

Participatory Governance

Participatory governance includes a number of strategies within quasi-legislative and quasi-judicial administrative tools employed by public administrators to leverage greater citizen control and involvement. Bingham, Nabatchi, and O'Leary (2005 pp. 547, 552) identify the legal framework from which the public administrator can utilize participatory governance:

> *Quasi-legislative processes* ... include deliberative democracy, e-democracy, public conversations, participatory budgeting, citizen juries, study circles, collaborative policy making, and other forms of deliberation and dialogue among groups of stakeholders or citizens.
>
> *Quasi-judicial processes* include alternative dispute resolution such as mediation, facilitation, early neutral assessment, and arbitration [and include] ... minitrials, summary jury trials, fact finding ...

Quasi-legislative and quasi-judicial processes are avenues for network managers to leverage citizen participation in collaborative policy making. Bingham, Nabatchi, and O'Leary outline a wide range of examples at the international, federal, state, and local levels that exemplify citizen inclusion strategies of public service governance. The authors conclude their work with a call for extended research with regard to process choices, quality, representation, policy cycle connection, impact, implementation, and institutionalization (pp. 554–55).

As an added dimension to the legal framework of participating governance possibilities, Archon Fung (2006) has developed a framework to interpret various participatory strategies and their influence with respect to the democratic outcomes of legitimacy, justice, and effectiveness of public action. The framework provides participatory designs based upon ranges of three governance dimensions: participant selection, communication and decision, and authority and power. In this effort, each design is examined in light of the ability to achieve democratic outcomes. Fung argues that "no single participatory design is suited to serving all three values simultaneously; particular designs are suited to specific objectives," and "direct participation should figure prominently in contemporary democratic governance" (2006, p. 74.)

Additional research has been accumulated to assist public managers with specific participatory governance strategies by focusing on public deliberation (Lukensmeyer and Torres, 2006). This research seeks to overcome the institutional barriers of implementing public deliberation strategies (policy fragmentation about citizen engagement and poor knowledge sharing about civic engagement) in order to offer managerial guidance and examples of various kinds of face-to-face and online deliberative democracy examples. Lukensmeyer and Torres (2006) provide a managerial guide to participatory governance alternatives that cover tools of participation (informational, consultation, engagement, and collaboration) as well as a framework for selecting engagement techniques that is reflective of a range of engagement parameters. In their review of eight models of deliberative democracy, the authors offer numerous examples of model applications.

Citizen-administration consensus-oriented deliberation (Yankelovich, 1991) continues to receive a great deal of attention that suggests a basis for optimism in neighborhood councils (Berry, Portney, and Thomson, 1993), urban neighborhoods (Fung, 2004), and a number of other sectors, such as participatory budgeting (Weeks, 2000) and environment and land use planning (Lukensmeyer and Torres, 2006).

While there is a great deal of optimism with regard to the promise and exercise of the various kinds of participatory governance, there remain a number of issues that concern how participatory governance is designed and implemented. One concern centers upon the political nature of governance where participatory governance cannot overcome the trade-offs between democratic values and norms, and pragmatic realities fueled by the desire for greater efficiencies or tacit power struggles (Roberto, 2004).

Another concern is related to the way in which participatory governance is designed and perhaps misapplied by government. Klijn and Skelcher note how some of this literature "starts from the theoretical premise that networks are predominantly characterized by horizontal relationships, self-steering and pluralism, and that too easily draws an association with deliberative forms of democracy, when, in essence, their dynamics are inherently more complex" (2007, p. 605). Citizen governance strategies that are mandated by law, such as public hearings and citizen advisory boards, may influence governance practices very differently than strategies that are based on citizen-centered or bottom-up initiatives.

Rodriguez et al. (2007) studied the dynamics within governance networks devised to coordinate the delivery of health care within Canada. Quasi-governmental boards worked with networks of large, regional hospitals and local health clinics, all of which were forced through legislative mandate to collaborate in efforts to coordinate health care delivery within their regions. They found that in this setting, at least, top-down oversight from the quasi-governmental board was needed in order to advance and deepen coordinated activities. In those instances in which actors were left to reach consensus around objectives of their own volition, tangible results were hard to come by (Rodriguez et al., 2007).

A related concern is the use of participatory governance strategies for bureaucratic rather than network-wide interests. A factor hampering the proliferation of deliberative forums concerns the coupling of deliberative processes to tangible decision making within the governance network itself. The results of citizen deliberations may be effectively communicated to actors within the governance network, only to have this feedback summarily ignored or reframed to meet the desired ends of the real power brokers within the network. In essence, deliberative forums may do more to co-opt citizens than provide them with real power within networks.

Clearly, the infusion of deliberative processes into the functioning of governance networks is by no means a simple feat. Consensus-oriented decision making is not easy (Priem and Price, 1991; Klijn, 2001; Roberto, 2004), nor, many argue, is it appropriate in all cases. Efforts to promote issue forums, study circles, etc., are hampered by challenges associated with reaching consensus when diverse interests and perspectives are introduced into these forums. While deliberative processes are gaining attention, there are serious barriers to greater citizen participation in such forums. Finally, the challenge of implementing these kinds of participatory processes calls upon a different set of skills of the public administrator. As Bingham, Nabatchi, and O'Leary (2005) assert, "Both quasi-legislative and quasi-judicial new governance processes require analogous skills from public administrators, including convening, conflict assessment, negotiation, active listening and reframing, facilitation, and consensus building" (p. 548).

The role of the governance network administrator needs to be framed within both quasi-legislative and quasi-judicial processes and will entail a wide range of participatory and deliberative options. Based upon evidence from a number of research efforts, it is clear that the skills of the administrator will focus on the ability to facilitate multiple stakeholder interests in complex settings and require the balancing of both network and hierarchical demands. Those areas in need of balance will be the basis for creating legitimacy. The key feature of this legitimacy will rest in the social construction of the service design and implementation that finds a balance among public service design alternatives and participatory processes. Those writing about collaborative and participatory governance often view the public manager as playing a central role in achieving this balance.

Boundary Spanning and Brokering

A critical feature of governance network administration is the capacity of network managers to take on boundary spanning or brokering strategies. In Chapters 3 and 4 we laid out a range of actor and tie characteristics. We noted how the network metaphor—grounded in the tinker toy metaphor of nodes and links/actors and ties—lies at the heart of this descriptive architecture. More than simply a metaphor, the management of network actors and the kinds of ties forged between them requires creating the capacity to span social and epistemic borders and boundaries. Network managers can serve as boundary spanners who, according to Agranoff and McGuire, may transcend boundaries that are both vertically and horizontally arranged (2003, p. 16).

In laying out a theory of communities of practice, Etienne Wenger discusses the role that brokers play in managing networks. "Brokers are able to make new connections across [organizations] and communities of practice and enable coordination." He goes on to add that "if they are good brokers [their efforts lead to] opening new possibilities for meaning" (Wenger, 1998, p. 109). Wenger describes brokering activity as an interplay of translation, coordination, and alignment—a relationship that is represented visually in Figure 8.1.

"Brokering provides a participative connection ... because what brokers press into service to connect practices is [the broker's] experience of multimembership and the possibilities for negotiation inherent in participation [within and across these groups]" (Wenger, 1998, p. 109). Wenger describes brokering as a process of translating knowledge and information, opinions, and perspectives into reference frames that are comprehendible to network actors. Brokering also requires some measure of coordination, aspects of which may be found in our previous discussion of facilitation and participatory governance. As a result of generative translations

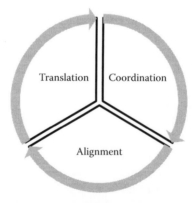

Figure 8.1 Components of a brokering strategy. (Modified from Wenger, ***Communities of Practice: Learning, Meaning, and Identity,*** **Cambridge University Press, Cambridge, 1998.)**

and efforts at coordination, the broker may assist in achieving of some alignment between network actors. Brokers need enough legitimacy to influence the development of a practice, mobilize attention, and address conflicting interests. Brokering also requires the ability to link practices by facilitating transactions between them, and to cause learning by introducing into practice elements of another. Brokering strategy inevitably calls for the mobilization of a network management, human, social, and political capital.

Ronald Burt's "structural hole" theory of social networks underscores the importance that boundary spanning and brokering can play within networked environs. Burt describes how most social networks possess structural holes within them (1997).

Burt's studies of structural holes in organizational settings have led him to conclude that the existence of structural holes may actually provide a better environment for the diffusion of innovation. Following Granovetter's strength of weak ties hypothesis, Burt asserts that "networks rich in structural holes present opportunities for entrepreneurial behavior" (Burt, 1997, p. 342). Network managers who serve as brokers can play a role in fostering greater innovation.

The manager who is capable of "filling in" a structural hole through linking two nodes that had not been previously linked "has a say in whose interests are served by the bridge" (Burt, 1997, p. 342). Brokering and boundary spanning may position a network manager to be highly influential. As Burt notes, "When coordination is based on negotiated informal control, as in network organization, more successful managers will be the managers with better access to the information and control benefits of structural holes" (Burt, 1997, p. 360).

Filling in structural holes across organizations possesses its own hazards to the broker. Wenger warns that "brokers must often avoid two opposite tendencies: being pulled in to become full members and being reflected as intruders. Indeed, their contributions lie precisely in being neither in nor out" (1998, p. 110). Thus, network managers may face somewhat of an identity crisis as they seek to span boundaries and possibly serve two masters.

Systems Thinking

A critical skill set and strategy that governance network administrators should employ is centered on the concept of systems thinking. Popularized by Peter Senge and others who integrated systems theory into organizational development and managerial leadership, systems thinking encompasses a capacity to see and act upon an appreciation of the "interrelatedness within and among systems." Systems thinkers hold on to this capacity to see the interrelatedness between the parts of the system and the whole by maintaining a time span of interest long enough to see patterns of interaction and behavior to appear (van den Belt, 2004, p. 22).

Endsley observes that administrators with situational awareness seek to classify and understand the situation around them. They rely on "pattern-matching mechanisms to draw on long-term memory structures that allowed them to quickly understand a given situation." Situational awareness "is the perception of the elements in the environment within a volume of time and space, the comprehension of their meaning, [and] the projection of their status in the near future." Situational awareness should explain dynamic goal selection, attention to appropriate critical cues, expectancies regarding future states of the situation, and the tie between situation awareness and typical actions (Endsley, 1995, p. 34).

The situational awareness that is derived through systems thinking then needs to be applied through the execution of administrative discretion and operationalization of goals. Network managers may seek to identify and act upon the "leverage points" providing opportunities to intervene in the system. Donnella Meadows' listing of the twelve leverage points is provided in Figure 8.2.

Meadows (2008) views the leverage points within a system as points where power may be executed. Systems thinking, when applied to the coordination of

---

1. Harness the power to transcend paradigms

2. Change or maintain the mindset or paradigm out of which the system arises

3. Modify the goals of the system

4. Add to, change, evolve, or support the self-organization of the system structure

5. Change the (explicit and/or implicit) rules of the system

6. Structure of the flow of information across the system

7. Try to drive the intensity of positive feedback loops impacting the system

8. The strength of the negative feedback loops impacting the system

9. Monitor and modify the length of delays, relative to the rate of systems changes

10. Structure of the material flow of capitals through the system

11. Alter the available stocks of resource capitals available to the system

12. Alter the constants, parameters, numbers used to determine performance standards

---

Figure 8.2 Places to intervene in the system. (Compiled from: Meadows, *Thinking in Systems*, Chelsea Green Publishing, White River Junction, VT, 2008.)

governance networks, leads to the identification of bifurcation points within the system that, when pushed, pulled, or enacted, lead to changes in the system's dynamics. In Chapter 7 we characterized network administrative practice as a form of feedback rendered on or within a system. To this end, the execution of systems thinking within the context of governance network administration involves the conscious manipulation, facilitation, and coordination of the variety of forms of feedback that guide the system's dynamics.

Ralph Stacey distinguishes between systems thinking and "complex responsive processes," criticizing some of the first-generation systems thinking as ignoring the emergent, adaptive characteristics of the system. Rather than pulling the levers and exploiting discernable leverage points to elicit responses, his view of what we might characterize as second-generation systems thinking focuses less on thinking in terms of what already exists and more on "thinking in terms of patterns that are continually reproduced and potentially transformed" (2001, p. 197). Stacey emphasizes the intersubjective creation of shared meaning that only emerges through the interactions of social actors. This position echoes the calls for more phenomenological interpretations of administrative action made by Ralph Hummel (2002). Stacey, Hummel, and others concerned about the reign of positivist interpretation of network administration and performance underscore the need to view systems thinking as an important contributor of the social construction of social reality.

We argue that a systems thinking approach to network administration needs to be viewed within the context of organizational learning (Senge et al., 1994; Argyris and Schon, 1995). According to proponents of systems thinking as social learning, "the key ... is not analytical method, but organizational process; and the central methodological concern is not with isolation of variables or the control of bureaucratic deviations from centrally defined blueprints, but with effectively engaging the necessary participation of system members in contributing to the collective knowledge of the system." Suggesting that social learning be integrated into administrative practices, David Korten goes on to observe that "the more complex the problem and the greater the number of value perspectives brought to bear, the greater the need for localized solutions and for value innovations, both of which call for broadly based participation in decision processes" (2001, p. 485). Thus, we conclude that systems thinking, and the kind of situational awareness arising from it, becomes an essential feature of all governance network administration. In other words, for any of the skills and strategies outlined in this chapter to succeed, the administrator employing them must possess a view of the whole and envision ways that his or her actions can support the network's capacity to learn.

Decision Architectures, Communities of Practice, and Administrative Discretion

The successful execution of any of the network management skills and strategies introduced in this chapter hinges on the capacity of individual administrators and intranetwork groups or communities of practice to make decisions. Within complex governance networks the following questions are of critical importance and oftentimes not easily answered: Who makes decisions? How are they made? Who decides who will make the decisions? These relatively simple questions are addressed by most decision-making theories. Answering them can provide a sense of the "decision architecture" (Price Waterhouse Change Integration Team, 1996; Cox, 2000) for a group, organization, or even a network of organizations. Empirical studies and contemporary theories of decision making reveal that the act of deciding often occurs within a multifaceted array of actors and situations (Allison, 1971; Cohen, March, and Olsen, 1972; Pressman and Wildavsky, 1973; Koppenjan and Klijn, 2004). These deciders exist within a complex system of actors spanning the individual, group, organization, and interorganizational levels.

Koppenjan and Klijn (2004) describe decision making as unfolding within a complex environment involving the individual, group, organizational, and interorganizational levels, with decisions occurring within and across these levels. Table 8.6 shows how they break decision making down in terms of social scale.

Herbert Simon recognized the complexity of decision making within organizations, laying out the proposition that at best, decisions are made by individuals operating within a "bounded rationality" context (1957). Simon recognized that no decision maker has access to perfect information, knows all possible alternatives, has all the time needed to weigh all alternatives, or possesses the capacity to perfectly implement his or her decisions. Charles Lindblom noted how decision makers rely on past experience, limited information, and "satisficing" behaviors when making decisions (1959). In short, he suggested that decision making was vastly a product of environmental and phenomenological factors. These factors are inherently shaped by the human social dynamics within which most decisions get made.

Historically, such dynamics have been couched in terms of small group behavior. Most theories of group decision making are premised on the assumption that "group outcomes are a function of the match between (a) the demands placed on the group and the resources provided it, and (b) the communicative processes the group enacts to meet these demands and deploy its resources" (Poole and Hirokawa, 1996, p. 13). Such communicative functions include the processes used to make decisions, suggesting that decisions do not spring out of nowhere; they emerge through group dialogue that includes the sharing of opinions and perspectives and, in some cases, the evaluation of evidence (Frey, 1996).

Other developments in decision-making theory recognized the role that the timely synchronicity of events and actors plays within the decision-making process. Cohen, Olsen, and March advanced the notion of the garbage can model of

Table 8.6   Multi-Social-Scale Approaches to Decision Making

Level	Nature of Decision Making	Central Insights	Useful Theories
Individual	The individual (central) decision maker assesses alternatives on the basis of his or her own objectives and with as much information as possible	Limitation of information processing capacity: bounded rationality	Rationality, incrementalism, and mixed scanning (Simon, 1957; Lindblom, 1959; Etzioni, 1967)
Group	Decisions are made in groups, where the group process influences course and outcome	Group processes influence information provisions, value judgments, and interpretations	Social psychology of groups (Janis, 1982); community of practice theory (Wenger, 1998)
Organization	Organizations make decisions in relative autonomy; the structure and function of the organization matter	Organizational filters, intraorganizational contradictions, and attention structures influence information processes and the decisions based upon them	Organizational process model; bureau-political model (Allison, 1971); garbage can model (Cohen et al., 1972); community of practice theory (Wenger, 1998)
Interorganizational	Decisions between mutually dependent organizations are taken in different configurations of vertical and horizontal settings in a highly disjointed nature	Subjective perceptions, power relations, dynamics, and coincidence influence information and decision making	Policy stream model (Kingdon, 1984); complexity theory (Koppenjan and Klijn, 2004); policy implementation (Pressman and Wildavsky, 1973)

Source: Adapted from Koppenjan and Klijn, *Managing Uncertainties in Networks*, Routledge, London, 2004, p. 44.

decision making (1972), viewing a decision within the context of a host of other decisions that require some combination of alignments between problems, solutions, and participants (Koppenjan and Klijn, 2004, p. 52). Allison's classic study of the Cuban Missile Crisis illustrated the bureau-political model through which decisions get made through a complex interplay between different governmental agencies (1971). Pressman and Wildavsky's study of the Economic Development Administration (1984) shed new light onto the role of decision making across organizations. Tracking the number of decision points occurring within an implementation chain, they noted just how difficult it was to achieve agreement around not only policy goals, but the manner in which the prescribed solutions should be enacted (1984). Kingdon's "policy stream" model suggests that decisions get made when problems, policies, and politics streams are fully or particularly coupled (1984). All of these models acknowledge the role that politics and other social dynamics play in decision making.

The bounded rationality/incrementalist perspectives on decision making focus on the role of the individual as *the* decision maker. Policy implementation studies, the garbage can, bureau-political, and policy streams models all suggest that decision making be viewed within the context of social systems comprised of individuals, groups, and organizations. The challenges to analyzing decision making amidst such complexity have long been recognized (Poole and Hirokawa, 1996). In addition to the problem of isolating "the decision" from a host of other functions undertaken within the social system, decisions are, as Simon (1957) first articulated, embedded in a means-ends hierarchy, in which "it serves both a means for a larger choice and as the end of the more restricted choices" (Poole and Hirokawa, 1996, p. 10). Decisions occur across chains of actors (Cohen, March, and Olsen, 1972; Pressman and Wildavsky, 1984) that are inherently nonlinear and networked (Koppenjan and Klijn, 2004). By examining how decision making occurs within communities of practice we are able to describe and analyze the dynamics of the component parts of the system. As the decision-making dynamics of each community of practice get identified, we may then develop a model for how the decision architecture of the organization, construed within this context as a system, exists.

Systems theories are particularly useful in describing and analyzing these intricacies, as they are grounded in assertions regarding the "mental models" (Senge et al., 1994) that exist within and across multiple layers of individuals, groups, organizations, and networks of organizations within ever-widening social systems. Systems theorists (Bertalanffy, 1950; Boulding, 1956) assume that organizations are not closed containers, with fixed boundaries, roles, responsibilities, functions, and behaviors that adhere to rational order. While the early proponents of rationalism saw the stability of such entities as an indicator of rational thought and action, general systems theorists view stability as a matter of equilibrium. Within the context of a community of practice framework, such equilibrium is best understood within the context of the interplay within and across communities of practice (CoPs).

The community of practice has emerged as a unit of analysis that situates the role of organizational learning, knowledge transfer, and participation among people as the central enterprise of collective action. Community of practice theory has been used most extensively within the knowledge management and learning organization fields. It has also been employed to explore the nature of professional practice within the context of collective learning (in the form of professional development (Parboosingh, 2002; Buysse, Sparkman, and Wesley, 2003)) and practice (in terms of evolving professional competencies (Nicolini, Gherardi, and Yanow, 2003; Adams and McCullough, 2003)).

Community of practice theory has come to be applied to both intra- and inter-organizational settings. Within CoP theory, organizations and networks of organizations can be viewed as essentially constellations of communities of practice. Individual identity is said to be shaped by one's membership and "trajectories" within communities of practice in which he or she finds himself of herself (Wenger, 1998). CoP members may also serve as boundary spanners to other CoPs. Such roles are not mutually exclusive from being an insider, outbound, inbound, or on the periphery. CoPs that contain many peripheral members will likely be loosely coupled, while those with many insiders are more tightly coupled.

"Communities of practice are 'groups of people who share a concern, a set of problems, or a passion about a topic, and who deepen their knowledge and expertise in this area by interacting on an ongoing basis.' They operate as 'social learning systems' where practitioners connect to solve problems, share ideas, set standards, build tools, and develop relationships with peers and stakeholders" (Snyder, Wenger, and de Sousa Briggs, 2003, p. 17). Taking this definition of communities of practice and applying it to real-life settings, we find CoPs "existing everywhere" as "an integral part of our daily lives" (Wenger, 1998, pp. 6, 7). As such, the community of practice is a decidedly phenomenological entity, manifesting as a body of common experience between three or more people.

Although the concept of communities of practice has been applied extensively across multiple social science disciplines and professional fields, it has only recently been applied to the fields of public administration, public policy, and political science. CoP theory has been used to study innovative practices within police departments (de Laat and Broer, 2004) and army units (Kliner, 2002). Burk writes from his role as the senior knowledge officer for the Federal Highway Administration (FHWA) about his agency's utilization of CoP development to stimulate knowledge transfer (2000). Garcia and Dorohovich (2005) discuss their role in developing guidelines for the U.S. Department of Defense designed to foster the intentional cultivation of CoPs as a means to support information sharing and innovation. Dekker and Hansen (2004) discuss how CoP theory can be used to study the impact of politicization on public bureaucracies.

In discussing the potential role of CoPs in the analysis of cross-sector collaborations relating to the provision of public goods and services, Snyder, Wenger, and de Sousa Briggs (2003) assert:

> The boundary-crossing organizational structures that we describe here serve not only to accomplish agency missions better. In the longer term, they provide also a foundation for a new kind of national governance model that emphasizes participation, inquiry and collaboration.… Communities of practice—addressing issues ranging from E-Government to public safety, and operating across organizations, sectors, and levels—can address national priorities in ways no current organizational structure can match. (p. 6)

A review of the literature finds several instances in which researchers applied CoP frameworks to the analysis of interorganizational and cross-sector collaborations with a focus on public policy, including within the health care arena (Lathlean and le May, 2002; Gabbay et al., 2003; Dewhurst and Cegarra Navarro, 2004), intergovernmental collaborations (Zanetich, 2003; Drake, Steckler, and Koch, 2004; Bouwen and Taillieu, 2004), transnational governmental organizations (Luque, 2001; Somekh and Pearson, 2002), interindustry alignments (Starkey, Barnett, and Tempest, 2004), and networks of nongovernmental organizations (White, 2004; Rohde, 2004).

Implications of CoP theory for policy development, specifically health care policy (Gabbay et al., 2003; Popay et al., 2004), literacy education (Wixson and Yochum, 2004), standards-based school reforms (Gallucci, 2003; Hodkinson and Hodkinson, 2004), and environmental policies (VanWynsberghe, 2001; Attwater and Derry, 2005), have been made, pointing to the potential of CoP theory to help inform new and existing public policy initiatives. Citizen interface with public policies has been examined by Popay et al. (2004), who apply the concept of CoPs to explore issues of agency in professional practice. Youngblood's (2004) study of the role of CoPs in political parties points to the utility of CoP theory in the deconstruction of the often complex set of actors involved in policy development and execution.

These applications of CoP frameworks to the field of public administration and public policy have not, to date, focused on the individual and the ways in which an individual public administrator is immersed within, and impacted by, his or her membership within, various communities of practice.

We are able to discern the types of decision processes and the roles that CoP members play when making decisions. For example, decision makers within the CoP can be distributed (in which consensus or voting is used) or concentrated (in which there is a particular decision maker). Decisions can be made by a single member of a group, a smaller subset of the group, or be based on the discretion of the entire group. Group members may play deliberative or consultative roles in decision making (Vella, 2002). Deliberative roles are substantive in nature. Deliberative decisions makers are those with the ultimate authority to make the decision. Consultative decision makers take on a secondary role, providing input or advice, but deferring to the deliberators to make the ultimate decision.

Table 8.7   Group Decision-Making Process

Group Processes	Consultative Roles	Deliberative Roles
Consensus	None	All deliberative
Voting	None	All deliberative, with majority opinion holding sway
Decisions made by a subset of the group	Those outside the subset may provide input into the decision	Subset of the group makes the decision
Single decision maker in the group	Group members may provide input into a decision to be made by the individual decider	Single member (or nonmember) possesses authority to make decision
Group provides input into an issue or decision	All consultative	Authority to make the decision falls to some other person or CoP

Table 8.7 illustrates the different kinds of configurations that may take place within a CoP.

The role and function of decision making within groups often encompasses a complex set of arrangements. For example, some decisions may be left to the discretion of the group, with all members playing a deliberative role. This model can be viewed in terms of consensus or majority rule (e.g., voting). Other decisions can be the subject of discussion, with most members playing consultative roles and one or a small number of members making the final decision (playing the deliberative role).

The implications of this discussion of decision making as a function of governance network administrator should be relatively clear. If the social level of the decision and the processes used to make the decision are clear, it is easier to undertake all of the skills and strategies mentioned in this chapter. In some cases, network managers can help to shift the scale of the decision or the process used to make a decision; in other cases, the network manager can bring clarity to the structure and process of decision making.

How Does Governance Network Administration Differ across Social Sectors?

The challenges associated with serving two (or more) masters are not to be resolved within the traditional hierarchical arrangement. The "unity of command" in hierarchies allows for a subordinate to be accountable to one supervisor. As we contemplate the role that network managers play within governance networks, we must consider the relationship between the network manager's sectoral allegiances and his or her participation with a governance network. Our consideration of network management, most particularly as referenced in the discussion of participatory governance, has been grounded in a basic assumption: Network managers managing within governance networks are, by definition, public administrators. In this section we discuss the relationship between network management and some of the basic, core tenants that have distinguished public administration from other managerial practices and professions. We begin the discussion by laying out the traditional view of the public administrator as an agent of government. We proceed to discuss how trends such as privatization, contracting out, and devolution have forced the field of public administration to integrate nonprofit management into its sphere of influence. Given the recognition that governance networks are managed to greater or lesser degrees by actors situated across the social sector, we ask the question of whether, under certain conditions, agents of for-profit businesses and corporations can or should be considered public administrators. As Bogason and Musso note, "network governance introduces ambiguity into the role of the public administrator" (2006, p. 6). We tackle this ambiguity in this section.

Public administrators as agents of the government. The definition of the public administrator as an agent of governments at whatever geographic level has been the classical view of the field. At the "street level" governments are represented within governance networks by those public administrators who represent their interests as a result of either being elected, politically appointed, or a member of the civil service and government workforce. Although we have noted how this representation can get complicated (Kootnz et al., 2004), the roles that public administrators who are agents of governments play within governance networks are of critical importance to effective network governance and operations. Government agents bring a measure of "democratic anchorage" to the network, a point that we will turn to in Chapter 9. They may be mandated to ensure that network actors comply with regulations or contractual agreements. They may be stewards of the government resources, coming in all forms of capital resources.

Public administrators as agents of nonprofit organization. In recent decades, it has been increasingly recognized that nonprofit managers are public administrators. The differences between government and nonprofit operations are noted, not the least of which is differing governance structures (a topic we turn to in Chapter 9). Nonprofit organizations exist as a legally discrete social sector actor, an argument that we made in the opening chapter. They play different roles in grant and contract agreements (where they are almost always the recipients of government funds) and public-private partnerships than their government and business counterparts.

However, many of the obligations that nonprofit organizations have to their interest groups or "publics" provide them with some measure of democratic anchorage. As voluntary associations, nonprofit organizations help to form the basis of civil society. The importance of civil society to the health and vibrancy of democratic societies has been widely noted (Couto, 1999). From its early origins in the chartable associations of the 1800s, the nonprofit sector has been an instrumental actor in identifying and meeting public needs. To some degree, nonprofits have carried out similar functions as governments. Given this, the leap to consider nonprofit managers as public administrators of a certain type (much like we may distinguish city and town managers from federal level bureaucrats)* is a relatively simple one.

Public administrators as agents of for-profit organization. The leap to consider the manager of a for-profit organization participating in a governance network as a public administrator may be harder to make. In order to determine whether we could consider a corporate or business manager a public administrator, we must ask questions relating to the characteristics of the private sector. On one hand, corporations are at liberty to pursue their self-interests as long as they remain within the law. As for-profit entities, they will most likely seek to maximize their profit. In order to accomplish this, they will likely seek the role that places them in the most advantageous positions leading to achieving their goals. This profit motive very likely filters down most directly into the role of the business or corporate manager. These managers owe their allegiances to their supervisors, owners, and shareholders, a fact that leads to a fundamental distinction between public managers and private managers. It is difficult to think that an agent of a for-profit organization will bring democratic anchorage to the governance network of his or her own volition.

We have noted how corporations possess the rights provided to all legal citizens of the nation. In the United States, these rights have been won through a series of Supreme Court rulings. We must ask, however, with these rights, are corporations and other forms of for-profit organizations asked to carry out the responsibilities that are often ascribed to citizenship? Is it possible for corporations to sense an obligation to interests that lie beyond their self-interests? More importantly, is it possible for these more altruistic interests to actually shape behavior? Viewed from the lens of voluntary compliance, in which compliance is forged through the sharing of common norms, it is very unlikely that a case for considering business managers as public administrators can be made.

A more solid case for considering agents of for-profit organizations as public administrators can be made when coercive or remunerative forms of compliance are considered. Contract agreements are most often based on terms negotiated between government principles and for-profits agents. The structure for resource exchanges is crafted as a series of remunerative agreements. A measure of codependence is achieved as a result. In theory, when compliance with remunerative agreements is met, a business or corporate manager must share the same accountability structures that guide public administrative actions. The same may be said for instances of compliance with regulations and mandates. Thus, we may argue that a for-profit

---

* The proliferation of nonprofit concentrations within MPA programs across the United States speaks to the inherent acceptance of nonprofit managers as public administrators within the field.

firm's participation within a governance network renders the business managers representing their firm's interests accountable to serving the public interest in much the same way as public administrators working out of governments and nonprofits do.

We do not suggest that we have resolved this matter here. We conclude, however, that more consideration must be given to the relationship between the sectoral characteristics of a governance network manager's organizational "home" and his or her identify as a public administrator. In the next chapter, we now know "sector blurring" may be leading to the blurring of public administrative principles and practices. This concern has been raised within the substantial critiques of NPM (see Denhardt and Denhardt, 2003). These same critiques hold true within a network context. What is different here is distinguishing governance networks from other forms of interorganizational networks (such as supply chains or other types of strategic alliances forged to pursue private gain). By grounding network structures and functions within a framework of democratic governance, we assert that governance network management rightly belongs among the other public administration paradigms.

Summary Implications for the Role of Managing Mixed-Actor Governance Networks

In summary, in this chapter we have emphasized that the three paradigms of public administration factor into or sediment onto a fourth, emergent paradigm that may best be labeled "governance network administration." We believe that several themes are likely to shape the role of the public administrator in governance networks: interdependencies, ambiguity, personal influence, and repoliticization.

For Myrna Mandell, "network management implies the need to manage interdependencies" (1990, p. 49). In this regard, the mobilizing of behavior and resources will be a critical skill—perhaps a gestalt—in orchestrating governance networks.

> The linkage between strategy formulation and strategy implementation is less clear when managing in an inter-organizational network. Unlike the intra-organizational perspective, a manager's ability to correctly analyze the environment, in and of itself, will not be the overriding determinant of whether his or her strategies will prove effective. Instead, the idea of mobilization behavior and the marshaling of resources in order to first create a more viable environment will dominate behavior in an inter-organizational network. (Mandell, 1990, p. 49)

Second, it seems clear the public administrator, as they have in the past, will be faced with ambiguity in the management of governance networks. Bryson, Crosby, and Stone have observed that network structures are "likely to change over time because of ambiguity of membership and complexity in local environments" (2006, p. 49). This ambiguity will be centered on how to accomplish network goals and to do so under the scrutiny of multiple forms of accountability, a topic that we will turn to in Chapter 9. According to Bogason and Musso (2005), "network governance introduces ambiguity into the role of the public administrator and raises issues related to public accountability and efficiency" (Bogason and Musso, 2005, p. 6). The proliferation of such ambiguities leads to many of the central concerns raised within the literature concerning the hollowing of the state.

As we have noted in our discussion of boundary spanning and brokering, personal influence in the network, while difficult, will play a central role in achieving both network outcomes and network legitimacy. According to Mandell,

> effective network management therefore relies on members' ability to influence others in horizontal, as well as hierarchical, relationships. To accomplish this, members will need to build pockets of commitment both within and outside the network. The ability to achieve this relates to the social and political environment. (Mandell, 1990, p. 42)

Extending personal influence within the governance network to ensure accountability and effectiveness will likely mean the repoliticization of the role of the public administrator. This repoliticization process has a significant bearing on the relationship between the sectoral allegiances of a manager's main organization and his or her allegiances to the governance network. According to Bogason and Musso, "network governance … repoliticizes public administration in a healthy manner by broadening the conceptualization of politics beyond the party." This reconceptualization "provides opportunities for cooperation, flexible responses, and collective social production" (Bogason and Musso, 2005, p. 6). We may argue that governance networks, dating back to some of their early foundations discussed in Chapter 1, have always been spaces for administrative as well as political processes and practices. The political nature of intergovernmental relations, the role of politics in contracting practices, and the existence of regulatory capture all point to the active role that politics has always played within and across network dynamics.

The role of the public administrator in governance networks will not be reflected in a list of singular action steps that, if followed, will result in success. More likely, their roles will emerge from an understanding and reckoning of these four themes. These four themes help to form the basis of a public administration gestalt for network management. In discussing this gestalt, Mandell references Porter and Warner, who "found that public administrators build a 'gestalt' (or understanding) as to which tasks will be performed by which organizations and from where resources will be drawn" (Mandell, 1990, p. 41). The role of the public administrator is to shape and be shaped by the nature of the interdependences of relationships, the ambiguity of those relationships and conditions, as well as by the goals the governance network seeks to achieve. This will undoubtedly be influenced by how interests and motivations are mustered by the public administrator and network participants. A theory of governance networks will need to embrace the role of the public administrator and the range of possibilities that will emerge from these themes.

Concerns regarding the proper role of the state as an actor within governance networks need to be articulated as a juxtaposition of sectoral differences, beyond the simple market vs. polis distinctions raised in most critiques of the new public management.

CRITICAL QUESTIONS AND CONSIDERATIONS

Revisiting your governance network again, we focus on the roles of individual governance network administrators operating within the governance network.

■ Who are the individual leaders of this governance network? Has leadership of the network changed over time? What are the skills and strategies that these leaders have undertaken as network administrators? How much situational awareness or systems thinking do these leaders exhibit?

■ If possible, pull out an instance when this network needed to be facilitated. Or pull out an instance when an important item of collective interest needed to be negotiated. Or describe an instance when the network purposely involved citizens in the network's governance process.

■ How are decisions made in this network? Are decisions made by one or a few actors, or are they made collectively? Where are critical decisions made? By whom?

■ How much do individual network administrators identify with the governance network's policy functions or policy domains? To what extent do network administrators identify more with the goals and missions of their "home" organization?

Chapter 9

The Hybridized Accountability Regimes of Governance Networks*

Adding actors does more than complexify, it tilts the balance of power.

—Laurence O'Toole and Kenneth Meier (2004a, p. 684)

Governance and Accountability

In previous chapters we make the case that governments are, unto themselves, network configurations formed through a complex array of inter- and intragovernmental relations. We have recognized that the state and its requisite governmental institutions coordinate activities and exchange resources with private and nonprofit organizations, resulting, at times, in the sharing of power with stakeholders from other social sectors. A picture of polycentric systems of governance emerges (Mathur and Skelcher, 2007). We have noted how these realizations have begun to shift emphasis away from the role of *government* to the proper configurations of the processes of *governance* that unfold amidst complex networks of individuals, organizations, and institutions. We have noted how the shift in focus to governance has coincided with the network turn in public administration, observing that governance becomes "the property of networks rather than as the product

* This chapter was written with assistance from Daniel Bromberg and Russell Mills.

225

of any single centre of action (Johnston and Shearing, 2003, p. 148)" (Crawford, 2006, p. 458).

We argue that accountability is a critical element in governing processes and practices. Writing about governing complex societies, Jon Pierre and Guy Peters observe that "the governance process is feedback, with the actions of instruments in the past being jointly evaluated and put back into the decision-making process. Governance has the same root word as 'cybernetics' and hence implies some connection to the environment and a continual adjustment of instruments (and perhaps even goals) in light of the success and failure of actions taken in the past" (2005, p. 15). We have already noted that governance may be understood as the processes that regulate the flow of feedback to and within the social system (Katz and Kahn, 1978). Such feedback may be derived through the internal dynamics occurring across the network or unfolding within individual actors of the network. Feedback may also be directed to the system from its external environment. We argue that accountability structures operate in most any administrative setting as negative feedback loops, playing a critical role in governing systems dynamics.

In Chapter 1, we noted A. W. Rhodes's assertion regarding the relationship between policy networks and governance. As one of the first scholars to deeply consider the relationship between governance and interorganizational networks, he argued that governance processes are guided by interdependencies shaped through their continuing interactions. He observed that these interactions take on "game-like" qualities (1997).

"Accountability is traditionally defined as the obligation to give an account of one's actions to someone else, often balanced by a responsibility of that other to seek an account" (Scott, 2006, p. 175). In essence, accountability structures arise when a certain measure of interdependency exists between those rendering accounts and those to whom accounts should be rendered. In this chapter we discuss governance as a matter of accountability, with feedback taking place as processes of rendering accounts to particular constituencies, relying on certain explicit standards and tacit norms to do so. Therefore, we assert that network accountability is as a system-level construct—one that is shaped by the accountability structures of the individual parts of the network, and the emergence of "hybridized accountability regimes" of the network as a whole (Mashaw, 2006).

Referring to the trend toward governance networks, O'Toole and Meier have noted that "adding actors does more than complexify, it [can] tilt the balance of power" (2004b, p. 684). Page (2004), Posner (2002), Newman (2004), Behn (2001), and Van Slyke and Roch (2004) have all noted the accountability challenges associated with governance networks, recognizing their complexity and the potential competing aims inherent to the organizations operating within them. Mashaw calls for the comparison of accountability regimes operating within and across network structures in order to "evaluate their differential capacities, and perhaps articulate hybrid regimes that approximate optimal institutional designs" (Mashaw, 2006, p. 118). In cases where a governance network is comprised of nonprofit and for-profit organizations working with governments, the accountability regimes historically ascribed to governments are not sufficient. "Conventional accountability narratives, emphasizing ex post and hierarchical forms of accountability, with only very limited reach beyond the state actors, are unable to support the burden of providing a narrative of accountability that can legitimate governance structures involving diffuse actors and methods" (Scott, 2006, p. 190).

It is apparent to those who have examined the accountability challenges associated with governance networks that new accountability models are needed to recognize their inherently intersectoral nature. We need to recognize that the accountability structures of individual organizational actors interrelate with the accountability structures of other organizations in the network. For example, within a simple binary network relationship between a government entity and a for-profit firm, the government's adherence to political or bureaucratic accountability structures may compete against the firm's need to earn a profit. Rarely have these kind of trade-offs been explored in a systematic way.

Each of the three social sectors that we have examined thus far, including the public, private, and nonprofit sectors, are constructed around particular compositions of accountability frames and types. Although we recognize the principle of holism that asserts that the whole amounts to more than the sum of its parts (Degenne and Forse, 1999), we must recognize the extent to which the governance frameworks of particular network actors will have an impact on the hybridized accountability regimes that emerge through the ongoing operations of a governance network. In the sections to follow we explore the differences between modes of governance across the three social sectors, drawing distinctions and similarities occurring between them.

Modes of Sector Governance

One way to examine the accountability structures of different governance network actors is to review the literature pertaining to accountability within the public (Romzek and Dubnick, 1987; deLeon, 1998; Denhardt and Denhardt, 2003), corporate (Smith, 1998; Scott, 2006), and nonprofit (Kearns, 1996; Brooks, 2002; Stone and Ostrower, 2007) sectors, in addition to the literature that looks at the differences between accountability structures across sectors (Behn, 2001; Riemer, 2001; Minow, 2002; Mashaw 2006). In Chapter 4, we introduced the possibility that the sectoral characteristics of particular network actors will influence their goal orientations toward their participation in governance networks. Considering the potential for sector blurring that may occur in some mixed-form governance networks, we must consider how and to what extent distinctions between the governance and accountability structures of governments, for-profit firms, and nonprofit organizations contribute to the development of network-wide accountability regimes.

Corporate governance can be framed in terms of the interplay of owners or shareholders, boards of directors, managers, and consumers (Anand, 2008), as well as adherence to legal requirements dictated by laws and regulations sanctioned by the state. Although critical theorists and neo-Marxist social scientists have raised concerns about the growing influence of corporate power within democratic societies, very few of these critiques have found their way into mainstream considerations of privatization and public-private partnerships. Corporations exist, first and foremost, to earn profits for their owners/shareholders. Although there has been increased interest in adding corporate social responsibility norms into the existing corporate governance formula (Fox et al., 2002), the essence of corporate governance remains one of the interplay between boards of directors, shareholders, and managers and the legal system that sets viable parameters around corporate activities. An argument can be made to add consumers into this framework, a point we will return to later in this chapter. The overarching performance standard of the private sector is profit.

Interest group theories assert how citizens join or associate with voluntary associations, organizing their collectivized interests into formal or informal interest groups. Nonprofit organizations also exist to meet unmet societal needs, providing public services and, essentially, filling gaps left in government's direct delivery of public goods and services (Salamon, 2002a). Within the literature, the governance structures of nonprofits have been understood in terms of board composition and development (Stone and Ostrower, 2007, p. 419). In summing up this literature, Stone and Ostrower observe: "Findings suggest that within nonprofits themselves, there are widely varying perspectives and expectations among board members and between the board and CEO concerning board roles and responsibilities. Furthermore, external factors, such as variations in funding environments, may significantly influence board composition and what a board does" (2007, p. 421). Of the three sectors that can participant within governance networks, the governance structures of nonprofit actors appear to be the most contextual and fluid. The overarching performance standard of the nonprofit sector is meeting the organizational mission, another facet of nonprofit governance that is highly context specific and situational.

Although the prestige of government has suffered over the years, the relevance of state sovereignty and the contractual obligation that states have to their citizens are still extremely critical to the functioning of governance networks. We argue that executive agencies of government most often actively represent government interests in governance networks. Governments bring several critically important functions and resources to governance networks, including funneling symbolic power and cultural authority to the network; informing public perceptions of the network, lending it legitimacy; and allocating distinctive (tactical) resources and providing sources of information through which interests are pursued (Crawford, 2006, p. 459). Governments lend legitimacy to a governance network; they formally (via elected officials) and informally (through representative bureaucracies) represent citizens in general as well as particular interest groups, contribute resources to the network, share and redistribute risks, and play a vital role in framing public problems and potential solutions.

The governance of governments is probably best understood in the context of sovereignty and the balance of powers across the branches of government. Government has traditionally been construed in terms of the iconic public bureaucracy, through which elected officials make political appointments, who in turn work with career civil servants. Citizens play a critical role in the governance of governments in democratic societies by actively selecting their representatives and possessing the capacity to directly interface with government (see the discussion of the collaborative and participatory governance literature cited above). Elected officials also play a pivotal role in ensuring that governments operate democratically. The performance standard unique to the state sector is meeting public needs and delivering public policy.

Table 9.1 illustrates a basic overview of the differences between the public, private, and nonprofit sectors. We define interests to mean those points of view and perspectives that either in theory or in practice govern organizations' capacities to act and exchange resources. We define representative interests as the formal or informal agents to whom accounts must be rendered. As contributors to organizations' accountability structures, interests influence how organizations behave, make decisions, and distribute resources. We describe accountability structures in terms of the governance characteristics of governments, corporations, and

Table 9.1   Characteristics of Sector Governance

Social Sector	Organizational Actors	To Whom Accountabilities Are Rendered	Predominant Performance Standard(s)
Public	Governments (national, state, regional, local)	Citizens and interest groups; elected officials	Policy goals; meeting public needs; implementing policies
Nonprofit	Nonprofit organizations (NGOs)	Citizens and interest groups; boards of directors; clients	Fulfillment of mission
Private	Corporations, firms, businesses (for-profit organizations)	Owners/ shareholders; customers; boards of directors	Profit

nonprofit organizations. Table 9.1 provides a basic overview of critical sectoral characteristics.

By considering sectoral differences of the governance structures of organizational actors within governance networks, we recognize the importance that nodal governance plays vis-à-vis the governance of the entire system. "Nodal governance … [focuses] attention on bringing more clarity to the internal characteristics of nodes and thus to the analysis of how power is actually created and exercised within a social system. While power is transmitted across networks, the actual points where knowledge and capacity are mobilized for transmission is the node (Burris, 2004, 341)" (Crawford, 2006, p. 458). At this juncture, very little is known about how the different governance structures of the nodes (informed, at least in part, through sectoral characteristics) inform the governance of the entire governance network. A view of the difference in performance standards across the public, private, and nonprofit sectors connotes a continuum of clearly defined measures: near universal measures (such as profit), to the ambiguity-riddled challenges of measuring successful public policies (Stone, 2002), to the highly context-specific and mostly localized performance standards ascribed to individual nonprofit organizations (Stone and Ostrower, 2007).

Corporate Governance

There are multiple influences that may affect the operations of a corporation. These influences may be external factors, such as legal implications or customer preferences. They may also be internal factors, such as organizational culture, governing structure, or investor relations. The complexity of these varying influences may challenge corporations to respond effectively to multiple demands. Much of an organization's response is determined by its mechanisms of corporate governance. Although corporate governance is rarely defined in clear, concise terms, it is generally understood as the macro composition of a corporation's governing and operating structure.

It is within a framework of corporate governance that managers function and determine the most appropriate responses to all internal and external influences. According to the Organization for Economic Cooperation and Development (OECD, 2004), there is "no single model of good corporate governance" (p. 13). Rather, there are numerous best practices that exist and certain principles that should be followed to ensure appropriate governance structures. In a 2004 document the OECD defined a set of principles of corporate governance:

> This document defined corporate governance as involving a set of relationships between a company's management, its board, its shareholders and other stakeholders. Corporate governance also provides the structure through which the objectives of the company are set, and the

means of attaining those objectives and monitoring performance are determined. (OECD, 2004, p. 11)

The OECD (2004) identifies six principles in which structures of corporate governance should be situated. These principles provide a general framework for corporate governance, yet remain adaptable to accommodate the needs of a specific corporation.

1. The corporate governance framework should promote transparent and efficient markets, be consistent with the rule of law, and clearly articulate the division of responsibilities among different supervisory, regulatory, and enforcement authorities....
2. The corporate governance framework should protect and facilitate the exercise of shareholders' rights....
3. The corporate governance framework should ensure the equitable treatment of all shareholders, including minority and foreign shareholders. All shareholders should have the opportunity to obtain effective redress for violation of their rights....
4. The corporate governance framework should recognize the rights of stakeholders established by law or through mutual agreements and encourage active cooperation between corporations and stakeholders in creating wealth, jobs, and the sustainability of financially sound enterprises....
5. The corporate governance framework should ensure that timely and accurate disclosure is made on all material matters regarding the corporation, including the financial situation, performance, ownership, and governance of the company....
6. The corporate governance framework should ensure the strategic guidance of the company, the effective monitoring of management by the board, and the board's accountability to the company and the shareholders. (pp. 17–24)

Corporate governance has been described in terms of agency theory, in which corporations are conceived as two parties—managers and investors—with corporate governance often seen as the mechanism used to bridge these two separate parties (Johnson, Daily, and Ellstrand, 1996). Agency theory typically depicts managers as self-interested entities; therefore, corporate governance structures are enacted not only to bridge the gap between managers and investors, but to protect investors from self-interested managers (Johnson, Daily, and Ellstrand, 1996). Primarily, the idea behind agency theory is to separate those who finance the corporation from those that manage it (Shleifer and Vishny, 1997). One would want to ensure structures that limit the potential of managers taking unwarranted salaries or other types of compensation arrangements.

The extent to which a corporation's accountability structure extends beyond the binary relationship between owners and management is a matter that is of critical importance when considered in light of governance networks. A continuum may stretch from those who believe corporations hold responsibilities to the greater society that they function within, to those who assert that a corporation's account-ability should be almost exclusively to the owners of the company. This continuum is anchored by two extremes that Dunfee (1999) refers to as the monotonic view and the pluralist view.

Economist Milton Friedman is often associated with the monotonic view. The monotonic view places the owner or shareholder as the only principal to whom accounts should be rendered. In 1970 he claimed that the expansion of corporate accountability to a broader array of stakeholders was "pure unadulterated social-ism," and that business executives' responsibilities lie with the desires of "the own-ers of the business to make as much money as possible" (1970, p. 17). He and other advocates of the monotonic view believe in increasing shareholders' profits, placing very little emphasis on the wider community within which the corpora-tion operates. This view is referred to by legal scholars as the *shareholder primacy norm*, in which "corporate directors have a fiduciary duty to make decisions that are in the best interests of the shareholders" (Smith, 1998, p. 278). Advocates of this view believe that corporate operations that accomplish goals outside of increasing shareholder profit should be forbidden, or in the very least not the subject of much consideration (Dunfee, 1999). Shareholders, it is held, invest in corporations to increase their own wealth (Bainbridge, 1993).

Although there is discrepancy concerning the rationale for shareholder primacy, it is believed to be a common and "obvious" corporate philosophy (Sundaram and Inkpen, 2004, p. 350). Justifications in favor of shareholder primacy include the promotion of entrepreneurial risk for managers, providing managers with one clear objective rather than a vague array of goals, and a lack of legal protection for share-holders that can readily be sought by stakeholders in the legal and political environ-ment (Sundaram and Inkpen, 2004).

On the other side of the continuum lies the pluralist view. Those advocating this view see the corporation as a member of a larger public and stress that it must act in congruence with the public interest. The pluralist view acknowledges respon-sibility to both the shareholders and the stakeholders of the corporation (Dunfee, 1999). Stakeholders encompass a broader constituency that can be identified as "suppliers, distributors, creditors, local communities, consumers, and the federal or state government" (Dunfee, 1999, p.29). Within this broadened view, the corpora-tion is asked to consider a more pluralist array of interests when making its deci-sions. Advocates of this view usually try to strike a moderate tone, claiming that it is not necessary for the corporation to please all of these stakeholders; however, it is of great importance that the corporation makes responsible, ethical decisions concerning these stakeholders.

This view may be traced back, philosophically, to Rousseau's notion of the social contract (2006), as well as to considerations given to the nature of exter-nalities that exist in any economic transaction (Tullock, 1996). Lastly, sys-tems theorists remind us that individuals and organizations do not persist in a vacuum, suggesting that all actors, including corporations, need to rely on reciprocating systems of social organization. Corporations rely on public infrastructures across all functions of their business operations. Obvious examples, such as roads, clean air, EMT services, and even the judicial system, are necessary public goods and expenditures utilized by corporations. As such, a corporation carries with it certain obligations to contribute to the public good. Therefore, to a certain degree, all corporations need to be mindful of their stakeholders, very broadly construed.

Turnbull (1997) identifies a much broader scope in which to study corporate governance. His perspective is shaped around a wider array of influences on corporate governance, encompassing all factors that may affect a corporation. Turnbull (1997) also suggests viewing corporate governance through the lenses of culture, power, and cybernetics. Each of these views provides a different vantage point, but each relies on the interaction of various influences on the corporation. These viewpoints allow corporate governance to be examined from the perspective of broad influences such as social interactions, cultural norms, and power relationships. Corporate governance therefore is a product of multiple influences that are not accounted for within classical agency theory.

If for-profit firms are implicated within a governance network, the range of possible stakeholders exerting influence on the corporation's behaviors get mitigated through the dominance of one performance measure in particular: profit. To the owners of a company, whether they are private owners or shareholders (in the case of publicly traded companies), the capacity of the firm to make a profit becomes paramount. We argue that the profit motive derived through shareholder/owner

EXTERNAL INFLUENCES ON A CORPORATION

Customer
Competitors
Shareholders
Employees
Unions
Suppliers
Bankers & Financers
Professional Associations
Trade Associations
Directors & Advisors
Regulators

Source: **Turnbull,** *Corporate Governance: An International Review,* **5,**
180–205, 1997.

accountability serves as the principal performance standard around which a business or firm is measured. A firm's performance is, of course, mediated through markets. We argue that customers, the target of most firms' business, also wield significant power within a corporation's governance structure.

Later in the chapter we discuss the extent to which a corporation's involvement in a governance network leads to a widening of the scope of stakeholders to whom a corporation needs to render accounts. These stakeholder may not only include those most directly involved in a firm's day-to-day practices, but wider, more publicly construed, interests captured within the drives for corporate social responsibility and the triple bottom line.

Nonprofit Governance

Although there are multiple influences that may impact the actions of nonprofit organizations, the board of directors has been widely recognized as the chief focus of the nonprofit governance literature for the past twenty years. Ultimately, "nonprofit organizations can only be said to articulate their objectives and formulate their plans when their governors—their boards of directors or executive officers—take action" (Smith and Lipsky, 1993, p. 72). However, nonprofit organizations contribute to civil society and "are important to our concepts of community and citizen empowerment because they represent the efforts of people to take collective action outside the umbrella of government" (Smith and Lipsky, 1993, p. 72). As voluntary associations, we have already noted that nonprofit organizations play a significant role in mediating the relationships between interests and the policy process. We may view the range of actors to whom nonprofit organizations are accountable through monocentric and pluralistic lenses—ranging from governance residing exclusively on the shoulders of boards of directors to the multiple constituencies of nonprofit organizations, including clients, funders, and represented interests.

In surveying the depth and breadth of the nonprofit governance literature, Melissa Stone and Francie Ostrower observed that there is "a widely held belief that governance in non-profit organizations is the province of their boards of directors and has to do with organization-level control, accountability, and managing resource dependencies (Stone, 1987; Miller-Millesen, 2003)" (Stone and Ostrower, 2007, p. 418). They note how "nonprofit legal scholars ... address governance as fulfilling legal and fiduciary responsibilities, most particularly the need for the board to comply with duty of care and duty of loyalty standards" (Stone and Ostrower, 2007, p. 417). The 2002 Sarbanes-Oxley Act has impacted nonprofits by focusing federal attention on nonprofit governance issues, shedding particular light on the role of nonprofit boards in carrying out their critical, fiduciary responsibilities (Stone and Ostrower, 2007, p. 430). It has been observed that the greater the stress placed on fiduciary accountability over other governing responsibilities, the more that nonprofit boards tend to micromanage (p. 429). Despite the attention given to boards to date, "very few studies … have asked whether and how board composition affects measures of organizational performance" (Stone and Ostrower, 2007, pp. 419–20).

Because nonprofit organizations "mediate between the interests of their constituents and public policy or the political process" (Couto, 1999, pp. 46–47), many other stakeholders may be implicated in their accountability structures, "including executive directors, staff, volunteers, donors, and beneficiaries," all of whom "are likely to influence organizational mission, major policies, executive director performance, and external relationships" (Stone and Ostrower, 2007, p. 418). The pluralistic view of nonprofit governance broadens the scope of stakeholders, shedding light on the "external boundaries of non-profits (Chait, Ryan, and Taylor, 2005; McCambridge, 2004)" (Stone and Ostrower, 2007, p. 418). These external boundaries extend into the murky waters of interest group formation and representation.

Summarizing studies of nonprofit governance, Stone and Ostrower suggest rather fluid and contextually-driven accountability structures:

> Findings suggest that within nonprofits themselves, there are widely varying perspectives and expectations among board members and between the board and CEO concerning board roles and responsibilities. Furthermore, external factors, such as variations in funding environments, may significantly influence board composition and what a board does. (Stone and Ostrower, 2007, p. 421)

Due to the lack of research in this area, the extent to which boards are attentive to external interests is not known. The lack of understanding of the impact of boards on nonprofit performance led Stone and Ostrower to ask, "Do boards see themselves as solely responsible for doing what is best for their organizations or do they see themselves as charged with a responsibility to a wider public, and how do they define that public?" They add: "What we know virtually nothing about, however, is whether and how nonprofit board members think about their relationship to the broader public interest as well as their own organization" (2007, p. 428).* They conclude that "board effectiveness is a negotiated and highly contingent concept" (Stone and Ostrower, 2007, p. 422).

---

* Stone and Ostrower lay out the following questions that are still unresolved: "Do nonprofit boards actually know the wider legal obligations and policy expectations that pertain to their work? Do boards understand the structure of policy fields, including differences among funding streams and regulations (federal, state, and local) as well as the normative expectations attached to each? How do they take this information into account when formulating strategic direction or evaluating organizational performance? Do boards see themselves as willing and able to influence specific policy expectations as well as policy formulation?" (Stone and Ostrower, 2007, p. 431).

The interpersonal dynamics of nonprofit boards of directors will likely play a significant role in determining how and to what extent boards are stronger or weaker entities to whom accounts need to be rendered. Likewise, the extent to which nonprofit organizations are accountable to interest groups, their clientele, and citizens at large may tend to be forged on weak ties. We consider the impact of what the governance structures of nonprofit actors bring to a governance network later in this chapter, when we discuss the implications of sector blurring.

Governance of Governments

Vested with sovereign authorities, governments are purposively constructed to be accountable to the multiple stakeholders found within and across a pluralistic, democratic society. We have already noted how the separation of powers structures the nature of network relations arising between branches of government. The separation of powers also plays a role in the accountability and operational structures of individual governmental actors, particularly those found in the executive branch. David Rosenbloom's application of separation of powers to public administrative theory suggests the ways that the administrative branches of government actors are shaped through a pluralistic array of managerial, political, and legal forces. "The basic concept behind pluralism within public administration is that since the administrative branch is a policy-making center of government, it must be structured to enable faction to counteract faction by providing political representation to a comprehensive variety of the organized political, economic, and social interests that are found in the society at large" (Rosenbloom, 2004, p. 449).

Rosenbloom discusses the managerial factors shaping public administration in terms of the public bureaucracies of the executive branch, and the command and control authorities that are said to persist in them. Much has been written regarding the managerial functions of public bureaucrats, most classically represented in Gulick's POSDCORB model (1937). Managerial relationships get structured through the principles of unity of command and the span of control. The classical view of management is grounded in hierarchical, vertically aligned organizational structures. The chief historical concerns arising here have been focused on the limits of rationality (Simon, 1957), ethical neutrality, and the potential dehumanizing effects that public bureaucracies bring to both the people who work in them and whom they serve.

The multiple forms of authority that exist within governance networks give rise to new managerial frameworks. We have already noted how the command and control administrative authorities found within the classical public bureaucracy do not sufficiently account for the possibilities of collaborative, horizontal ties, and the compromises and concessions found in the diagonal ties found in negotiated and bargaining authorities. In governments, the managerial principals to whom accounts need to be rendered are those situated at the top of the public bureaucracy.

The role of politics in the administration of public bureaucracies has been a widely discussed topic within the public administration field, ranging from Wilson and Goodnow's early calls for the separation of politics and administration, to Appleby's recognition that politics plays a big role in the day-to-day practices of most public bureaucracies, to Selznick's discussion of the role of politics and citizen participation as a form of cooptation, to Minnowbrook I's call for public administrators to promote social equity and justice. Across these threads of discussion has been the assumption first captured by Karl Mannheim, that "bureaucracy turns all political issues into matters of administration" (1936, p. 118). Echoing this observation, a general consensus has emerged that public administrators are political actors and, more specifically, policy makers when they interpret and enforce rules and regulations set forth in laws and statutes. Frederick Mosher discussed the role of politics in the life of public administrators this way:

> Public administrators are heavily engaged in policy and politics a good share of their time, but much of this activity is of a different order of politics from that represented by political parties, elections, and votes in the Congress. It is controversy, competition, and negotiation among different factions within the bureaucracy itself. It consists in dealing with, responding to, or resisting clienteles and other interest groups outside the bureaucracy, and dealing with Congressional groups and other individual congressmen. (Mosher, 1982, p. 95)

March and Olsen define politics as "aggregating individual preferences into collective actions by some procedures of rational bargaining, negotiation, coalition formation, and exchange (Riker, 1962; Coleman, 1966; Downs, 1967; Niskanen, 1972; Taylor, 1975)" (March and Olsen, 1995, p. 7). In essence, politics both results from and contributes to negotiation and bargaining processes. Lowercase *p* politics unfolds as the result of negotiated meaning, positioning, and other "games" (Rhodes, 1997) that result through the phenomena of everyday actors and resource exchanges. Capital *P* politics can be found in the electoral process, the role and influence of political parties, and the creation of interest group coalitions designed to impact the decisions and actions of sovereign governments.

The role of capital *P* politics in the accountability structures of democratic governments may be found in the deference paid to elected representatives and citizens. Democratic governments are chiefly accountable to the public at large, vested with the authority to carry out the public's interest. As sovereign authorities, governments are contractually anchored to their citizenry. This relationship requires that governments have the legitimate authority to make decisions and carry out actions on behalf of the public. Citizens, in turn, have the legitimate authority to

ACCOUNTABILITY PRINCIPLES OF THE LEGAL SYSTEM

Procedural due process: "The term stands for the value of fundamental fairness and is viewed as requiring procedures designed to protect individuals from malicious, arbitrary, capricious, or unconstitutional harm."

Substantive rights: "Maximization of individual rights and liberties as a positive good and necessary feature of U.S. political system."

Equity: "Stands for the value of fairness in the result of conflicts between private parties and the government. It militates against arbitrary or invidious treatment of individuals, encompasses much of the constitutional requirement of equal protection, and enables the courts to fashion relief for individuals whose constitutional rights have been violated by administrative action."

Source: **Rosenbloom, in Shafritz et al., Eds.,** *Classics of Public Administration,* **5th ed., Wadsworth/Thomson Learning, Belmont, CA, 2004, pp. 451–52.**

petition their government, and attempt to exert their influence over the government through the election of representatives, the passing of referendums, etc. As elected representatives, presidents, governors, mayors, legislators, and in some cases, judges get elected to serve the interests of their constituencies. Elected officials play a major role as principals in the accountability structures of governments.

Rosenbloom reminds us that governments are also vested with legal authorities, and in some cases government agencies "begin to function more like courts and consequently legal values come to play a greater role in their activities" (Rosenbloom, 2004, p. 451). The legal values of procedural due process, substantive rights, and equity become factors in ensuring the legal accountabilities of governments.

Courts and judges play pivotal roles in mediating conflicts, interpreting and enforcing laws, and ensuring contractual agreements are adhered to. As particular governmental actors, courts play a privileged role in governance networks, most often serving as peripheral actors who may wield significant authority to hold network actors accountable.

The accountability structures of governments have been widely discussed, ranging from Robert Dahl's considerations of democratic structures and norms in the 1940s to Maas and Radway's articulation of the responsibilities of government. Table 9.2 presents an overview of Maas and Radway's overview of governments' responsibilities, including the "working bias" that has historically coincided with them.

Table 9.2 Maas and Radway's Accountabilities of Government

Government Agencies Are Responsible to	Working Bias	Accountability Rendered to
People at large	"An administrative agency cannot and should not normally be held directly responsible to the people at large." (p. 166)	Citizens
People— pressure groups	"An administrative agency should be responsible to pressure groups so far as necessary to equalize opportunities for safeguarding interests, to acquire specialized knowledge, and to secure consent for its own program." (p. 167)	Citizens
Legislature	"An administrative agency should be responsible to the legislature, but only through the chief executive, and primarily for broad issues of public policy and general administrative performance." (p. 169)	Elected representatives
Chief executive	"An administrative agency should be directly responsible for conforming to the general program of the chief executive and for coordinating its activities with other agencies of the executive branch." (p. 173)	Elected representatives
Political parties	"An administrative agency cannot be held independently responsible to the organization or policies of political parties." (p. 175)	Citizens
Profession	"An administrative agency should be responsible for maintaining, developing, and applying such professional standards as may be relevant to its activities." (p. 176)	Professions
Courts	"Judicial review is largely a negative, post hoc, and unduly ritualized check addressed to errors of commission." (p. 178)	Courts

Source: Adapted from Maas and Radway, 2001.

Democratic Anchorage

Accountability in democratic societies has traditionally been predicated on the legitimacy that accompanies the kinds of sovereign entities found in local, state, and national governments. The substantial shift from accountability predicated on governments to accountability found within and across governance networks focuses attention on the fate of state sovereignty and the qualities of democratic anchorage that have been traditionally ascribed to it.

Studies of social cliques and group think within interpersonal networks demonstrate how social capital, coupled with insularity, can give rise to the exercise of power free of accountability or of the knowledge and insights that flow through permeable network boundaries. Bogason and Musso summarize the potential threats that antidemocratic networks pose to democratic accountability: "There are dangers that interest groups and political insiders will manipulate the system for their own gains and to the dis-advantage of those who do not have the resources to organize.… And in any democratic system, there is a tendency for more powerful factions to overwhelm the weak and to perpetuate their advantage through institutional means" (Bogason and Musso, 2006, p. 14).

A governance network's capacity to support or hinder democratic accountability hinges on its capacity to be what Eva Sorensen and Jacob Torfing (2005) describe as democratically anchored. Sorensen and Torfing assert that "governance networks are democratically anchored to the extent that they are properly linked to different political constituencies and to a relevant set of democratic norms that are part of the democratic ethos of society" (2005, p. 201). They go on to define democratic anchorage as comprising some kind of combination of:

A. Control by democratically elected politicians;
B. Accountable to the territorially defined citizenry;
C. Representation of the membership basis of the participating groups and organizations; and
D. Following the democratic rules specified by a particular grammar of conduct. (Sorensen and Torfing, 2005, p. 201)

The democratic anchorage of a governance network is thus construed as a matter of degree, not in absolute terms. We have noted how governments, as sovereign entities, play a critical role in governance networks. States contribute to the democratic anchorage of a governance network most directly through the privileged position that elected officials play as representatives of territorially defined citizenry. If government actors play informal or weak roles in a governance network, the anchorage that their ties to the network bring will be limited. The resultant networks tend to "resist government steering, develop their own policies and mould their environment" (Kickert, Klijn, and Koppenjan, 1997a, p. xii).

GOVERNMENT ROLES

- Funnel symbolic power and cultural authority to the network;
- Inform public perceptions of the network, lending it legitimacy;
- Allocate distinctive (tactical) resources and provide sources of information through which interests are pursued; and
- Being a back-up of last resort with regard to other forms of control.

Source: Crawford, *Theoretical Criminology*, 10, 459, 2006.

Sorensen and Torfing do not assume that democratic anchorage lies squarely on the shoulders of government actors. Taking into account the role that civil society plays, anchorage depends on the degree of democratic legitimacy voluntary associations bring to the network. For interest groups and collective action organizations to bring a measure of democratic anchorage to a governance network, they need to legitimately represent the membership basis of its participating individuals, groups, and organizations. Nonprofit, voluntary associations have been described as playing the role of mediating institutions. "They mediate between the interests of their constituents and public policy or the political process; they play roles within the game of politics as government and governing" (Couto, 1999, pp. 46–47). Governments as sovereign entities as well as most nonprofit, voluntary associations possess certain measures of discursive legitimacy. Discursive legitimacy "allows some organizations and individuals to speak on behalf of issues because of their ability to mobilize support from [interest] groups ... (Benson, 1975)" (Rodriguez et al., 2007, p. 155).

Another dimension of democratic anchorage of a governance network will hinge on the extent to which democratic norms, rules, and "grammar of conduct" are employed in the coordination of network activity. Presumably, a democratic grammar of conduct is shaped by legal standards (constitutional law, the rule of law, etc.), political norms (appeals to equity, liberty, and fairness), and administrative practice (sound and fair bargaining and negotiation practices). Democratic rules are also informed by the central norms associated with building horizontal ties: honesty, trust, and reputation.

We are left to conclude that democratic anchorage is rooted in the legitimacies that accompany the involvement of sovereign governments and their agents, the representative interests of nonprofit organizations, and the democratic processes undertaken in governance networks. We may draw parallels between democratic anchorage and democratic legitimacy. It was Max Weber who first understood administrative authority as legitimated power. Thus, the kind of legitimacy that accompanies democratic anchorage carries certain powers and authorities, as well as an essence of trust in the capacities of legitimate authorities to act in good faith on behalf of those interests to whom they are accountable.

In Chapter 8 we asserted that the emerging network administration paradigm that needs to arise when governance networks are considered is rooted in the public administrator's ongoing "search for public value" (Stoker, 2005, 2006). It is not the public administrator's role to actually determine what is of public value, but rather to ensure that the processes, functions, and structures are in place to make sure that the public value of governance network activities is (1) collectively determined via the kind of democratic anchorages discussed above, and (2) collectively monitored through the development of robust accountability regimes.

Accountability in Terms of Relationships between Network Actors

Scott defines accountability as "the obligation to give an account of one's actions to someone else, often balanced by a responsibility of that other to seek an account" (Scott, 2006, p. 175). The obligations are structured and enforced through the adoption of explicit standards and implicit norms (Kearns, 1996), and a recognition and responsiveness to particular individuals, groups, or organizations (Maas and Radway, 1959; Mashaw, 2006).

Kearns defines *explicit* standards as being "codified in law, administrative regulations, bureaucratic checks and balances, or contractual obligations to other organizations" (Kearns, 1996, p. 66). In essence, explicit standards are reified "artifacts" that provide stable parameters used to structure coordinated action. Such standards are often put into writing and appear as contracts, regulations, laws, performance standards, and formal rules, and are explicitly stated within performance measures.

Kearns defines *implicit* standards as "ill-defined and, perhaps, shifting notions of what constitutes responsible or appropriate behavior" that "are rooted in professional norms and social values, beliefs, and assumptions about the public interest, the public trust, and how (and to whom) organizational behavior should be explained … they can involve powerful sanctions for nonperformance or noncompliance" (Kearns, 1996, pp. 66–67). Implicit standards exist as "theories-in-use" (Argyris and Schon, 1995) that rely on the active participation of actors to create, re-create, enforce, and object to them. Implicit standards may be understood as a weaker accountability tool because they are often predicated on tacit knowledge. Implicit standards may include principal-agent norms (Milward and Provan, 1998), democratic values (Sorenson and Torfing, 2005), policy goals (Stone, 2002), and reciprocity and trust (Behn, 2001).

Accountability structures require that actors be responsive and responsible to particular constituencies. The eight different accountability types that we will explore may be understood in terms of the set of actors to whom accountability must be rendered. These actors, be they elected representatives, citizens, courts, supervisors, professionals, owners, consumers, or collaborators, are placed in the position of judging the performance of the agents that are being held accountable. Those to whom account is rendered (the "accounter") will inevitably prioritize different

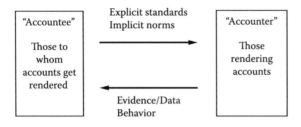

Figure 9.1 The accountability dyad.

combinations of policy goals, performance measures, and other desired procedures and outcomes, placing value on and rendering judgment of performance differently (Gruber, 1987; Radin, 2006). It is also imperative that those to whom accounts are rendered are capable or interested in fulfilling their roles. Figure 9.1 illustrates the relationship between accountee and accounter.

A Governance Network Accountability Framework

Democratic anchorage is one of the central governance features of the governance networks. Governance also needs to be considered in light of network structure—the roles that vertical, horizontal, and diagonal relations play in relation to the leadership structure and flow of power and authority. Governance also needs to be understood in the context of the accountability frameworks that persist within each node as well as across nodes. If states and, to a certain extent, interest groups play a role in bringing democratic anchorage to a governance network, other sectoral characteristics need to be considered as well. The confluence of sectoral governance characteristics needs to be considered in light of an accountability framework that (1) allows for the consideration of accountability across sectors (particularly the public and private sectors); (2) draws upon the existence of vertical, horizontal, and diagonal ties within and across governance networks; (3) distinguishes between strong and weaker forms of accountability relationships; and (4) recognizes the existence of both explicit and implicit standards and norms. Table 9.3 lays out the governance network accountability framework that we will discuss in some detail.

Barbara Romzek and Mel Dubnick's model of accountability is arguably the most influential framework used to analyze the accountability structures of governmental organizations. Drawing upon a study of the Space Shuttle *Challenger* explosion, they illustrate the four different accountability structures at work within NASA, and government actors in general: political, legal, bureaucratic, and professional (1987). In their 2 × 2 accountability model, Romzek and Dubnick conjoin four different accountability frames to considerations of external and internal control, and high and low degrees of control. Within the context of interorganizational

Table 9.3 Governance Network Accountability Framework

Accountability Frame	Accountability Type	To Whom Is Account Rendered?	Strength of Accountability Ties	Explicit Standards	Implicit Norms
Democratic	Elected representative	Elected officials	Strong (weaker when "lame duck")	Laws, statutes, regulations	Representation of collective interests; policy goals
	Citizen	Citizens	Weak (stronger during elections)	Maximum feasible participation; sunshine laws; deliberative forums	Deliberation; consensus; majority rule
	Legal	Courts	Strong	Laws; statutes; contracts	Precedence; reasonableness; due process; substantive rights
Market	Shareholder/owner	Shareholders/owners	Strong	Profit; performance measures	Efficiency
	Consumer	Consumers	Weak	Consumer law; product performance measures	Affordability; quality; satisfaction
Administrative	Bureaucratic	Principals; supervisors; bosses	Strong	Performance measures; administrative procedures; organizational charts	Deference to positional authority; unity of command; span of control
	Professional	Experts; professionals	Weak (stronger when capacity to revoke licenses exists)	Codes of ethics; licensure; performance standards	Professional norms; expertise; competence
	Collaborative	Collaborators; peers; partners	Weak	Written agreements; decision-making procedures; negotiation regimes	Trust; reciprocity; durability of relationships

networks, control may be predicated on an individual network actor's degree of centrality within the network. Romzek and Dubnick also suggest that degrees of control may be understood in terms of strength of ties. Presumably, stronger ties elicit higher levels of control. Within governance networks, the degrees of centrality and the relative strengths of the "controlling" entities are often highly contextual and contingent on the positionality of the organizational actors within the governance network.

Within a governance network framework, power gets interpreted in terms of the vertical and horizontal nature of relationships between actors *to whom* and *from whom* accountability is being rendered. The exercise of vertically oriented power has been well documented within theories pertaining to organizational hierarchies (Gulick, 2004), and later, relationships between principals and agents (Donahue, 1989; Milward and Provan, 1998). Social capital and social network theories have focused on the exercise of horizontally oriented power that manifests between network actors, often mitigated through norms of reciprocity and trust (Behn, 2001). Each accountability frame will be considered in light of the relational power that exists between actors within governance networks.

By building on these assertions, we seek to give shape to the "narrative of accountability" (Scott, 2006) that needs to be developed for governance networks. An accountability framework applied to governance networks needs to account for its democratic anchorage; the possibility that market-oriented businesses, corporations, or firms are implicated in and by network activity; and the interplay of both bureaucratic and collaborative ties within the operationalization of network structures. Two familiar dichotomies posed within the public administration and political science fields are useful here: the "politics-administrative dichotomy" (Goodnow, 2004) and the distinction between democracy and markets (Stone, 2002).

That it takes a combination of political and administrative accountabilities to effectively govern public institutions has been a widely accepted assumption in public administration (Appleby, 2004). However, the division between political and administrative functions in public administration theory is still widely assumed (see Rosenbloom, 2004; Romzek and Dubnick, 1987). Stone draws a distinction between the market and the polis (democracy) as a means for understanding how policy is framed through goals, problems, and solutions (2002). Distinctions between democracy and markets have been interpreted through neoliberal, neocorporate, neoconservative, and critical lenses, all of which may be useful in determining the apparent trade-offs existing between them (Miraftab, 2004).

We construct a three-pronged theory of accountability for governance networks encompassing democratic, market, and administrative frames. Such a tripartite framework takes into account the existing accountability structures that have been applied to public sector organizations (historically framed in terms of the politics-administrative dichotomy (Goodnow, 2004)) or as trade-offs between political and bureaucratic accountabilities (Romzek and Dubnick, 1987). Our model integrates the role that markets and market forces play within governance networks. It also

246 ■ *Governance Networks in Public Administration and Policy*

acknowledges the existence of both vertical ties (classically defined in terms of command and control) and horizontal ties (as discussed within social network and social capital literature).

Many have noted how the shift from a monocentric system of *government* to a polycentric system of *governance* raises some serious accountability challenges (Behn, 2001; Posner, 2002; Page, 2004; O'Toole and Meier, 2004b; Pierre and Peters, 2005; Goldsmith and Eggers, 2004; Scott, 2006; Mashaw, 2006; Mathur and Skelcher, 2007). Because it can no longer be assumed that the state possesses the same kind of authority as traditionally ascribed to public organizations, governing these interorganizational networks gives rise to new accountability challenges. These challenges arise when states are displaced as central actors, market forces are considered, and cooperation and collaboration are recognized as an integral administrative activity. We introduce a tripartite accountability framework for discerning how accountability is structured within governance networks that include democratic, market, and administrative accountability frames, through which eight accountability types emerge.

Discerning the accountability structures amidst the complexity that emerges in cross-sector, cross-jurisdictional settings requires us to consider the dynamics at work when the accountability structures of one network actor comingle, compete, or complement the accountability structures of other network actors. As a result of unpacking these dynamics, we may be able to ascertain the extent to which "hybrid accountability regimes" (Mashaw, 2006, p. 118) emerge within governance networks.

Democratic Frame

Romzek and Dubnick referred to political accountability as responsiveness to the needs and concerns of political constituents and public stakeholders. Under the expectations inherent to political accountability, "public agencies are expected to be responsive to other actors within the political system, particularly to elected politicians aiming to control their activities" (Mulgan, 2000, p. 566). Political accountability structures also rely on public access to governmental decision-making processes directly through open meeting laws, freedom of information acts, maximum feasible participation requirements, and sunshine laws, or indirectly through representation of elected officials. In essence, political accountability confers the vestiges of "democratic anchorage" onto public bureaucracies. The depth and breadth of the democratic anchorage of a governance network is said to depend on the roles of elected officials and public administrators, the accountability regimes at work within the network, and the extent to which the existence of the network expands the capacity for citizens to access networks and benefit from the outputs and outcomes of network activity (Sorensen and Torfing, 2005). In democratic systems, political accountability may be framed as democratic accountability through which both citizens and the representatives they elect serve as the actors to whom accountability must be rendered. The standards and norms used by citizens and elected officials to hold public bureaucracies accountable may be understood in terms of the laws and regulations passed by elected officials, the rights of citizens to exercise their voice, and the kind of norms often ascribed to deliberations about public policy (Stone, 2002).

We refine Romzek and Dubnick's sense of political accountability by narrowing in on the critical roles that elected officials and citizens play, recasting political accountability as the democratic frame through which *elected representative accountability* empowers elected representatives to serve as the principal actors in the legislative and executive branches of democratic governments. Although voted into office by citizens, elected representatives become the principals of public bureaucracies through their powers to allocate resources, mandate certain actions, and monitor the day-to-day administration of the executive branch.

Elected officials, however, are subject to pressures put on them from those to whom they feel obliged to render accounts. These actors may be the very citizens that elect them, or they may be interest groups. Writing about the kinds of pressures that interest groups can place on elected officials, Teske observes that "like vectors in a physics model, the interest group pressure will act on politicians from different directions and with differential force. The groups that are able to 'push' regulators harder are more likely to get resultant outcomes that they prefer, though perhaps not exactly congruent with what they want" (2004, p. 38).

Citizens, by contrast, may directly hold public organizations accountable through the more horizontal (and essentially weaker) ties forged through maximum feasible participation regulations, sunshine laws, and deliberative forums. The importance of *citizen accountability* for the democratic frame of governance networks is recognized within the literature pertaining to deliberative democracy (Fung, 2006), participatory governance (Bingham, Nabatchi, and O'Leary, 2005), collaborative governance (Ansell and Gash, 2008), and, to an extent nonprofit governance. Nonprofit organizations, as voluntary associations, have been long understood as important mediating institutions through which citizens directly contribute to a nation's civic culture. Citizen accountability may therefore exist for both governmental and nonprofit actors.

Romzek and Dubnick suggest that a *legal accountability* structure stresses the role that judiciary and quasi-judiciary procedures play in ensuring the execution of sound and reasonable judgments within an organization. Although they differentiate legal from political accountability, we follow Mashaw's (2006) lead in equating legal accountability with a democratic frame of reference. Legal accountability is ensured through laws and other explicit standards, such as due process, substantive rights, and legal agreements found in binding contractual arrangements. Presumably, all types of formal organizations and individuals are held to some measure of legal accountability, often predicated on adherence to the rule of law, constitutional law, civil and criminal laws, and legislative mandates. Legal accountability distinguishes itself through the centrality of the legal system and the roles that judges and juries play as principal actors within it. Also, it is important to note that public managers have been recognized as taking on quasi-judicial roles as well (Rosenbloom, 2004; Bingham, Nabatchi, and O'Leary, 2005). Thus, we may equate legal accountability with more vertically oriented ties, although the use of juries and the complexities of legal precedence do provide for greater opportunities for horizontal ties to manifest themselves through legal accountability frames.

Market Frame

A market frame may be understood by differentiating between capital and production markets (Mashaw, 2006, p. 122). The profit-making obligations of businesses dominate private sector accountability structures (Mulgan, 2000). In the private sector, accountability applies to owners and shareholders who have rights to call the company's managers to account for the company's performance, and then, secondarily, to customers whose main right is to refuse to purchase (Mulgan, 2000, p. 569). Thus, a market frame of accountability may be divided into two distinct, but interrelated components: shareholder accountability and consumer accountability (Scott, 2006). It should be noted, however, that this interpretation of corporate accountability structures does not take into consideration that a broader interpretation of stakeholder accountability exists in U.S. constitutional law (Nace, 2005) and more recently within the corporate social responsibility literature (Fox et al., 2002). Nor does it take into consideration labor as its own distinct accountability type. We believe there to be room to incorporate broadened stakeholder account-ably types at some future point, building upon the notion of the rights of organized labor and appeals to corporate social responsibility.

American legal scholars have advanced the "shareholder primacy norm" through which "corporate directors have a fiduciary duty to make decisions that are in the best interests of the shareholders" (Smith, 1998, p. 278). Shareholders or, in the case of privately owned businesses, owners are thought to be motivated by the maximization of profit. *Shareholder accountability* calls for the alignment of performance measures with profitability. Shareholder accountability requirements push companies to undertake the most efficient set of practices possible in order to maximize profits. Shareholder accountability is mediated through the monitoring of certain parameters that are used to determine the company's profitability. Shareholders and owners exist as principals within the corporate governance structure.

Consumerist accountability is a market-based accountability predicated on the ability of consumers to choose between alternative, competing goods or services. Through a consumer's choice or refusal to purchase, the consumer may be understood as holding a corporation accountable. "The central mechanism of this modality is competition. Thus, a standard is set through the interaction of buyers and sellers, which also forms the basis for monitoring and rewarding compliant behavior through loyalty and for punishing deviant behavior through exit" (Scott, 2006, p. 178). Mulgan observes that "while a customer may hold a private sector provider accountable in the case of a faulty individual purchase or contract, he or she has no general right to demand that the private provider offer services that meet his or her perceived needs. In a competitive market, the main mechanism of responsiveness is consumer choice, the capacity of the consumer to exit to an alternative provider" (2000, p. 569). Thus, the consumer exists in a horizontal arrangement with the corporation. Within the context of governance networks, consumerist accountability may be understood within the new public management edict to treat "citizens as customers" of public goods and services.

Administrative Frame

An administrative frame of governance network accountability may be viewed in terms of the vertical and horizontal ties within hierarchical bureaucracies and flatter collaborative arrangements. The administrative frame encompasses the implementation of policies and decisions (Chandler and Plano, 1982) and is directed at the relationships between actors who, by virtue of their positional authority within (and across) organizations, interact with each other to achieve some collective ends. The administrative frame focuses on the processes, procedures, and practices that are employed in the administration and management of formally organized social networks. Our chief concern here is distilling administrative relationships down to their basic processes and exploring how accountability may be framed administratively in terms of the dynamics operating between principals and agents, experts and laypersons, collaborators, and other contributors.

Bureaucratic accountability structures are characterized by hierarchical arrangements through which there are clear relationships between subordinates and superiors who rely on the classical principles ascribed to hierarchical, bureaucratic structures, such as the "unity of command" and "span of control" (Gulick, 1937). These principles may be embodied within the formal operating standards and procedures in place, along with stated rules and regulations. Bureaucratic accountability structures rely on an adherence to intraorganizational rules and procedures and, more informally, principal-agent norms. This form of accountability stresses the importance of authority embodied in vertically arranged relationships within formal organizations. Individual nonprofit organizations may rely on bureaucratic accountability structures, as do hierarchically arranged businesses.

Within the context of Romzek and Dubnick's accountability framework, *professional accountability* structures rely on the skills and expertise of professionals to inform sound judgments and discretion (1987). They assert that "professional accountability is characterized by placement of control over organizational activities in the hands of the employee with the expertise or special skills to get the job done" (p. 187). Professional accountability may also be maintained through compliance with profession or industry best practices, rules, or codes of ethics. The relationship between public administration and professionalism is another enduring theme within the literature (Mosher, 1982). Professional practice has been equated with ethical behavior, competence, discretion, and responsiveness. Professional account-ability is manifested through networked relationships between other professionals and the means by which they associate with one another. Such associations usually take place through interpersonal networks that transcend organizational bound-aries. Professional accountability may be understood in terms of the horizontal ties that exist between social networks of professionals who voluntarily associate with each other (Mashaw, 2006). It has also been framed as a matter of verti-cally oriented relationships that exist between experts and laypersons (Romzek and Dubnick, 1987).

Both individual network actors (Weick, 1976) and governance networks as a whole (Agranoff and McGuire, 2003) are predicated on the relative strengths or weaknesses of horizontal ties. When two actors enter into a horizontal relation-ship they are not beholden to the traditional principal-agent dynamics of vertically arranged relationships. Instead, social network theorists have equated horizontal relationships with cooperative behaviors, and norms of trust and reciprocity. The *collaborative accountability* that binds actors as peers or partners exists at the inter-personal level during the course of daily interactions with others (Mashaw, 2006). It should be noted that even within the most hierarchically arranged organizations workers interact with each other as peers or partners organized around collective endeavors, a fact that is particularly documented within the literature on teamwork and small group behavior (Mintzberg, 1979; Langfred and Shanley, 2001) and dis-cussions of clan governance (Ouchi, 1980; Rodriguez et al., 2007). We have already noted how horizontal ties may be understood within the context of social capital, and the normative foundations that give shape to social networks.

The application of game theory to the study of cooperative behavior reveals that "the foundation of cooperation is not really trust, but the durability of the relationship." Durability is built up over time through what Axelrod views as a "trial-and-error learning about possibilities for mutual rewards" and imitation of past successful relationships (1980, p. 182). Durability also requires network actors to not tolerate deviant behaviors. Axelrod's study of the iterated prisoner's dilemma underscores the need for networked actors to challenge such behaviors in an effort to bring about cooperative behaviors (1980, p. 184). Thus, the "reputational capital" of network actors becomes a key element within the establishment of durable, hori-zontally aligned relationships (Kreps and Wilson, 1982). Reputation becomes an important element in the bargaining, negotiating, and mutual adjustment activities undertaken in networked relationships (Morris, Morris, and Jones, 2007, p. 95).

Overlapping Accountability Frames

We suggest that governance networks draw upon a combination of some or all of the accountability types identified above, ultimately creating hybrid accountability regimes (Mashaw, 2006). These regimes are structured by the sectoral characteristics of network actors, with state actors bringing with them the democratic anchorage to representatives and citizens, and the private sector actors bringing a market frame of owners and consumers. These regimes are also structured as a complex array of vertically and horizontally aligned relationships, some of which persist through the operational characteristics of bureaucracies and collaboratively arranged social networks. There are substantive challenges to defining the hybridized accountability regimes of governance network as the aggregate of discrete accountability types. We argue that these discrete types combine, comingle, and compete with each other, often forming the basis of trade-offs. Where trade-offs are evident, confusion over which accountability type trumps others is bound to persist, a point that was first articulated by Romzek and Dubnick (1987).

Koliba, Mills, and Zia (accepted for publication) have applied the governance network accountability framework presented above to the case of the response and recovery efforts following landfall of Hurricane Katrina upon the Gulf Coast in August 2005. They discuss the accountability couplings and trade-offs arising within some of the "several overlapping networks for disaster management … in place in southeastern Louisiana, largely in response to federal stimuli" (Kiefer and Montjoy, 2006, p. 125). They cite how the lack of certain couplings and trade-offs, particularly between the Federal Emergency Management Agency (FEMA) and the Red Cross, led to some of the policy implementation failures evident in the studies that have been conducted.

Implications of Sector Blurring

The model of governance network accountability presented here takes into consideration the accountabilities that encompass different social sectors. We have described democratic accountabilities as being anchored within the preexisting accountability structures of democratic governments and, to a certain extent, the capacity of nonprofit organizations, as contributors to civil society, to represent, advocate for, and act on behalf of certain collective interests and constituencies. We have integrated private sector accountability structures into the model through the introduction of market accountabilities. Lastly, we recognized the administrative accountability structures that exist across all forms of social organization. When and where accountability structures overlap we recognize instances where accountability structures complement or even combine with each other. One implication of the coupling of accountability structures between different network actors within governance networks is the possibility of the blurring of accountability boundaries and borders, resulting in instances of "sector blurring." Sector blurring may result in any number of possibilities. Figure 9.2 suggests the range of possibilities that may result when sectors blur.

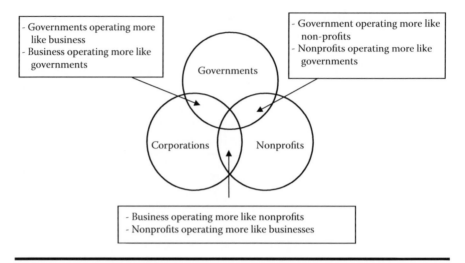

Figure 9.2 Overlapping sectors.

Nonprofit-Government Accountability Alignments

Writing about the implications of government's increasing influence over nonprofit organizations within grant and contract agreements, Steve Smith and Michael Lipsky have identified the impacts that the receipt of government funding bears upon nonprofit organizations. They discuss how government funding changes the scale of the nonprofit organization and increases administrative demands to remain in compliance (1993), an observation echoed later by Phillip Cooper (2003). The pursuit or maintenance of government grants and contracts leads to a deeper involvement of nonprofits in regulation-writing, the legislative process, and government budgeting cycles. Smith and Lipsky were also one of the first to recognize that such involvement has increasingly "professionalized" the management of nonprofit organizations (1993, p. 90). Richard Couto has recognized that "this development implies a shift of norms from those of the local community to those of the government agency providing funds" (1999, p. 63).

We may view the impacts of this particular form of sector blurring as a matter of comingled accountability types. The bureaucratic accountability structures of government funders are imported into the nonprofit agents. Cooper notes that "the same political abilities that allow NGOs to be supportive also allow them to resist change and to fend off accountability efforts" (Cooper, 2003, p. 66). The comingling of these accountability regimes results not only in certain transaction costs, as many have noted (Kelman, 2002; Cooper, 2003), and greater professionalization, but the possibility that a common normative framework can be forged. As the accountability feedback loops of the public and nonprofit sector blur, the representative interests of nonprofit organizations attempt, sometimes with great success, to influence regulation writing, the legislative process, and the government budgeting cycle. As nonprofits interface with governments in this way, through either their development of grant and contract agreements, their involvement within interest group coalitions, or active engagement in public-private partnerships, they impact the accountability regimes of the government actors in their governance networks. As civil society organizations, nonprofit organizations vie to have their interests integrated into the democratic accountability structures of governments.

Couto discusses the mediating roles that nonprofit organizations may follow to reach their democratic potential. Nonprofits serve as civil society "mediating organizations" when they "produce, directly or through advocacy of social and political provision, new forms and larger amounts of social capital, including the economic base of human community; when they provide their members representation and participation in the sociopolitical organizations of neighborhood, community, state, and nation; and when they expand their members' sense of common bonds with others and thus increase trust, cooperation, and collaboration" (Couto, 1999, p. 68). Thus, nonprofit organizations that are based upon premises of voluntary association bring a measure of democratic accountability to a governance network through the social capital they bring/provide. The relationship of social capital to the promulgation of civil society and, most particularly, the levels of engagement of ordinary citizens has been laid out by Robert Putnam (1993, 2000). Nonprofit organizations will likely be critical actors in the kind of participatory governance strategies highlighted in Chapter 8.

Corporation-Government Accountability Alignments

The blurring of corporate and government accountability structures is evident in the long-standing discussions within public administration regarding the comparison of business and government administrative practices. We note the instances of sector alignment in the efficiencies that were to be found within scientific management and later evolving into government reforms built around the goal of making governments run more like businesses. Critics of the new public management paradigm have made compelling arguments concerning the efficacy of treating citizens as customers (Denhardt and Denhardt, 2003), letting market forces dictate public investments of resources, and efficiency being the primary or only rationale for making decisions. These arguments may be interpreted through our accountability framework as trade-offs between citizen and customer accountability, trade-offs between democratic and market accountabilities more broadly, and the coupling of market and administrative accountabilities.

Regulatory capture that arises within certain regulatory subsystems may be construed in terms of accountability trade-offs and couplings. When special interests or private businesses try to become those critical actors with whom elected representatives decide to form allegiances, they will likely modify either the explicit or tacit accountability structures of government actors to varying degrees of success.

When the coupling of these accountability structures does occur, it may be said that private interests are vested into the accountability structures of public sector actors who also still have constitutional obligations to be accountable to a citizenry and their freely elected representatives. We posed the challenges associated with this kind of sector blurring as a matter of deepened democratic anchorage or the withering capacity of a hollowed-out state in Chapter 1.

With this concern in mind, we may look toward the implications that sector blurring bears on the accountability structures of private sector actors. We may examine these impacts in terms of two visible considerations. The first is the recent interest in nationalization, and the long-standing interest in the regulation, of business, industry, and aspects of the market economy. The second concerns the capacity of the corporate social responsibility movement and other attempts at socially responsible business practices to modify the accountability structures of private actors in word as well as deed.

Contemplating what the lasting effect of the financial crisis of 2008 will have on the relationship between the public and private sectors, Donald Kettl suggests that the crisis is of such large proportions that it has led to a new social contract between governments and businesses. This contract is guided by three factors: more public money in the private economy, more rules to shape how the private sector behaves, and more citizen expectations that government will manage the risks we face (2009). Kettl then goes on to suggest that the problem with this new contract is that "we're making it up as we go along, and we're not sure where we're going."

Johnathan Koppell's analysis of hybrid organizations (2003) sheds a great deal of light on the relationship between accountability and sector blurring. According to Koppell, quasi-governmental or hybridized organizations "allow government to harness the power of markets. They are capable of steering private, profit-seeking organizations into arenas improved by their presence" (Koppell, 2003, p. 185). Hybrid organizations are initiated by governments to address specific public policy purposes. They are "owned in whole or part by private individuals or corporations and/or generate revenue to cover [their] operating costs" (p. 12). Perry and Rainey distinguish between types of hybrid organizations: government corporations, government-sponsored enterprises, regulated enterprises, governmental enterprises, and state-owned enterprises (1988). In the United States, these hybridized organizations include Fannie Mae and Freddie Mae in the housing and mortgage arenas, Amtrak in the transportation arena, regulated telecommunication and utility industries, and regional port authorities. Hybridized organizations are also developed to serve multiple nations with global jurisdictions. Koppell discusses how international entities such as the World Bank and the International Monetary Fund have been devised to maintain international markets and monetary flows between the developed and developing worlds (2003, p. 7). Koppell's analysis of hybridized organizations provides an extensive examination of the role that governmental regulators play in providing oversight over these profit-seeking enterprises. These hybridized organizations all operate within regulatory subsystems.

Although Rainey and Perry add government contractors to their list of quasi-governmental organizations, Koppell suggests that government contractors differ from hybridized organizations because "a.) the contracting agency typically bears responsibility for delivery of some service or good by contractors; b.) as a consequence, expectations for accountability and public control do not apply" (2003, p. 12). It should be noted that in addition to Perry and Rainey, Kettl (1993) and Bozeman (1987) both claim that contractors and hybridized organizations are indistinguishable. The extent to which the democratic accountability structures of governments extend to government contractors becomes a critical consideration here. The more that democratic accountabilities extend to private contractors, as well as the kind of quasi-governmental entities listed above, the more sectors blur and the more that private firms behave like governments. The uniting factor that arguably exists in all forms of hybridized organizations, including government contractors, is the simultaneous pursuit of programmatic objectives aligned with the pursuit of public goals and profitability (Koppell, 2003, p. 104).

Another avenue through which private firms will take on the accountability characteristics of public sector entities is through the advancement of corporate social responsibility (CSR).* The contemporary corporate social responsibility movement is premised upon the voluntary (and essentially normative) efforts of corporations to achieve public goals (Davis, 1976). This movement emerged in the latter half of the twentieth century, marking a departure from the deference that was given to competitive market regulation in the early twentieth century (Hay and Gray, 1974). Two key developments in the 1930s opened the door for a corporate social responsibility framework: "the increasing diffusion of shares of American corporations and the development of a pluralistic society" (Hay and Gray, 1974, p. 136). Due to these developments, two central groups entered the accountability structures of private firm shareholders and labor unions (Hay and Gray, 1974).

In the 1960s and 1970s, the civil rights movement brought elevated concerns of ethical business practices into the mainstream social consciousness (Lantos, 2001). During this period the literature was mainly concerned with defining CSR (see Davis, 1960; Heald, 1970). Keith Davis (1976), a prominent early scholar on CSR, wrote: "Social responsibility implies that business decision makers recognize some obligation to protect and improve the welfare of society as a whole" (p. 14). Davis believed that there was an incongruence between the beliefs of general society and the actions taken by business. The "economic abundance" no longer outweighed concerns for a "declining social and physical environment" (Hay and Gray, 1974, p. 137). In 1971, the Committee for Economic Development (CED) published *Social Responsibilities of Business Corporations* and noted that businesses were taking on broader responsibilities for meeting public interests. The CED was comprised

---

* This discussion of CSR was greatly informed by the master thesis of Daniel Bromberg.

of members of the academic and business communities, demonstrating that both recognized the emergence of CSR as a viable movement shaping corporate behavior (Carroll, 1999).

There are multiple interpretations of what constitutes CSR. Generally, it is viewed as a corporation's effort to respond to issues relating to the environment, labor practices, and human rights (GAO, 2006). CSR concerns are defined by the General Accounting Office (GAO, 2005, pp. 9–10) as:

- **Business Ethics**—Business actions addressing the CSR concern of business ethics involve values such as fairness, honesty, trust and compliance, internal rules and legal requirements....
- **Corporate Governance**—Business actions addressing the CSR concern of corporate governance involve the broad range of policies and practices that boards of directors use to manage themselves and fulfill their responsibilities to investors and other stakeholders....
- **Community Development**—Business actions addressing the CSR concern of community development involve business policies and practices intended to benefit the business and the community economically, particularly for low-income and underserved communities....
- **Environmental Protection**—Business actions addressing the CSR concern of the environment involve company policies and procedures to ensure the environmental soundness of its operations, products, and facilities....
- **Preservation of Human Rights**—Business actions addressing the CSR concern of human rights involve assuring basic standards of treatment to all people, regardless of nationality, gender, race, economic status, or religion....
- **Workplace Equity**—Business actions addressing CSR workplace concerns generally involve human resource policies that directly impact employees, such as compensation and benefits, career development, and health and wellness issues.
- **Marketplace**—Business actions addressing CSR marketplace concerns involve business relationships with its customers and such issues as product manufacturing and integrity; product disclosures and labeling; and marketing, advertising, and distribution practices....

Much more could be written regarding the composition of these concerns, their origins and assumptions, and the ways in which they are shaped and informed by policy discussions. Space precludes such an examination. However, all of these issue areas can be understood within the context of the pluralistic view of corporate behavior. All encompass a perspective that adopts a broader view of to whom the corporation is accountable. Community development issues are, by definition, concerns for many interests and stakeholders. Environmental issues, by necessity, require a broadened view of interests and stakeholders. Valuing the quality of life for those beyond our immediate communities can be understood as an expression of concern for human rights issues. The focus of CSR concerns on the quality of the workplace suggests that stakeholder interests extend internally as well to workers, suggesting to us the possibility for integrating workers' rights into the market accountability framework introduced here.

The World Bank has defined corporate social responsibility as "the commitment of business to contribute to sustainable economic development—working with employees, their families, the local community and society at large to improve the quality of life in ways that are both good for business and good for development" (Fox et al., 2002, p. 1). This definition does not exclude a corporation's ability to earn a profit; however, it does provide for other considerations, including accounting for a firm's environmental impacts, community impacts, and quality of employee relations.

Davis (1973) wrote that CSR refers to "the firm's considerations, and response to, issues beyond the narrow economic, technical, and legal requirements of the firm" (p. 312). He goes on to say:

> A firm is not being socially responsible if it merely complies with the minimum requirements of the law, because this is what any good citizen would do. A profit maximizing firm under the rules of classical economics would do as much. Social responsibility goes one step further. It is a firm's acceptance of a social obligation beyond the requirements of law. (1973, p. 313)

Within this definition, the socially responsible corporation must go "beyond compliance." Arguably, the motivation to move beyond compliance is grounded in the corporation's value base, or its normative foundation. We suggest that we have provided researchers with some ways for considering the authenticity of a corporation's democratic anchorage. Good faith negotiation; the meaningful contribution and provision of the private sector entity's capital resources (financial, human, physical, political, social, cultural, and knowledge in nature); attempts to mobilize resources for purposes that lie beyond the pursuit of their own narrow interests; and efforts to facilitate and broker solutions to pressing public problems may all be indicators of shared accountabilities between the owners of private capital and the publics that they may be said to serve.

The voluntary nature of CSR is subscribed to by many of the leading research and advocacy groups supporting the CSR movement. Organizations such as the Business for Social Responsibility, the Center for Corporate Citizenship at Boston College, and Harvard's Kennedy School for Government's Corporate Social Responsibility Initiative all promote voluntary action on the part of the corporation. These groups support networks of more local and regional associations designed to support a business's voluntary pursuit of CSR objectives. Rather than waiting to react to the regulatory system to initiate socially responsible mandates, corporations are encouraged to preemptively act in responsible ways. Hence, corporations can prevent regulations from occurring with their own voluntary actions (Davis, 1973).

Although we have noted this possibility in our ongoing consideration of regulatory capture, we open the door, at least, for the consideration of those instances when business interests and accountability structures align with the democratic accountabilities that anchor governments and many nonprofit organizations.

Hybridization of Accountability Regimes

There is mounting evidence that reflects the evolving nature of accountability structures at the network-wide as well as individual network actor level. The resultant "hybridized accountability regimes" (Mashaw, 2006) that contributed to sector blurring are leading to new forms of "quasi governmental" (Koppell, 2003) and quasi nonprofit (Smith, 2007) organizational structures.

Revisiting Romzek and Dubnick's analysis of NASA following the *Challenger* Space Shuttle tragedy, we find instances in which more than one accountability structure was in play. They premised the accountability failures in this case as a series of trade-offs between the political, bureaucratic, and professional accountability structures in play. Koliba, Mills, and Zia's (accepted for publication) study of some of the failures in the response and recovery efforts following Hurricane Katrina reveals the lack of articulation of new accountability regimes that are in place during times of emergency, and the resultant conflicts over which accountability regimes were at work in the emergency management governance networks implicated in the Gulf Coast response and recovery efforts.

Conflicts over "to whom" accounts are bound to prevail within governance networks. By introducing a theoretical framework through which we may describe and ultimately evaluate how accounts are rendered within complex governance networks, we hope to provide practitioners with options for designing network accountability systems. If design or redesign is difficult, we hope to, at least, provide practitioners with a way of describing the trade-offs that arise when accountability structures compete, as well as comprehend the consequences when accountability structures are imported and exported across organizational, group, and individual boundaries and borders. The capacity of a governance network to negotiate such borders crossings and boundary blurring can be tangibly reified in the performance management systems at work within a governance network, a subject that we turn to in the next chapter.

By positing accountability in terms of the relationships between two or more actors, we set the stage for developing an empirical basis for studying and evaluating how and to what extent accountability is rendered.

CRITICAL QUESTIONS AND CONSIDERATIONS

Taking note of the critical actors implicated in your governance network, what is the relationship between the governance structures of these actors and the governance of the network on the whole?

- To what extent do individual network actors exhibit the qualities and characteristics of other actors within the network?
- To whom are individual networks accountable? How do these accountabilities combine, comingle, or compete with each other?
- May this network be said to possess a network-wide accountability regime? Where are there apparent trade-offs between accountabilities?
- Can you recognize any instances of sector blurring arising in this network?
- What can be done, or is being done, to ensure that the network is accountable?

Chapter 10

Governance Network Performance Management and Measurement

An ounce of performance is worth pounds of promises.

—Mae West (Thinkexist.com)

We have grounded our exploration of interorganizational governance networks in the concept of governance and the range of accountabilities that must be associated with democratic governance systems. In Chapter 9 we discussed the extent to which accountability in a governance network is informed by the accountability structures of the network's component parts. We discussed, extensively, the potential roles that actors' sectoral characteristics may contribute to the governance network's hybridized accountability regimes. We differentiated between the accountabilities associated with vertical and horizontal administrative relationships and defined accountability in terms of the relationships between those being held accountable and those to whom accounts are rendered. We discussed how accountability relationships are shaped by explicit standards, laws, and rules, as well as implicit norms characterized by deference to authority and the creation of trust and reciprocity. In this chapter we discuss particular kinds of explicit standards: those equated with performance and performance measures. We recognize some of the major challenges and problems associated with performance management in general (Poister, 2003; Radin, 2006; Moynihan, 2008), and those performance management challenges arising within the kinds of interorganizational governance networks that we discuss in this book (Radin, 2006; Frederickson and Frederickson, 2006). We position governance network performance in terms of the use of data flowing through feedback loops and anticipate the role that communities of practice play in the effective design, collection, and use of performance data.

Governance and Performance

Those who have studied the role of performance measurement and management in public administration and policy studies have often equated performance with questions of governance (Moynihan, 2008). Likewise, those proposing that the field advance a "logic of governance" often frame governance with "performance or outcomes of public programs at the individual or organizational level as the ultimate dependent variable (Lynn et al., 2000)" (Stone and Ostrower, 2007, p. 423). Performance and performance measurement may be viewed as attempts to apply systematic and, ultimately, standardized criteria through which to assess the success of a social entity, be it at the individual, group, organization, or interorganizational levels.

Throughout this book we have described governance in terms of feedback loops occurring within any social systems aligned around policy functions. We have equated governance with management and the range of managerial functions undertaken within vertically and horizontally arranged administrative relationships. We have discussed the intimate connection between governance and accountability. In this chapter we interpret governance as a matter of monitoring performance. We assert, following Moynihan (2008), that performance management is a critical function in the effective governance of not only public bureaucracies, but entire governance networks as well. We also ground the monitoring of performance as a crucial feedback function within a governance system.

The application of fair and effective performance measurement in public administration and policy studies is no easy task. Beryl Radin, for instance, warns that "despite the attractive quality of the rhetoric of the performance movement, one should not be surprised that its clarity and siren call mask a much more complex reality" (2006, p. 235). It should come as no surprise at this juncture that we concur with her observations here. Performance management is a complicated matter within *individual* organizations, let alone interorganizational networks. Herbert Simon (1957) and Charles Lindblom (1959) were some of the first to discuss the limits of rationality within social organizations. As we will explore later in this chapter, the same factors that lead to "bounded rationality" and incrementalism in the course of day-to-day management and policy making cloud performance management practices across interorganizational network contexts.

Just what amounts to effective performance is a matter of perception. Performance data and standards come about through the social construction of knowledge (Moynihan, 2008). Gregory Bateson has noted that "the processes of perception are inaccessible; only the products are conscious" (1972, p. 32). Performance data, performance measures, and ultimately, performance management are complicated by the question of whose perceptions matter. Building on our discussion of accountability in Chapter 9, we assert that, presumably, those to whom accounts need to be rendered are in the best (or most legitimate) position to determine what it means for any social entity to perform, and presumably, perform effectively.

We need to note that perception is guided by one's assumptions about what kind of information matters (Bateson, 1972). The performance measurement movement often privileges information presented as numbers and the kinds of categories that arise when things are counted. A critical presentation of performance measurement ignores the extent to which measures and numbers are defined and prioritized through a decidedly political process (Stone, 2002; Radin, 2006). Thus, performance measurement needs to be understood within the context of how and what kinds of knowledge matter, particularly the distinctions raised in the differentiation between the quantifiable dimensions of positivism and the descriptive and qualitative characteristics of interpretivism. Without grounding our consideration of performance management in these critiques, we run the risk of positioning performance measurement as the superimposing of "managerial logic and managerial processes on inherently political processes embedded in the separation of powers (Wildavsky, 1979; Rosenbloom, 2004; Aberbach and Rockman, 2000; Radin, 2006)" (Frederickson and Frederickson, 2006, p. 177). Performance measurement, if wielded acritically, inevitably re-creates a politics-administrative dichotomy that bears little significance within the actual governance of governance networks. We argue that performance measurement and performance management are already playing a significant role in the governance of governance networks. However, ascertaining how performance management and measurement play a role in governance networks calls us to again consider the challenges that arise when accountability and interests comingle, combine, and compete. In the next section we discuss how the modern performance measurement movement has been implemented as a series of initiatives occurring across all levels of government.

The Performance Measurement Movement

Initiatives geared toward collecting and using performance data in governments have their roots in the performance management systems used in the private sector. The reinventing government reforms of the 1990s were fueled by the new public management's (NPM) assumptions regarding the efficacy of running governments more like businesses. We have already discussed the kinds of performance standards adopted by the public, private, and nonprofit sectors. The private sector, in particular, is governed by the pursuit of one performance measure in particular: profit. The systematic collection of corporate performance data has been a critical element of publicly traded firms. The successful functioning of financial markets

**CONTEMPORARY USES OF PERFORMANCE MEASURES
IN GOVERNMENT AND NONPROFIT ORGANIZATIONS**

- Monitoring and reporting
- Strategic planning
- Budgeting and financial management
- Program management
- Program evaluation
- Quality improvement
- Contract management
- External benchmarking
- Communication with the public

See Poister (2003, pp. 9–15) for a breakdown of these functions.

is premised on the availability and use of information regarding the performance of firms. A major assumption guiding the use of corporate performance data is the coupling of efficiency and profits. Advocates of NPM often believe that the "hidden hand" of markets may be applied to the functions of government. Market forces operate efficiently when "perfect" information is exchanged between buyers and sellers. The adoption of performance measurement systems across government was presented by reinventing government gurus David Osborne and Ted Gaebler (1992) as a way to unleash the entrepreneurial energies most often equated with markets and market forces.

Historically, the move to assess and manage performance has been most often characterized as an effort to bring about greater accountability within organizations. Donald Moynihan asserts that the "performance management doctrine is based on the logic that the creation, diffusion, and use of performance information will foster better decision making in government, leading to dividends in terms of political and public accountability, efficiency and budget decisions" (Moynihan, 2008, p. 10).

The modern application of performance management systems to the operations of governments has its origins in the scientific management movement of the early twentieth century. The father of scientific management, Frederick Taylor, was one of the early proponents of the systematic collection of performance data and the use of such data to advance effective and efficient practices. In later decades reforms to governmental budgetary systems such as planning programming and budget systems and zero-based budgeting in the 1960s and 1970s were attempted in efforts to link performance data to decision making. The performance measurement movement came into full fruition with the reinventing government initiatives of the early 1990s. The Clinton administration's National Performance Review (NPR) led to the Government Performance and Results Act (GPRA) that has subsequently been extended in thirty-three states (Moynihan, 2008). GPRA has been institutionalized across the federal government through the Office of Management and Budget (OMB) through the extensive implementation of the Program Assessment Rating Tool (PART) (Frederickson and Frederickson, 2006; Moynihan, 2008).

Performance Management Systems

Viewed through the lens of organizational behavior (Mintzberg, 1983), complex systems dynamics (Boland and Fowler, 2000), and organizational learning (Moynihan, 2008), performance management systems operating across organizational and interorganizational contexts are interlocking processes that are intentionally designed to manage the flow of feedback within or across units.

Donald Moynihan observes that "performance management systems are designed to take information from the environment, through consultation with the public, stakeholders, public representatives, and [other relevant actors]." Performance management systems provide a means by which critical actors "engage in coding, interpreting and refining information from the external environment and internal stakeholders into a series of information categories such as strategic goals, objectives, performance measures, and targets" (2008, p. 6). To be an effective performance management system, this analysis must be used by policy makers and other key decision makers to guide collective action.

Dialogue around performance data "will not necessarily engender consensus and agreement." Moynihan asserts that "this depends greatly on the homogeneity of the actors involved, their interpretation of the data, their ability to persuade others, and their power in the decision process" (2008, p. 112). Performance management systems facilitate the use of "dialogue routines" that "require a commitment of time by staff and a setting where performance data that might otherwise be ignored is considered.... Such routines provide an opportunity to access information, make sense of this information, and persuade others" (Moynihan, 2008, p. 110). In effective performance management systems, actions and strategies are collectively agreed upon, and "those made responsible are not only given the task but also the rationale, thus, enabling them to understand the 'what' and 'why.' Through understanding this, there [is] an increased likelihood of implementation" (Savas, 2005, p. 136). Within performance management systems, "dialogue forms a basis of social cooperation," and where commitments around common agreements are reached. Moynihan concludes that "interactive dialogue therefore acts as a social process that helps to create shared mental models, has a unifying effect, and helps to develop credible commitment for the execution phase" (2008, p. 111).

Performance *management* systems are guided by the performance *measurement* theories that inform the mental models and decision heuristics of critical actors. These mental models are often shaped by certain assumptions regarding the ascription of causality, and assumptions regarding the relationship between inputs, processes, outputs, and outcomes. It has been suggested that the greater the consensus around the relationship between causes and effects, the more robust the performance management system (Moynihan, 2008). Henry Mintzberg referred to these processes as "performance control systems" (1983, p. 145).

Moynihan asserts that the rationale for advancing performance management systems is "based on the logic that the creation, diffusion, and use of performance information will foster better decision making in government, leading to dividends in terms of political and public accountability, efficiency and budget decisions" (2008, p. 10). In short, it is assumed that "performance measurement is a stimulus to strategic behavior" (De Bruijn, 2001, p. 21) that should, in theory, ultimately lead to effective outcomes.

Beryl Radin (2006, p. 19) describes the traditional assumptions that have guided the introduction of performance management systems:

- Goals can be defined clearly and set firmly as the basis for the performance measurement process.
- Goals are specific and the responsibility of definable actors.
- Outcomes can be specified independently of inputs, processes, and outputs.
- Outcomes can be quantified and measured.
- Outcomes are controllable and susceptible to external timing.
- Data are available, clear, and accurate.
- Results of the performance measurement can be delivered to an actor with authority to respond to the results.

These assumptions mirror the kind of rational assumptions that have guided the traditional policy cycle. The clarity of goals, the measurability of performance standards, the availability and accessibility of data, and the utilization of those data to guide decision making and action are all said to be critical components of an effective performance management system. Figure 10.1 illustrates the flow of data collection to analysis to action.

Figure 10.1   Performance management systems. (Compiled from: Poister, 2003, pp. 15–17.)

TYPES OF PERFORMANCE MEASURES

Resource
Workload
Output productivity
Efficiency
Service quality
Effectiveness
Cost-effectiveness
Customer satisfaction
Integrated sets of measures

See Poister (2003, pp. 49–50) for breakdown.

Theodore Poister describes performance measurement as a continuous cycle of inquiry that encompasses the collection and processing of data, the analysis of these data, and the utilization of this analysis to adjust actions and behaviors. Poister posits that the analysis of data is carried out through the act of rendering comparisons over time, against internal targets, across units, and against external benchmarks (2003, p. 16). The analysis of data may lead to decisions regarding strategy, program delivery, service delivery, day-to-day operations, resource allocation, goals and objectives, and performance targets, standards, and indicators (2003, p. 16).

Performance measurement implies certain assumptions regarding causality, namely, that inputs into the system (however defined) shape the processes undertaken, which in turn produce certain outputs leading to short-, intermediate-, and long-term outcomes. In Chapter 7, we discussed how systems dynamics have been described in terms of inputs, processes, outputs, and outcomes. This model of systems dynamics has been adopted in some types of performance measurement initiatives, particularly those associated with the evaluation of programs. The input, process, output, and outcome model is often called the logic model (Poister, 1978, 2003). The logic model is a commonly adopted form of performance evaluation used in government and nonprofit organizations.

Input measures are often framed in terms of resources contributed to the system that may take any number of different forms of capital (financial, physical, human, social, natural, and knowledge). "Performance advocates often argue that organizations emphasize the importance of inputs to the exclusion of other elements and, as a result, equate the availability of these resources with success" (Poister, 1978, p. 15). "Information in this category deals with the amount of resources actually used in the operation of a policy or program" (Radin, 2006, p. 191). "Inputs are recognized as valuable only insofar as they produce desired outputs and measurable results" (Savas, 2005, p. 12).

Process measures usually involve information that may be collected about the activities being undertaken within the social system. Variables employed to study and evaluate organizational behavior and management practices are sometimes defined as process measures. Process measures may also include actors' perceptions of the practices undertaken. Paul Posner describes process measures in the context of governance networks this way:

> Goals emerge from the interaction of actors in the network. Implementation and performance are evaluated based on the capacity to cooperate and solve problems within networks. The focus is not on goal achievement but on whether conditions encourage the formation and sustainability of positive interactions across the network. Criteria for network management include creating win-win situations that make non-participation less attractive, limiting interaction costs, promoting transparency, and securing commitment to joint undertakings. (Posner, 2002, p. 546)

Given the wide array of potential process dynamics, "processes are often counted in varying or inconsistent ways: as a result, aggregated statistics about processes can be misleading" (Radin, 2006, p. 191). Additionally, more attention needs to be paid to the development of process measures that are constructed around democratic norms and rules (Klijn, 2001).

Output measures hinge on results that may be directly ascribed to the activities undertaken within the system. Outputs are generally the most tangibly visible, measurable representation of "the amount of work performed or the volume of activity completed" (Poister, 2003, p. 40). "Outputs are products and services delivered. Outputs are completed products of internal activity: the amount of work done within the organization or by its contractors" (Poister, 2003, p. 15). Outputs may also be used to assert a causal relationship between the actions undertaken and the impacts of those actions on the wider social and natural environment. "This category measures the amount of products and services completed during the reporting period … tabulations, calculations, or recordings of activity or effort that [can] be expressed in a quantitative or qualitative manner. In some cases, process measures are subsumed within this category" (Radin, 2006, p. 191). "Outputs are best thought of as necessary but insufficient conditions for success" (Poister, 2003, pp. 38–39). We have highlighted how the universality of the one output measure guiding market accountability, profit, is taken into consideration in governance networks within which for-profit firms are implicated.

Outcome measures are often the most difficult to determine because they are constructed out of a chain of causality that must take into account all of the inputs, processes, and outputs implicated in the social system. "Outcomes … are the substantive impacts that result from producing these outputs" (Poister, 2003, p. 40). Much has been written regarding the complexities of coming to agreement around the construction of causal relationships. Outcome indicators are "a numerical measure of the amount or frequency of a particular outcome" (Radin, 2006, p. 15). Often implicated in society's most "wicked problems," governance networks operate in a highly politicized environment through which policy outcomes get framed by stakeholders differently (Stone, 2002). Outcomes are an "event, occurrence, or condition that is outside the activity or program itself and is of direct importance to program customers or the public" (Poister, 2003, p. 15). "Outcome information defines the events, activities, or changes that indicate progress toward achievement of the mission and objectives of the program" (Radin, 2006, p. 191). Outcomes may be registered in the short to long term. "Intermediate outcomes are activities that are expected to lead to a desired end but not ends in themselves" (Radin, 2006, p. 192). An "end outcome" is described in terms of "the end result that is sought" (Poister, 2003, p. 15).

Challenging the Performance Paradigm

Donald Moynihan concludes that "there is likely to be no single definitive approach to a.) interpreting what performance information means and b.) how performance information directs decisions" (2008, p. 102). He goes on the add that "information selection and use occurs in the context of different beliefs, preferences, and cognitive processes, and they will reflect organizational power and politics. Information providers will try to shape outcomes by choosing what information will be collected and highlighted. Each measure is representative of values and accompanied by the assumption that the organization should be making efforts that will have an impact on the measure" (2008, p. 106). Just why this is so has been the subject of extensive analysis.

George Frederickson (2000) and Beryl Radin (2006) have noted that the major challenges associated with performance measurement concern the fallacies regarding the chains of causality that arise between inputs, processes, outputs, and outcomes; the measurability of performance indicators; and relatedly, the availability and quality of data. Radin has deemed the traditional view of performance measurement as being overtly rationalistic and naïve, observing how performance measurement traditionalists view information as readily available and value neutral (2006, pp. 184–85). We find these critiques of performance measurement to be tied to discussions of the limits of positivism, the assertion that knowledge and information are a product of social construction, and critiques of rational action. Although these concerns have been raised within the context of performance measurement within a single organization, we find these challenges accentuated when more actors are added. Before moving to particular challenges relating to performance management within governance networks, we believe it is worth considering some of the major challenges associated with the performance measurement paradigm that is so prevalent today. We define these challenges in terms of the dualisms created through the correlation of causes and effects, questions concerning the validity of data, and the challenges associated with the costs of data.

Exploring the challenges associated with managing complexity in the public services, Phillip Haynes observes that one of the dangers of performance management lies in "seeing issues in terms of simplistic cause and effect rather than complex entanglements and changing dynamics." He goes on to add that "this is the nature of the problem that complexity has with performance management. It is potentially a dualism, a false separation of two aspects, an erroneous separation of means and ends, process and outcome" (Haynes, 2003, pp. 90–91).

In a performance measurement framework, the relationship between inputs, processes, outputs, and outcomes is premised on certain assumptions regarding the chain of causality that exists between these elements. Poister warns that "if the underlying program logic is flawed—if the assumptions of casual connections between outputs and results don't hold up in reality—then the desired outcomes will not materialize, at least not as a result of the program" (Poister, 2003, p. 39). In discussing the policy paradox, Deborah Stone has underscored how causality and assumptions about the relationships between causes and effects are socially constructed (2002). As critics of performance measurement have noted, definitions of performance and the outcomes that result from performance are subject to the perceptions and interpretations of stakeholders and faulty assumptions regarding the relationship between means and ends. The complexity argument laid out by Haynes is very similar to the one laid out by Deborah Stone, who observes how the ascription of causal relationships is, in the realm of public policy and management, wrought with ambiguities (2002).

Radin has warned that "one needs to take care and avoid ascribing events to a single cause" (2006, p. 2370). Claims regarding the validity of particular couplings of causes and effects, and ultimately, problems and solutions, are made by and through certain policy actors, and as we will assert here, networks of policy actors operating within and across mixed-form governance networks. In a sense, the building of a performance management system around a set of assumptions regarding a relationship between causes and effects, inputs and outputs, and outputs and eventual outcomes, is grounded in validity claims made by certain combinations of stakeholders who are implicated in one or more of the accountability relationships discussed in Chapter 9. Critiques of performance management systems highlight the limits of rationality and a growing a wariness of the complexities inherent to most collective endeavors.

Critics of performance measurement are concerned about the equation of data with "facts," and the air of objectivity that accompanies the presentation of data as facts. Sociologists dating back to Emile Durkheim have explored, at length, how social facts get socially constructed and mediated through social interactions (Collins, 1988). Social scientists have long understood that the validity of certain social facts and assertions linking causes and effects is determined through any number of validity claims. "Face," "consensual," "correlational," "predictive," "democratic," "catalytic," and "outcome" validity can all be used to justify the claims made about performance data (Poister, 2003, p. 91).

Validity claims are also shaped by perceptions regarding the measurability of social facts. Deborah Stone has documented how the capacity to describe social facts through numbers helps to shape perceptions of public problems and solutions. She recognizes that the choices made around what to measure (e.g., what to count) define what is important. The fear here is that, as David and George Frederickson observe, "the measurable drives out the important" (Frederickson and Frederickson, 2006, p. 102), with the measurability of the input, process, output, or outcome dictating the goals and functions that are ascribed to. In essence, the emphasis placed on the measurable performance indicators leads to goal displacement, and potentially away from what is actually important or desirable.

Performance measurement is often advanced under a certain set of assumptions that data are available, consistent, accurate, and inexpensive (Frederickson and Frederickson, 2006, p. 16). These assumptions mask the very real transaction costs that come with any performance management system. Following Francis Fukuyama's line of thought, Beryl Radin observes that "formal systems of monitoring and accountability … either entail very high transaction costs or are simply impossible because of the lack of specificity of the underlying activity." Further, she notes that "the effort to be more 'scientific' than the underlying subject matter permits carries a real cost in blinding us to the real complexities of public administration as it is practiced in different societies" (Radin, 2006, p. 6).

Brent Milward and Michael Provan have recognized that "high transactions costs are associated with monitoring performance.… In the absence of a price mechanism to determine cost—and in the absence of outcome data to determine quality—trust and the reputation for credible commitments become important in determining who it is that agencies contract with, and for what services" (1998, p. 3). Performance management systems may tend to exacerbate principal-agent problems. As Paul Posner observes, "Inputs and level of effort are more easily assessed and tracked by principals. By contrast, the link between a given level of funding and prospective or actual performance is often more uncertain and difficult for principals to ascertain independent of agents" (Posner, 2002, p. 541).

Recognizing the possibility of principal-agent dynamics within any performance management system leads to the inevitable concern regarding information asymmetries. When considered at the level of governance networks, information asymmetries may be compounded as questions of who owns data and who has access to data become points of contestation. When data are viewed as the property of some network actors and not others (as in the case of certain forms of proprietary data that private contractors claim), the capacity to share, analyze, and make decisions using the type of analysis process found in Figure 10.1 is seriously compromised.

CHALLENGES ASSOCIATED WITH PERFORMANCE MEASUREMENT INITIATIVES

- Inadequate training and technical know-how for developing performance measures;
- Lack of resources for measurement design, data collection, and monitoring;
- Different expectations about what performance measures are designed to do and for what they will be used;
- Fear by agencies that they will be asked to develop outcomes measures for results that are not easily measured, that are shaped by factors outside their control ... and that are not amenable to assigning responsibility to particular actors.

Source: **Durant, in Golembiewski, Ed.,** *Handbook of Organizational Behavior,* **2nd ed., Marcel Dekker, New York, 2001, pp. 702–3.**

Referencing the arguments made in favor of extending performance management systems across governments, Frederickson and Frederickson observe that "it is argued that performance measurement in government reduces information asymmetry and thereby provides information that enables policymakers and agencies to refine or improve policy or its implementation." They go on to add that "information derived from performance measurement is, however, used not only to improve policy and its implementation but also to arm policy makers with arguments for or against policy" (Frederickson and Frederickson, 2006, p. 15).

On a practical level, transaction costs also surface when performance management systems require the infusion of financial, physical, human, and knowledge capitals. The tangible costs of collecting, analyzing, and using performance data to make decisions and hold actors accountable can be debilitating (Cooper, 2003). Thus, there is a real need to make sure that the right kind and appropriate volume of data are collected. "If there is a large range of performance measures covering different areas, the danger then becomes that services are over-audited and this creates too much data collection and analysis work for middle managers" (Haynes, 2003, p. 104).

Challenges for Performance Management Systems in Governance Networks

All of the challenges associated with performance management described in the previous section surface in the more relatively simple contexts of an organization.

The validity of data, the social construction of what gets counted and why, and the role of transaction costs can be found within performance management systems operating within a single organizational domain. Frederickson and Frederickson (2006) conclude that when multiple actors, across multiple scales of government, businesses, and nonprofits, get implicated as critical actors within a governance network, these challenges only get accentuated.

In writing about the challenges of performance measurement in networked contexts, Beryl Radin observes that "the construct of the American political system calls for an assumption that the multiple actors within the system have different agendas and hence different strategies for change. Performance measurement should thus begin with the assumption of these multiple expectations and look to the different perspectives found [across the spectrum of network actors]" (2006, pp. 239–40). Thus, in complex, networked contexts, not only do the costs of data and the challenges of access to data pervade, but questions concerning what performance data are to be collected, which data matter, and how these data are used to inform decisions are vaulted into ever more complex multi-institutional arrangements. These challenges may be particularly visible in the processes that networks undertake to define, collect, analyze, and use performance data to guide decision making and collective action. When performance management systems are employed across a governance network, "the ability of any single actor to establish its own blueprint for a performance management model, define the meaning of performance information, or determine how performance information is used" is limited (Moynihan, 2008, p. 10). The potential loss of control over how performance is measured and managed may be viewed as a potential transaction cost that some network actors may find too steep to bear.

A second factor that impacts how performance management systems operate within governance networks concerns the state of the existing performance management systems and "performance measurement culture" (Frederickson and Frederickson, 2006) that specific network actors bring to the network. As Radin observes, "Organizations are likely to vary considerably in the data systems that they have put in place; even if the system is considered to be effective when viewed within the organization's boundaries, most of the systems that have been devised are not easily converted to integrated data systems" (2006, p. 206).

In studying how performance management systems operate across organizational domains, Moynihan (2008, pp. 112–13) formulates the following set of assumptions that need to be considered as performance management systems are described and evaluated:

- Different actors can examine the same programs and come up with competing, though reasonable, arguments for the performance of a program based on different data.

- Different actors can examine the same performance information and come up with competing, though reasonable, arguments for what the information means.
- Different actors can agree on the meaning of performance information/program performance and come up with competing solutions for what actions to take in terms of management and resources.
- Actors will select and interpret performance information consistent with institutional values and purposes.
- Forums where performance information is considered across institutional affiliations will see greater contesting of performance data.
- Use of performance information can be increased through dialogue routines.

The definition of what constitutes effective outcomes for a governance network is a critical question to be addressed. There have been some studies conducted that look at the efficacy of network structures in achieving ascribed outputs or outcomes (see as a representative: Marsh and Rhodes, 1992; Heinrich and Lynn, 2000; Koontz et al., 2004; Imperial, 2005; Frederickson and Frederickson, 2006; Koliba, Mills, and Zia, accepted for publication; Rodriguez et al., 2007). The highly contextual nature of the environments that governance networks operate within, coupled with the highly contextual nature of most of the perceptions of the network actors within the network, renders the development of consensus around common definitions of viable network performance measures very difficult to achieve.

An additional challenge to performance management within governance networks pertains to differences in the geographic scale of individual network actors. Locally oriented network actors will likely focus on performance indicators that fall within their domain, while regionally, nationally, or internationally oriented network actors will look toward performance indicators that capture the scale and scope of their domains. One way that scale differences are handled is through the aggregation of data from multiple data points. However, aggregated data are not enough to compensate for geographic differences among actors, particularly when the identities (and by inference, ascriptions of causalities) of local actors get lost when their data are combined with other data points of either similar or dissimilar geographic scale. Ultimately, the central problem with performance management systems in complex governance networks lies in "determining which party defines the outcomes that are expected" (Radin, 2006, p. 157). Furthermore, the differences in geographic scale may be combined with a "lack of capacity for experimentation, the conservative identities of actors who want to preserve the status quo, and the failure to resolve the internal conflicts between the actors that struggle over the assessment of experiments and the formulation of strategies for institutional reform" (Sorensen and Torfing, 2008, p. 105). As a process of active experimentation, the theories of causality that are either implicitly or explicitly assumed when

CHALLENGES ASSOCIATED WITH HOLDING COLLABORATORS ACCOUNTABLE

- Reasonable people may disagree about which results to measure, and appropriate data can be difficult to track.
- Some collaborators may resist being held accountable for results, fearing they will not perform well—either because they doubt their own capacity, or because circumstances beyond their control may influence results they are asked to achieve.
- Measuring particular results may focus implementation efforts so narrowly that desirable policy goals that are harder to measure are displaced (teaching to the test).
- A "complete mental reorientation" on the part of public managers, their authorizers and stakeholders, their staff and collaborators, and citizens themselves is needed (Behn, 2001a).

Source: **Page,** *Public Administration Review, 64,* **591–92, 2004.**

data on performance are collected become highly problematic when more actors are added and as the wickedness of problems get compounded.

In order to develop more sophisticated understandings of how performance management can successfully unfold in complex networked environments, more emphasis needs to be placed on "the entanglement of the stages of performance management that go further than a cause and effect understanding." It is within this context that our considerations of governance networks as complex systems comes into the fore. "Complexity accounts will … focus on the interaction and resulting feedback between different elements of the process and outputs. Complexity theory implies that it is the feedback process itself that offers us the best understanding of how performance is constructed" (Haynes, 2003, p. 96).

Differences in the views of what theories of causality reign, what types of feedback to listen to, and the determinant standards through which performance is set and, most importantly, successful performance is to be promoted and used are shaped, in part, by the sectoral characteristics of network actors. The performance standard unique to the state sector is meeting public needs and delivering public policy. The overarching performance standard of the private sector is profit. Observing the distinctions between public sector and private sector performance goals, Radin states:

> The elements in a democracy lead one to acknowledge that much of public action carries multiple and often conflicting goals. As a result, unlike the private sector where profit becomes the ultimate measure of success, it is difficult to establish a standard against which to measure outcomes. (2006, p. 38)

The overarching performance standard of the nonprofit sector is meeting the organizational mission, another facet of nonprofit governance that is highly context specific and situational. A view of the difference in performance standards across the public, private, and nonprofit sectors connotes a continuum of clearly defined measures: near-universal measures (such as profit), to the ambiguity-riddled challenges of measuring successful public policies (Stone, 2002), to the highly context-specific and mostly localized performance standards ascribed to individual nonprofit organizations (Stone and Ostrower, 2007).

Determining how performance is defined between collaborators is complicated by the capacity of collaborators to possess their own unique perspectives around what matters, what counts, and why. As Page puts it, "reasonable people may disagree about which results to measure, and appropriate data can be difficult to track" (2004, pp. 591–92). Despite these challenges, the application of performance measurements to governance networks is important because of the link between performance measurement and accountability. Those to whom accountability must be rendered may be inclined to rely on certain kinds of performance measurement data (construed here in terms of both quantitative and qualitative forms) in the execution of their obligations as accountants. As we have argued, governance networks are held accountable by a complex array of accountants operating through one or several different accountability frameworks.

Using Data to Drive Decisions and Actions

In Chapter 7 we alluded to the role that performance management systems play in facilitating systems feedback. Performance management systems should be designed to serve as the proverbial thermostat for the network, facilitating the flow of data through some kind of comparator that compares performance data with goals and benchmark indicators. When or if the data and goals are out of line, administrative systems are in place to bring the network back into its desired state. Performance management systems have been described as providing a form of double-loop feedback operating within the system (Haynes, 2003, p. 95).

Moynihan has suggested that effective performance management systems serve as the space where "interactive dialogue" between critical stakeholders takes place. He grounds this assertion in the classical performance management doctrine discussed earlier in this chapter by claiming that "performance management doctrine is based on what is essentially a theory of learning. Decision makers are expected to learn from performance information, leading to better-informed decisions and improved government performance." He goes on to add that "performance management doctrine has been relatively weak in identifying routes to learning" (Moynihan, 2008, p. 164). The identification of "routes to learning" serves as a critical feature of performance management systems within governance networks. According to Moynihan, these routines to learning are predicated on the design and use of dialogue routines that are "specifically focused on solution seeking, where actors collectively examine information, consider its significance, and decide how it will affect action" (2008, p. 167). By grounding performance management systems in organizational learning theory, Moynihan provides a solid conceptual link between the evaluation of performance data, the dialogue about these data, and presumably, decisions leading to action. Educational theorist Jonathan Goodlad and colleagues (2004) referred to this process as a "cycle of inquiry," illustrated in Figure 10.2.

Conceptually, the cycle of inquiry draws from John Dewey's (1963a, 1963b) pragmatic philosophy of the social construction of thinking and learning from experience, Kurt Lewin's (1947) theory of action research, and David Kolb's (1984) experiential learning cycle. The cycle of inquiry is predicated on the assumption that groups that share common practices, interests, or roles, and who have a space in which to engage with each other, can be said to be immersed within a cycle of dialoguing, deciding, acting, and evaluating (DDAE) (Gajda and Koliba, 2007).

The DDAE cycle of inquiry provides a crucial theoretical link between concepts of social learning and knowledge management, and decision-making theory. Within governance networks, the cycles of inquiry that supposedly anchor performance management systems take place through a "forum" comprised of members of the network. Such forums likely function at the group level and operate as communities of practice. Radin refers to these communities of practices as "performance partnerships" (2006, p. 168). In an ideal sense, "dialogue forms a basis of social cooperation, and people feel committed to the agreements researched in such a context. Interactive dialogue therefore acts as a social process that helps to create shared mental models, has a unifying effect, and helps to develop credible commitment for the execution phase" (Moynihan, 2008, p. 111).

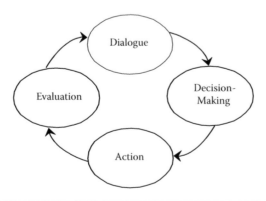

Figure 10.2   DDAE cycle of inquiry.

Performance Management and Network Accountability

The dialogue, decision-making, action, and evaluation cycle of inquiry that results from the effective implementation of performance management systems hinges on the capacity of these processes to be integrated into accountability regimes of the governance network. If those to whom accounts are to be rendered are not actively engaged in these cycles of inquiry, any attempts to systemically collect performance data will be undertaken for naught. Without an audience to engage in an interactive dialogue around performance data, there exists little possibility that accountability and performance management systems will be aligned.

Although "availability of performance information lends legitimacy" to a governance network (Moynihan, 2008, p. 68), performance data must still be used to "maintain both internal and external accountabilities" (Moynihan, 2008, p. 36). Table 10.1 outlines some questions regarding performance measurement that arise as we consider accountability through each accountability type that we introduced in Chapter 9.

The performance management questions raised within each of the accountability types are certainly not offered as an exhaustive list. Nor do the critical considerations assigned to each accountability type convey the complete scope of possible critical considerations that arise when different accountability types are considered within a performance management context.

The point remains that when the performance management systems of a governance network are devised, due consideration must be given to those for whom performance data matter. We have cited some of the challenges that arise when the performance indicators that matter to both those to whom accounts are rendered and those responsible for rendering the accounts do not align. We acknowledge Stephen Page's ascertainment that "reasonable people may disagree about which results to measure" (Page, 2004, pp. 591–92). Some actors implicated in an accountability structure may be more centered on the political implications of performance data, viewing the data as a means to "score points" or achieve policy objectives that lie well beyond the scope of the governance network's operations. We also recognize the potential that some actors who should be paying attention to performance data are not, whether it is because the data are technically inaccessible, one lacks the time to seriously consider performance data, or one lacks the interest. All of these potential challenges to coupling accountability structures with performance management systems persist.

Systems theorist Russell Ackoff notes that "system performance depends critically on how the parts fit and work together, not merely on how well each performs independently; it depends on interactions rather than on actions. Furthermore, a system's performance depends on how it relates to its environment—the larger system of which it is a part—and to other systems in that environment" (1980, p. 27). We believe, following those who have promoted the "logic of governance" as one that is anchored in the coupling of accountability and performance management

**FACTORS CONTRIBUTING TO THE SUCCESSFUL
INTEGRATION OF PERFORMANCE MANAGEMENT
SYSTEMS WITHIN GOVERNANCE NETWORKS**

- Commitment of agency leadership (both principals and agents)
- A belief in the logic of performance measurement as a means of ensuring accountability
- A highly developed organizational culture
- Adequate funding for the performance measurement framework
- Performance is thought by agency executives or their third parties to increase the prospects for agency effectiveness; they will embrace it and make it work

Source: **Frederickson and Frederickson,** *Measuring the Performance of the Hollow State,* **Georgetown University Press, Washington, DC, 2006, pp. 63, 172.**

(Lynn, Heinrich, and Hill, 2000), that those responsible for rendering accounts and those to whom accounts are rendered actively engage in interactions around the collective review of the governance network's performance.

Both practitioners within and researchers of governance network performance will need to focus on those communities of practice operating within the governance network that routinely collect, analyze, discuss, and make decisions based on performance data. These spaces where "performance partnerships" (Radin, 2006) take place have been documented in the study of performance management systems operating with the networks facilitated by regional metropolitan planning organizations (Koliba, Campbell, and Zia, 2009). The designation of committees to collect, process, discuss, and make decisions based on performance data has been mandated by the U.S. Department of Transportation. These guidelines are presented in Figure 10.3 (U.S. DOT, 2009).

The designation of members of the regional planning governance networks to work within committees to process performance data suggests a great deal of foresight on the part of federal funders and regulators. Although much more empirical work is needed to study the composition and make-up of these committees, we surmise that it is these types of groups, operating as communities of practice, engaged in interactive dialogue and continuous cycles of inquiry, that serve as critical agents around which the governance of complex governance networks can (and in many cases does) take place. As Moynihan aptly notes, these performance management processes "require a commitment of time by staff and a setting where performance data that might otherwise be ignored is considered.… [These processes] provide an opportunity to access information, make sense of this information, and persuade

Table 10.1 Performance Measurement Considerations by Accountability Type

Accountability Type	Performance Management Questions	Critical Concerns
Elected representative	• How and to what extent do elected officials place value on certain measures over others? • When might political considerations override the implications drawn from analyzing performance data?	• "Elected officials are rarely interested in performance information" (Moynihan, 2008, p. 12). • Performance data may be politicized and interpreted to suit a predetermined policy frame (Frederickson and Frederickson, 2006).
Citizen/ collective interests	• How and to what extent do citizens and other interest groups place value on certain measures over others? • What technical skills and shared mental models do citizens need to comprehend performance data?	• Citizens are also rarely interested in performance information, particularly information relating to higher levels of government (Moynihan, 2008, p. 63). • Performance data may be politicized and interpreted to suit a predetermined policy frame. • Citizens may ascribe accountability to wrong actors (Van Slyke and Roch, 2004).
Legal	• How might performance data be used to bring about legal compliance? • To what extent can network actors be held legally accountable for poor performance?	• Enforcing contract law is costly (Cooper, 2003). • Many instances of network governance are not premised on contract law.
Owner/ shareholder	• How and to what extent does profit trump all other possible performance indicators?	• Owners may be less than forthright in publicly stating their performance goals when engaged in a grant and contract agreement or PPP.

Table 10.1   Performance Measurement Considerations by Accountability Type (continued)

Accountability Type	Performance Management Questions	Critical Concerns
Consumer	• How and to what extent do consumers take performance data into consideration? • What technical skills and shared mental models do they need to comprehend performance data?	• Consumers' interests in performance data do not extend beyond consideration of themselves or their households.
Bureaucratic	• Who determines which measures count? Who collects and analyzes data? • Who shoulders the burden (e.g., the transaction costs) of data collection and reporting?	• Failure to cut off funding due to lack of reporting of performance data (Frederickson and Frederickson, 2006, p. 60). • "Performance measurement may be used to attempt to give administrative answers to inherently political questions" (Frederickson and Frederickson, 2006, p. 172).
Professional	• How and to what extent do professional standards shape the choice of which performance indicators matter?	• Multiple professional lenses may be evident within the network. • Professionals may be distanced from actual decision making (Romzek and Dubnick, 1987).
Collaborator	• How do peers and partners agree on which performance indicators matter? • Who shoulders the burden (e.g., the transaction costs) of data collection and reporting?	• "Reasonable people may disagree about which results to measure" (Page, 2004, p. 591–92). • Collaborators "are especially unlikely to find acceptable units of comparison across different types of programs" (Moynihan, 2008, p. 97). • Conflicts over performance measures may break down trust.

1. *Create an MPO committee that addresses performance measurement.* The process of developing and implementing performance measures requires a commitment of time and resources. One way to acknowledge this reality from the outset is to plan for a sustained group of practitioners devoted to the complex tasks of selecting measures, identifying data sources and tools, and deciding the best frequency of analysis and distribution of performance findings.

2. *Discuss what measures are ideal and use them to motivate data and tool development.* Given the rapid evolution of automated travel data collection technology, it is helpful to discuss performance measures beyond those that are supported by current capabilities. As one element of a performance measurement effort, transportation agencies within a region may jointly wish to define the most appropriate measures and associated data needs.

3. *Build performance measurement into traveler information programs.* A number of regions have developed systems to provide the public with real-time information on the condition of the transportation system (e.g., location and severity of delays, location and status of accidents, status of the transit network, weather-related traffic problems, disruptions from special events).

4. *Develop a regular performance report.* Many transportation agencies are reporting transportation performance measures on a regular basis. Even a very simple report providing one or two performance measures can have a positive effect on broadening the discussion over investment priorities.

5. *Involve managers with day-to-day responsibility for operations in the process of developing performance measures.* Agencies responsible for major investment decisions often take the lead in developing performance measures. However, it is critical that this process involve practitioners who are concerned primarily with day-to-day operations of the transportation system.

Figure 10.3   Federal Highway Administration performance management system guidelines.

others" (2008, p. 110). The composition of these committees and the efforts made to convey the results of data analysis to external stakeholders to whom the network is accountable may provide a great deal of information about the extent to which performance management and accountability structures are effectively integrated within governance networks. We believe, then, that the study of these governing communities of practice provides an important place to focus administrative, political, and empirical attention.

It is assumed by those who advocate for the application of performance measurement to governance networks that this exercise, when done effectively, may ensure that the resources devoted to them are being used wisely. Performance measures may be one way to guard against the proliferation of ineffective networks and may lead to improvements in public policy outcomes, deepen citizen engagement, provide for some measure of transparency, ensure that accountability exists within and across the network, provide for the equitable distribution of power, and sustain effective networks (Bovaird and Loffler, 2003, p. 322).

The extent to which performance measures can be used to guard against "dark networks" is another matter. Dark networks are potentially dangerous to democratic systems because they are not transparent, lack adequate democratic anchorage, and pursue aims that are said to harm society. Should performance measures be applied to dark networks, one of the major factors shaping their identities as threats to democracy has been mitigated. To couple performance management with the accountability structures of governance networks inevitably requires some measure of transparency and inferences regarding the relationship between network activity and outcomes.

In the end, Moynihan reminds us that "performance data, or simplified assessments of performance data, fails to tell us: Why performance did or did not occur [and] the context of [the] performance" (2008, p. 104). He concludes, "There is likely to be no single definitive approach to a.) interpreting what performance information means and b.) how performance information directs decisions" (2008, p. 102). These important caveats suggest that focusing on performance management systems cannot, nor should not, replace larger and perhaps more tacit accountability considerations. To overemphasize performance management and measurement serves to perpetuate an oversimplification of what performance management is capable of delivering on. This is why we suggest that performance management systems be viewed as an important, but not exclusive, component of a governance network's hybridized accountability regime.

The development of performance measures, however, hinges on how the governance network defines the problem; i.e., what social, political, economic, physical, chemical, and biological factors are assessed as key causes of the policy problem that needs to be addressed by a governance network? Ulrich (1998) calls this management choice the "system of concern" or "boundary judgment." We call this dynamic the phenomenon of micro- or macro-scoping: Micro-scoping occurs when a governance network shrinks its spatial and temporal boundaries to define a system of concern (or define a policy problem). Conversely, macro-scoping occurs when a governance network expands the boundaries of a system of concern. Micro- or macro-scoping leads to a differential development in the choice of performance measures by a governance network.

CRITICAL QUESTIONS AND CONSIDERATIONS

■ How, if at all, is your governance network defining high performance or measuring performance? Who determines which performance indicators matter? Does the network exhibit conflict over how to measure and manage performance?

■ Does the network have a discernable performance management system? Where are data collected and analyzed? To what extent are evaluation data used to inform decision making and collective action?

■ Is there a discernable relationship between accountability and performance? How is the performance of the network perceived differently by different accountants?

Chapter 11

Governance Networks Analysis: Implications for Practice, Education, and Research

> Every great advance in science has issued from a new audacity of imagination.
>
> **—John Dewey (1929, p. 310)**

In the introduction to this book we defined as one of our central goals providing the reader with a sense of the characteristics that make up the governance networks within our midst. Synthesizing a wide range of literature drawn from a variety of academic fields and disciplines, we sought to provide the reader with a foundation for conducting governance network analysis as a function of one's practice, one's education, and one's research agenda. We have argued that governance, as understood in terms of network and systems dynamics as well as democratic anchorage, is a critical and important feature distinguishing governance networks from other forms of interorganizational networks. Following the long line of public administration theorists and practitioners (March and Olsen, 1995; Pierre and Peters, 2005; Sorensen and Torfing, 2008), we have sought to anchor this conception of governance within the context of democratic theory. By integrating network and systems constructs with theories of governance premised on the consideration of accountability and performance standards, we have suggested that governance needs to serve as the modifier of a certain genre of interorganizational networks. In the process, we have attempted to elevate governance processes, structures, and practices as the critical competencies that accompany a public administrator into his or her roles as a network manager.

In this chapter we point to the implications that this taxonomy has for administrative practice, education and training, and research. We discuss some of the *practitioner* questions and applications that may arise when governance networks are critically considered. We then consider the implications that the turn toward governance and networks, embodied in the extensively rich and multifaceted literature presented here, has for the *education and training* of present and future public administrators who are finding (or will find) themselves operating as governance network managers (leaders and followers alike). We then offer some considerations pertaining to the *empirical study of governance networks*, focusing particular attention on the potential for greater case studies, hypothesis testing, and modeling. We conclude with a discussion of action research methods and designs.

Deepening Our Situational Awareness of Governance Networks

In Chapter 8 we discussed the role that situational awareness has in developing a network administrator's systems thinking skills and strategies. To restate a definition, *situational awareness* "is the perception of the elements in the environment within a volume of time and space, the comprehension of their meaning, [and] the projection of their status in the near future" (Endsley, 1995). Situational awareness should explain dynamic goal selection and give attention to appropriate critical cues and expectancies regarding future states of the situation (Endsley, 1995, p. 34). "If we want to operate within a complex and dynamic system, we have to know not only what its current status is but what its status will be or could be in the future, and we have to know how certain actions we take will influence the situation. For this, we need structural knowledge, knowledge of how the variables in the system are relaxed and how they influence one another" (Radin, 2006, p. 24). We believe the taxonomy presented in this book can be used to advance our structural knowledge of governance networks.

This body of work has been premised on a set of assumptions regarding the framing of a network perspective, discussed here by Bressers and O'Toole:

> An advantage of a network perspective is that it can be used to direct attention to the larger structures of interdependence. Instead of assuming that influence takes place only through direct and observable interactions, whether as personal relationships or among representatives of institutional interests, a network approach—applied to portions of a

policy process as varied as formulation and implementation—can investigate how the larger structure can have systematic effects on the behavior of individual actors as well as on the content of decisions, policy responses, and implementation efforts. A network approach thus offers the chances to continue both interpersonal and structural explanations for policy-relevant events. (2003, p. 147)

We believe that the kind of structural knowledge inherent in Bressers and O'Toole's observation can contribute to the answering of these and many other questions:

- *What capital resources, types of ties, policy tools, administrative strategies, accountability structures, and performance management systems need to be in place to ensure that networks function properly?* In essence, those administrators operating inside of or outside of a governance network need to be capable of accessing and using a range of administrative tools and strategies at their disposal.
- *Which actors should be involved in a governance network?* Public administrators may be playing the role of network activitator (Salamon, 2002a) or catalyst (Fox et al., 2002), and have an instrumental role in determining which actors are in the governance network. They may choose which actors to contract or partner with. They may broaden or narrow the range of actors implicated under their regulatory and oversight authority.
- *When should we attempt to enter into a governance network?* When should a nonprofit organization or private business pursue a grant or government contract? When should actors decide to cooperate in an effort to share and pool resources?
- *What do we do about the governance networks we are already operating within?* We may be already operating within the belly of a governance network, without much capacity to exit it. How do we clarify our roles within the governance network? To what extent do we have the power or authority to modify the flow of capital resources in the network? How might we devise accountability and performance management systems to govern this network? Why might we want to consider leaving the network?
- *What are the functions of the governance network?* Does it have discernable boundaries and borders?
- *What is our role within this governance network?* Does our organization understand that we're participating in the network on its behalf? Do we have adequate resources?
- *To whom are we accountable?* To what extent are these accountabilities forged on weak or strong ties? To what extent is there a clear understanding of to whom accounts are to be rendered within the governance network?
- *When should we actively seek to alter the accountability structures of our own organizations in order to pursue network-wide goals?* How do we manage to handle accountability trade-offs? Accountability couplings? What kinds of skills and strategies are needed to operate within a hybridized accountability regime?

- *How is network performance defined? Who is doing the defining? How is network performance measured and managed?* Where within the governance network are network performance data discussed, used to make decisions, and acted upon?
- *Is it possible to design a governance network?* What are the few simple rules that set governance network activity in place?

Bressers and O'Toole's articulation of "contextual-interaction theory" may be useful in developing a conceptualization of situational awareness. This theory is "open to considering all kinds of situational factors" while channeling all of these factors "through (that is, considers their potential influence as shaping) a limited number of 'core variables' that are used to build deductive frames [*sic*] of analysis" (2003, p. 148). They suggest that emphasis be given to the processes and procedures that govern the structures, functions, and actions of governance networks.

> Thinking in terms of policy processes suggests emphasizing their character as patterns of social interaction. Doing so shifts the central focus from the semifinished "products" and ultimate end results of the policy-implementation process to the actors participating in the process itself. The basic assumption of the theory is thus that the course and outcomes of the processes depend not only on inputs (in this case, the characteristics of the policy instruments), but primarily on the characteristics of the actors involved, particularly their motivations, information, and relative power. All other factors that influence the process do so because, and insofar as, they influence the core characteristics of the actors involved. (2003, p. 149)

Integration of Governance Network Analysis into Formal Education and Training

During his 2004 keynote address at the National Society for Schools of Public Affairs and Administration (NASPAA) Annual Conference in Indianapolis, Indiana, Lester Salamon threw down a gauntlet to higher education administrators and graduate program directors. After laying out the conditions that give rise to a new governance perspective, he called for curricular reforms that prepare present and future public administrators to "design and manage the immensely complex collaborative systems that now form the core of public problem-solving and that seem likely to do so increasingly in the years ahead" (Salamon, 2005, p. 10). He was quick to note as well, as did Charles Goodsell a year later (2006), that the new public management framework geared toward reforming public bureaucracies to be more like businesses does not adequately prepare networked administrators.

For public administration educators there would appear to be a growing need to provide a curriculum devoted to the study of governance networks. Given the proliferation, complexity, and need for greater accountability for and within governance networks, the need to provide students of public administration with greater opportunities to critically examine governance networks and ascertain where and how public administrators are to play a role within them is only increasing. To this end, courses and training need to be developed to provide students with an overview of the trends and factors shaping governance networks.

Koliba (2006) lays out a series of learning outcomes that are needed to prepare students to administer within these complex, networked environments:

■ *Identify the reforms and trends in governance that have given rise to the evolution of governance networks.* They must be able to situate a governance network perspective within the context of the public administration's core themes and history. This will ultimately call for the extension of the public administration cannon to account for these shifting paradigms (Goodsell, 2006).

■ *Explain the roles and motivations that various actors take on through networked relationships.* In light of the new public management's focus on business practices, a serious look at the complementary and competing governance and accountability structures of different sectors is called for. Students should be encouraged to engage in serious, critical discussions regarding the role that profit-making and market mechanisms bear not only on the assumed improved efficiencies, but also on maintaining the normative basis of the public administration field.

■ *Understand how policy tools and public action tools mobilize, or are utilized by, governance networks.* As we think about the defining characteristics of networked activities, the roles of policy tools (Salamon, 2002b; Howlett, 2003) and other public action tools (Agranoff and McGuire, 2003) become important. Not only do these tools mobilize network activity, but they are used to monitor and critique it. In essence, students must learn the extent to which governance networks are implicated within the public policy process and the coupling of policy streams.

■ *Understand some of the challenges and factors involved in the successes and failures of networked activities, including the importance of goal alignment and functional compatibilities.* There is a growing body of literature that looks at network failure and successes. These may be used to provide students with insight into the kinds of conditions necessary to ensure network effectiveness. Case studies of network failures (as in the cases of responses to 9/11 (Comfort, 2002) and the failed response in the aftermath of Hurricane Katrina (GAO, 2006; Kiefer and Montjoy, 2006)) may be juxtaposed against cases of success or near success (Provan and Milward, 1995; Agranoff and McGuire, 2003; Wines and Roberts, 2003; Townsend, 2004; Guo and Acor, 2005) to highlight central issues pertaining to governance within networked environs.

■ *Identify the kinds of skills and functions that public administrators take on within the context of networked relationships.* The public administration field has historically focused on the structure and functioning of vertical relationships within public bureaucracies. However, the growing recognition that public administrators must "cross boundaries" (Kettl, 2006) and work horizontally across departmental and even organizational lines calls for the study of collaboration and the situations and conditions within which collaborative arrangements are feasible and effective. Students must be exposed to case studies and expert practitioners skilled in building collaborative partnerships. In the process, they must be prepared to execute "coordinating strategies of actors with different goals and preferences" (Kickert, Klijn, and Koppenjan, 1997a, p. 10).

■ *Draw upon some of the relevant theoretical foundations to analyze governance networks.* Students should be exposed to transdisciplinary theoretical frameworks that may be used to better understand the intricacies of complex governance systems. Social capital theory, rooted in assumptions regarding the relative value of social relations and the levels of trust, reciprocity, and norms developed within them, is useful in assessing the qualities of networks (Putnam, 1993, 2000; Baron, Field, and Schuller, 2000). Network theory, originating out of the field of sociology, has focused on the nature of exchanges that take place between actors involved in a network (Marsden and Laumann, 1984; Milward and Provan, 1998). Community of practice theory, emerging from the organizational learning and knowledge management fields, is useful in describing and assessing inter- and intraorganizational relationships between actors (Snyder, Wenger, and de Sousa Briggs, 2003). Complexity theory builds upon a systems analysis framework, underscores the self-organizing capacities of groups, and can be utilized in describing complicated network activities and patterns (Haynes, 2003; Koppenjan and Klijn, 2004; Morcol and Wachhaus, 2009).

■ *Critically assess how and where accountability and accountability regimes work within network structures.* The complexity that coincides with networked activities generates additional accountability challenges (Posner, 2002; Page, 2004). As network governance continues to gain prominence in the field, it will become increasingly vital that frameworks and structures are in place to hold actors from different sectors accountable to the public at large. This is a daunting task: Accountability structures vary across sectors, and the mechanisms to enforce public accountability become blurred as the number of actors in a network increase (Behn, 2001; Dowdle, 2006; Mashaw, 2006). Public administration students must be encouraged to look at the nature of the accountability regimes (Mashaw, 2006) at work within governance networks. Arguably, the rise of a governance network perspective makes this task all the more challenging.

Why should we be concerned about developing an empirical and theoretical framework to describe and analyze governance networks? Ultimately, the systemic examination of the governance network as an empirical construct will lead to certain utilities for practitioners, citizen groups, and educators. That governance networks proliferate virtually everywhere (Sorensen and Torfing, 2005) should be cause enough to warrant the mounting of such a research enterprise. By advancing governance networks as a unit of analysis, generalizations regarding the interplay of network variables may be rendered. Ultimately, these generalizations should yield insights into the design, administration, and monitoring of governance network activity. Issues of democracy, accountability, and fairness in network governance may also be proposed as important metacriteria for developing theoretical frameworks.

Case Study Analysis

The most extensive body of empirical research on governance networks exists in the form of written case studies that are often rich in detail and categorization (to cite a few of the book-length studies of multiple cases: Agranoff and McGuire, 2003; Koontz et al., 2004; Frederickson and Frederickson, 2006; Agranoff, 2007). In all of these cases, extensive field studies were rendered involving direct observation, interviews, surveys, and the analysis of secondary data. Case studies provide an opportunity to render "thick descriptions" (Geertz, 1973) of social phenomena. Case studies may identify critical individual actors—those network administrators operating inside the network who are either succeeding or failing. We believe that there is greater need to focus on describing and analyzing the governing committees, teams, boards, and other communities of practice responsible for network governance and administration, as has been done by Koontz et al. (2004) and Agranoff (2007).

In the classes that we have taught using this framework, students have been asked to apply the framework to existing case studies. For those seeking more in-depth applications, we have found two studies to be instructive: (1) David and George Frederickson's (2006) *Measuring the Performance of the Hollow State*, which focuses on performance management in health care networks, and (2) Thomas Koontz et al.'s (2004) book, *Collaborative Environmental Management: What Roles for Government?*, which features comprehensively written case studies of environmental management networks. We found the case studies in these two books to be extremely useful in this regard. Students have also applied the framework to governance networks of their own choosing. A guide for those interested in applying the framework to new or existing case studies of governance networks is provided in Appendix B.

The case study template found in Appendix B provides some tools for generating case studies of governance networks, beginning with an initial identification of network actors and network-wide characteristics. Out of this initial framing, fuller case studies with focused attention given to the critical governing apparatus may be given. Students have used these templates to analyze existing written cases and devise their own case studies.

At the conclusion of most chapters of the book we have given some guidance to the reader around studying a governance network of their choosing in the "Critical Questions and Considerations" section. We believe that these questions, combined with the template provided in Appendix B, provide the reader with some basis for rendering a case study of a governance network.

The case study approach not only allows the researcher or analyst to render a thick description of the network, but can allow us to compare one case to another. Rendering comparative case studies requires the use of a standard framework through which we may compare one network to another.

Hypothesis Generation: Deductive Testing Leading to Generalization

The capacity to test hypotheses is a central feature of deductive social science. Hypotheses are "links in a theoretical causal chain" that aid in determining the "direction and strength of a relationship between two variables" (Neuman, 2000, p. 131). Appendix A presents a comprehensive display of the range of characteristics and variables discussed throughout this book.

Within a given study, any combination of variables may be viewed as independent, dependent, or intervening. In Table 11.1 we introduce a set of potential independent and dependent variables. We distinguish between four types of potential hypothesis:

- Actor characteristics impacting actor behaviors (*actor-to-actor relations*)
- Actor characteristics impacting network-wide characteristics and behaviors (*actor-to-network interactions*)
- Network-wide characteristics impacting actor characteristics and behaviors (*network-to-actor interactions*)
- Network-wide characteristics to network-wide behaviors (*network-to-network relations*)

Table 11.1 outlines some of the ways that hypotheses may be generated across these types.

A much more comprehensive review of the range of hypotheses that have been generated and tested across the literature is needed. For some of these variable parings we drew on the hypothesis laid out by Michael Provan and Patrick Kenis based on their network governance model (2007).

Hypothesis testing requires that independent and dependent variables be quantifiable. In some instances, variables are naturally reported and conceived of numerically (as in the case of money and other financial resources). Others require systemic attempts to define an "operationalizable" that adequately matches abstract constructs with empirically quantified values.

Table 11.1   Range of Potential Hypotheses to Be Generated from a Governance Network Taxonomy

Levels of Interaction	Independent Variable(s)	Dependent Variable(s)	Example of Generic Hypothesis
Actor to actor	Individual network actor's contribution of capital resources	Network actor's roles; functions; ties within the network	Network actors contributing higher levels of capital resources to the network are positioned as principals within the network
	Social sector of network actors	Network actor's roles; functions; ties within the network	Public sector network actors are more likely to play a lead organization role than non-governmental actors under *x* circumstances
			Private sector actors are less likely to contribute financial resources to a governance network under *y* circumstances
Actor to network	Actor perceptions of trust of other network actors	Governance structures	Where trust between network actors is high, a shared governance structure is more apt to form
			Where trust is intermediate, a network administrative organization is more apt to form
			Where trust is low, a lead organization structure is more apt to form
			(Extrapolated from Provan and Kenis, 2007)

(continued)

Table 11.1   Range of Potential Hypotheses to Be Generated from a Governance Network Taxonomy (Continued)

Levels of Interaction	Independent Variable(s)	Dependent Variable(s)	Example of Generic Hypothesis
	Actor perceptions of trust of other network actors	Performances outcomes	Those networks that exhibit high levels of trust between network actors are more apt to perform than those networks with low levels of trust
	Citizen, elected representatives, interest groups, courts' interest in governance network performance	Performance outcomes	The existence of democratic accountabilities ensures more effective network performance
	Actor social sector Geographical scale	Network governance structures; network functions	The more homogenous actors' sector and geographic scale, the more likely that ...
Network to actor	Network performance	Actor acquisition of capital resources	Networks performing at a high level infuse network actors with Z kinds of capital resources
	Network governance structure	Actor perceptions of trust in other members	Shared governance structures generate higher degree of trust between actors than either lead organization or network administrative organizations (extrapolated from Provan and Kenis, 2007)

Table 11.1   Range of Potential Hypotheses to Be Generated from a Governance Network Taxonomy (Continued)

Levels of Interaction	Independent Variable(s)	Dependent Variable(s)	Example of Generic Hypothesis
	Network governance structures; network functions	Actor social sector; geographic scale	Actor participation in governance network of certain structures and functions contributes to sector blurring, or changes in their scope of geographic focus
Network to network	Network governance structures	Network policy function; network policy domain function	Certain governance structures are more amenable to the pursuit of particular policy functions and policy domain functions than others
	Network policy function; network policy domain function	Network governance structure	*X* governance network functions lead to *A* network structures
	Network governance structure	Network performance	Certain governance structures lead to better network performance than others within a particular policy domain
	Network functions	Network performance	Governance networks that take on *Y* functions are more apt to perform better than those networks that do not take on those functions
	Network performance indicators and performance management systems	Network performance outcomes	Quality of performance management systems lead to better network performance

(continued)

Table 11.1   Range of Potential Hypotheses to Be Generated from a Governance Network Taxonomy (Continued)

Levels of Interaction	Independent Variable(s)	Dependent Variable(s)	Example of Generic Hypothesis
	Network governance structure	Network change and adaptation	Networks of *B* network structure are more apt to change and adapt than those of *C* network structure

Modeling Complex Governance Networks

Combining elements of case study analysis with the quantifiable elements of hypothesis testing, the tools of network analysis and computer-based modeling are employed in the study of governance networks. The most extensive applications of social network analysis to the study of governance networks within the public administration literature have been undertaken by Louise Comfort (2002, 2007) and Naim Kapucu (2006a, 2006b), who have applied the tools of social network analysis (and their related software applications) to the study of emergency management networks. These tools are particularly useful in studying the nature of the ties occurring between network actors. Social network analysis allows for the coding of ties based on strength, types of resource flows, and formality. The position of actors vis-à-vis their networks may be studied, providing a capacity to not only test the kind of hypotheses discussed above, but also re-create holistic systems models of existing governance networks. Dynamic models may be employed to anticipate the emergence of future structures and functions (Miller and Page, 2007).

Miller and Page describe modeling as an "attempt to reduce the world to a fundamental set of elements (equivalent classes) and laws (transition functions), and on this basis ... understand and predict key aspects of the world" (2007, p. 40). Social network analysis provides one set of elements that may be relied upon to build a model. "Modeling proceeds by deciding what simplifications to impose on the underlying entities and then, based on those abstractions, uncovering their implications" (Miller and Page, 2007, p. 65). Social network analysis simplifies the structures of networks into a series of nodes and ties.

Those who are viewing social networks in terms of complex adaptive systems have begun to ascribe agency to actors in the network into agent-based models (ABMs). Miller and Page describe the difference between ABMs and forms of complex systems dynamics models:

> The agent-based object approach can be considered "bottom up" in the sense that the behavior that we observe in the model is generated from the bottom of the system by the direct interactions of the entities

Table 11.2 Computations as Theory

	Simple Structure	*Complicated Structure*
Agent-Based Objects	Bottom-up modeling (e.g., artificial adaptive agents)	Bottom-up simulation (e.g., artificial life)
Abstraction-Based Objects	Top-down modeling (e.g., computable general equilibrium)	Top-down simulation (e.g., global warming)

Source: Miller and Page, *Complex Adaptive Systems: An Introduction to Computational Models of Social Life*, Princeton University Press, Princeton, NJ, 2007, p. 67. Permission granted by Princeton University Press.

> that form the basis of the model. This contrasts with the "top-down" approach to modeling where we impose high-level rules on the system—for example, that the system will equilibrate or that all firms profit maximize—and then trace the implications of such conditions. Thus, in top-down modeling we abstract broadly over the entire behavior of the system, whereas in bottom-up modeling we focus our abstractions over the lower-level individual entities that make up the system. (2007, p. 66)

They relate the complexity of the structure to the bottom-up or top-down nature of the objects studied in Table 11.2.

Bottom-up models of governance networks will start with the characteristics of each actor in the network, including the roles that individuals, groups, and organizations play. In dynamic agent-based models, the behaviors of these agents are ascribed certain characteristics or some ranges of intensity around certain characteristics, with the system virtually "taking on a life of its own." Top-down models deduce the essential properties to be modeled and construct nonlinear models to predict outcomes.

Utilizing Action Research and Modeling to Inform Planning Design and Practice

"Action research" is another way to frame the role of evaluation within complex adaptive systems. French and Bell define action research as

> the process of systematically collecting research data about an ongoing system relative to some objective, goal, or need of that system; feeding these data back into the system; taking actions by altering selected

variables within the system based both on the data and on hypothesis; and evaluating the results of actions by collecting more data. (1999, p. 130)

Chris Argyris and Donald Schon (1995) view action research as intervention experiments through which evaluative data are used to inform organizational practices. To structure such inquiries as interventions, a certain measure of intentionality in the design of the action research process must be taken (Koliba and Lathrop, 2007). Action research processes are grounded in theories of organizational and experiential learning. Action research projects may employ a wide range of research methods, including all of the methodological approaches mentioned in this chapter.

Action researchers will likely collect data that may be used by a performance management system to generate greater understanding of existing practices. This systemic evaluation leads to the development of sense making, "based on the assumption that interventions purported to enhance learning in practice should focus more on bringing out people's natural information-seeking and learning behaviors" (Parboosingh, 2002, p. 234). By integrating action research designs and processes into their performance management system, groups of individuals within a governance network will form communities of practices designed to share information, learn, and transfer and build knowledge (Fetterman, 2002; Foth, 2006; Gajda and Koliba, 2007; Koliba and Gajda, 2009). By intentionally situating action research processes within governance network operations at this level, we believe it is possible to integrate action research practices into the performance management systems of governance networks.

The key to utilizing action research and performance management in this way is to understand how consensus among stakeholders relates to the degree of understanding and application of system dynamics (and situational awareness) to current thinking. Marjan van den Belt describes the relationship between combinations of systems thinking and consensus and the kind of action research interventions possible in Table 11.3.

We believe that this typology is helpful in distinguishing the different ways that action research and modeling can be applied to the operations of governance networks. When there is little to no consensus around goals and little degree of systems thinking, there exist very little opportunities for strategic change to be undertaken—the status quo reigns. When there is goal consensus but little adaption of systems thinking and situational awareness, good discussions are possible that may or may not lead to constructive decisions and actions. Little goal consensus, but a high degree of systems dynamics yields expert-driven models of complex adaptive systems, but the interface between experts and decision makers may be limited (as they will likely be when there is little consensus on goals).

Van den Belt suggests that mediated modeling processes may be devised when goal consensus is high and there is a widely understood appreciation of systems dynamics. She describes mediated modeling in terms of a distinct, staged process

Table 11.3   Interventions: Understanding of Systems Dynamics vs. Degree of Consensus

		Degree of Consensus among Stakeholders	
		Low	High
Degree of understanding of the system dynamics	Low	**Status quo** Typical result Confrontational debate and no improvement	**Mediated discussion** Typical result Consensus on goals or problems but no help on how to achieve the goals or solve the problems
	High	**Expert modeling** Typical result Specialized model whose recommendations never get implemented because they lack stakeholder support	**Mediated modeling** Typical result Consensus on both problems/goals and process, leading to effective and implementable policies

Source: van den Belt, *Mediated Modeling: A System Dynamics Approach to Environmental Consensus Building*, Island Press, Washington, DC, 2004, p. 18. Reproduced by permission of Island Press.

that mirrors the cycle of inquiry discussed in the previous chapter. Modelers work with key stakeholders to determine the critical values and variables that matter most to them. Models are constructed based on these preferences. Other forms of action research found within the organizational and experiential learning literature and applied across every policy domain make the most sense when consensus is high and system thinking prevails. Van den Belt (2004) focuses her attention to the use of STELLA models that develop by using stocks and flow and feedback factors in the design, but we believe ABMs may also be employed in this manner.

Governance Networks, 2.0

We began the chapter with a look at the ways in which practitioners can apply some of the constructs of this book to their own practice. The educational imperative that we derive from our analysis was discussed. We suggested tools to use to begin to describe governance networks through case studies. We anticipated the range of possible combinations of independent and dependent variables possible to build into hypotheses. We then discussed the role that modeling, in its many forms, can play in describing, evaluating, and predicting governance network behavior. We concluded with some considerations for integrating empirical inquiry into the very operations of governance networks. The interrelationship between theory and practice may play itself out through any number of "governance network, 2.0" activities.

This book presents what we may label as an initial rendering of governance networks. The model of governance networks that we present here is static. It is the bare bones of a body of practice and inquiry that is still emerging. The evidence for this emergence may be found in the works listed in our bibliography, in addition to the mountain of research and practice not touched on here.

The next version of this work will need to begin where we leave off. We have purposely opted to not write about the development of governance network "theory." We are mindful of Ostrom's distinctions between conceptual frameworks, theories, and models (2005, p. 6).

We argue that what we have introduced here is a conceptual framework that is something in between a modest set of variables and a paradigm. Further theory development is already emerging from the extensive case studies and hypothesis testing being undertaken across the field. Models of governance networks are yet to be fully constructed. The continual evolution of a conceptual framework informed by theories and models will mark future iterations of this work.

Chapter 12

Conclusion: Smart (Democratic) Governance Systems

> The question we ask today is not whether our government is too big or too small, but whether it works.
>
> **—Barack Obama, Inauguration Speech (2009)**

We conclude by discussing the two major themes woven throughout this book:

1. The democratic imperative of governance network analysis
2. The increasing need to build the capacities of all governance network actors, particularly governments, to be more strategic in their orientation to the governance networks in their midst.

In this concluding chapter, we consider what it means to operate "smart" governance systems. Part of the Web 2.0 culture that marks the era within which this book is written centers on developing the capacities of systems to behave more effectively. There exists considerable interest in creating a "smart grid" to manage our energy infrastructure. Transportation planning systems are utilizing real-time data to monitor traffic flows and critical incidents. Simulation models are used to train soldiers, train and teach managers, and entertain adults and children. The central feature behind all of these systems is a belief in the capacity of human invention and technology to garner a firmer grasp on how natural, engineered, and social systems work, and apply this knowledge to the effective stewardship of the natural environment, more effective design-engineered systems, and the effective management, administration, and governance of certain types of social systems.

Smart Systems as Ensuring Democratic Anchorage

We are unabashedly clear that smart governance systems need to be construed as smart, *democratic* governance systems. Over the course of this book we have made a concerted effort to incorporate some of the most important normative considerations facing the future of network governance. Building on the long-standing assumptions regarding the role of the state and its sovereign obligations and the basic tenets of democratic theory, we have asserted that governance networks operating within a democratic context, at least, need to bear a significant democratic anchorage in order to be deemed legitimate in the eyes of their democratic "accountees." We assume that such an anchorage is crucial to ensure that certain overarching policy goals are achieved.

The notion of sovereignty within a democratic context is that those doing the governing need to obtain the consent of the governed. Considered within the context of traditional governance arrangements, consent was to be delivered through a combination of electoral processes and other forms of deliberative process designed to ensure authentic citizen involvement within the governance process. However, as we have noted in Chapter 1, these arrangements have either always been complicated or are increasingly becoming complex. The capacities of elected representatives and citizens to essentially anchor governance within a robust application of democratic accountability are continually evolving. The extent to which democratic anchorage erodes to the point where the essence of state sovereignty ceases to exist in the structures and functions of governance networks needs to continue to be one of our most pressing points of concern.

Some may argue that the democratic anchorage of governance networks is being eroded when certain groups capture the interests of governance networks, inevitably leading to behaviors and actions that mimic those interests captured in the process. We see this as evident within instances of "regulatory capture," the obtuse operations of some interest group coalitions and iron triangles, and the whole scale privatization of certain functions of sovereign governments.

We believe that these efforts will be greatly enhanced by the advancement of public interest and public values frameworks. Barry Bozeman's (2007) extensive discussion of these frameworks is useful here, and may be found in his book *Public Values and Public Interest*. We replicate some of Bozeman's provisional definitions of public concepts in Table 12.1.

According to Bozeman, publicness is determined through the exercise of political authority. We may equate political authority to democratic accountably. He views publicness as well as privateness in terms of matters of degree. In Bozeman's

Table 12.1 The Provisional Definitions of *Publicness*

Key Term	*Provisional Definition*
Public interest	An ideal public interest refers to those outcomes best serving the long-term survival and well-being of a social collective construed as a "public."
Public values	A society's public values are those providing normative consensus about (1) the rights, benefits, and prerogatives to which citizens should (and should not) be entitled; (2) the obligation of citizens to society, the state, and one another; and (3) the principles on which governments and policies should be based.
Public value criteria	Public value criteria are used to investigate the extent to which public values seemed to have been achieved. Public value failure occurs when neither the market nor public sector provides goods and services required to achieve public values.
Publicness	"An organization is 'public' to the extent that it exerts or is constrained by political authority" … "An organization is 'private' to the extent that it exerts or is constrained by economic authority" (Bozeman, 1987, pp. 84–85).
Normative publicness	An approach to values analysis assuming that a knowledge of the mix of political and economic authority of institutions and policies is a prerequisite of understanding the potential of institutions and policies to achieve public values and to work toward public interest ideals.

Source: Bozeman, *Public Values and Public Interest: Counterbalancing Economic Individualism*, Georgetown University Press, Washington, DC, 2007, p. 18. Reproduced with permission from Georgetown University Press.

view, organizations may be described in terms of the extent of their publicness or privateness, giving theoretical and philosophical credence to the possibility of sector blurring. Publicness becomes a normative value that may be applied to the complicated arrangements found within governance networks. Recalling our discussion of sector blurring in Chapter 9, we suggest that an organization or institution that is implicated within a governance network will be subjected to influences that may affect the extent to which it is more or less public. Captured governments within a regulatory subsystem will be influenced more by the economic authority of the regulated entities. Nonprofit organizations receiving government grants may become beholden to the political authorities that dictate the actions of their public funders. Private businesses may voluntarily or involuntarily integrate consideration of the public interests into their rhetoric, behaviors, and actions.

Determining what the public interest is requires that we consider which public we are referring to, giving rise to the possibility that there are, in reality, many publics whose interests must be considered (Bozeman, 2007). Couple this with the wickedness of the publics' problems, and it is logical to conclude, as many have done, that what defines the publics' interests depends on whose interests are accounted for and how those interests are framed. The shift in the literature from public interest to public value has arisen, in part, as an attempt to render a clear set of criteria through which the public interest (however it ultimately gets defined) is met (Stoker, 2005, 2006). Public values are derived out of the fundamentals of democratic theory. Public values are those that exist when the sovereign relationship between a democratic state and its citizens is legitimately honored. We believe that we have contributed something to our understanding of how we may describe, evaluate, and model how public values are being upheld or not within governance networks. This was the point that we were making when we considered the overlap between accountability and performance in Chapter 10. By choosing to view accountability and performance as two of the major critical considerations necessary to the study of governance network, we point to some ways through which we may observe the democratic anchorage of a governance network in practice.

Smart Systems as Governing Dynamic Networks

The taxonomy presented in this book did not spring from the minds of the authors and onto the pages of this book. As we discussed in Chapter 2, the frameworks and theories discussed here have evolved over the course of decades of study and consideration of governments, public policies, nonprofit organizations, and market forces. In this book we have presented a framework for describing and eventually evaluating governance networks. By appealing to practitioners and students as well as researchers and theorists, we have assumed that a good theory (or conceptual framework, to borrow Ostrom's term) is good for practice. We argue that democratically accountable network managers will need to utilize the tools of analysis and the strategies of implementation presented here.

In our discussion of modeling in Chapter 11 we alluded to the possibility of developing models of governance networks in much the same way as natural and engineered systems are being modeled. Through these tools and techniques the governance of dynamic systems may be studied and designed. We believe that the increasing computing capacity of high-speed computers will make it possible to map, model, and simulate governance networks, with applications that defy explanation (Koliba, Zia and Lee, 2010; Zia, Metcalf, Koliba, and Widener, 2010).

We are also quick to note that individual public administrators and policy makers are already immersed in the governance of dynamic systems. We have argued that governance has always been a complex endeavor, beginning with the first conflicts to arise between two actors in Thomas Paine's thought experiment. Governance has always encompassed the interplay of public, private, and voluntary sectors. Challenges pertaining to geographic scale have always accompanied civilized human development (as rural-urban tensions, as city-state–nation-state tensions, etc.). Actors immersed within governance networks have always traded some form of capital resources while pooling others. These dynamics have not emerged with the development of the nuclear bomb, color television, or performance-based contracting. These dynamics have persisted since the dawn of recorded history. *The contexts and situations have changed and evolved.* The wickedness of problems has become more endemic. Some actors have gained power, others have lost it. Some new skills and strategies have emerged to more effectively manage complex dynamics, while some other skills and strategies have been used to hold back progress. What is clearly "new" in all of this has been our growing capacity to describe, evaluate, and design these complex dynamic systems. Applying these new skills, tools, and techniques serves as the basis of a smart governance system populated by actors serving as accounters, accountees, resource providers, resource takers, leaders, followers, peers, owners, consumers, citizens, interest groups, and network managers. Those possessing a deeper awareness of complex system dynamics will be at an advantage. Let us hope that we may extend these tools to all with a stake in the future. We believe that the integrity of our very democracy may rest on it.

Bibliography

Aberbach, J. D., & Rockman, B. A. (2000). *In the web of politics: Three decades of the U.S. federal executive.* Washington, D.C.: Brookings Institution

Ackoff, R. L. (1980). The systems revolution. In M. Lockett & R. Spear (Eds.), *Organizations as systems.* Milton Keynes, UK: Open University Press.

Adams, G. (1981). *The iron triangle: The politics of defense contracting.* New York: Council on Economic Priorities.

Adams, R., & McCullough, A. (2003). The urban practitioner and participation in research within a streetwork context. *Community, Work and Family, 6*(3), 269–287.

Adams, S., & Kriesi, H. (2007). The network approach. In P. A. Sabatier (Ed.), *Theories of the policy process* (pp. 129–154). Boulder, CO: Westview Press.

Adkins, N. F. (Ed.). (1953). *Thomas Paine: Common sense and other political writings.* New York: Liberal Arts Press.

Agranoff, R. (2006). Inside collaborative networks: Ten lessons for public managers. *Public Administration Review, 66*(6) (Special Issue), 56–65.

Agranoff, R. (2007). *Managing within networks: Adding value to public organizations.* Washington, DC: Georgetown University Press.

Arganoff, R. (2008). Enhancing performance through public sector networks: Mobilizing human capital in communities of practice. *Public Performance and Management Review, 31*(3), 320–347.

Agranoff, R., & McGuire, M. (2003). *Collaborative public management: New strategies for local governments.* Washington, DC: Georgetown University Press.

Agranoff, R., & McGuire, M. (2004). Another look at bargaining and negotiation in intergovernmental management. *Journal of Public Administration Research and Theory, 14*(4), 495–513.

Albert, L., Gainsborough, J., & Wallis, A. (2006). Building the capacity to act regionally: Formation of the regional transportation authority in South Florida. *Urban Affairs Review, 42*(2), 143–168.

Allison, G. T. (1971). *Essence of decision.* Boston: Little, Brown and Company.

Anand, S. (2008). *Essentials of corporate governance.* Danvers, MA: John Wiley & Sons.

Anderson, P. (1999). Complexity theory and organizational science. *Organization Science, 10*(3), 216–232.

Ansell, C., & Gash, A. (2008). Collaborative governance in theory and practice. *Journal of Public Administration Research and Theory, 18*(4), 543–571.

307

Appleby, P. (2004). Government is different. In J. Shafritz, A. C. Hyde, & S. J. Parkes (Eds.), *Classics of public administration* (5th ed., pp. 131–135). Belmont, CA: Wadsworth/ Thomson Learning.

Argyris, C., & Schon, D. A. (1995). *Organizational learning II: Theory, method, and practice.* Reading, MA: Addison-Wesley Publishing.

Attwater, R., & Derry, C. (2005). Engaging communities of practice for risk communication in the Hawkesbury Water Recycling Scheme. *Action Research, 3*(2), 193–209.

Axelrod, R. (1980). *The evolution of cooperation.* New York: Basic Books.

Axelrod, R., & Cohen, M. (1999). *Harnessing complexity: Organizational implications of a scientific frontier.* New York: Free Press.

Ayres, I., & Braithwaite, J. (1992). *Responsive regulation: Transcending the deregulation debate.* New York: Oxford University Press.

Bainbridge, S. (1993, Fall). In defense of the shareholder wealth maximization norm: A reply to Professor Green. *Washington and Lee Law Review,* 1423–1450.

Barabasi, A. (2003). *Linked.* Cambridge, MA: Penguin Books.

Bardach, E. (1998). *Getting agencies to work together: The practice and theory of managerial craftsmanship.* Washington, DC: Brookings.

Baron, S., Field, J., & Schuller, T. (2000). *Social capital: Critical perspectives.* New York: Oxford University Press.

Bateson, G. (1972). *Steps to an ecology of mind: Collected essays in anthropology, psychiatry, evolution, and epistemology.* Chicago: University of Chicago Press.

Baumgartner, F. R., & Jones, B. D. (1993). *Agendas and instability in American politics.* Chicago: University of Chicago Press.

Baumgartner, F. R., & Jones, B. D. (Eds.). (2002). *Policy dynamics.* Chicago: University of Chicago Press.

Beam, D. R., & Conlan, T. J. (2002). Grants. In L. A. Salamon (Ed.), *The tools of government: A guide to the new governance* (pp. 340–380). Oxford: Oxford University Press.

Behn, R. D. (2001). *Rethinking democratic accountability.* Washington, DC: Brookings Institution Press.

Berle, A., & Means, G. (1968). *The modern corporation and private property.* New York: Harcourt, Brace & World.

Berry, F. S., Choi, S. O., Goa, W. X., Jang, H., Kwan, M., & Word, J. (2004). Three traditions of network research: What the public management research agenda can learn from other research communities. *Public Administration Review, 64*(5), 539–552.

Berry, J. M., Portney, K. E., & Thomson, K. (1993). *The rebirth of urban democracy.* Washington, DC: Brookings Institution.

Bertalanffy, L. V. (1950). The theory of open systems in physics and biology. *Science, 111*(2872), 23–29.

Bingham, L. B., Nabatchi, T., & O'Leary, R. (2005). The new governance: Practices and processes for stakeholder and citizen participation in the work of government. *Public Administration Review, 65*(5), 547–558.

Bingham, L. B., & O'Leary, R. (Eds.). (2008). *Big ideas in collaborative public management.* Armonk, NY: M.E. Sharpe.

Birkland, T. A. (2001). *An introduction to the policy process: Theories, concepts, and models of public policy making.* New York: M.E. Sharpe.

Block, S. R. (2001). A history of the discipline. In J. S. Ott (Ed.), *The nature of the nonprofit sector* (pp. 97–111). Boulder, CO: Westview Press.

Bogason, P., & Musso, J. A. (2006). The democratic prospects of network governance. *American Review of Public Administration, 36*(1), 3–18.

Boland, T., & Fowler, A. (2000). A systems perspective of performance management in public sector organizations. *International Journal of Public Sector Management, 13*(5), 417–446.

Borgatti, S. P., & Foster, P. C. (2003). The network paradigm in organizational research: A review and typology. *Journal of Management, 29*(6), 991–1013.x

Boris, E. (1999). Nonprofit organizations in a democracy: Varied roles and responsibilities. In E. Boris & E. Steurle (Eds.), *Nonprofits and government: Collaboration and conflict* (pp. 2–29). Washington, DC: Urban Institute Press.

Boulding, K. E. (1956). General systems theory: The skeleton of science. *Management Science, 2*(3), 197–208.

Bourdieu, P. (1986). The forms of capital. In J. G. Richardson (Ed.), *Handbook for theory and research for the sociology of education* (pp. 241–258). New York: Greenwood Press.

Bouwen, R., & Taillieu, T. (2004). Multi-party collaboration as social learning for interdependence: Developing relational knowing for sustainable natural resource management. *Journal of Community and Applied Social Psychology, 14*(3), 137–153.

Bovaird, T. (2004). Public-private partnerships: From contested concepts to prevalent practice. *International Review of Administrative Sciences, 70*(2), 199–215.

Bovaird, T. (2005). Public governance: Balancing stakeholder power in a network society. *International Review of Administrative Sciences, 71*(2), 217–228.

Bovaird, T., & Loffler, E. (2003). Evaluating the quality of public governance: Indicators, models and methodologies. *International Review of Administrative Sciences, 69*(3), 313–328.

Bozeman, B. (1987). *All organizations are public: Bridging public and private organizational theories.* San Francisco: Jossey-Bass.

Bozeman, B. (2007). *Public values and public interest: Counterbalancing economic individualism.* Washington, DC: Georgetown University Press.

Brass, D. J., & Burkhardt, M. (1993). Centrality and power in organizations. In N. Nohria & R. G. Eccles (Eds.), *Networks and organizations: Structure, form and action* (pp. 191–215). Boston: Harvard Business School Press.

Bressers, H. T. A., & O'Toole, L. J. J. (2005). Instrument selection and implementation in a networked context. In P. Eliadis, M. M. Hill, & M. Howlett (Eds.), *Designing governance: From instruments to governance.* Montreal: McGill-Queen's University Press.

Brooks, A. (2002). Can nonprofit management help answer public management's "big questions?" *Public Administration Review, 62*(3), 259–266.

Brown, R. H. (1976). Social theory as a metaphor: On the logic of discovery for the sciences of conduct. *Theory and Event, 3*(2), 169–197.

Bryson, J., Crosby, B., & Stone, M. (2006). The design implications of cross-sector collaborations: Propositions from the literature. *Public Administration Review, 66*(6), 44–55.

Buckley, W. (1998). *Society—A complex adaptive system: Essays in social theory.* Amsterdam: Overseas Publishers Association.

Burk, M. (2000). Communities of practice. *Public Roads, 63*(6), 18–22.

Burns, J. M. (2003). *Transforming leadership.* New York: Atlantic Monthly Press.

Burt, R. S. (1997). The contingent value of social capital. *Administrative Science Quarterly, 42*, 339–365.

Buysse, V., Sparkman, K. L., & Wesley, P. W. (2003). Communities of practice: Connecting what we know with what we do. *Exceptional Children, 69*(3), 263–278.

Carroll, A. B. (1999). Corporate social responsibility: Evolution of a definitional construct. *Business and Society, 38*, 268–295.

Carroll, T., & Burton, R. M. (2000). Organizations and complexity: Searching for the edge of chaos. *Computational & Mathematical Organization Theory, 6*, 319-337.

Carson, R. (1962). *Silent Spring*. Boston: Houghton Mifflin.

Carver, C. S., & Scheier, M. F. (1998). *On the self-regulation of behavior*. Cambridge: Cambridge University Press.

Casey, K. (2008). *Defining political capital: A reconsideration of Bourdieu's interconvertability theory* (pp. 1–24). Paper presented at Annual Illinois State University Conference for Students of Political Science.

Catlaw, T. J. (2008). Governance and networks at the limits of representation. *The American Review of Public Administration 39*(5), 478–498.

Chandler, C. R., & Plano, C. J. (1982). *The public administration dictionary*. New York: John Wiley & Son.

Chatzkel, J. L. (2003). *How knowledge-based enterprises really get built knowledge capital*. Oxford: University Press.

Cigler, B. (2007a). The "big questions" of Katrina and the 2005 great flood of New Orleans. *Public Administration Review, 67*(s1), 64–76.

Cigler, B. (2007b). *Hurricane Katrina: Two intergovernmental challenges*. Paper presented at AACPM Conference.

Cigler, B. A. (2001). Public administration and the paradox of professionalization. In C. Stivers (Ed.), *Democracy, bureaucracy, and the study of administration* (pp. 355–391). Oxford: Westview Press.

Clayton, M. (2002). *Frank Lloyd Wright field guide: His 100 greatest works*. Philadelphia, PA: Running Press Book Publishers.

Cleveland, H. (1972). *The future executive*. New York: Harper & Row.

Coglianese, C., & Lazer, D. (2003). Management-based regulation: Prescribing private management to achieve public goals. *Law and Society Review, 37*, 691–720.

Cohen, M. D., March, J. G., & Olsen, J. P. (1972). A garbage can model of organizational choice. *Administrative Science Quarterly, 17*(1), 1–25.

Cole, K. C. (1999). *First you build a cloud and other reflections on psychics as a way of life*. New York, New York: W. Morrow Co.

Coleman, J. (1986). Micro foundations and macrosocial theory. In S. Lindenberg, J. Coleman, & S. Nowak (Eds.), *Approaches to social theory*. New York: Russell Sage Foundation.

Coleman, J. (1988). Social capital in the creation of human capital. *American Journal of Sociology, 94*, s95–s121.

Coleman, J., Katz, E., & Menzel, H. (1977). The diffusion of an innovation among physicians. In S. Leinhardt (Ed.), *Quantitative studies in social relations* (pp. 107–124). New York: Academic Press.

Collins, R. (1988). *Theoretical sociology*. San Diego: Harcourt Brace Jovanovich.

Comfort, L. (2002). Managing intergovernmental responses to terrorism and other events. *Publius, 32*(4), 29–51.

Comfort, L. (2007). Crisis management in hindsight: Cognition, communication, coordination, and control. *Public Administration Review, 67*(Suppl.), 189–197.

Cooper, P. (2003). *Governing by contract: Challenges and opportunities for public managers*. Washington, DC: CQ Press.

Cordes, J. J. (2002). Corrective taxes, charges, and tradable permits. In L. A. Salamon (Ed.), *The tools of government: A guide to the new governance* (pp. 255–281). Oxford: Oxford University Press.

Costa, L. D. F., Rodrigues, F. A., Travieso, G., & Villas Boas, P. R. (2007). Characterization of complex networks: A survey of measurements. *Advances in Physics, 56*(1), 167–242.

Costanza, R., d'Arge, R., de Groof, R., Farber, S., Grasso, M., Hannon, B., et al. (1997). The value of the world's ecosystem services and natural capital. *Nature, 387*(253–260).

Cox, R. (2000). Creating a decision architecture (public administration). *Global Virtue Ethics Review, 2*(1), 19–42.

Crawford, A. (2006). Networked governance and the post-regulatory state? Steering, rowing and anchoring the provision of policing and security. *Theoretical Criminology, 10*(4), 449–479.

Crenson, M. A., & Ginsberg, B. (2002). *Downsizing democracy: How America sidelined its citizens and privatized its public.* Baltimore: Johns Hopkins University Press.

Cuoto, R., & Guthrie, C. S. (1999). *Making democracy work better: Mediating structures, social capital, and the democratic prospect.* Chapel Hill, N.C.: University of North Carolina Press.

Daly, H. E., & Farley, J. (2004). *Ecological economics.* Washington, DC: Island Press.

Davenport, T. O. (1999). *Human capital: What it is and why people invest in it.* San Francisco: Jossey-Bass Publishers.

Davis, K. (1960). Can business afford to ignore social responsibilities? *California Management Review, 2*, 70–76.

Davis, K. (1973). The case for and against business assumption of social responsibilities. *Academy of Management Journal, 16*, 312–322.

Davis, K. (1976). Social responsibility is inevitable. *California Management Review, 19*, 14–20.

De Bruijn, H. (2001). *Managing performance in the public sector.* London: Routledge.

De Bruijn, J. A., & ten Heuvelhof, E. F. (1997). Instruments for network management. In W. J. M. Kickert, E.-H. Klijn, & J. F. M. Koppenjan (Eds.), *Managing complex networks: Strategies for the public sector* (pp. 119–136). London: Sage Publications.

Degenne, A., & Forse, M. (1999). *Introducing social networks.* London: Sage Publications.

DeHoog, R. H., & Salamon, L. A. (2002). Purchase-of-service contracting. In L. A. Salamon (Ed.), *The tools of government: A guide to the new governance* (pp. 319–339). Oxford: Oxford University Press.

Dekker, S., & Hansen, D. (2004). Learning under pressure: The effects of politicization on organizational learning in public bureaucracies. *Journal of Public Administration Research and Theory, 14*(2), 211–230.

de Laat, M., & Broer, W. (2004). CoPs for cops: Managing and creating knowledge through networked expertise. In P. Hildreth & C. Kimble (Eds.), *Knowledge network: Innovation through communities of practice* (pp. 58–69). New York: Idea Group Publishing.

deLeon, L. (1998). Accountability in a reinvented government. *Public Administration, 76*(3), 539–558.

De Vita, C. (1998). Nonprofits and devolution: What do we know? In E. T. Borris & C. E. Steurle (Eds.), *Nonprofits and government: Collaboration and conflict* (pp. 213–233). Washington, D.C.: The Urban Institute Press.

Denhardt, J. V. A., & Denhardt, R. B. (2003). *The new public service: Serving, not steering.* Armonk, NY: M.E. Sharpe.

Derthick, M. (2007). Where federalism didn't fail. *Public Administration Review, s1*(67), 36–47.

Dewey, J. (1929). *The quest for certainty.* New York: Minton.

Dewey, J. (1963a). *Experience and education.* New York: Collier Books.

Dewey, J. (1963b). *The process of thought, from how we think.* Chicago: Encyclopedia Britannica.

Dewhurst, F. W., & Cegarra Navarro, J. G. (2004). External communities of practice and relational capital. *The Learning Organization: An International Journal, 11*(4–5), 322–331.

Dodder, R., & Sussman, J. (2002). *The concept of a CLIOS analysis illustrated by the Mexico City case* (MIT Engineering Division Working Paper, ESD-WP-2003-01.07). Cambridge, MA: MIT.

Doern, B. G., & Phidd, R. W. (1992). *Canadian public policy: Idea, structure, and process.* Toronto: Methuen.

Donahue, J. D. (1989). *Public ends, private means.* New York: Basic Books.

Dorough, B. (1973). Conjunction junction [Television series episode]. In *Schoolhouse Rock.*

Dowdle, M. W. (2006). *Public accountability, conceptual, historical, and epistemic mappings.* Cambridge: Cambridge University Press.

Drake, D. B., Steckler, N. A., & Koch, M. J. (2004). Information sharing in and across government agencies: The role and influence of scientist, politician, and bureaucrat subcultures. *Social Science Computer Review, 22*(1), 67–84.

Dunfee, T. (1999). Corporate governance in a market with morality. *Law and Contemporary Problems, 62,* 129.

Durant, R. F. (2001). A way out of no way? Strategy, structure, and the "new governance." In R. T. Golembiewski (Ed.), *Handbook of organizational behavior* (2nd ed., pp. 689–723). New York: Marcel Dekker.

Endsley, M. R. (1995). Toward a theory of situation awareness in dynamic systems. *Human Factors, 37*(1), 32–64.

Etymology of governor. (2009). Retrieved May 23, 2009, from http://www.spiritus-temporis.com/governor/etymology.html

Etzioni, A. (1964). Modern organizations. Englewood Cliffs, NJ: Prentice-Hall.

Etzioni, A. (1967). Mixed-scanning: A "third" approach to decision-making. *Public Administration Review, 27*(5), 385–392.

Farkas, G. (1996). *Human capital or cultural capital? Ethnicity and poverty groups in an urban school district.* Hawthorne, NY: Walter de Gruyter.

Farkas, G. (2003). Cognitive skills and noncognitive traits and behaviors in stratification processes. *Annual Review of Sociology, 29,* 541–562.

Farley, J., Baker, D., Batker, D., Koliba, C., Matteson, R., Mills, R., et al. (2007). Opening the policy window for paradigm shifts: Katrina as a focusing event. *Ecological Economics, 63*(2–3), 344–354.

Feldman, R. (2002). Government insurance. In L. A. Salamon (Ed.), *The tools of government: A guide to the new governance* (pp. 186–216). Oxford: Oxford University Press.

Fetterman, D. M. (2002). Empowerment evaluation: Building communities of practice and a culture of learning. *American Journal of Community Psychology, 30*(1), 89–102.

Fischer, F. (2000). *Citizens, experts and the environment: The politics of local knowledge.* Durham, NC: Duke University Press.

Fisher, R., Ury, W., & Patton, B. (1991). *Getting to yes.* New York: Penguin Books.

Foldvary, F. E. (2006). The complex taxonomy of the factors: Natural resources, human actions, and capital goods. *American Journal of Economics and Sociology, 65*(3), 787–802.

Foth, M. (2006). Network action research. *Action Research, 4*(2), 205–226.

Fox, T., Ward, H., & Howard, B. (2002). *Public sector roles in strengthening corporate social responsibility: A baseline study.* Washington, DC: The World Bank.

Frederickson, D., & Frederickson, H. G. (2006). *Measuring the performance of the hollow state.* Washington, DC: Georgetown University Press.

Frederickson, H. G. (1999). The repositioning of American public administration. *Political Science and Politics, 32*(4), 701.

Frederickson, H. G. (2007, December). Filling up the hollow state: The state of agents project. *PA Times,* 11.

Frederickson, H. G., & Meek, J. W. (2008). *Bureaucratie sans frontieres: Legitimacy, authority, accountability in geo-governance systems.* Paper presented at the Fourth Transatlantic Dialogue on the Status of Intergovernmental Relations and Multi-Level Governance in Europe and the United States.

French, W. L., & Bell, C. (1999). *Organizational development: Behavioral science interventions for organization development* (6th ed.). Saddle River, NJ: Prentice-Hall.

Frey, B. B., Lohmeier, J. H., Lee, S. W., & Tollefson, N. (2006). Measuring collaboration among grant partners. *American Evaluation Association, 27*(3), 383–392.

Frey, L. (1996). *Remembering and re-membering: A history of theory and research on communication and group decision making* (2nd ed.). Thousand Oaks, CA: Sage Publication.

Friedman, M. (1970, September 13). A Friedman doctrine—The social responsibility of business is to increase profits. *New York Times,* (Sept. 13, 1970).

Fung, A. (2004). *Empowered participation: Reinventing urban democracy.* Princeton, N.J.: Princeton University Press.

Fung, A. (2006). Varieties of participation in complex governance. *Public Administration Review, 66,* 66–75.

Gabbay, J., Le May, A., Jefferson, H., Webb, D., Lovelock, R., Powell, J., et al. (2003). A case study of knowledge management in multi-agency consumer-informed "communities of practice": Implications for evidence-based policy development in health and social services. *Health, 7*(3), 283–310.

Gage, R. W. (1990). Key intergovernmental issues and strategies: An assessment and prognosis. In R. W. Gage & M. P. Mandell (Eds.), *Strategies for managing intergovernmental policies and networks* (pp. 127–150). New York: Praeger.

Gage, R. W., & Mandell, M. P. (Eds.). (1990). *Strategies for managing intergovernmental policies and networks.* New York: Praeger.

Gajda, R. (2004). Collaboration theory to evaluate strategic alliances. *American Journal of Evaluation 25*(1), 65–77.

Gajda, R., & Koliba, C. (2007). Evaluating the imperative of intra-organizational collaboration: A school improvement perspective. *American Journal of Evaluation, 28*(1), 26–44.

Galbraith, J. R. (1977). *Organization design.* Reading, MA: Addison-Wesley.

Gallucci, C. (2003). Communities of practice and the mediation of teachers' responses to standards-based reform. *Education Policy Analysis Archives, 11*(35).

Garcia, J., & Dorohovich, M. (2005). The truth about building and maintaining successful communities of practice. *Defense A R Journal, 12*(1).

Gazley, B., & Brudney, J. L. (2007). *Collaboration and partnership: Preparing local network for emergency situations.* Paper presented at the Ninth National Public Management Research Conference.

Geertz, C. (1973). *The interpretation of cultures.* New York: Basic Books.

Goldsmith, S., & Eggers, W. (2004). *Governing by network.* Washington, DC: Brookings.

Goodlad, J., Mantle-Bromley, C., & Goodlad, S. J. (2004). *Education for everyone: Agenda for education in a democracy.* San Francisco: Jossey-Bass.

Goodnow, F. J. (2004). Politics and administration. In J. Shafritz, A. C. Hyde, & S. J. Parkes (Eds.), *Classics of public administration* (5th ed., pp. 35–37). Belmont, CA: Wadsworth/Thomson Learning.

Goodsell, C. (2006). A new vision for public administration. *Public Administration Review, 66*(4), 623–635.

Government Accountability Office. (2006). *Hurricanes Katrina and Rita: Coordination between FEMA and Red Cross should be improved for 2006 season* (GAO-06-712). Washington, DC: Congressional Committees.

Granovetter, M. (1973). The strength of weak ties. *American Journal of Sociology, 76,* 1360–1380.

Gray, B. (1989). *Collaborating: Finding common ground for multiparty problems.* San Francisco: Jossey-Bass.

Greenleaf, R. K. (2002). *Servant leadership: A journey into the nature of legitimate power and greatness* (25th ed.). New York: Paulist Press.

Grimshaw, D., Marchington, M., Rubery, J., & Willmott, H. (2005). Introduction: Fragmenting work across organizational boundaries. In M. Marchington, J. Grimshaw, J. Rubery, & H. Wilmott (Eds.), *Fragmenting work: Blurring organizational boundaries and disordering hierarchies.* Oxford: Oxford University Press, 1–38.

Gruber, J. (1987). *Controlling bureaucracies: Dilemmas in democratic governance.* Berkeley: University of California Press.

Gulick, L. (2004). Notes on the theory of organization. In J. Shafritz, A. C. Hyde, & S. J. Parkes (Eds.), *Classics of public administration* (5th ed.). Belmont, CA: Wadsworth/Thomson Learning.

Guo, C., & Acar, M. (2005). Understanding collaboration among nonprofit organizations: Combining resource dependency, institutional, and network perspectives. *Nonprofit and Voluntary Sector Quarterly, 34*(3), 340–361.

Hall, R. H. (1980). Organizational goals. In M. Lockett & R. Spear (Eds.), *Organizations as systems* (pp. 129–131). Milton Keynes, UK: Open University Press.

Hammond, D. (2003). *The science of synthesis: Exploring the social implications of general systems theory.* Boulder, CO: University Press of Colorado.

Hanaki, N., Peterhansl, A., Dodds, P. S., & Watts, D. J. (2007). Cooperation in evolving social network. *Management Science, 53*(7), 1036–1050.

Hawken, P. (1988). *Growing a business.* New York: Simon and Schuster.

Hay, G., & Gray, E. (1974). Social responsibility of business managers. *Academy of Management Journal, 17,* 135.

Haynes, P. (2003). *Managing complexity in the public services.* London: Open University Press.

Heald, M. (1970). *The social responsibilities of business: Company and community, 1900–1960.* Cleveland, OH: Case Western Reserve University Press.

Heclo, H. (1978). *Issue networks and the executive establishment.* Washington, DC: American Enterprise Institute.

Heinrich, C. J., & Lynn, L. E. (Eds.). (2000). *Governance and performance: New perspectives*. Washington, D.C.: Georgetown University Press.

Heinrich, C. J., Hill, C. J., & Lynn, L. E. (2004). Governance as an organizing theme for empirical research. In P. W. Ingraham & L. E. Lynn (Eds.), *The art of governance: Analyzing management and administration*. Washington, DC: Georgetown University Press.

Henton, D., & Melville, J. (2008). Collaborative governance: A guide for grantmakers. Retrieved August 5, 2008, from http://www.hewlett.org/Publications/collaborativegovernance.htm

Hertting, N. (2008). Mechanisms of governance network formation—A contextual rational choice perspective. In E. Sorensen & J. Torfing (Eds.), *Theories of democratic network governance* (pp. 43–60). New York: Palgrave Macmillan.

Hill, M., & Hupe, P. (2002). *Implementing public policy: Governance in theory and in practice*. Thousand Oaks, CA: Sage Publications.

Hirst, P. (1997). *From statism to pluralism*. London: UCL Press.

Hodkinson, P., & Hodkinson, H. (2004). *A constructive critique of communities of practice: Moving beyond Lave and Wenger*. Leeds, UK: University of Leeds.

Holland, J.H. (1995). *Hidden order: How adaptation builds complexity*. New York: Helix Books.

Hood, C. C. (1984). *The tools of government*. London: MacMillan.

Horne, C. S., Van Slyke, D. M., & Johnson, J. L. (2006). Charitable choice implementation: What public managers should know about public opinion and the potential impact of government funding on private giving. *International Journal of Public Administration*, *23*(10–11), 819–836.

Houston, K. (2009). *Rural road conflict case study*. Unpublished class project.

Hovey, H. (1999). *The devolution revolution: Can the states afford devolution?* New York: Century Foundation.

Howard, C. (2002). Tax expenditures. In L. A. Salamon (Ed.), *The tools of government: A guide to the new governance* (pp. 410–444). Oxford: Oxford University Press.

Howard, J. (1999) *Families*. New Brunswick, New Jersey: Transaction Publishers. (found on p. 234)

Howlett, M. (2005). What is a policy instrument? Tools, mixes, and implementation styles. In P. Eliadis, M. M. Hill, & M. Howlett (Eds.), *Designing government: From instruments to governance*. Montreal: McGill-Queen's University Press.

Hula, K. W. (1999). *Lobbying together: Interest group coalitions in legislative politics*. Washington, DC: Georgetown University Press.

Hummel, R. P. Stories managers tell: Why they are valid as science. In C. Stivers (Ed.), *Democracy, Bureaucracy, and the Study of Administration* (pp. 87–109). Boulder, CO: Westview Press.

Hutter, B. (2001). Is enforced self-regulation a form of risk taking? The case of railway health and safety. *International Journal of Sociology of Law*, *29*, 379–400.

Imperial, M. T. (2005). Using collaboration as a governance strategy. *Administration & Society*, *37*(3), 281–320.

Ingram, H., & Schneider, A. (1993). Constructing citizenship: The subtle messages of policy design. In H. Ingram & S. R. Smith (Eds.), *Public policy for democracy*. Washington, DC: Brookings Institution Press.

Janis, I. L. (1982). *Groupthink: Psychological studies of policy decisions and fiascoes*. Boston: Houghton Mifflin.

Janoski, T. (1998). *Citizenship and civil society: A framework of rights and obligations in liberal, traditional, and social democratic regimes*. Cambridge: Cambridge University Press.

Jarosz, L. (2004). Understanding agri-food networks as social relations. *Agriculture and Human Values, 17*(3), 1572–8366.

Johnson, H. (2001). Corporate social audits—This time around. *Business Horizons, 44,* 29.

Johnson, J. L., Daily, C. M., & Ellstrand, A. E. (1996). Boards of directors: A review and research agenda. *Journal of Management, 22*(3), 409–438.

Jones, B. D. (1994). *Reconceiving decision-making in democratic politics*. Chicago: University of Chicago Press.

Kapucu, N. (2006a). Public-nonprofit partnerships for collective action in dynamic contexts of emergencies. *Public Management, 84*(1), 205–220.

Kapucu, N. (2006b). Interagency communication networks during emergencies: Boundary spanners in multi-agency coordination. *American Review of Public Administration, 36*(2), 207-225.

Karkkainen, B. C. (2004). Post-sovereign environmental governance. *Global Environmental Politics, 4*(1), 72–76.

Kathi, P., & Cooper, T. L. (2005). Democratizing the administrative state: Connecting neighborhood councils and city agencies. *Public Administration Review, 65*(5), 559–568.

Katz, D., & Kahn, R. (1978). *The social psychology of organizations*. New York: Wiley.

Kaufmann, S. (2004). Autonomous agent. In J. D. Barrow, P. C. W. Davies, & C. L. Harper, Jr. (Eds.), *Science and ultimate reality: Quantum theory, cosmology, and complexity*. Cambridge: Cambridge University Press.

Kearns, K. (1996). *Managing for accountability: Preserving the public trust in public and non-profit organizations*. San Francisco: Jossey-Bass.

Keast, R., Mandell, M. P., Brown, K., & Woolcock, G. (2004). Network structures: Working differently and changing expectations. *Public Administration Review, 64*(3), 363–371.

Keifer, J., & Montjoy, R. (2006). Incrementalism before the storm: Network performance for the evacuation of New Orleans. *Public Administration Review, 66*(6), 122–130.

Kelman, S. J. (2002). Contracting. In L. Salamon (Ed.), *The tools of government: A guide to the new governance* (pp. 282–318). Oxford: Oxford University Press.

Ketcham, R. (Ed.). (1986). *The anti-federalist papers and the constitutional convention debates*. New York: Nal Penguin.

Kettl, D. F. (2006). Managing boundaries in American administration: The collaborative imperative. *Public Administration Review, 66*(6), 10–19.

Kettl, D. F. (1993). *Sharing power: Public governance and private markets*. Washington, DC: Brookings Institution Press.

Kettl, D. F. (2002). Managing indirect government. In L. Salamon (Ed.), *The tools of government*. Oxford: Oxford University Press.

Kettl, D. F. (2009, March 3, 2009). Heading for disaster. *GovernmentExecutive.com*. from http://www.govexec.com/story_page.cfm?articleid=41926.

Kezar, A. (2001). Investigating organizational fit in a participatory leadership environment. *Journal of Higher Education Policy and Management, 23*(1), 85–101.

Kickert, W. J. M., Klijn, E.-H., & Koppenjan, J. F. M. (1997a). Introduction: A management perspective on policy networks. In W. J. M. Kickert, E.-H. Klijn, & J. F. M. Koppenjan (Eds.), *Managing complex networks: Strategies for the public sector* (pp. 1–11). London: Sage Publications.

Kickert, W. J. M., Klijn, E.-H., & Koppenjan, J. F. M. (Eds.). (1997b). *Managing complex networks: Strategies for the public sector*. London: Sage Publications.

Kickert, W. J. M., Klijn, E.-H., & Koppenjan, J. F. M. (1997c). Managing networks in the public sector: Findings and reflections. In W. J. M. Kickert, E.-H. Klijn, & J. F. M. Koppenjan (Eds.), *Managing complex networks: Strategies for the public sector* (pp. 166–188). London: Sage Publications.

Kickert, W. J. M., & Koppenjan, J. F. M. (1997). Public management and network management: An overview. In W. J. M. Kickert, E.-H. Klijn, & J. F. M. Koppenjan (Eds.), *Managing complex networks: Strategies for the public sector* (pp. 35–60). London: Sage Publications.

Kiefer, J., & Montjoy, R. (2006). Incrementalism before the storm: Network performance for the evacuation of New Orleans. *Public Administration Review, 66*(6), 122–130.

King, M. L. (1986). Letter from a Birmingham jail. In J. M. Washington (Ed.), *A Testament of hope: The essential writings and speeches of Martin Luther King, Jr.* (pp. 289–302). San Francisco: Harper Collins.

Kingdon, J. W. (1984). *Agendas, alternatives and public policies.* Boston: Little, Brown and Company.

Klijn, E.-H. (2001). Rules as institutional context for decision making in networks: The approach to postwar housing districts in two cities. *Administration and Society, 33*(2), 133–164.

Klijn, E.-H., & Skelcher, C. (2007). Democracy and governance networks: Compatible or not? *Public Administration, 85*(3), 587–609.

Klijn, E.-H., & Snellen, I. (2009). Complexity theory and public administration: A critical appraisal. In G. Teisman, A. van Burren, & L. Gerritis (Eds.), *Managing complex governance systems* (pp. 17–36). New York: Routledge.

Knight, F. H. (1965). *The economic organization.* New York: Harper Torchbooks.

Knoke, D. (1990). *Organizing for collective action: The political economies of associations.* New York: Aldine de Gruyter.

Kolb, D. A. (1984). *Experiential learning: Experience as the source of learning and development.* Englewood Cliffs, NJ: Prentice-Hall.

Koliba, C. (2006). Serving the public interest across sectors: Assessing the implications of network governance. *Administrative Theory & Praxis, 28*(4), 593–601.

Koliba, C., Campbell, E., & Zia, A. (2009). *Performance measurement considerations in congestion management networks: Aligning data and network accountability.* Paper presented at the American Society of Public Administration Annual Conference, Miami, FL.

Koliba C., Zia, A., Lee, B. (2010). The analysis of complex governance system dynamics: Emergent patterns of formation, operation and performance of regional planning networks. Decision Theater Workshop on Policy Informatics. Arizona State University. Tempe, AZ.

Koliba, C., & Gajda, R. (2009). Communities of practice as an empirical construct: Implications for theory and practice. *International Journal of Public Administration, 32,* 97–135.

Koliba, C., & Lathrop, J. (2007). Inquiry as intervention: Employing action research to support an organization's capacity to learn. *Administration & Society, 39*(1), 51–76.

Koliba, C., Mills, R., & Zia, A. (Accepted for publication). Accountability in governance networks: Implications drawn from studies of response and recovery efforts following Hurricane Katrina *Public Administration Review.*

Koontz, T., Steelman, T., Carmin, J., Korfmarcher, K., Moseley, C., & Thomas, C. (2004). *Collaborative environmental management: What roles for government?* Washington, DC: Resources for the Future.

Koppell, J. G. S. (2003). *The politics of quasi-government.* Cambridge: Cambridge University Press.

Koppenjan, J. F. M. (2008). Consensus and conflict in policy networks: Too much or too little? In E. Sorensen & J. Torfing (Eds.), *Theories of Democratic Network Governance* (pp. 133–152). New York, New York: Palgrave Macmillan.

Koppenjan, J., & Klijn, E. (2004). *Managing uncertainties in networks.* London: Routledge.

Korten, D. C. (2001). The management of social transformation. In C. Stivers (Ed.), *Democracy, bureaucracy, and the study of administration* (pp. 476–497). Boulder, CO: Westview.

Krane, D., Ebdon, C., & Bartle, J. (2004). Devolution, fiscal federalism, and changing patterns of municipal revenues: The mismatch between theory and reality. *Journal of Public Administration Research and Theory, 14*(4), 513–533.

Krause, G. A. (1997). Policy preference formation and subsystem behaviour: The case of commercial bank regulation. *British Journal of Political Science, 27*(4), 525–526.

Kreps, D., & Wilson, R. (1982). Reputation and imperfect information. *Journal of Economic Theory, 72,* 253–279.

Laffont, J. J., & Tirole, J. (1991). The politics of government decision making: A theory of regulatory capture. *Quarterly Journal of Economics, 106*(4), 1089–1127.

Landry, R., & Varone, F. (2005). The choice of policy instruments: Confronting the deductive and the interactive approaches. In P. Eliadis, M. M. Hill, & M. Howlett (Eds.), *Designing governance: From instruments to governance.* Montreal: McGill-Queen's University Press.

Langfred, C. W., & Shanley, M. T. (2001). *Small group research: Autonomous teams and progress on issues of context and level of analysis.* New York: Marcel Dekker.

Lantos, G. (2001). *The boundaries of strategic corporate social responsibility.* Retrieved January 12, 2006, from http://faculty.stonehill.edu/glantos/Lantos1/PDF_Folder/Pub_arts_pdf/Strategic%20CSR.pdf

Lathlean, J., & le May, A. (2002). Communities of practice: An opportunity for interagency working. *Journal of Clinical Nursing, 11*(3), 394–398.

Leach, W. D., & Pelky, W. N. (2001). Making watershed partnerships work: A review of the empirical literature. *Journal of Water Resources Planning and Management, 127,* 378–385.

Leinhardt, S. (Ed.). (1977). *Social networks: A developing paradigm.* New York: Academic Press.

Lepoutre, J., Dentchev, N., & Heene, A. (2007). Dealing with uncertainties when governing CSR policies. *Journal of Business Ethics, 72*(4), 391–408w.

Lesser, E., & Prusak, L. (2000a). *Communities of practice, social capital and organizational knowledge.* Boston: Butterworth Heinemann.

Lesser, E., & Prusak, L. (2000b). Communities of practice, social capital, and organizational knowledge. In E. L. Lesser, M. A. Fontaine, & J. A. Slusher (Eds.), *Knowledge and communities* (pp. 123–132). Boston: Butterworth Heinemann.

Lesser, E. L. (2000). *Knowledge and social capital: Foundations and applications.* Boston: Butterworth Heinemann.

Levine, M. E., & Forrence, J. L. (1990). Regulatory capture, public interest, and the public agenda: Toward a synthesis. *Journal of Law Economics and Organization, 6,* 167–198.

Levy, S. (1993). *Artificial life: A report from the frontier where computers meet biology.* New York: Random House.

Lewin, K. (1947). Frontiers of group dynamics: Concept, method, and reality in social science: Social equalibria and social change. *Human Relations, 1,* 5–41.

Lewis-Beck, M. S., & Alford, J. R. (1980). Can government regulate safety? The coal mine example. *American Political Science Review, 74*(3), 745–756.

Lindblom, C. E. (1959). The science of "muddling through." *Public Administration Review, 19*, 79–88.

Linder, S. H. (2000). Coming to terms with the public-private partnership: A grammar of multiple meanings. In P. V. Rosenau (Ed.), *Public private partnerships* (pp. 19–36). Cambridge, MA: MIT Press.

Linder, S. H., & Rosenau, P. V. (2000). *Mapping the terrain of the public-private policy partnership*. Cambridge, MA: MIT Press.

Lipsky, M. (2004). Street-level bureaucracy: The critical role of street-level bureaucrats. In J. Shafritz, A. C. Hyde, & S. J. Parkes (Eds.), *Classics of public administration* (5th ed., pp. 414–422). Belmont, CA: Wadsworth/Thomson Learning.

Loomis, B. A., & Cigler, A. J. (2002). The changing nature of interest group politics. In B. A. Loomis & A. J. Cigler (Eds.), *Interest group politics* (6th ed., pp. 1–33). New York: CQ Press.

Lopez, E. (2002). The legislator as political entrepreneur: Investment in political capital. *Review of Austrian Economics, 15*(2–3), 211–229.

Lowi, T. (1969). *The end of liberalism: Ideology, policy, and the crisis of public authority*. New York: W.W. Norton and Company.

Lowndes, V. (2001). Rescuing Aunt Sally: Taking institutional theory seriously in urban politics. *Urban Studies, 38*(11), 1953–1971.

Lukensmeyer, C. J., & Torres, L. H. (2006). *Public deliberation: A manager's guide to citizen engagement*: IBM Center for the Business of Government.

Luque, E. (2001). Whose knowledge (economy)? *Social Epistemology, 15*(3), 187–200.

Lynn, L. E., Heinrich, C. J., & Hill, C. J. (2000). Studying governance and public management: Why? How? In C. J. Heinrich & L. E. Lynn (Ed.), *Governance and performance: New perspectives* (pp. 1–33). Washington, DC: Georgetown University Press.

Maas, A., & Radway, L. (1959). Gauging administrative responsibility. *Public Administration Review, 19*, 182–193.

Macedo, S., et al. (2005). *Democracy at risk: How political choices undermine citizen participation and what we can do about it*. Washington, DC: Brookings Institution Press.

Macey, J. R. (1992). Organizational design and political control of administrative agencies. *Journal of Law, Economics and Organization, 8*(1), 93–125.

Mandell, M. P. (1990). Network management: Strategic behavior in the public sector. In R. W. Gage & M. P. Mandell (Eds.), *Strategies for Managing Intergovernmental Policies and Networks*. New York, New York: Praeger.

Mandell, M., & Steelman, T. (2003). Understanding what can be accomplished through interorganizational innovations. *Public Management Review, 5*(2), 197–224.

Mannheim, K. (1936). *Ideology and utopia*. New York: Harcourt, Brace and World.

March, J. G., & Olsen, J. P. (1995). *Democratic governance*. New York: Free Press.

Marion, R. (1999). *The edge of organization: Chaos and complexity theories of formal social systems*. Thousand Oaks, CA: Sage.

Marsden, P. V., & Laumann, E. O. (1984). Mathematical ideas in social structural analysis. *Journal of Mathematical Sociology, 10*, 271–294.

Marsh, D., & Rhodes, R. A. W. (Eds.). (1992). *Policy networks in British government*. Oxford: Clarendon Press.

Mashaw, J. L. (2006). *Accountability and institutional design: Some thoughts on the grammar of governance*. Cambridge: Cambridge University Press.

Mathur, N., & Skelcher, C. (2007). Evaluating democratic performance: Methodologies for assessing the relationship between network governance and citizens. *Public Administration Review, 67*(2), 228–237.

May, P. (2002). Social regulation. In L. A. Salamon (Ed.), *The tools of government: A guide to the new governance* (pp. 156–185). Oxford: Oxford University Press.

Mayntz, R. (1993). Modernization and the logic of interorganizational networks. In J. Child, M. Crozier, & R. Mayntz (Eds.), *Societal change between markets and organization* (pp. 3–18). Aldershot, UK: Avebury.

McDonnell, L. M., & Elmore, R. F. (1987). *Alternative policy instruments.* Santa Monica, CA: Center for Policy Research in Education.

McNabb, D. E. (Ed.). (2007). *Knowledge management in the public sector: A blueprint for innovation in government.* Armonk, NY: M.E. Sharpe.

Meadows, D. H. (2008). *Thinking in systems.* White River Junction, VT: Chelsea Green Publishing.

Midgley, G. (2000). *Systemic intervention: Philosophy, methodology, and practice.* New York: Kluwer Academic/Plenum Publishers.

Miller, D. Y. (2002). *The regional governing of metropolitan America.* Boulder, CO: Westview Press.

Miller, J. G. (1955). Toward a general theory for the behavioral sciences. *American Psychologist, 10*(9), 513–531.

Miller, J. H., & Page, S. E. (2007). *Complex adaptive systems: An introduction to computational models of social life.* Princeton, NJ: Princeton University Press.

Milward, H., & Provan, K. (1998). Principles for controlling agents: The political economy of network structure. *Journal of Public Administration Research and Theory, 8*(2), 203–222.

Milward, H., and Provan, K. (2006). *A manager's guide to choosing and using collaborative networks.* Washington, DC: IBM Center for the Business of Government.

Minow, M. (2002). *Partners, not rivals.* Boston: Beacon Press.

Mintzberg, H. (1979). *The structure of organizations: A synthesis of the research.* Englewood Cliffs, NJ: Prentice-Hall.

Mintzberg, H. (1983). *Power in and around organizations.* Englewood, Cliffs, NJ: Prentice-Hall.

Miraftab, F. (2004). Public-private partnerships: The Trojan horse of neoliberal development? *Journal of Planning Education and Research, 24*, 89–101.

Mischen, P. A., & Jackson, S. K. (2008). Connecting the dots: Applying complexity theory, knowledge management and social network analysis to policy implementation. *Public Administration Quarterly, 32*(3), 314–338.

Moe, R. (1987). Exploring the limits of privatization. *Public Administration Review, 48*, 453–460.

Moe, T. M. (1989). The politics of bureaucratic structure. In J. E. Chubb & P. E. Peterson (Eds.), *Can the government govern?* Washington, DC: Brookings Institution Press.

Morcol, G., & Wachhaus, A. (2009). Network and complexity theories: A comparison and prospects for a synthesis. *Administrative Theory & Praxis, 31*(1), 44–58.

Morris, J., Morris, E., & Jones, D. (2007). Reaching for the philosopher's stone: Contingent coordination and the military's response to Hurricane Katrina. *Public Administration Review, 67*(s1), 94–106.

Mosher, F. (1982). *Democracy and the public service.* New York: Oxford University Press.

Moynihan, D. P. (2008). *The dynamics of performance management: Constructing information and reform.* Washington, DC: Georgetown University Press.

Mulder, K., Costanza, R., & Erickson, J. (2006). The contribution of built, human, social, and natural capital to quality of life in intentional and unintentional communities. *Ecological Economics, 59*(1), 13–23.

Mulgan, R. (2000). Accountability: An ever-expanding concept? *Public Administration Review, 78*(3), 555–573.

Nace, T. (2005). *Gangs of America: The rise of corporate power and the disabling of democracy.* San Francisco: Berrett-Koehler Publishers.

Neuman, W. L. (2000). *Social research methods: Qualitative and quantitative approaches* (4th ed.). Boston: Allyn and Bacon.

Newell, W. H. & Meek, J. (2005). Complex systems and the conjuctive state. Proceedings of the 11th ANZSYS/Manaiging the Complex V conference. Christchurch, New Zealand.

Newman, J. (2004). Constructing accountability: Network governance and managerial agency. *Public Policy and Administration, 19*(4), 17–33.

Nicolini, D., Gherardi, S., & Yanow, D. (2003). *Introduction: Toward a practice-based view of knowing and learning in organizations.* Armonk, NY: M.E. Sharpe.

Nownes, A. J. (2001). *Pressure and power: Organized interests in American politics.* Boston: Houghton Mifflin.

Obama, B. (January 20, 2009). Inauguration speech, presented at the U.S. Capitol. Transcript retrieved from http://www.msnbc.msn.com/id/28751183/ns/politics-inauguration/page/2/

OECD. (2004). *Principles of corporate governance.* Retrieved from Organization for Economic Cooperation and Development (OECD): http://wwww.oecd.org/dataoecd/32/18/31557724.pdf

O'Leary, R., & Bingham, L. B. (2007). *A manager's guide to resolving conflicts in collaborative networks.* Washington, D.C.: IBM Center for the Business of Government

Osborne, D., & Gaebler, T. (1992). *Reinventing government: How the entrepreneurial spirit is transforming the public sector.* New York: Addison Wesley Publishing.

Ostrom, E. (1990). *Governing the commons: The evolution of institutions for collective action.* New York: Cambridge University Press.

Ostrom, E. (2007). Institutional rational choice: An assessment of the institutional analysis and development framework. In P. A. Sabatier (Ed.), *Theories of the policy process* (pp. 21–64). Boulder, CO: Westview Press.

O'Toole, L. J. (1990). Multiorganizational implementation: Comparative analysis for waste-water treatment. In R. W. Gage & M. P. Mandell (Eds.), *Strategies for managing policies and networks.* New York: Praeger Publishers.

O'Toole, L. J. (1997). The implications for democracy in a networked bureaucratic world. *Journal of Public Administration Research and Theory, 7*(3), 443–459.

O'Toole, L. J. (2000). Research on policy implementation: Assessment and prospects. *Journal of Public Administration Research and Theory, 10*(2), 263–288.

O'Toole, L. J. J. (1997). Treating networks seriously: Practical and research-based agendas in public administration. *Public Administration Review, 57*(1), 45–52.

O'Toole, L. J., & Meier, K. J. (2004a). Desperately seeking Selznick: Cooptation and the dark side of public management in networks. *Public Administration Review, 64*(6), 681–693.

O'Toole, L. J., & Meier, K. J. (2004b). Public management in intergovernmental networks: Matching structural networks and managerial networking. *Journal of Public Administration Research and Theory, 14*(4), 469–495.

Ouchi, W. G. (1980). Markets, bureaucracies, and clans. *Administrative Science Quarterly, 25*(1), 557–582.

Page, S. (2004). Measuring accountability for results in interagency collaboratives. *Public Administration Review, 64*(5), 591–606.

Paquet, G. (2005). *The new geo-governance: A baroque approach.* Ottawa, Canada: University of Ottawa Press.

Parboosingh, J. T. (2002). Physician communities of practice: Where learning and practice are inseparable. *Journal of Continuing Education in the Health Professions, 22*(4), 230–236.

Parsons, T. (1951). *The social system.* Glencoe, IL: Free Press.

Patton, C. V., & Sawicki, D. S. (1986). *Basic methods of policy analysis and planning* Englewood Cliffs, N.J.: Prentice-Hall.

Peltzman, S. (1976). Toward a more general theory of regulation. *Journal of Law and Economics, 19,* 211–240.

Perri 6, University of Birmingham. (2004). Joined-up government in the western world in comparative perspective: A preliminary literature review and exploration. *Journal of Public Administration Research and Theory, 14*(1), 103–138.

Perrow, C. (1961). The analysis of goals in complex organization. *American Sociological Review, 26*(6), 853–861.

Perrow, C. (1967). A framework for the comparative analysis of organizations. *American Sociological Review, 32*(2), 194–208.

Perry, J., & Rainey, H. G. (1988). The public-private distinction in organizational theory. *Academy of Management Review, 13*(2), 182–201.

Peter, L. J. (1982). *Peter's Almanac.* Entry for September 24. New York, New York: William Morrow & Co.

Peters, B. G. (2005). *Institutional theory in political science: The "new institutionalism"* (2nd ed.). London: Continuum.

Peters, B. G. (2008). Virtuous and vicious circles in democratic network governance. In E. Sorensen & J. Torfing (Eds.), *Theories of democratic network governance.* New York: Palgrave Macmillan.

Pierre, J. (Ed.). (2000). *Debating governance: Authority, steering, and democracy.* Oxford: Oxford University Press.

Pierre, J., & Peters, B. G. (2005). *Governing complex societies: Trajectories and scenarios.* New York: Palgrave Macmillan.

Podolny, J. M., & Page, K. L. (1998). Network forms of organization. *Annual Review of Sociology, 24,* 57–76.

Poister, T. H. (1978). *Public program analysis: Applied research methods.* Baltimore, MD: University Park Press.

Poister, T. H. (2003). *Measuring performance in public and nonprofit organizations.* San Francisco, CA: Jossey-Bass.

Poole, M. S., & Hirokawa, R. (1996). Introduction: Communication and group decision-making. In R. Hirokawa & M. S. Poole (Eds.), *Communication and group decision making* (2nd ed.). Thousand Oaks, CA: Sage Publication.

Popay, J., Mallinson, S., Kowarzik, U., MacKian, S., Busby, H., & Elliot, H. (2004). Developing public health work in local health systems. *Primary Health Care Research and Development, 5*(4), 338–351.

Porter, D. O. (1990). Structural pose as an approach for implementing complex programs. In R. W. Gage & M. P. Mandell (Eds.), *Strategies for managing intergovernmental policies and networks*. New York: Praeger.

Posner, P. (2002). *Accountability challenges of third-party government*. New York: Oxford.

Powell, W. W. (1990). Neither market nor hierarchy: Network forms of organization. *Research in Organizational Behaviour, 12*, 295–336.

Pressman, J., & Wildavsky, A. (1973). *Implementation*. Berkley: University of California Press.

Pressman, J., & Wildavsky, A. (1984). *Implementation* (3rd ed.). Berkeley: University of California Press.

Price Waterhouse Change Integration Team. (1996). *The paradox principles*. Chicago: Irwin Professional Publishers.

Priem, R. L., & Price, K. H. (1991). Process and outcome expectations for the dialectical inquiry, devil's advocacy, and consensus techniques of strategic decision making. *Group & Organization Studies, 16*(2), 206–225.

Provan, K., Fish, A., & Sydow, J. (2007). Interorganizational networks at the network level: A review of the empirical literature on whole networks. *Journal of Management, 33*(3), 479–516.

Provan, K. G., & Kenis, P. (2007). Modes of network governance: Structure, management and effectiveness. *Journal of Public Administration Research and Theory, 18*, 229–252.

Provan, K. G., & Milward, H. B. (1995). A preliminary theory of interorganizational network effectiveness: A comparative study of four community mental health systems. *Administrative Science Quarterly, 40*(1).

Putnam, R. (2000). *Bowling alone: The collapse and revival of American community*. New York: Simon Schuster.

Putnam, R. D. (1993). *Making democracy work: Civic traditions in modern Italy*. Princeton, NJ: Princeton University Press.

Raab, J., & Milward, H. B. (2003). Dark networks as problems. *Journal of Public Administration Research and Theory, 13*(4), 413–439.

Radcliffe-Brown, A. R. (1940). On social structure. In S. Leinhardt (Ed.), *Quantitative studies in social relations*. New York: Academic Press.

Radcliffe-Brown, A. R. (1997). On social structure. In S. Leinhardt (Ed.), *Social networks: A developing paradigm*. New York: Academic Press.

Radin, B. (2006). *Challenging the performance movement: Accountability, complexity and democratic values*. Washington, DC: Georgetown University Press.

Ravasz, E., & Barabasi, A. (2003). Hierarchical organization in complex networks. *Physical Review, 67*, 1–6.

Reagan, R. (1981, January 20). Inauguration speech. Presented at the U.S. Capitol.

Reed, J., & Koliba, C. (1995). Facilitating reflection: A guide for leaders and educators. Retrieved November 30, 2009, from http://www.uvm.edu/~dewey/reflection_manual/index.html

Rhodes, R. (1997). *Understanding governance: Policy networks, governance, reflexivity and accountability*. Buckingham, UK: Open University Press.

Rhodes, R. (2007). Understanding governance: Ten years on. *Organization Studies, 28*(8), 1243–1264.

Richardson, J. G., Gough, M. Z., & Puentes, R. (2003). *Is Home Rule the answer? Clarifying the influence of Dillon's Rule on growth management*. Discussion paper for the Brookings Institution Center on Urban and Metropolitan Policy. Retrieved 11/16/06: from www.brookings.edu/es/urban/publications/dillonsrule.htm

Riemer, D. (2001). Government as administrator vs. government as purchaser: Do rules or markets create greater accountability? *Fordham Urban Law Journal, 28*, 1715.

Rittel, H. W. J., & Webber, M. M. (1984). Planning problems are wicked problems. In N. Cross (Ed.), *Developments in design methodology* (pp. 135–144). Chichester, UK: John Wiley & Sons.

Roberto, M. A. (2004). Strategic decision-making processes: Beyond the efficiency-consensus trade-off. *Group & Organizational Management, 29*(6), 625–658.

Rodriguez, C., Langley, A., Beland, F., & Denis, J.-L. (2007). Governance, power, and mandated collaboration in an interorganizational network. *Administration & Society, 39*(2), 150–193.

Rohde, M. (2004). *Find what binds: Building social capital in an Iranian NGO community system.* Cambridge, MA: MIT Press.

Romzek, B., & Dubnick, M. (1987). *Accountability in the public sector: Lessons from the Challenger tragedy.* Boulder, CO: Westview Press.

Rosegrant, S. (1996). Witchita confronts contamination. In R. Stillman (Ed.), *Public administration: Concepts and cases* (6th ed., pp. 148–156). Boston: Houghton Mifflin.

Rosen, S. (2008). Human capital. In S. N. Durlauf & L. E. Blume (Eds.), *The new Palgrave dictionary of economics.* New York: Palgrave Macmillan.

Rosenau, J. (1992). Governance, order and change in world politics. In J. Rosenau & E.-O. Czempiel (Eds.), *Governance without government.* Cambridge: Cambridge University Press.

Rosenbloom, D. H. (2004). Public administrative theory and the separation of powers. In J. Shafritz, A. C. Hyde, & S. J. Parkes (Eds.), *Classics of public administration* (5th ed., pp. 446–457). Belmont, CA: Wadsworth/Thomson Learning.

Rousseau, J. (2006). *Autobiographical, scientific, religious, moral and literary writings* (C. Kelly, Trans.). Hanover, NH: Dartmouth College Press.

Sabatier, P. A. (Ed.). (2007). *Theories of the policy process* (2nd ed.). Boulder, CO: Westview Press.

Sabatier, P. A., & Jenkins-Smith, H. C. (1993). *The advocacy coalition framework: An assessment.* Boulder, CO: Westview Press.

Sabatier, P. A., & Mazmanian, D. (1981). Relationships between governing boards and professional staff. *Administration & Society, 13*, 207–248.

Salamon, L. (2001). Scope and structure: The anatomy of America's nonprofit sector. In J. S. Ott (Ed.), *The nature of the nonprofit sector* (pp. 23–39). Boulder, CO: Westview Press.

Salamon, L. (2002). Economic regulation. In L. M. Salamon (Ed.), *The tools of government* (pp. 117–155). New York, New York: Oxford University Press.

Salamon, L. (2002a). The new governance and the tools of public action. In L. Salamon (Ed.), *The tools of government: A guide to the new governance* (pp. 1–47). New York: Oxford University Press.

Salamon, L. (Ed.). (2002b). *The tools of government: A guide to the new governance.* New York: Oxford.

Salamon, L. (2005). Training professional citizens: Getting beyond the right answer to the wrong question in public administration. *Journal of Public Affairs Education, 11*(1), 7–20.

Savas, E. S. (2005). *Privatization in the city: Successes, failures, and lessons.* Washington, DC: A Division of Congressional Quarterly.

Schaap, L. (2008). Closure and governance. In E. Sorensen & J. Torfing (Eds.), *Theories of democratic network governance* (pp. 111–132). New York: Palgrave Macmillan.

Schaap, L., & van Twist, M. J. W. (1997). The dynamics of closedness in networks. In W. J. M. Kickert, E.-H. Klijn, & J. F. M. Koppenjan (Eds.), *Managing complex networks: Strategies for the public sector* (pp. 62–76). London: Sage Publications.

Schmidt, M. R. (2002). Grout: Alternative kinds of knowledge and why they are ignored. In C. Stivers (Ed.), *Democracy, bureaucracy, and the study of administration* (pp. 110–122). Boulder, CO: Westview Press.

Scott, C. (2006). *Spontaneous accountability*. Cambridge: Cambridge University Press.

Scott, R. W. (1987). *Organizations: Rational, natural, and open systems* (2nd ed.). Englewood Cliffs, NJ: Prentice-Hall.

Selznick, P. (2003). The cooptative mechanism. In J. Shafritz, A. C. Hyde, & S. J. Parkes (Eds.), *Classics of public administration* (5th ed., pp. 155–161). Belmont, CA: Wadsworth/Thomson Learning.

Senge, P., Kleiner, A., Roberts, C., Ross, R., & Smith, B. (1994). *The fifth discipline fieldbook*. New York: Currency Doubleday.

Senge, P. M. (1990). *The fifth discipline: The art and practice of the learning organization*. New York: Doubleday Currency.

Shane, S., & Nixon, R. (2007, February 4). U.S. contractors becoming a fourth branch of government.www.nytimes.com (retrieved March 10, 2007).

Shils, E. (1975). *Center and periphery: Essays in macrosociology*. Chicago: University of Chicago Press.

Shleifer, A., & Vishny, R. (1997). The limits of arbitrage. *Journal of Finance, 52*, 33–55.

Simon, H. (1957). *Administrative behavior: A study of decision-making processes in administrative organization*. New York: MacMillan.

Simon, H. (1966). Thinking by computers. In G. C. Robert (Ed.), *Mind and cosmos: Essays in contemporary science and philosophy* (pp. 3–21). Latham, MD: Center for the Philosophy of Science.

Smith, D. G. (1998). The shareholder primacy norm. *Journal of Corporation Law, 23*, 277.

Smith, M. J. (2007). From policy community to issue network: Salmonella in eggs and the new politics of food. *Public Administration, 69*(2), 235–255.

Smith, S. R., & Lipsky, M. (1993). *Nonprofits for hire: The welfare state in the age of contracting*. Cambridge, MA: Harvard University Press.

Snyder, W. M., Wenger, E., & de Sousa Briggs, X. (2003). Communities of practice in government: Leveraging knowledge for performance; learn how this evolving tool for cross-organizational collaboration currently is being used in a variety of public sector settings and how it can help you cultivate improved performance outcomes in your backyard. *The Public Manager 32*(4), 17–22.

Somekh, B., & Pearson, M. (2002). Intercultural learning arising from pan-European collaboration: A community of practice with a hole in the middle. *British Educational Research Journal, 28*(4), 485–502.

Sorensen, E. (2006). Metagovernance: The changing role of politicians in processes of democratic governance. *American Review of Public Administration, 36*(1), 98–114.

Sorensen, E., & Torfing, J. (2003). Network politics, political capital and democracy. *International Journal of Public Administration, 26*(6), 609–634.

Sorensen, E., & Torfing, J. (2005). The democratic anchorage of governance networks. *Scandinavian Political Studies, 28*(3), 195–218.

Sorensen, E., & Torfing, J. (Eds.). (2008). *Theories of democratic network governance*. New York: Palgrave Macmillan.

Sporleder, T. L., & Moss, L. E. (2002). Knowledge management in the global food system: Network embeddedness and social capital. *American Journal of Agricultural Economics*, 85(5), 1345–1352.

Springsteen, B. (1980). The ties that bind. *On The River* [Album]. New York, New York: Columbia Records. In text citation: (Springsteen, 1980, Side 1) *Track 1.

Stacey, R. D. (2001). *Complex responsive processes in organizations: Learning and knowledge creation*. London: Routledge.

Stanton, T. H. (2002). Loans and loan guarantees. In L. A. Salamon (Ed.), *The tools of government: A guide to the new governance* (pp. 381–409). Oxford: Oxford University Press.

Starkey, K., Barnett, C., & Tempest, S. (2004). Beyond networks and hierarchies: Latent organizations in the UK television industry. In K. Starkey, S. Tempest, & A. McKinlay (Eds.), *How organizations learn: Managing the search for knowledge* (2nd ed., pp. 259–270). London: Thomson.

Stephenson, M. (1991). Whither the public-private partnership: A critical overview. *Urban Affairs Quarterly*, 27, 109–127.

Steuerle, C. E., & Twombly, E. C. (2002). Vouchers. In L. A. Salamon (Ed.), *The tools of government: A guide to the new governance* (pp. 445–465). Oxford: Oxford University Press.

Stevenson, W. B., & Greenberg, D. (2000). Agency and social networks: Strategies of action in a social structure of position, opposition, and opportunity. *Administrative Science Quarterly*, 45(4), 651.

Stewart, T. (1997). *Intellectual capital: The new wealth of nations*. New York: Currency Doubleday.

Stivers, C. (1993). *Gender images in public administration: Legitimacy and the administrative state*. Newbury Park, CA: Sage Publications.

Stivers, C. (2004). Toward a feminist perspective in public administration theory. In J. Shafritz, A. C. Hyde, & S. J. Parkes (Eds.), *Classics of public administration*. Belmont, CA: Wadsworth/Thomson Learning, 477–486.

Stoker, G. (1995). Regime theory and urban politics. In D. Judge, G. Stoker, & H. Wolman (Eds.), *Theories of urban politics*. London: Sage Publications, 54–74.

Stoker, G. (2005). *Public value management (PVM): A new resolution of the democracy/efficiency trade-off*. Manchester, UK: Institute for Political and Economic Governance, University of Manchester.

Stoker, G. (2006). Public value management: A new narrative for networked governance? *American Review of Public Administration*, 36(1), 41–57.

Stone, C. (1989). *Regime politics: Governing Atlanta 1946–1988*. Lawrence: University Press of Kansas.

Stone, D. (2002). *Policy paradox: The art of political decision making*. New York: Norton.

Stone, M. M., & Ostrower, F. (2007). Acting in the public interest? Another look at research on nonprofit governance. *Nonprofit and Voluntary Sector Quarterly*, 36(3), 416–438.

Sundaram, A., & Inkpen, A. (2004). The corporate objective revisited. *Organization Science*, 15, 350–363.

Svendsen, G. L. H., & Sorensen, J. F. L. (2007). There's more to the picture than meets the eye: Measuring tangible and intangible capital in two marginal communities in rural Denmark. *Journal of Rural Studies*, 23, 453–471.

Swartz, D. (1990). Pierre Bourdieu: Culture, education and social inequality. In F. M. K. J. H. Doughtery (Ed.), *Education and society: A reader* (pp. 70–80). Orlando, FL: Harcourt, Brace, Jovanovich.

Swidler, A. (1986). Culture in action: Symbols and strategies. *American Sociological Review*, *51*(2), 273–286.

Teske, P. (2004). *Regulation in the states*. Washington, DC: Brookings Institution Press.

Thinkexist.com (2010). Mae West Quotes, from http://thinkexist.com/quotation/an_ounce_of_performance_is_worth_pounds_of/144829.html

Thompson, G. (2003). *Between hierarchies & markets: The logic and limits of network forms of organization*. Oxford: Oxford University Press.

Thrift, N. (1999). The place of complexity. *Theory, Culture, and Society*, *13*(3), 31–69.

Thurber, S. (1922). *Shakespeare's as you like it*. Boston: Allyn and Bacon. (found on p. 39)

Townsend, W. A. (2004). Systems changes associated with criminal justice treatment networks. *Public Administration Review*, *65*(4), 607–617.

Tullock, G. (1996). Provision of public goods through privatization. *KYKLOS*, *49*(2), 221–225.

Turnbull, S. (1997). Corporate governance: Its scope, concerns and theories. *Corporate Governance: An International Review*, *5*(4), 180–205.

Ulrich, W. (1998). *Systems thinking as if people mattered: Critical systems thinking for citizens and managers*. Lincoln, UK: Lincoln School of Management, University of Lincolnshire and Humberside.

van den Belt, M. (2004). *Mediated modeling: A system dynamics approach to environmental consensus building*. Washington, DC: Island Press.

Van Slyke, D. M., & Roch, C. H. (2004). What do they know, and whom do they hold accountable? Citizens in the government-nonprofit contracting relationship. *Journal of Public Administration Research and Theory*, *14*(2), 191–209.

VanWynsberghe, R. (2001). Organizing a community response to environmental injustice: Walpole Island's Heritage Centre as a social movement organization. *Research in Social Problems and Public Policy*, *8*, 221–243.

Vella, J. (2002). *Learning to listen, learning to teach: The power of dialogue in educating adults*. San Francisco: Jossey-Bass.

Wasserman, S., & Faust, K. (1994). *Social network analysis: Methods and applications*. Cambridge: Cambridge University Press.

Watkins, M. (1999). Negotiating in a complex world. *Negotiation Journal*, *15*(3), 245–270.

Wattanasupachoke, T. (2009). Sufficiency economy principles: Applications of organizational management strategies. *Journal of American Academy of Business*, *14*(2), 263–270.

Waugh, W. (2007). EMAC, Katrina, and the governors of Louisiana and Mississippi. *Public Administration Review*, *67*(s1), 107–113.

Weber, E. P. (1999). The question of accountability in historical perspective: From Jackson to contemporary grassroots ecosystem management. *Administration & Society*, *31*(4), 451–494.

Webster's Encyclopedic Unabridged Dictionary. (1989). Avenel, NJ: Gramercy Books.

Weeks, E. C. (2004). The practice of deliberative democracy: Results from four large-scale trials. *Public Administration Review*, *60*(4), 360–373.

Weick, K. E. (1976). Educational organizations as loosely coupled systems. *Administrative Science Quarterly*, *21*(1), 1–19.

Weininger, E. B., & Lareau, A. (2007). Cultural capital. In G. Ritzer (Ed.), *Encyclopedia of sociology*. Oxford: Blackwell. Retrieved 4/22/10: http://www.sociologyencyclopedia.com/public/tocnode?query=cultural+capital&widen=1&result_number=1&from=search&fuzzy=0&type=std&id=g9781405124331_yr2010_chunk_g97814051243319_ss1-170&slop=1

Weiss, J. A. (2002). Public information. In L. A. Salamon (Ed.), *The tools of government: A guide to the new governance*. Oxford: Oxford University Press.

Weissman, R. (2008). Deregulation and the financial crisis. *The Huffington Post*. from <http://www.huffingtonpost.com/robert-weissman/deregulation-and-the-fina_b_82639.html>?

Wenger, E. (1998). *Communities of practice: Learning, meaning, and identity*. Cambridge: Cambridge University Press.

White, N. J. (2004). Click, connect and coalesce for NGOs: Exploring the intersection between online networks, CoPs and events. In P. Hildreth & C. Kimble (Eds.), *Knowledge networks: Innovation through communities of practice* (pp. 282–294). Hershey, PA: Idea Group Publishing.

Wildavsky, A. B. (1979). *The politics of the budgetary process* (3rd ed.). Boston: Little, Brown.

Wilson, D. S. (2007). *Evolution for everyone: How Darwin's theory can change the way we think about our lives*. New York: Delacorte Press.

Wines Smith, L., & Roberts, J. W. (2003). Death for a terrorist: Media coverage of the McVeigh execution as a case study in interorganizational partnering between public and private sectors. *Public Administration Review*, *63*(5), 515–524.

Wise, C. (1994). The public service configuration problem: Designing public organizations in a pluralistic public service. In A. Farazmand (Ed.), *Modern organizations*. Westport, CT: Praeger.

Wixson, K. K., & Yochum, N. (2004). Research on literacy policy and professional development: National, state, district, and teacher contexts. *The Elementary School Journal*, *105*(2), 219–243.

Wohlstetter, P., Smith, J., & Malloy, C. L. (2005). Strategic alliances in action: Toward a theory of evolution. *Policy Studies Journal*, *33*(3), 419–443.

Wolf, J. F., & Farquhar, M. B. (2005). Assessing progress: The state of metropolitan planning organizations under ISTEA and TEA-21 (Intermodal Surface Transportation Efficiency Act of 1991) (Transportation Efficiency Act for the 21st Century). *International Journal of Public Administration*, *28*(13–14), 1057–1079.

WordNet 2.0. (2003). Retrieved June 13, 2009, from http://wordnet-online.com/capital.shtml

Worsham, J., Eisner, M., & Ringquist, E. (1997). Assessing the assumptions: A critical analysis of agency theory. *Administration & Society*, *28*(4), 419–440.

Wright, D. S. (2000). *Models of national, state, and local relationships*. Washington, DC: CQ Press.

Yang, K., & Bergrud, E. (Eds.). (2008). *Civic engagement in a network society*. Charlotte, NC: Information Age Publishing.

Yankelovich, D. (1991). *Coming to public judgment: Making democracy work in a complex world*. Syracuse, NY: Syracuse University Press.

Youngblood, J. W. (2004). Learning for political party partisanship and participation. *Dissertation Abstracts International A: The Humanities and Social Sciences*, *65*(6), 2350.

Zanetich, J. T. (2003). Knowledge management in the public sector: A case study of the inter-governmental response to the West Nile Virus epidemic in New York State. *Dissertation Abstracts International A: The Humanities and Social Sciences, 64*(3), 1072.

Zia, A., Metcalf, S., Koliba, C., Widener, M. (2010). Management of complex governance networks: Opportunities and challenges for agent based models of policy analysis. American Society of Public Administration Annual Conference. San Jose, CA.

Appendix A: Governance Network Taxonomy

Table A.1 A Taxonomy of Governance Networks 1.0

Level/Type of Variable	Variable	Variable Descriptors
Actor	Social scale	Individual Group Organizational/institutional Interorganizational
	Social sector (organizational level)	Public Private Nonprofit
	Geographic scale	Local Regional State National International
	Role centrality	Central-peripheral Trajectory
	Capital resources actor provides (as an input)	Financial Physical Natural Human Social Cultural Political Knowledge

(continued)

Table A.1   A Taxonomy of Governance Networks 1.0 (Continued)

Level/Type of Variable	Variable	Variable Descriptors
	Providing accountabilities to	Elected representatives Citizens and interest groups Courts Owners/shareholders Consumers Bureaucrats/supervisors/principals Professional associations Collaborators/partners/peers
	Receiving accountabilities from	Elected representatives Citizens and interest groups Courts Owners/shareholders Consumers Bureaucrats/supervisors/principals Professional associations Collaborators/partners/peers
	Performance/output and outcomes criteria	Tied to policy function and domain
Ties	Resources exchanged/pooled	Financial Physical Natural Human Social Cultural Political Knowledge
	Strength of tie	Strong to weak
	Formality of tie	Formal to informal
	Administrative authority	Vertical (command and control) Diagonal (negotiation and bargaining) Horizontal (collaborative and cooperative) Competitive

Table A.1   A Taxonomy of Governance Networks 1.0 (Continued)

Level/Type of Variable	Variable	Variable Descriptors
	Accountability relationship	Elected representatives Citizens and interest groups Courts Owners/shareholders Consumers Bureaucrats/supervisors/ principals Professional associations Collaborators/partners/peers
Network-wide characteristics	Policy tools	Regulations Grants Contracts Vouchers Taxes Loans/loan guarantees
	Operational functions	Resource exchange/pooling Coordinated action Information sharing Capacity building
	Policy functions	Define/frame problem Design policy solution Coordinate policy solution Implement policy (regulation) Implement policy (service delivery) Evaluate and monitor policy Political alignment
	Policy domain functions	Health, environment, education, etc.
	Macro-level governance structures	Lead organization Shared governance Network administrative organization

(continued)

Table A.1   A Taxonomy of Governance Networks 1.0 (Continued)

Level/Type of Variable	Variable	Variable Descriptors
	Network configuration	Intergovernmental relations Interest group coalitions Regulatory subsystems Grant and contract agreements Public-private partnerships
Systems-wide	Properties of network boundaries	Open-closed permeability
	Systems dynamics	Systems-level inputs, processes, outputs, and outcomes
	Feedback loops via	Policy tools Representation Administrative authority Accountability Performance management
	Hybridized accountability regimes	Elected representatives Citizens and interest groups Courts Owners/shareholders Consumers Bureaucrats/supervisors/principals Professional associations Collaborators/partners/peers
	Performance management system	Governing communities of practice Data collection regimes Decision heuristics

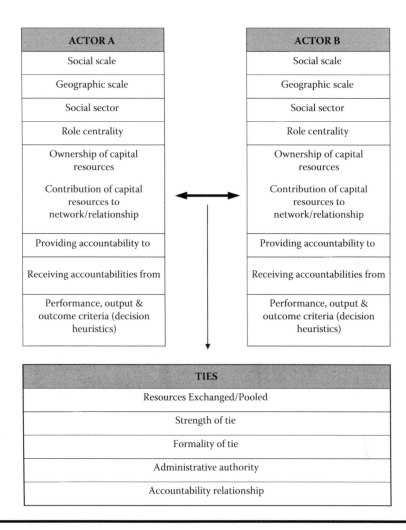

Figure A.1   Actor and tie characteristics.

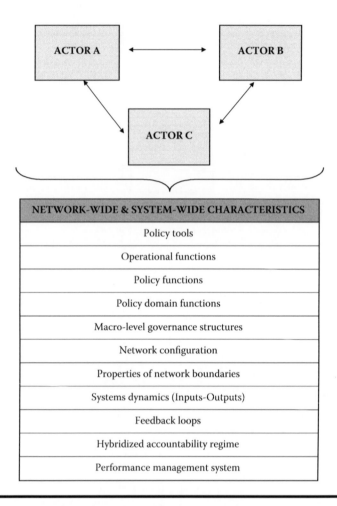

Figure A.2   Network- and systems-wide characteristics.

Appendix B: Case Study Template

Governance Network Analysis Case Study Template

Network name: _____

A. Network policy function (adapted from Bovaird, 2004)
  _____ Problem definition
  _____ Policy design and planning
  _____ Policy coordination
  _____ Policy implementation (regulatory)
  _____ Policy implementation (service delivery)
  _____ Political alignment
  _____ Policy monitoring/evaluation

B. Network policy domain(s) (Baumgartner and Jones, 2003)
  _____ Macroeconomics
  _____ Civil rights, minority issues, and civil liberties
  _____ Health
  _____ Agriculture
  _____ Labor, employment, and immigration
  _____ Education
  _____ Environment
  _____ Energy
  _____ Transportation
  _____ Law, crime, and family issues
  _____ Social welfare
  _____ Community development, housing issues
  _____ Banking, finance, and domestic commerce

_____ Defense
_____ Space, science, technology, and communications
_____ Foreign trade
_____ International affairs and foreign aid
_____ Government operations
_____ Public lands and water management

Integrated domains:
_____ Climate change
_____ Regional planning
_____ Emergency management
_____ Other: _____

C. Organizational network actors

Actor	Social Sector (Public, Private, Nonprofit)	Geographic Scale (Local to International)	Level of Involvement (Center, Periphery, Intermediate)

D. Distribution of power
Where is power situated in this network? Who has it and how is it used?

E. Apparent challenges to network management
What are the apparent challenges/problems associated with the functioning of this network?

F. Policy tools utilized

Policy Tools Implicated in Network Functioning

Tool Type	Actors Implicated

G. Capital resource flows

Capital Flows in Network Systems Analysis

Type of Capital Flow	Provider of Capital (Contributor of Capital as Input)	Evidence of Capital as Network Output
Financial		
Physical		
Natural		
Human		
Social		
Political		
Cultural		
Knowledge		

H. Governing communities of practice

Communities of Practice Operating in This Network

Community of Practice	Members	Function(s)	Decision-Making Authority	Decision-Making Process

What is the relationship between membership and decision-making authority of these communities of practice?

What does this relationship tell us about the relative power that the community of practice has?

What is the relationship between these communities of practice? Sketch out the dynamics to help explain the relationships.

I. System dynamics

Inputs	Processes	Outputs	Short-Term Outcomes	Long-Term Outcomes

J. Accountability regimes

How do actors within this network hold each other accountable? Whose accountability structures hold sway?

Evidence of Accountability Types

Accountability Type	Actor Level	Network Level
Elected representatives		
Citizens/interest groups		
Legal		
Owner/shareholder		
Consumer		
Bureaucratic		
Professional		
Collaborative		

K. Performance management
How is performance defined/measured?

Performance Indicator	Network Actors Responsible for Collecting These Data	Communities of Practice Responsible for Analyzing the Data	Scale of Performance Indicator

L. Systems map
Render a visual articulation of the "hubs" and "spokes" structure of the network.

What do the lines connecting the nodes signify? (direction of financial resources, direction of human resources, direction of physical capital, direction of information)

M. Macro-level governance structure (Provan and Kenis, 2008)
_____ Lead organization: _____
_____ Network administrative organization: _____
_____ Shared governance

N. Type of governance configuration
_____ Intergovernmental relations
_____ Interest group coalition
_____ Regulatory subsystem
_____ Grant and contract agreement
_____ Public-private partnership

O. Major milestones for the network

Date	Milestone	Actors Implicated	Why Relevant?

Index

343